THE GREAT

FRAUD

FIGHTBACK

The true story of one woman's
struggle against an international
crimewave

AMBER WAHEED

ISBN:
Print: 978-1-8383776-1-8
iBooks: 978-1-8383776-0-1
Kindle: 978-1-8383776-2-5

Copy proof and cover text by Ted McDermott
Book concept by Mark Reid
Book design by Cal Sharpe
Book formatting by Amber Waheed and Sohail Liaqat

To all the victims of fraud

AUTHOR'S NOTE

᷍ We should always stand for justice as a matter of principle, even if it seems justice sides against us ᷍

F raud is fraud.

It is using deception to gain financially.

I think that focusing on types of fraud can take us away from the simplicity of both the act of fraud and the means to fight it. Fraud is nothing more than a lie intended to produce monetary gain. It doesn't matter if the victim is an employer, a business partner, a government, a consumer, a supplier or a customer. If something of value is provided based on a lie, it is fraud. That conduct may be called money laundering, corruption, embezzlement, or something else. But the common element is a lie – sometimes a lie by omission. As soon as one scheme to defraud becomes successful it is often mimicked, and then as it proliferates systems are adopted to fight that particular scheme. A focus on the lie common to all forms of fraud is the key to minimising its risk. Not merely chasing the fraud du jour.

It is human nature to believe that while fraud exists, it is 'out there' and wouldn't be committed by 'our people'. The desire to trust your own and distrust others is natural. But it is a human reaction that fraudsters take advantage of every day. Unfortunately, this aspect of human nature often blinds close-knit groups to the substantial risk of fraud from within. Friendship circles are made up of human beings who have the same blind spots and natural desire to trust their own as any other person. The key is to recognise these blind spots and the fact that they create the greatest risk of fraud.

We are passing through an uneasy and uncertain time, witnessing fraud, deception, and destruction in many parts of an increasingly interdependent world. People of conscience need to be a voice for justice and say enough is enough. It's time to bring madness and insanity to an end. Otherwise, history will not forgive us. There is no denying that remaining silent in the face of injustice is tantamount to taking part in it and that is a grave offence by any standard.

CHAPTERS

PART 2

PART 3

PROLOGUE

๑ A true story comes to life in a book ๑

Independent Financial Advisor Neil Ramsay Pringle Grant seemed like a dream come true for thousands of Dubai expats. Then an investment fraud of staggering proportions came to light, costing them their savings, their livelihoods and their future financial security.

My story describes the kind of experience that will be familiar to millions of people: being trapped in a relationship with a financial advisor, the maddening tactics of financial institutions and the smoke and the mirrors that keep you trapped for so long.

The idea for this book came from the victims of the financial advisory industry who clubbed together to try to understand how all these parties fitted into the picture and how they worked together and appeared bulletproof when it comes to the law which somehow legalised the taking of other people's money. Slowly, we were able to unravel these complexities and finally piece the whole fiasco together.

And so, the book details my entire experience of investing with a rogue financial advisor; pursuing the legal process and the court systems in Dubai as well as the legal process and court systems in Jersey, to administer a little drop of justice against the rogue and his enablers.

My goal with the book was to write it for a general reader who knows nothing about the financial advisory industry and who wants to learn more about it before they start investing, and to learn how they can best protect themselves. But most importantly, I am hopeful that highlighting this particular case will prevent other vulnerable, trusting people being exploited in similar ways, and prevent similar tragedies.

The book also acts an educational piece for victims of financial advisory fraud and how exactly they were scammed, and what legal recourses they have available to them, offering a roadmap to help other people navigate similar complex legal cases. By the time the reader reaches the end of the book, they will know what they can and cannot do about their current financial situation. The not-knowing is what freezes people and makes them feel powerless. That was the problem with Dubai's most notorious Independent Financial Advisor – as expats, we didn't know where to start.

And for investors who feel stuck, confined, and imprisoned by their current financial investment circumstances, there are steps we can take together, along with specialised experts who educate thousands of investors on the different financial markets and products.

My story isn't simple. Parts of this book may shock you, and there are parts which may make you laugh.

Fortunately, I had kept regular contemporaneous notes of crucial moments, meetings, encounters and emails. Sometimes this was for my own amusement, usually because I was a control freak, and often to make sure I had my back covered – for what, I didn't know. Back then, never in my wildest dreams would I have imagined that I was going to take my financial advisor – my friend – to court in years to come, and this information was going to save me. I never quite knew why I was hoarding it, but I guess I subconsciously thought it might come in handy one day. They were fascinating papers to revisit during the court cases – there were so many red flags, where I had displayed a shocking lack of common sense, based purely on too much misguided trust. It wasn't until seven years later after I began questioning things that I had the courage to follow my instinct and take my brain with me.

Since my story became public, I've had so many victims from all walks of life who have supported me, powered me up and poured out their problems and devastating stories. Every single story has troubled my heart and has helped me, and I'm thankful to all of those people who sort me out. We are not that powerful alone. Success always requires cooperation and teamwork. So, this book is for all the victims of fraud.

One last thing – whilst some scattered names throughout the book have been changed for various reasons, mainly to protect our collective stupidity, I've elected not to change the names of those who are pivotal to the message of the story. There are quite a few people mentioned, often only by their first name. To help you keep track of who I am talking about, you may find it useful to refer to the cast of characters at the back of the book.

In the vernacular of financial services, financial books are by default technical and rather formulaic for most people. And so I realised that the best way to tell my story was as a story. Because nothing beats the drama and sheer readability of a good emotional rollercoaster.

PART 1

CHAPTER 1

THE PERFECT HUNTING GROUND

⟋ A gilded plot silhouetted against a golden setting sun ⟋

F inancial advisors are a universal problem but it so happens my story is set in the United Arab Emirates (UAE), a federation of seven monarchies, each with its own laws.

Hundreds of thousands of British tourists flock to the UAE every year, drawn by the duty-free high-end shopping and the permanent sunshine. In a country of just nine and a half million people, British expatriates make up 5.1 percent of its total population, many of them working in hospitality, law, medicine, construction and finance.

Dubai is the most glamourous and popular emirate. A city that has so much going for it: the energy, the optimism; the wonderful fact that it can reinvent itself just at the moment when it looks to be finished. It has maintained a stable economy with a high standard of living and with extremely low unemployment. There is a complete infrastructure of a modern society and a good place for families to live. Thousands and thousands of high-net-worth individuals working for hundreds of multinational companies reside in the big communities. For financial advisors it's potentially a huge new market.

It's also the perfect hunting ground for financial predators who fail to make it in places like the UK and come and set up in Dubai, where the regulation and comeback on them is virtually non-existent. To them, Dubai felt like a caveman discovering fire – a glittering scene for an equally glittering guest list that included lawyers and engineers, managers, and regional heads. And that is what makes this story all the more extraordinary – it's not that the rogue preyed on particularly soft, credulous targets.

The novice

I didn't know the first thing about investing. And I had long made it a point to avoid joining the financial and investment fray.

The first and only time I had heard of a financial advisor was in 1992 when I saw pictures of the Duchess of York, Sarah Ferguson, having her toes sucked by her 'financial advisor', the Texan oil tycoon John Bryan – the same year she separated from Prince Andrew.

For several years a series of bad investments saw the Duchess on the brink of bankruptcy. This led to her being caught in a tabloid newspaper sting selling access to her former husband for half a million pounds. The cash-strapped Duchess was taped accepting a $40,000 cash down-payment to introduce her ex, who then worked as a UK trade envoy, to an undercover reporter posing as an international businessman. She immediately apologised for the embarrassment it had caused him and her family and admitted she only accepted the money because she was in financial difficulty after her investments crashed.

The story alone was enough to put me off investing for decades.

But some time after moving to Dubai, I realised I had to think about my future. The global financial crisis of 2008, a financial catastrophe caused in part by uncalculated risk-taking and blindness to threat, cost tens of millions of people their savings. As interest rates fell, putting money in the bank no longer paid dividends. The property market was also affected and unstable as housing prices were plummeting. It was all very dark and bleak. For many the priority is to save as much of their earnings as possible and invest them in a long-term future, whether that involves protection for their families, school or university fees or a retirement home. As savings were nil, people had to do something about the future and buy financial security.

If I wanted financial security, protection and independence, I knew that I would have to consider investing – asset allocation and diversification amongst others. A monthly income alone was not going to give me that security. At New Year in 2010 I, along with everyone else, was trying to juggle the inevitable lists of resolutions: change job, lose weight, join the gym, take up a hobby. I realised maybe it was time ignore the defiant refusal to leave the comfort zone – it was time for me to invest.

And that led me to turn to the financial advisory industry.

But financial investment is complicated. Bankers know to make the right calls about sectors, understand different types of funds and where to invest. Who else has the time or knowledge to understand it?

And that leads us to seek out 'professional help'. The idea that something can be pre-arranged by an expert appeals to us. All of a sudden, we drift off into a daydream that someone else can handle all of this for us.

With business, we frequently hire advisors and consultants who help us grow the company and make it successful. That strategy works wonders for us. When we start to invest, we think that the same would apply to investing. That's perhaps, the biggest myth. That these professionals are leading you, signalling which way you go, which way your money grows. That they pick the funds and vet them, so you think they are what you need and match your investment profile, and that their intentions are honest and they want the same for you.

With finances, I was neither the sharpest nor the brightest and so, when a financial advisor came knocking on my door, I was so grateful that someone could sort everything out for me.

The rogue

Neil Ramsay Pringle Grant was introduced to me as an Independent Financial Advisor; six foot, over 200 pounds, deep close-set blue eyes, and a dry Scottish humour.

Taking advantage of the young financial advisory services market in Dubai, Grant saw a golden opportunity to set up a company called Prosperity Offshore Investment Consultants, to advise expats, predominantly British expats, within his social circle on where to invest their hard-earned savings for their future and for their children.

I believed I could trust Grant at first based on close friends who vouched for and recommended him as a knowledgeable financial professional.

"He is very, very good," they said to me, "extremely personable, very trustworthy," and, "I've known him for years, his kids play with my kids … all my friends are with him".

In Dubai you become friends-like-families, a famous hashtag in the emirate, where expats are away from home and their social circle and friends and colleagues become their second family. I soon realised that most of my circle had indeed signed up with Grant and had worked with him for years – all of who were advocating Grant as the 'go to man' to sort out your financial affairs. Such was the influence, that Grant's details were included in the induction pack that some companies gave to new arrivals. Endorsed by human resources, it seemed every new high-profile appointment must, by rights, now be forwarded to the financial advisor. It was the ultimate triumph for Grant that gave him complete credibility, and his business a veneer of legitimacy.

As the cherry on the top, he had written a couple of articles in respected media publications offering expert advice on what people should do with their money. "It is never too late to get help," he said. The discussions on financial planning and his guides on how to avoid 'rogue' financial advisors were already smoothing my natural first doubts. In a series of bullet points on how to spot fraud, he warned: "Even clever investors sometimes fall for the most ambitious fraudsters".

To me Grant presented a trustworthy figure. There were no red flags.

That's the reason I didn't think of checking Grant's background. I just assumed someone along the way had vetted him and that's why he was being referred around.

In hindsight – a silly reason.

I preferred to deal with someone who was 'independent'. The big firms had too many people, too many heavyweights, too many accounts, where you were simply a number to them. 'Independent' meant better service; personal and tailored by simply one man. A man who was the money manager for the uber-rich set in Dubai. People knew that he had a lot of wealthy individuals on his books. During the Dubai boom between 2006 and 2009, he hit it out of the ballpark. A lot of powerful men liked him and trusted him to manage their savings. Although the world of financial advisory was perceived to be like the old Wild West, with plenty of cowboys, there were good financial consultants in the market and with his Scottish good looks, neat shave and Mont Blanc crisp suits, Grant was just the man to burnish the industry's image.

Grant himself was making money and living a life most people dream about. If you have money in Dubai people think they can buy their way into any society. Some of the protectiveness, some of the clannishness – it's definitely a very insular world. There is almost a hermetic seal around it. It's not just an extremely wealthy emirate, it's a whole different world and I learnt that it almost has a psychological effect on the very wealthy people who move there, because there is a sense of being untouchable; a feeling that Grant had grown accustomed to.

So, I took the plunge, and I agreed to meet him, this so-called saviour of so many of my friends' finances. I first met him at his offices, a rented office space in one of the prestigious Business Centres in a top Dubai hotel along the iconic Sheikh Zayed Road. Entering the shared reception area on the 21st floor, the first thing visitors saw was an impressive board listing prestigious companies as having offices in the centre.

Sessions would usually take place in one of the shared meeting rooms which Grant's administrative assistant would book prior to your arrival. It meant that you never saw his office where normally the academic certificates and company licenses are hanging off the walls; you never saw his physical set up.

His assistant greeted you in the reception area and took you directly into a meeting room. This is where you learned it was just Grant and the assistant – overheads were kept to a minimal. After making you comfortable she left and Grant himself appeared.

"Welcome," he said dramatically, with a broad grin, as if what was to follow was an event the memory of which I would cherish forever.

Our first meeting was a long visit filled with lots of chitchat.

"You have been highly recommended," I said, and Grant couldn't suppress a proud smile.

He was extremely friendly and personable just as they said, and he mentioned my friends by their first name, and he knew their kids names too – and you instantly felt in safe, warm family-knit hands. I think when you are an expat in any country, we are all vulnerable. We instantly look for someone who we can relate to at some level, even if it is just sharing the same nationality.

My impression was that he was just a very private guy, who was approaching a huge milestone in his life: 50 years of age. He arrived in Dubai with his wife Abigail in the 1990s from Scotland. With their four young boys, the family settled effortlessly into the expat community. At the beginning, I felt like I had this painting of Grant that he was this perfect family man, with the perfect wife and perfect kids, and that I was very lucky to ever be introduced to him.

Those who knew Grant away from work held him in similarly high regard. In the respectable suburb of Dubai, where he and his wife lived in a villa for which they paid high-end rent of over £50,000 a year, neighbours recalled his willingness to 'do good turns' such as mending things for you, and helping you find employment through using his contacts.

On the surface they were a typical outgoing Scottish family. He was a dutiful husband, forever decorating the house and the garden; a proud and devoted father; a family stalwart who hosted regular Friday brunches for his family and friends. Every Ramadan and Christmas he would send out greeting cards and well wishes to spread some cheer and hand out gifts. And he was a part of the expat high-end charities, golf clubs, and director of some football club back in his hometown – all very lucrative.

His wife, who was described as a devoted mother and a 'sweetheart', with her petite trim figure and luxuriant deep brown hair, was the Martha Stewart type, heavily involved in the local community, charities, and immersing herself in her boys' schools; a kindly woman to whom friends could turn in a crisis.

Apparently the couple had acquired no bad habits, and led a clean life. Neither smoked, and there was no evidence they drank much. He liked to jog early morning before work; she was very active in church.

The couple befriended their clients on Facebook and she often showcased her designer home and renovation projects on social media, becoming obsessively house-proud. The ultimate seal of approval, of course. If we trusted him enough to add him to our Facebook, well, we trusted him enough to manage our money.

And so he presented himself as the perfect vehicle to sort out my finances. I understood why clients were queuing up to meet, greet, wine and dine him, asking *him* to be *their* financial advisor.

There are just so many myths about financial advisors – I thought I had a good egg.

I didn't bat an eye.

The conversation turned to the need to diversify my savings. Long-term, low-risk, illiquid, within reach – all wonderful sounding words and the melody was like a flower to a honeybee.

"Yes, yes, I agree property is not a good investment at the moment," and, "let's park that and get you some savings and secure your future". It was like I'd given him the script playing in my mind and he was reading it back to me. What could possibly go wrong? We were on the same page. He made me feel terrific and responsible.

He reassured me that he spent hours polishing his knowledge, at becoming an expert at finding the best investment funds for his clients to keep their money safe. He was a devoted advisor with high moral standards, physically frowning on the rogues that decorated the market. And you agreed he was very knowledgeable – like he really understands this stuff, so you don't need to worry about it, like you don't need to worry about the dentist and the doctor looking after your kids. It's all in hand – in safe hands.

He managed to use the word 'rogue' a few times as he reassured me: "Don't worry. I'm not one of those rogue financial advisors who fleece their clients". I agreed. No, of course he's not. I thought I was so lucky to have him, and I'd dodged all the other bullets.

He gave me a compelling story, a dream within my reach. And I saw him as a solution. He promised, in fact he "guaranteed", I would be able to see healthy returns through social and environmental means as well as gaining a good financial return, if I followed his personal advice.

My first immediate reaction or thought that came to my mind was this was great. This was my ticket to financial management, become a serious saver, secure my financial future.

I felt it was all very exciting. And safe. Because my overriding specification was that my capital remained safe, viewing all these investments as a savings tool – like a piggy bank. The money that I would get out of them when they matured was a bonus that I had 'saved' and didn't fritter away.

You have to trust your finance partner, which is a factor, but you also have a unique bond that comes from creating a secure future together.

That's the power of money and the excitement of finance.

Who could resist such an offer?

This is the start of it.

And so I opened up my wallet. Just like that. I did whatever he needed, signed whatever he wanted. I agreed to sign up to four different plans thinking it is smart of him to suggest that to me.

He advised me to open an offshore bank account with Anglo Irish; invest in a short-term five-year Vision Life Insurance policy in Guernsey (£10,000); a long-term off-shore Trust with Guardian Trust Company Ltd in Jersey (£50,000), and a Hansard Policy in the UK (£40,000) that never came to fruition due to an administration error on behalf of Grant's assistant. The applications were rejected by Hansard as they were not completed properly, and the writing ineligible for the bank to follow its instructions to make the transaction. This forced us to submit them again, although this time I was to complete them which I never got round to do.

Unprompted, he let me see a copy of the Terms and Conditions he has set up with Guardian Trust Company Ltd, to smooth any doubts I may be having. As I glazed through the posh letterheaded document on thick, crisp, pure paper, I couldn't help but be impressed by what I was reading. According to the document, in 2004 Grant already had four hundred clients on his books investing their money with him. For an individual, that is a staggering impressive book of business. It was now 2010, and the likelihood was that his total number of clients had grown considerably higher. I was so blinded by that fact I failed to register that number should have been a warning sign. Anything above one hundred clients or so for any individual would suggest he couldn't devote the time he needed to me and was more focused on selling commission-based products. It should have been clear from the numbers he was addicted – to easy targets, easy money. And here I was making it even easier for him.

The document also revealed he had paid himself generously, making a turnover of £670,381 tax-free in the year 2004 alone, leaving me suitably impressed at his accomplishments. The outlet looked like a regular version of a successful professional company.

He never specifically asked for money to be directed to him. Instead, he managed the process and asked me to send my money directly to the financial institutions and then handled the money from there, putting it into investment funds that I thought were solely benefitting me. By insisting on this, I thought he was wonderfully transparent.

I'd never heard of the investment funds he was investing my money into and their funny peculiar names. But it's like a doctor mentioning different parts of your anatomy to you which you have never heard before or able to pronounce. But you trust they do exist, and they are performing their jobs, and you need the advised operation to ensure they continue to do their task to keep you healthy and live longer.

It was maybe the second or third time I went to him when he asked whether I had any friends I could introduce. He said he would give me entertainment vouchers worth AED 500 if they signed up to any of the policies.

"Of course," I said and soon I was dropping his name in conversations with colleagues and friends describing him as a respected Independent Financial Advisor, doing all the work for him – lionised as a visionary advisor.

A friendship bloomed. We talked often.

He would say, "How are you? How is everything? How's your family?"

He wanted you to think he was a friend and that he cared.

We spoke about our lives, his children – we would have so many conversations about everything and anything and everyone. He was not only my financial advisor; he became a close confidante. Many hours were passed together in his office and the meetings used to turn into personal therapy sessions for me. He went out of his way to get me to open up emotionally. The trust ran that deep. With some of my friends, his friendship had him entering their homes, selling investments. It was one of the most intimate sales situations imaginable, not into a boardroom or a car dealership, but inside a potential clients' home, selling them a product that would help them feel financially secure in that home.

All the while, he reassured me over the years that the individual funds were performing, as was the overall long-term Trust and the short-term policy. As confirmation, the figures in the quarterly valuation statements that he personally sent to me were there, in black and white.

I never once thought of actually asking him for his credentials or trade licence. Even when times got tough, I found myself making excuses for him, and having sympathy for him when he told me people were getting tough on him, blaming him for their investments losing money because of the economic climate. "You can't possibly be held responsible for that?" I reassured him.

As time went by, he started to ask me for more money

to top up my investment which of course he always has a reason as to why, and I continued to believe he was very plausible. Financial advisory fraud is not as obvious as a black eye or a split lip: over the years, he exerted more and more subtle control over my financial affairs.

And so, in the beginning, I didn't query anything. I had left everything to Grant. After all, and as he frequently reminded me, he was hired by these financial institutions to manage my finances, so I didn't have to. He always told me my investments were safe, my financial future was secure, and that I was doing the right thing. And as far as I was aware, he was paid directly from these financial institutions: the Financial Service Providers (where all your policies and Trusts are kept), the Provident Providers (life insurance companies who sell life insurance investment funds) and the Fund Managers (who sell the investment funds). And I could see that no fees were ever being paid from my own pocket. It all looked wonderfully transparent.

Little did I know that financial advisory fraud has been simmering for years, and I had now become part of it; that the region was a tinderbox just waiting for a little spark to ignite into a huge fireball.

CHAPTER 2

THE PURSUIT OF SOMETHING...

It was simply the principle of the thing

T hings started to change a year or two into the relationship. I had given Grant £60,000, a significant amount of cash, but now I was feeling particularly anxious about the Trust he had set up with Guardian Trust Company Ltd in Jersey and the short-term five-year Vision Life Insurance policy in Guernsey. Mysterious shortfalls were starting to plague my valuation accounts and the Trust itself continued to flag up baffling losses. The main issue to me was that there was no rhyme or reason as to why.

Grant had been attempting to convince me that this was normal and temporary. He frequently moved cash and funds around in the Trust, to combat the shortfalls. Although my friends helped ease my woes at first, it left me with a constant, horrible tight feeling of worry.

By 2013, the value of the overall Trust was down £10,000 from its original inception and losing cash rapidly. This was surprising as the investment funds within the Trust were meant to be low-risk and long-term – some fluctuation was expected but suspension of funds? How was that even possible?

After finishing university and securing my first job, I gifted my first salary to my father as a thank you for supporting me in my education. In return, he bought himself a tie with the money, and then did what every responsible father would do for their child, and poured the rest into a traditional low-risk long-term investment fund for me. Before I knew it, I was committed to putting £100 into it every month from my salary. It was not quite the gift I had in mind and I made a mental note to just buy him aftershave next time. However, a decade or so later, I was of course grateful. It acted more like a piggy bank. It was a low-risk fund that dipped now and then but only marginally and, on the whole, it was a steady incline and I realised that I had a pretty good savings account.

It's exactly what I had in mind when I approached Grant only the results were far different and my experience started questioning everything, and I had this nagging insecurity that this just did not all add up. My suspicious mind then suddenly noticed a few subtle contradictions in what Grant was saying to me – so subtle that you could have missed them. When I started to ask probing questions about the Trust and the funds related to it, he was no longer answering my calls so quickly, and I noticed he was fobbing me off. But again, I argued myself out of my own misgivings.

2015, five years into the relationship, my money was almost gone in both the Trust and in the five-year Vision Life Insurance policy and Grant wasn't coming up with any real answers for the losses. At this time, I couldn't even comprehend why and how that had happened. All of the funds in the Trust were suspended yet showing a healthy return on paper. I couldn't make out the real value of the Trust itself or how much of it was liquid that I could actually get my hands on. Being vulnerable to the financial world and trying to handle financial affairs on my own, it was just overwhelming, so I continued to go back to Grant.

But by now, Grant was straight out avoiding me.

"I've been trying to reach you over and over again, and you haven't bothered to answer. Tell me anything that could reasonably explain why I haven't been able to get hold of you?"

Grant shrugged. He had no explanation. And I remember thinking that he seemed so different to when I first met him – abrupt, arrogant almost downright rude on occasion.

And that's when I realised that I really knew nothing about Grant's professional background and business – and neither did anyone else. Yes, they have known Grant for a long time, but did they really know him? Had anyone actually checked him out?

The problem was that Grant had always been extremely reluctant to talk about his business. Whenever we met, he skimmed over discussions on our investment portfolios and focused entirely on personal matters. One day I decided to write down everything I'd ever known about him and his company set up. I ended up sitting in front of a blank piece of paper, holding my pen in my hand. Even though Grant and I had spent a lot of time together, he had never told me anything about his business, his partners, his qualifications or mentioned where he'd gone to school or university.

That in itself should have set off the alarm bells. People always reveal little titbits about themselves in conversation, scraps of information that can give an overall picture of a personality that show what had made them into the character they'd become. The fact that he was so guarded about his background led to me discovering that no one really knew anything about him. We had just passed his name around for decades.

My friend Rupert had been the one who introduced me to him in 2010. Despite our vast age difference, Rupert and I were very good friends. We were two people that didn't look like we would be friends with each other. We are culturally different. We're an odd pair. He was a proper English gentleman, with a cut glass British accent. And I was, well, a northerner.

He had known Grant for a long time and had introduced at least twenty friends and colleagues to him in eight to ten years. If Rupert trusted him, it was bang on the money good enough for me. I trusted Rupert with everything, including log-ins and passwords to some of my accounts and sensitive information; he was the very embodiment of truth and integrity. I don't think he's ever told a lie in his life – even a white lie. After hearing him on the phone to his bank querying over £50 I knew the referral was solid. He looked over everything; nothing got past him.

But now we were in a very precarious situation, and slightly out of control. Especially when I discovered Rupert had given Grant an additional £200,000 on top of the £50,000 initial investment. Rupert was coming up to retirement and I was also concerned for him. It became impossible to ignore that tight feeling of worry.

I first raised the question mark over Grant with Rupert and his response was disappointingly underwhelming.

"What's the sudden interest in Neil?"

"It's disturbing, that's all, that we're all losing money."

"No, it's not. It happens in investment. It comes in swings and roundabouts. Relax."

Up to that point there hadn't been a hint of suspicion about Grant, not so much as a wonder. And Rupert didn't want to even entertain the idea, and I didn't push the issue.

It led me to confide in some other friends about "our mate Grant" and that his actions over the past few years had led me to believe that maybe he simply lacked the training and experience to help guide our financial strategies.

But these conversations were held against an uneasy backdrop as Grant and his wife were hugely popular, with a very tight close circle and my concerns about him were always met with a wall of silence and little sympathy and faces of almost clownish incredulity.

"NO! Don't be ridiculous," they retorted.

"What are you on about ... he's a family man, he's got four kids."

"You need his help; you'll end up alienating him if you're not careful."

"It's just the climate."

"Just ask him to explain it to you ... sit down with him and it will be clear."

Oh, and yes, the inevitable: "Women and finances ... see ... they just don't go together". Some numpty was going to come up with that original comment.

"It's not what it seems, that's all," I would say repeatedly.

"Not this again. How is it not what it seems?"

"I don't know ... but I can feel it."

"It's probably indigestion." An unhelpful response.

During the years they'd all been working together Grant had never done anything to give them cause to distrust him. They realised that, yes, investments go up and they go down.

"Of course, one ill-judged investment does not undo all the good he has done, or call into question his many fine qualities." Grant was clearly an open book to them and they continued defending him: "In his line of work he must get blamed for absolutely everything. There must come a time when the elation of sitting there is replaced by a feeling of "Bloody hell, do I really need all this aggravation?"."

Perhaps.

Then again, perhaps not.

My comments started filtering back to Grant through our friends, and that I was showing a lot of concern that maybe he's not handling our finances well.

Well, he doesn't agree.

No, of course, he wouldn't.

Grant was well prepared ready to kill any arguments I made.

He emphatically denied anything was wrong. He blamed my lack of understanding of the financial industry. His indignant, flat denials were so convincing it left other people thinking that perhaps I was going mad. In the face of such certainty and insouciance, who wouldn't have been left doubting me?

The thought-provoking question for many in this sordid affair is how could Grant have preyed for so long on so many strong, Dubai professionals without anyone getting suspicious?

The short answer: because most of us didn't look at our policies or Trusts or follow them. I was the only one that had started to in our circle.

With most of us, Grant took full control of the family finances and was able to hide the extent of the damage. To compound the problem, my friends were not thought to 'regularly' read their valuation statements, instead depending on random updates from Grant on their investment portfolio, which had the effect of leaving them very poorly informed. This meant that no one knew what was exactly happening with their finances. That's how much the trust was in Grant and how ridiculous I sounded to them to now question that trust.

But unbeknown to me, I was unconsciously witnessing the kind of experience that will be only too familiar to millions of people: being trapped in a relationship with a 'gaslighter'.

That's the term for someone who, through subtle manipulation and sustained abuse of power, undermines their investor's self-confidence, self-belief and, ultimately, their sanity, in a bid to keep them under the thumb.

The term, well understood in psychiatric circles, is a form of control, often exercised by fraudsters who feed their narcissistic needs by sucking the confidence out of others. That Grant fits this pattern is not entirely surprising.

The spinning plates start to wobble

Then something happened. Something so small, I had initially missed it.

In January 2015, Grant sent an email circular informing all of his clients of a change in his company license. Due to changes in the UAE law from February 8th, 2015, he would be working under the umbrella of another company, and he was going to run his business through their licence.

He went on to write that he would continue to run Prosperity Management Consultancy.

Who?

I looked at it again, empty of premonition. What struck me was that in his email it was the first time he had mentioned 'Prosperity Management Consultancy' as he had always referred to his company as 'Prosperity Offshore Investment Consultants', as I had always known it to be. At no time during any correspondence or meeting had he referred to his company as 'Prosperity Management

Consultancy'.

Who are they?

I remember thinking it was odd and I told myself to ask him about it the next time I saw him. Maybe he had rebranded, which wasn't an unusual thing for companies to do, and I had somehow missed the announcement.

Months later I asked Grant for a copy of his trade licence to complete some documentation.

Cagey was not the word. I had put it down to him just being difficult. I had to request a copy of his trade licence eight times before he sent it to me and even then he didn't send me a copy of it; just the name and licence number on an email.

At first blush, I hadn't noticed anything about his email to me. But jotting down the details, I wondered why he didn't just give me a copy of his license, instead of actually going to the trouble of writing out the details himself. Something, *something* made me come back to the email.

Then I saw it. It was a throwaway line in his email that, well, threw me: "As you are aware this is the appropriate license for when you took out the Trust".

Those words weren't very significant to me in the beginning. But now, the question was: Why would you add that line? What is it about his email or details that he thinks I'm going to question?

Without that line, I probably wouldn't have looked at it again so closely.

And there's that name again: Prosperity Management Consultancy. It was on the email. His email signature and the company name on which he sent the email to me was Prosperity Offshore Investment Consultants.

Following my friends' advice, I had tried to put my suspicions about Grant to the back of my mind. But right now, this was a big red flag. All these little pieces started meaning something when I put them together. Although I knew I was onto 'something', I still felt none the wiser.

I was left in an utterly untenable situation. There was no choice, I was going to have to take this 'something' outside my social circle and get an opinion on Grant's whole situation.

But who?

I remembered somebody I had met two years earlier at a networking function at the luxurious hotel Burj Al Arab. During our conversation on whether or not that was real gold hanging from the ceiling, the gentlemen had mentioned that he dined at the hotel often because his financial advisor kept awarding him hotel vouchers every time he introduced a new client to him.

That sounds familiar. "Would that be Neil Grant by any chance?" I had asked.

Turns out it was and Grant was a good friend of his. Most of the construction industry had signed up with Grant because of him. Grant and his family had recently attended his wedding, so he was obviously very close to him, and he had struck me as a salt-of-the-earth type, hardworking and loyal.

I checked and miraculously I still had his number stored in my phone. Nathan Charlson.

I wasn't sure on whether to call him, or email him. How do you call someone after two years and ask them if there was any unusual activity with their investments? He may not even remember me and be offended. People don't like talking about money, let alone admitting to losing any. He may not want to get involved. He may put the phone down on me and tell Grant. And I was prepared for him to say and do all that. If that's the worst that could happen, I would take the risk. The desperate need for an unbiased ear was overwhelming. I decided to ignore any such scruples, which were far outweighed by my curiosity.

I checked his details on LinkedIn and he was now working for the Middle East arm of a global company – in a very senior position.

Pause. Maybe this is not such a great idea.

I was just going to ask a few questions, I reminded myself. It wasn't supposed to be anything more than that.

So I called him.

He picked up so fast, I was caught off guard.

"Hello," came the very British, crisp, professional voice of a mature man.

After the initial pleasantries, I prepared myself to bring up the real topic I wanted to discuss. "I know you're busy so I'm just going to get right to it. I need to ask you a question."

"Sure, fire away."

"It's quite sensitive."

"I'll try to answer."

"I just want to touch base with a matter that I'm, well, looking into – involving Neil Grant."

Pause.

"Okay." He drew the word out long. He was saying nothing. There was a brief silence that we both temporarily didn't feel like filling. It was understandable: he was unexpectedly being asked by a virtual stranger to talk about a good friend.

I pressed on to explain the situation with my finances and the manner in which they had plummeted. "My main concern, obviously, is that Neil is managing my money and yet I'm losing money, and some of my money appears to be trapped in funds that I can't seem to get to."

"Okay," again he drew the word out long, as he digested all this information.

"What can you tell me about that?"

A long pause followed. Then came the bombshell.

"I've lost hundreds of thousands."

My £60,000 loss all of a sudden paled in significance.

Now I was silent. It was such a strange sensation. On one hand I was relieved that my gut feeling was right, and I was not the only one to have lost all my money through Grant. This wasn't just a mad blip. On the other hand, this was a disaster. I was understandably rather unnerved by the scale of Nathan's losses.

I then explained the background in more detail. We spoke for over an hour, neither of us quite knowing what the situation really was but we both laughed at our own stupidity of handing over and ultimately losing so much money. What were we thinking? The feeling of just being able to talk to someone about it, and the relief of emptying our minds to an almost-stranger was wonderfully liberating.

Grant apparently has a list of favourite investment funds. Nathan was put in more or less the same funds as I was. So far, whoever I had spoken to, we were all in the same investment funds regardless of our investment profile. It begged the question: Why were we in the same funds when we had different goals and were at different stages in our lives?

Nathan maintained his good cheer despite the story of disaster he proceeded to tell. He had worked hard all his life and managed to put away some money for retirement. But he'd got the idea from Grant that, despite having no experience in the markets, he should invest in some low-risk funds that he had been convinced was a no-lose investment.

Everything was going so well at the beginning that it hardly seemed worth mentioning he'd noticed small amounts being withdrawn from his portfolio. He was duped into spending tens of thousands of pounds as he was repeatedly reassured by Grant that his investments were "doing well", when in fact they were not. There was worse to come. He ended up with two plans from the same provider that were identical.

Nathan had recently remarried and by the sounds of it his wife was cleverer than all of us put together and the take-charge type. Whilst Nathan had been blinded by his friendship with Grant and just did what he told him to do, as a new-girl-in-the-group she saw right through Grant. She found his charm a shade too much and wondered if it was an act. She worried at her husband's passivity and started questioning everything and anything and took her time mulling over every detail – yeah, pretty much what we should have done. It had increasingly frustrated Grant who found himself working harder to get money out of Nathan. That had led to the initial tension between them.

"I haven't seen or spoken to him since that time," he said.

"Really?"

"Not a word."

"How did Neil explain the total loss of all your investment?"

"He blamed the market." That standard reply.

"And then he just disappeared?"

"Pretty much."

Nathan asked the Fund Managers if they could help recoup his losses. They could not. "It's gone," they told him. "You are never going to make that money back."

He asked what he'd done wrong. At the time, the Fund Managers simply put it down to a misreading of the market that had cost him his savings. Perhaps he shouldn't have been investing in such policies in the first place. Perhaps he'd risked far too much money and he should have limited his exposure to say five percent of his net worth. All advice he hadn't received from Grant who was looking to take more money off him. Their relations had deteriorated so badly that they were no longer on speaking terms.

Nathan had probably introduced thirty of his friends and colleagues to Grant. Those friends and colleagues also brought other friends and colleagues. It was like a train. He had made it so easy for him. He would casually bring Grant up in conversations and he would make the introductions. That's the level of trust he once had in Grant.

I asked Nathan if he had heard of a company called Prosperity Management Consultancy. It didn't reflect his experiences either. "No, I have no clue. Who are they?" I said I had no idea, and that I was puzzled by the name when I first came across it, too. Nathan made a mental note of it, and said he'd make some enquiries into it.

At this point in time, all Nathan and I had was that Grant had lost us all our investments whilst badly managing our portfolio.

But is this even a crime? How can we prove it? Can we get him to answer questions? Can we bring an action against him? If so, what action? Can we get our money back? At the time, I didn't know how the financial advisory industry worked, or how to describe it. I had zero experience on finance and local laws, and of this world. And I had no relationships within it to lean on for advice.

"We need to find all of this out," I said to Nathan as it would serve no purpose to keep speculating.

"I'll see what I can find out about this other company," offered Nathan, before pausing and asking, "and then what?".

"Then we have to do something."

"Such as?"

"I have no idea."

That was indeed the first and great question: What exactly were we pursuing? I had no idea. Literally no idea.

As a devotee of jigsaws, I saw this as a gigantic jigsaw puzzle to solve, and the first piece was where do you start in Dubai on bringing an action to get answers from your financial advisor? I wouldn't know *how* I was going to start it.

But I knew where to start.

Well, where else but at the heart of the financial community: Dubai Financial Services Authority or the commonly used acronym, DFSA in the Dubai International Financial Centre (DIFC). Dubai is full of acronyms – DED, DIA, DLA, SEC – which I was going to have to get used to. And I was also going to have to prepare myself for getting my knuckles severely wrapped occasionally.

To Grant, the spinning plates of his life were starting to wobble dangerously.

Dubai Financial Services Authority sow the seed

I've never had less of a plan in my life than I did upon arrival in the DFSA reception area.

"Is there anyone I can speak to about investment funds and a 'possible' situation with my financial advisor?" Can I be any more vague? The receptionist did a good job decoding my query, which clearly highlighted that I didn't know what situation I was in.

I didn't think for a minute this would come under the DFSA jurisdiction but I hoped that they may point me in the right direction. I was incredibly fortunate. Whilst sitting in reception, two British national directors on their way to an internal meeting, were waved over by the receptionist and they kindly offered to hear my story there and then.

Entering the sprawling ice-cold boardroom, the first thing visitors saw was a blown-up photograph on the wall of the Dubai's ruler, His Highness Sheikh Mohammed bin

Rashid Al Maktoum. A dozen leather chairs were arranged neatly around a table which was in the centre of the room. On the opposite wall, floor to ceiling windows looked over the entire DIFC complex. It was an ultra-posh set up.

The first time that I formally talked about the suspicions about Grant was with the DFSA, and sitting across from the two gentlemen I explained that there were possibly other clients in the same situation.

Holding the valuation statements of the Trust, and of the short-term Vision Life Insurance policy in their hands, they carefully, and without a trace of hurry, stared at the figures. In particular, they peered curiously at the names of the investment funds within the Trust. They gave it to me straight: they have never heard of any of them, or of Guardian Trust Company Ltd, the trustee. In their view, it looked like my advisor had chosen high-risk illiquid investments most of which failed either partly or entirely, which is why the five funds in the Trust had suspended and crashed so badly in the short-term. The funds looked to be start-up companies where the risk was inevitably high because they were largely unregulated but, as I was informed, the rewards for Grant would also be high. Money poured into investments of a start-up nature was every financial advisors' dream – they held the maximum commission for them.

I was momentarily dumbstruck. Grant never said nothing about this sort of set up for me.

Start-up. Short-term. High-risk. Illiquid. Each word hit me like a train. It's exactly what I asked Grant not to invest my money in. Were they sure?

And there was another surprise.

The Trust itself, they confirmed, was also lining Grant's pockets with regular financial advisory fees.

My eyebrows lifted. *Sorry, What!?*

Guardian Trust Company Ltd, the trustee, had not been paying Grant's fees all these years, as he had told me. I had been. Although Grant was not paid directly from my pocket, he was paid indirectly from the Trust itself. It is referred to as a 'hidden' fee. Other types of hidden fees they predicted would be huge marketing fees that are never fully disclosed which was also paid out of my Trust.

"It's that bad?" I asked, pointing at my financial statements spread across the table in front of them.

"Yes, it really is that bad." And they gave me the devastating news. Despite what the figures in the valuation statements were showing, my investments they predicted were worthless, and had been for some time. The figures that I received from Grant were just smoke and mirrors and not the actual value of the overall Trust.

They confirmed my worst fears. "I mean, yes, he hoodwinked you, clearly; he should have stuck to traditional companies for you." Sadly, they said, non-experienced cautious investors such as myself, all too often will be totally ill-advised, of the risks and illiquidity of the investments we are entered into, that are wholly inappropriate for our risk profile, goals and aims.

A lot of things raced through my mind as I listened to this. How much commission had he made? "Impossible to know exactly," they replied. "The only thing we can tell you is that these type of investment funds generate high commission for advisors between the four to eight percent bracket." Two sympathetic faces looked back at me, "so, yes, a lot of commission, we would imagine".

"How does it work?" I asked.

"Well," one of the gentlemen relaxed in his chair as he explained the basics of the remuneration to me. "With the five-year policy they will pay an initial indemnity commission, probably around AED 18,000 on a particular plan such as this."

"And the Trust itself?"

"It works as a straight up one-time introductory fee. If he sells ten of these Trusts a day, at £4,000 a pop, that's £40,000 a day. These are approximate figures, but you get an idea of what he is making off you; and then say quarterly advisory fees on top of that, which is a percentage of the value of the Trust."

As I sat across from them and absorbed this information, the boulder finally dropped on my head. Whilst my life savings were sinking faster than the Titanic, my financial advisor's personal wealth was leap frogging ahead.

And the reality sank in.

I'd been had.

I hadn't even suspected foul play, let alone that Grant might *purposely* be mis-advising me. The only person making money seemed to be Grant.

Asked if I knew he was regulated or not, I shook my head, and claimed to have "no idea". I realised how puerile that sounded.

"Probably not," was their verdict, "which will make it more difficult for you as there may be no complaints mechanism for you to pursue". This was, sadly, true. There wasn't a systematic investigation that could be undertaken if Grant was not regulated anywhere.

As for their advice?

It centred around one word: mis-selling.

To them it indeed appeared to be a typical case of mis-selling and mis-management.

Mis-selling and mis-management?

It didn't sound good. What had I got myself into?

That was the official industry confirmation and the insight that changed it all.

They advised I assemble all of the documentation that I had including valuation statements and they told me which appropriate formal bodies and organisations I needed to engage with to take forward the complaint, starting with the regulators in Dubai, the Insurance Authority. Grant could be open to some legal action as I had entered into an advisory agreement. Relevant considerations in the assessment of a complaint would include the extent to which the investments recommended to me from Grant were suitable for my circumstances and attitude to risk, and what exactly was disclosed to me at the time – but, I was warned, it was a long shot.

I waited for them to produce something more persuasive. When they didn't, I asked, "Impossible?".

"No, we wouldn't say so."

The truth was that they had no idea whatsoever. And the Insurance Authority was the best place to start, and they might be interested in helping me in some way.

Another suggestion they offered was to consider engaging in legal assistance. At this point I decided not to. I had to understand and make sense of it myself first.

The pair agreed with me that Grant was likely to have a lot more victims in a similar "investment" situation to myself, including other expats. It was somewhat cathartic hearing this and realising Nathan and I were maybe not his only victims because it took a personal element out of the sordid affair.

After the meeting, I shared my news with Nathan who was shocked by it: "Wow. That's a lot more serious."

A thought hit me, then I asked, "Do you know anyone who has actually made money with Grant?".

He paused. Slowly he said, "No".

"Lost money?"

"Not really. It's not really spoken about."

"That really would be interesting to find out if anyone has made money and how many have lost money."

"Well, they may think they are in the black." He had a point. Albeit a scary one.

Later that day, one of the directors I had met with sent me an email advising me to check with Guardian Trust Company Ltd to identify who has access to, or control over, my various fund investments. I previously had no direct contract with Guardian and he advised that I may need to explain in full the problems that I was currently experiencing.

I decided to do just that.

Unbeknown to me at the time, I was about to tip off a gentleman called Philip Van Neste; Grant's right-hand man in Jersey.

Insurance Authority and a very worrying insight

I had no idea who to ask for when I arrive at the Insurance Authority's offices. And of course, I didn't have an appointment. I hadn't phoned in advance, thinking that I might win an advantage by making a surprise visit. It just so happens, the manager, based in Abu Dhabi, was visiting their Dubai office that very day, and he was the person I needed to speak to.

He was in back-to-back meetings all day. I was told by a very friendly receptionist that I could wait for a possible window in-between his meetings and see if he will see me. The other alternative was to make an appointment to see him during his next visit to Dubai in one month's time. I decided to take her up on her suggestion and wait, and sure enough I managed to secure a meeting with him. I was led into his temporary office; a brightly lit, windowless, long room that looked like it was used for everything, with a small desk at one end of it and large swivel chairs and boxes randomly scattered around the rest of the room.

"Ahlan," he smiled warmly. He was tall, well over six feet and, although a local Emirati, had opted to wear a suit instead of the traditional dish dash. With his saturnine good looks, neatly trimmed goatee and drooping black moustache, he seemed just the man to burnish the regulator's image.

"Grab a chair," he said doing so himself, walking round to the front of his desk. He sat down, unbuttoned his jacket and pulled a small notebook and pen out of his pocket and laid it on his desk. I pulled a chair from the other side of the room and sat down opposite him.

I was bracing myself for some full-bore bombast of the 'we can't help you' and 'there's a procedure' type that was rumoured to be unleashed on anyone who dares to approach a government organisation without an appointment. But instead, we ended up having a cordial free rolling 45-minute exchange which gave me a fascinating insight into Grant's business activities and, more importantly, the man himself.

In between sips of Arabic coffee, I started by describing my story, then did my best to reconstruct conversations I had with the DFSA in their entirety on their view of my situation.

He listened to me, politely, without interrupting, smiling and shaking his head, like, 'isn't it so funny the things people do?'.

When I was finished, he asked, "Why did you give him so much money?" slowly shaking his head, "and you didn't check any of his details?". His face twisted in sympathy.

Yes, it was puerile. I'd never be able to explain.

"What nationality?" he asked.

"He's British … well Scottish."

He started giving his colleagues some instructions.

They returned one by one with typed documents in their hands to say there was no record within their systems of either Prosperity Management Consultancy, Prosperity Offshore Investment Consultants or of Neil Grant. Despite the Prosperity Offshore Investment Consultant's website saying he was regulated, he wasn't. That was indeed a blow. But there was more.

The manager was absorbed in the email Grant had sent to his clients informing them that from January 29th, 2015 he was running his business through the licence of a local insurance broker.

"This is not possible," he said tapping the paperwork with his thumb. "Legally, there are lots of problems with this." It was not possible for Prosperity to work under the licence of an insurance broker. Two companies could not operate from one business address or from one license, performing different activities.

Welcome to my highly confusing world, I thought.

Given this back-drop, the manager, decided to ask some questions of his own – to Grant himself.

"What is his number?" He picked up the phone and was about to call him.

I wasn't prepared for that. Grant had no idea I had come this far. He thought I was just causing a stir at Friday brunches and over family barbecues. In the UK, authorities don't want to reveal to people like Grant that they are being investigated, until they had an airtight case. In Dubai, they operate differently. It means, inadvertently Grant will be tipped off, and I didn't want that to happen. But at the same time this constituted a major escalation in intrigue.

It turns out I had no choice in the matter. The manager was determined, and all I could think was, why not? There were now so many questions. It was time Grant answered them. I whipped out my phone to pass him

Grant's mobile number.

He put him on speaker phone.

"Mr Neil Grant?" He sounded very official.

Silence.

"This is Neil Grant?" he repeated in his Arabic drawl.

"Yes. Who is this?"

"Manager from Insurance Authority. Good morning."

That's as far the pleasantries went between the two men.

The manager explained to Grant he was calling about a complaint against him that had just landed on his desk, and wanted to ask him some questions pertaining to it. He paused for effect.

"I don't know what you're talking about," Grant said somewhat unsteadily and without sufficient conviction. Undeterred, the Emirati pressed ahead.

Intriguingly, Grant then refused to answer any questions regarding Prosperity, his new employer who he had joined as senior partner earlier that year, or which Visa he was currently working on, simply on the basis that they were private information.

This early exchange set the scene for a fractious encounter between the two of them. Grant was in avoidance mode and the manager was in detective mode.

Things only got worse and heated as the conversation continued. Grant went on to refuse to answer any questions on the type of investments he handled and was uptight and defensive when the manager asked him about them.

"I don't have to answer anything or feel the need to explain this," he repeatedly said, before defiantly stating, "We've done nothing wrong."

I twisted my face into a cartoon-like-expression that said, 'strange response?'. At this point the manager hadn't said he had done anything wrong. It was a rash statement, and Grant was prepared to say anything just then. But the Emirati was staring hard at the phone. Grant didn't entirely recognise the magnitude of the call, and who he was speaking to. It was clear the manager did not like what he was hearing, or how he was being spoken to.

"You don't want to answer my questions, Mr Neil?" he asked, raising his voice slightly, trying to force a light-hearted moment as he flipped my papers in his hands. Not waiting for a response he said, "I'm looking at this portfolio, of Miss Waheed's. My question to you, are these products insurance-related?".

"I can't discuss my clients' portfolio with you on grounds of confidentiality." Abandoning the flippancy, he was quick of the mark with that comeback.

"She is sitting here with me." The Emirati gave me a quick wink.

Silence. It's awkward. Really awkward.

"She's there?"

"Yes, she is here."

There's a gap that no one's putting any words into. Do I sing out "Surprise"?

"I don't have to answer anything on the grounds that it is confidential," Grant said eventually, quite roughly. It was the first time I had ever heard him sound jittery.

"She's here, giving consent."

Maybe it was his sales training which had taught him divulge the minimum information, maybe it was his natural caution when dealing with something he didn't understand, but Grant said, "Best ask her yourself".

"Indeed." Undeterred the manager glanced at me and continued. Stroking his goatee, he now referred to the email from Grant dated January 29th, 2015 informing all of his clients of a change in his company licence and that due to changes in the UAE law from February 8th, 2015, he would be working under the umbrella of another company, and he was going to run his business through their licence.

"Which law are you referring to here?" the manager wanted to know, but Grant awkwardly refused to answer the question before finally conceding at this current moment he couldn't remember exactly. All the while I listened and I was left wondering who is this guy on the other end of the phone? Why is he evading questions?

The manager gave a slow nod to show he was getting the picture. He went on to explain to Grant that it was not possible for Prosperity, an offshore investment company, to be licensed by an insurance broker and regulated by the Insurance Authority, who deal only with insurance brokers and insurance-related products. He clarified to Grant that his employer, as insurance brokers, were licensed and regulated under the Insurance Authority, but Prosperity, a financial advisory company, was not.

When asked if Grant was aware of this, he fell silent.

Now, the Emirati once again asked if the products Grant sold were insurance-related, to which Grant now said they were not.

Gulp. This is, quite simply, not true. My mind flashed back to the short-term Vision Life Insurance policy and the Trust where he was advising on life insurance products as well as the Centurion (Life Insurance Settlement) investment fund. This meant, by law, he had to be regulated by the Insurance Authority.

The manager held up his hand as though he anticipated I was unable to keep a lid on my frustration any longer and I was about to blurt something out. Was there any point in saying anything? If a person won't admit they've been caught out and doesn't care what you think of them, what can you do? They're as free as they've always been to make up anything and don't need to convince anybody.

The manager again asked Grant questions about the Prosperity licence and its status, to which Grant replied that he did not have to share those details with him and that it was between him and the Department of Economic Development (DED) – the government body responsible for issuing the appropriate business licenses. Looked mildly irritated, the Emirati quickly regained his composure, and went on to ask what was his employer's business activity under DED.

"Why do you need to know that?" Grant's reply was swift and firm.

"I think it would be insurance brokers', which would be correct for them, but my question to you is if it allows anybody from the broker to act as a financial consultant?" He gave me another wink signalling he already knew the answer.

Grant was growing hostile and again stood firm and said he did not need to reply to that question either. In a counter move, he pointedly asked the manager for his details – full name, title and phone number, which the Emirati obliged, without a moment's hesitation, albeit bemused. I shook my head at the phone.

Why did Grant remain silent amid a growing list of questions from the Insurance Authority around his company licence and activities? With one simple answer he could have resolved this one way or another, and that would have put an end to it, but for him not to say anything at this stage was misjudged on his part. Question after question, and it bothered me that he didn't give the answer to a single one of them. And above all, why was he so secretive about his business affairs? All these questions were racketing around in my head throughout the phone call.

The Emirati exchanged glances with me. It was pointless to say more. We both knew that we weren't going to get anything else out of Grant. At least not for the time being. And just like that, he promptly ended the call. "He's not genuine," was his observation. And based on that call, I had to agree with him. I think it was obvious that was one of the worst mea culpas ever known to this man. I mean, if we didn't think Grant was suspicious before, after that conversation we now thought something had happened. Something was going on with his business activities and all these difference licences and I was starting to see a glimpse of the real Grant for the first time – and it was rather shady. It was a far cry from the image he represented that now looks hopelessly tarnished.

I went there hoping for answers. Instead, I felt as if I'd been given a bigger, more impossible puzzle than the one I came in with.

"Send an email to this company and check if Prosperity is regulated with them." The Emirati wrote down the email address of Securities and Commodities Authority (SCA). He explained that companies outside of the DIFC are regulated by the UAE Insurance Authority for all insurance-based products; and SCA for investment-based products.

"Then go to the police and file a report. He needs to be investigated." This urgent encouragement by the Insurance Authority worried me more than anything else. This was getting serious.

The police? Do they investigate this sort of thing? Apparently, they did. He explained it was a slow-moving process before he could hurl Grant or his employer before him for a meeting. And this was a far quicker call to action without getting bogged down by the system.

Meanwhile, he said he would make enquiries with Grant's employer and the DED. He promised my visit would not be the end of his inquiries.

What an extraordinary day.

I wrote an email to SCA and they confirmed that neither Prosperity Management Consultancy nor Prosperity Offshore Investment Consultants were regulated by them for any activity.

Okay, so he's not licensed – anywhere. I didn't know enough about the local law to go into any detail. I had no idea what charges I could even bring against him. Mismanagement of funds? Mis-selling? Was that actually a crime? Doesn't a car salesman mis-sell, over-sell a car to us every time? Clarity on his business activities and licenses was definitely required as he certainly didn't like any questions related to them. It was still too early for me to get my head around it as there were so many loose ends and bits of information here and there, and I didn't know how to tie them up, but I might get all the pieces to the puzzle from some help from the police. The next step, the only step I could think of, was to talk with the police, and get them to press Grant for some answers.

Not one to shy away from a challenge, whatever else it would be worth having a go. I just felt I had no other choice as Grant was not giving anything away.

I messaged Nathan on the amazing developments.

"Can you believe it?" I asked him.

"I'm not sure what to believe anymore." Every time I gave Nathan feedback he had the feeling that something was very wrong and something sinister was very possibly happening.

Nathan had become a friend; he had occupied a prime seat in the royal puzzle and as my relationship with Rupert went temporarily quiet, Nathan moved into the vacuum to give me the benefit of his advice and full support. Although I did have a laugh with him about my weird fixation on this matter, and let's just say that he was quite ticked with my quirky obsession with it, he was having a good old chuckle at my eccentric encounters with people around town. "Hilarious, brilliant – good luck. Go for it." He explained he was doing some of his own digging into Grant's companies and he would get back to me.

"Do you really think the police can do something?" he queried.

"Not sure." I knew nothing about how the Dubai police operated, and had managed to stay out of their way from the day I had landed in the sandpit. "At least we can open a dialogue with them, just in case something can happen."

"It'll be fun to see what happens tomorrow with them."

"I think we have a different definition of the word 'fun'."

Indeed. Just as you would expect from any good police drama, there was plenty of humour, tension, heartbreak and a healthy sprinkle of poignant one-liners.

The epitome of stupid

But proof? What proof did I have?

I arrived at the police station intending to just show up and see what happened. So far that strategy has worked for me. Ultimately, I believed I would be turned away. It was always going to be difficult to prove some wrongdoing had taken place. Grant didn't force us to do anything; he made us all complicit in our own undoing. He didn't steal from us. He didn't threaten us. He didn't put the money in his own pocket. We gave money willingly. That was the reality. And now I was going to explain this to someone, hoping that they may just get it.

Early morning, 7.30 am, I learnt fast, was the best time to visit a police station. There's hardly anyone around and the officers themselves are fresh and in a jolly mood because you've grabbed them just after a hearty breakfast.

I entered the reception area of the station, to see a police officer sat at the desk listening to members of the public and their grievances. One by one he directed them to various offices. It was all very robotic and business-like.

The mood of the police station was always one of total patience. Sometimes people must wait for hours before an officer gets a chance to take care of them, but, unlike Britain, they never so much as tap their feet or complain or roll their eyes in exasperation. There's just a different standard here for good behaviour in front of authorities.

"What's the complaint?" I was asked, when it was my turn to approach the desk.

"Financial. Mis-selling. Mis-management."

I was ushered into a non-descript office, with whitewashed walls where there were two police officers in an olive green shirt and trousers and a dark green beret sat at two tables at the back of the room in front of a row of folding chairs. The office consisted of one large room, so there was no possibility of closing a door for some privacy.

That morning, I was third in the waiting line. The first guy was immediately directed to the civil courts after being told after just two minutes into his story that his complaint was not criminal. He accepted the outcome and promptly left. The second guy in front of me was an Irish well-dressed young businessman – something to do with credit card fraud.

Whilst he was being questioned, I was called to the second officer. His big broad brown desk was completely empty except for a computer and a phone.

"What is the problem?" he asked me as I took a seat across from him.

I started to explain what happened, but two minutes into it I could see the officer was already lost. Too much alien information and too difficult to wade through it.

"This is civil," he eventually said.

"No, it's not its criminal," I replied firmly. I wasn't going to let him fob me off like he did to the first guy.

"Where is the contract?" He got right to the point.

Now, it was going to get tricky. The case was not black and white, and for a start there was no contract between Grant and myself. My contracts, I had learned, were directly with the financial institutions holding my Trust and my policy, not with my financial advisor. It was the same situation for Nathan.

"Which part is criminal?" the police officer was clearly confused. "You gave him the money. And you say you have no contract with him."

Begrudgingly, I nodded my head.

"Investments – you win you lose. Here you lose." He punched his desk with each word he said. He had a wonderful talent for keeping things simple. "No crime," was his final say, with a final fist punch of the desk. It was written all over his face as he looked past me – Next.

"But there's the mis-selling and mis-management element," I argued, positioning my face firmly back in his view. "He invested my money in things for his own benefit, to make money for himself. That's what I want you to investigate."

"All right," he says slowly, thinking. "So you're saying fraud?" He does a pantomime 'What now?' face. "There is nothing here of fraud."

"Well, no, I'm not saying that." There was certainly nothing to suggest fraud. "All I want you to do is to call him down here and just ask him some questions of how he managed my investments and why I lost it all."

He held his hands open wide as he asked, "on what reason am I going to call him here?". He started to repeat himself. "You gave him money. You have no contract. Where is the contract?" Since his vocabulary was limited, there wasn't much variety to his conversations. And he was not budging.

"That's a complicated question." How do you explain something you do not understand yourself? How did I not have a contract with Grant? How had I missed that? In fact, I couldn't find any paper trail between Grant and myself linking him to me as my financial advisor. Which was, in itself, utterly bizarre.

By now the room was filling up and I could see he was getting distracted again and he wanted to move on.

"What can I do now?" I pressed, leaving the question hanging and not budging myself. But the conversation was plunging headlong into nothingness, and I sensed the worst.

There was a pause, much too long, as if he couldn't decide. I couldn't criticise him for his reaction. This has been no ordinary story. And no way for me to come out of it well. He just saw it as a frivolous complaint, that was going to take up time, and most of all cost money in investigation fees, and that had no shred of solid evidence that will even help the case.

Slowly, he opened his drawer and he picked up a pen and wrote something in Arabic on a yellow Post-it Note and told me to go to office number nine and speak to the "manager", whom I guessed was his boss. "Tell him your story." Before I had a chance to say anything further he looked past me and bellowed, "Next." And with that, I was dismissed. If it got me to the next step, I liked his approach. I scurried from the room and went to find his manager.

It turned out there were two levels of approval required before a case is referred to the director and head of the station for final approval and it can be transferred to the prosecution office in the police station and then onto public prosecution, who ultimately decides if the case is to proceed before a judge in court.

I was already at step two.

As I made my way to office nine, I was chased down the corridor by the Irishman who had been sitting in the room listening to my story.

"You're wasting your time." I was told in a thick Irish accent. "They can't do anything here ... I know."

"How do you know?"

"I'm a financial advisor myself," he told me, which had to be the weirdest coincidence imaginable. "I can guess what this guy has done, and I can guess how he's done it. You're not going to get anywhere with this ... I don't want you to waste your time here ... seriously."

"Well, I'm here now ... let's see how far I get ... I can only try," I replied undeterred. He wasn't saying anything I didn't already know but I wanted to see how far I could take it before I was literally kicked out of there. It would either prove useful or it wouldn't. I thought it was worth a try.

"How do you know what he did?" I asked him, very deliberately, studying his face.

"Wild guess." He shrugged his shoulders, "Common knowledge within the industry". An intriguing answer. Grant is merely the latest on the list it appears. "There's a lot I can tell you, that I can't tell you here."

I took the Irishman's phone number, before continuing down the corridor.

Officer Salah was the name painted in dark red on the door of office number nine and he was sitting at his desk with his back to the window when I entered his office. The room was spacious and white with the cluttered dusty look one would expect to find in a police officer's room. One wall was lined with shelves holding three-ring binders, the other a large leather sofa. Diminutive in figure, he wore a different uniform to the previous officer; dark cream with badges on the collar reflecting his high rank, with a number of medals across his chest.

"Sabah al khair," fortunately, I had picked up a number of Arabic phrases during my years in the emirate, and could hold a decent conversation in the local language.

"Marhaba," he drawled in a deep voice, politely rising to his feet. There was one empty chair across from his desk and I looked hopefully at it. "May I?"

"Of course," he said. He carefully sat down, as if all movements needed forethought. Up close, his metal-rimmed glasses had the effect of magnifying his eyes. "What can we do for you?"

"I'm in a rather urgent situation." I explained that I was sent to him because my case "is a bit complicated". I then handed him the yellow Post-it Note the first officer had handed to me, which he quickly glanced at. And I had to tell the whole story again. For the first five minutes I recounted what had happened to me, starting with how I had been introduced to Grant. He allowed me to tell the story at my own pace. After I finished, the officer spoke using almost identical language to the previous officer.

"Where is the contract?"

"I don't have one. There wasn't a contract between us."

"You gave him money and there is no contract ... you gave him money, just like that?" His eyes widened in pure wonderment.

Yep, just like that. I had already endured my fair share of criticism. Experience was thrown away, common sense was withdrawn, scepticism gave way to belief, trust and ultimate power.

"Do you have any reason about why he might have deceived you?"

"Err ... money!"

The oldest, most common motive there is; pure intent, obsessive, entitled, money.

He paused to consider. I started to tell the whole story again, in a different way.

He interrupted me and held up his hand and said, "I understand, I'm asking, what you want me to do about it?".

For the next twenty minutes, I argued my case with the officer who just wasn't budging in light of the sketchy evidence, his arms permanently folded across his chest. But unlike the previous officer, he was really trying to understand why I thought I had a case and seemed to be amused by it. I pretty much felt like I was this weird creature to them with this bizarre belief that a crime had taken place.

"Have you tried dealing with this other person directly?" he finally asked, clasping his hands together.

"He's not responding to anything," I replied.

"This is not a police issue ..."

"Of course it's a police issue. He's mis-managing our money ..."

He quickly interjected, "you haven't entered into a contract with him, so there is no crime."

"I'm sorry, sir, but what you just said makes no sense to me at all."

He lets out a deep sigh. Where criminality is suspected there has to be good grounds on which to pursue it. It was clear that the only case he thought I had was for stupidity. Against me.

Moving on tenaciously, I hated to do this because I didn't want to put him on the spot, but it had to be said, so I just laid it out there. "Look, sir, I respect you and I respect your position, but I promise you I would not waste your time if I thought I did not have a case against him. It's not just a thought I had rolling out of bed this morning. And I need you to investigate him. We can't just let this go, we can't just ignore it. If you then decide there is no case I will accept it. But we have to at least try." I sat back in my seat and folded my arms before adding, "he may possibly be rogue even," as if that explained everything. Which, in fact, it actually did. I sincerely hoped that he would understand because this thing had to be resolved, one way or the other – in part, so I could move on.

"Rogue," he repeated, rolling his tongue around the letter 'R' for extra effect. He was chewing over what I had said, probably amused that I had given him my opinion on what I think he should do. But he bore all this with a slightly wintry smile.

He tapped his finger against his temple, straightened his glasses, and sighed. "But I really don't understand why you think we might be able to help you." A quiet mood had settled over the room. He needed some sort of concrete lead in order to move forward with an investigation. Caught between his instinct for caution, his urge to help, and his reluctance to point me in what might be a futile direction of hope.

"Alright ... okay," he finally sighed wearily, and, to his great credit given the huge pressure I was putting him under, relented and said he would ask Grant to come to the police station to answer a few questions.

"And let's see ... that's the best I can do." His hands clasped in prayer. But I would have to give a full statement. Did I have a problem with that?

"No," I said emphatically, as if I'd been waiting to say the word all my life. In fact, if it was official, they would have to follow through on the complaint.

"Okay, go back to the officer and tell him to take your statement."

"Thank you," I said bowing slightly.

I swiftly left his office and made my way back up the corridor to the first room, which had now filled up with more people and officers.

The first officer was perplexed, to say the least, when I gave him the message.

"Whalla," he sang out in a jolly tone, elaborately spreading his hands in front of him. Dubai police weren't known for being particularly tactful. His comment was met with laughter from the other officers in the room. He had not expected to see me again; that was clear. He thought for a second, and then picked up the phone – I was taking a wild guess to Officer Salah in office number nine – to get confirmation that his leg wasn't being pulled by this obviously deluded woman sitting in front of him.

And I must confess I rather enjoy his breezy, unselfconscious style; there aren't many people who would dare show their belief at what they thought was an absurd decision.

Finally, he put down the receiver and said "okay, sit". Gesturing with his hand, he turned all professional whilst I gave him my statement which he duly entered into the computer, tapping away as I spoke. The whole process took some twenty minutes. After I finished, he printed off the paper and I was asked to sign it. It was all in Arabic and as I don't read Arabic fluently, I had no idea what he had written and how much of what I had said he had captured. For all I knew he had just typed out his wife's shopping list. I rummaged through my handbag and found a pen, signed the bottom of the sheet and handed the paper back to him. He glanced at it and put it in his drawer.

"Okay, we'll call him," he told me, beginning to sort through a pile of messengers that had been left on his desk.

"And then?"

"We'll call you," he said, getting to his feet. As simple

as that.

"Yes – right, okay." I decided not to push it further. I wanted to ask when I could expect to hear from him, but I could see that the officer had no intention of saying anything more at the moment.

Instead, I thanked him exactly as I would if I were grateful for something, and leave. It was a result. Grant at least needed to answer some questions. He couldn't get off totally scot-free.

By now the police station had filled up. People were walking around and many had their Arabic translators with them. I had a feeling that if I had a translator with me I probably wouldn't have got the result that I did because the officers would have spoken directly to them and not to me. And they can dismiss things a lot quicker that way, especially with the minimal evidence I was offering.

As I left the police station, my phone rang. It was Nathan. You couldn't have scripted a more ironic, or pertinent segway.

"Where are you?" he asked.

I updated him. "They're not entirely convinced but they're going to call him and ask him a few questions ..."

He interrupted me.

"You're not going to believe this." Nathan's words on the phone, the barely suppressed excitement in his voice. He paused. "I've had the most extraordinary day, something of a breakthrough. Well, I think so anyway."

"Great. What?"

A small rush of breath while he framed the words. "I think we are dealing with fraud here. No ... in fact I know it is fraud."

My story took an unexpected turn.

"I don't know. I ..." I was lost for words. "The police officer asked me ... but how ... how is it fraud exactly?" He was right, I couldn't believe it. Just could not believe it. I always thought that maybe there was a good explanation for what Grant was doing with our investments, and that it wasn't fraud, or something less criminal.

Fraud sounded so deceitful and calculating and something I had never really had to deal with. And it completely changed the situation. Worryingly, I had just given my statement on the subject of mis-management and I had not mentioned fraud of any nature (something Grant's lawyers later pounced on in trial).

My first thought was, how do his actions become fraudulent?

The breakthrough

If Grant's present seemed blissful, his past was rapidly catching up on him.

During all this time, Nathan had been meandering around Grant's business affairs and had done some hard digging of his own into his former friend and advisor, presenting a view that differed from his 'official' narrative, and the pieces fell into place, in one swift second.

I had sent him the email that Grant had sent to me with his company licence details on it and the same throwaway line that had bothered me, now bothered him. He was distracted by the two companies Grant had mentioned in his email.

He noticed 'Prosperity Offshore Investment Consultants' was operating from the same office address as 'Prosperity Management Consultancy'. There appeared to be two companies under two licenses at the same office address, first at the Business Centre in the Dubai hotel and then in offices in Business Bay, a central business district in Dubai.

His curiosity had led him to the DED website, and he had done some snooping on the two companies, which led to a significant breakthrough in our search for some answers.

Later that night, I sat down to do the online search I probably should have done a long time ago to check out Nathan's story for myself.

The DED was a government body that registers companies and provides companies with the appropriate business licence.

Although Grant had set up a company called 'Prosperity Offshore Investment Consultants' there was no record of it with the DED. It simply did not exist. It transpired that the company trading as 'Prosperity Offshore Investment Consultants' was actually registered with the DED as 'Prosperity Management Consultancy' under the same licence number 559536, active from July 18th, 2004 until July 17th, 2016.

So what was Prosperity Management Consultancy?

One thing for sure, the list of activities they were legally allowed to do under their business licence did not include managing money or advising on money. The activity they were legally allowed to do was 'management consultancy' only. But advisory meetings and paperwork signing for financial advice and documentation signing for financial products all took place with partners and clients, including ourselves, in the Dubai offices of 'Prosperity Management Consultancy'. All correspondence showed that Prosperity Management Consultancy was operating as an offshore company based in Dubai under the DED licence number 559536.

In order to carry out financial advisory services, financial planning, and recommendations on savings and pension planning policies, and taking commission from policy providers from these recommendations, the company had to have the DED activity 'financial analysis and consultancy'.

To double-check this, Nathan had researched other companies who carried out financial advisory services to see what activities they had on their licences. He went through all the entities one by one. He found the following: Mondial have two activities. The first is 'financial analysis and consultancy' and the second activity is 'mortgage brokers'. Professional Investment Consultancies Middle East has the activity of 'financial analysis and consultancy'. Acuma has 'financial analysis and consultancy' activity under their licence number.

None of the above mentioned financial advisory consultancies operate under the activity of 'management consultancy'.

It was like a Polaroid getting clearer as you watch it develop.

What this meant was that Prosperity Management Consultancy had been acting wholly outside of the boundaries of their registered activity with the DED and were acting in the capacity of financial advisor and financial broker, based in Dubai.

Now it was blindingly obvious. Grant was misusing his licence.

He had set up Prosperity Management Consultancy, but as he was unable to obtain a financial advisory services licence, he deceptively traded as Prosperity Offshore Investment Consultants to make investors think they were an investment company.

In legal terms, this is licence fraud.

But in our case, there was another layer to this.

We had been given what we considered bad advice by Grant on which funds to sign up to, and we believed that this advice was provided predominantly on the basis of generating commission for Grant, where the funds recommended generated high commissions for him. This bad advice had left us with long-term policies, some for 25-year terms, that were making considerable losses. People were tied into these policies, unable to get out of them without forfeiting even further losses if surrendering these policies before the full term.

In legal terms, this layer amounted to criminal behaviour, a more serious, sinister type of fraud where it is described as a wrongful deception intended to result in financial or personal gain. We could dress up the language, but that was the gist of it.

Here was proof, but I felt no elation, no triumph, only a dull, persistent anxiety. It was so shocking and so horribly obvious that I couldn't believe I hadn't thought of it before.

Wait a minute. Then you have a light bulb moment. This was a planned, carefully executed, cunning and deceitful plan. Grant had us from day one. He had deliberately engineered a fake company the same time as he set up Prosperity Management Consultancy in 2004. He knew exactly what he was doing. It wasn't an opportunity that had presented itself to him.

It was this realisation that really hit us.

And there was even more.

Nathan then referred to the email from Grant dated January 29th, 2015 where it is stated that Prosperity will "continue to be your financial advisor", but will operate under the licence of a local insurance broker. Upon checking the DED licence activity of the insurance broker their only licence activity was that of 'insurance brokers'. Just as the manager at the Insurance Authority had said, Grant's employer did not hold the DED activity for 'financial analysis and consultancy'. In short, the details and description for Grant's employer's registered activity as per the DED did not allow them to employ any company or individual providing financial advice on savings or pension policies.

Nathan's amateur sleuthing might put one in mind of Peter Falk's tenacious character in the crime drama television series Columbo; the detective whose persistent behaviour teases out incriminating evidence.

The question that remained, however, was why didn't the DED permit Grant the licence to practice as a financial advisory company? What criteria did Grant not meet?

It was around this time I remembered the Irishman I had met at the police station. The financial advisor. I had a feeling he could answer that, but I also wanted to see if there was additional evidence to validate the information Nathan and I were collecting.

I called him and we agreed to meet the next day, when I gave him an update on what happened at the police station after he left.

"They took your statement?" he exclaimed. "Nothing will happen though, nothing can touch him … don't get your hopes up … they probably took pity on you."

Whatever. I'll take it where I can. My hopes undimmed.

I gave him a copy of the valuation statement for the Trust to look at, by now anticipating his response.

"This is not good is it?" He finally said in his rough Irish accent, just like a teacher reviewing an unfavourable report card, and then gave me a face as if to say 'Pinch me, is this real?'.

"I've never even heard of these funds." He leaned in towards me. "You know, he's just going to desperately, desperately hope that you'll walk away from this," tapping the paper with his fingers. He was right, the job required a borderline genius to make sense of the Trust before they could even think of turning it around.

I talked to him and gathered as much industry background as I could, or as much as he could give me. I learned that one of the reasons why the DED may not have issued Grant a licence to set up an advisory practice was clear from his academic profile. Although no qualifications or minimum standards is required in Dubai for Grant to practice as an Independent Financial Advisor, his most basic and antiquated qualifications did not meet DED's academic criteria to set up his own advisory business. The fact that Grant didn't even meet those standards for the DED licence, was pretty scary. Issued in 2004, the rules were no way as strict as they are now and back then he hadn't passed even that soft criteria.

That revelation was quite an eye opener. And it was not pretty.

His conclusion matched the verdict of the investment advisors at the DFSA, "I would sadly be very surprised if the total investment ever recouped its initial value, and the problem is due to the illiquidity of so much of it. You are potentially trapped in these high-risk and underperforming investments".

There was a short silence while we both concentrated on this for a moment.

"He is a fraudster," I said slowly, more of a statement to myself.

"Pretty much, sorry to say."

"I still can't believe it, you know. I can't ..." I felt a sudden upwelling of emotion as the truth kept insisting itself to me. 'Modern-day scam artist', tricking friends into a 'fraudulent relationship with their permission'.

In the wake of this, I realised the person we thought we knew did not exist. The 'charming family man' I had met was, in fact a rogue advisor who had devised an elaborate plot to con me and others so he could pocket commission and fees and fund a lavish lifestyle for him and his family.

"He isn't likely going to get into trouble over it though," the Irishman was speaking from years of experience from working within the industry. "He'll dodge everything, they always do."

This reality was the pivotal point because I now realised I was the victim of an insidious form of financial advisory fraud. You know – the one that you had read about and swore you would never be foolish enough to fall for.

CHAPTER 3

THE REALITY SINKS IN

✼ *Betrayed* ✼

Behind the neat façade of family, life for Grant was less straightforward. On the surface, it was almost impossible to imagine a less likely serial rogue than Grant. Impossible to imagine that this ostensibly kind, contemplative, mild-mannered man with a high-pitched voice, who would giggle and blush in awkward social situations, secretly harboured a savage lust for money, at all costs.

The realisation that we were now labelled as 'victims' hit hard, simply because of what the very word represents in society as a whole. Targeted. Weak. Defenceless. Powerless. Voiceless.

I didn't want to see myself or think about myself as a victim. No one does.

I didn't need to go mental. Nathan was able to come up with a few choice words of his own: "Unthinkably repugnant" is the only one I can repeat. I could come up with many less flattering nicknames. For the life of me, I couldn't understand how anyone with a conscience could behave the way Grant had done. Who would do such a thing? And to friends? All for the sake of making a profit. To throw us to the wolves like that. I'll never understand that. What I felt was anger at the selfishness of it, then betrayal. Total betrayal. How many victims were there? How far had he gone?

The questions fell like hard rain around me.

We supplied the narrative to him ourselves. We offered up everything – our life story, our finances, our relationships, our dreams, our future – and we were willing to go along with just about anything, putting our confidence in just a random guy we had met because someone else had referred him to us and for some reason we believed he could secure our future for us.

That was our story.

None of our friends and colleagues knew of Grant's set up because Nathan and I had yet to share the information with anyone. And for the meantime, we agreed to keep all the news we had discovered under wraps. At this point, although Rupert had shared with me that his Trust had lost tens of thousands, he was not convinced that Grant had done any wrongdoing. This was going to be a regular initial reaction. The thought that a good friend may have been deceiving us for decades was going to be difficult to comprehend for anyone, and I would have to think long and hard about how I was going to share this information. I knew I wouldn't get far on theory alone. I needed concrete proof. And I wasn't about to tell my friends our findings until we had that proof, because otherwise they might not believe me.

But first, I had to go back to the police and relay all this to them. And I needed them to help me get hard evidence linking Grant to fraud. Two very difficult tasks.

First, I had to get them to review all of the information Nathan and I had collected, and agree that Prosperity Management Consultancy and, subsequently, Grant's employer, had operated outside of the boundaries of their license, and accept that a significant number of other people may have been badly advised on financial matters by a company that was not qualified or registered to provide this advice or recommend policies. This resulted in us all losing a significant amount of money, running into thousands and hundreds of dollars, possibly millions.

Secondly and much harder, was to ask the police to request a statement from the DED evidencing Grant and Prosperity Management Consultancy were operating illegally under their business licence.

I didn't fancy my chances.

And apparently I was up against a clock.

All of a sudden I received a tip that Grant was going to be leaving Dubai for his summer family vacation.

My phone rang and it was a mutual friend of both Grant and mine, sounding very concerned. A row over management of finances is one thing – I would not be the first anxious investor – but might there be a still sharper anxiety that explains why Neil Grant now seems permanently on edge?

"No idea," I simply replied.

"Well, he's looking forward to his holiday, so he can take some time to unwind".

"When is he leaving?"

"Next week … the first I think he said."

My phone rang again and it was Officer Salah from the police station, requesting to meet with me the next day.

Make-or-break time

The mood couldn't quite be classified as festive – we were after all in a police station – but it was Eid Holidays and the chatter was noticeably lighter as officers and members of the public gathered and greeted one other.

I was outside Officer Salah's office at 7.30 am. The door stood open. He was sitting in his desk chair talking to another officer when he saw me. "Come in," he said, reaching for my file which was already on his desk. I entered his office as the other officer politely left.

"Sit," he offered me a chair across from his desk.

"Thank you." I leaned forward, elbows on his desk, ready to hear it. He started the conversation, and he sounded somewhat resigned.

Within the past two days, Grant had been called to the police station and his entire statement had been taken. He came back with his own story, a well-rehearsed response to the questions put to him, which was that I had lost my money and I was now afraid of the consequences of my gamble. The moral of his story is that investments can go up or down. If you want to put money, in an investment scheme you need to understand you can lose it. If you don't want to lose it put it in a bank. And he had explained all this to me, along with the risks. What part of the value of your investment may go up or down did she not understand he had asked the police officer. Although untrue, it will always remain his irresistible script: the kind advisor gently explaining to the pushy investor not to get too greedy. He followed that up with there was no contract between us.

I took the news with a straight face, even offered a very slight shrug, as if it say, 'So, what?'.

"He was very cooperative," said the officer, flicking aimlessly through the file. "He explained that you were unlucky. It's the game."

He didn't need to spell it out. Everything Grant said to him has sounded ultra-reasonable, and everything I'd said to him has sounded ultra-unhinged.

After a lull in the feedback, he went on to say Grant had told him that he had "never embarked on any kind of illegal activity" and that he had cooperated with "any lawful authority". The officer agreed, saying he had a clean record, implying that he had him checked out.

I gave him a look that told him he was way off the mark, to which he shrugged his shoulders and said, "he has no case to answer, and there is no contract". And with that he promptly shut my file. There didn't seem to be any further police interest.

"I totally disagree," I said to him. But it was going to make my task harder.

Generally there isn't actual proof for this kind of crime, which is why the fraudsters get away so easily and why lawyers advise you to not waste your time and money. The lack of a contract is the biggest problem. The contract angle is how rogues rely on the technicalities of the law to avoid charges. I was sure every question the officer threw at Grant, he tossed aside as if it were a triviality, as he kept trying to downplay the whole thing. And it was why Grant found it easy to fend off their questions, even without the need for a lawyer.

I went through all the evidence with the officer that Nathan had obtained from the DED website and he put on his reading glasses and read it all. But he wouldn't budge. The well-intentioned police officer was placed in an impossible position, due to the complexity of the case. He couldn't tell what case Grant had to meet.

In fact, he continued to be adamant that Grant had done no wrongdoing and I was simply someone who had lost a lot of money and was trying to blame someone – which sounded a lot like Grant had fed him that line.

"DED can provide the evidence," I explained to him, and that the statement from DED would prove that as per the law in Dubai, Grant under Prosperity Management Consultancy did not have a license to operate as a financial advisor nor was he permitted to have anything to do with money. "That includes dealing with money of any kind, or advising on money matters and investments," I further clarified to him.

No. Was the response. I swallowed hard.

My question: "Why can't we just request a statement?"

His reply, whilst taking off his glasses, was fascinating. "Why do we need to?"

He was shell-shocked and vaguely appalled that I thought he had the time or inclination to do this kind of thing.

He was clear. He was not going to ask the DED for anything. If the DED wish to file a case against Grant, they had to come down to the station. "The police don't ask people to open cases. We take statements when they file a case."

I paused for this to sink in. I saw his point. He had a point.

But without that statement I had nothing. I had no evidence to build a case of fraud. I couldn't get around the 'no contract' issue because no court of law would even consider it. I could steer the conversation away from the lack of a contract and onto the licence itself. A crucial shift. The DED would force them to think about the licence, not the lack of contract. With all the other bits of information that had been gathered I could support a case of fraud, but without the DED's support, I had nothing.

No. He was unwilling to concede. I refused to move. I'd come this far. There had to be some justice administered. I had to make one last effort.

"I have enough evidence for you to request a statement on whether or not I am right or wrong. It would be wrong to say there is no truth in any of it."

I then pointed to a paragraph on one of the papers I had given to him: "Unlicensed prescribing of a service that causes permanent losses," I read out, before adding, "he should face criminal charges, that's outrageous." No response. I then simplified what I had just said to him: "Sir, he set up a fake company to make lots of commission from people. And now I need your help."

"I understand," said the officer. Clearly he didn't.

I rubbed my forehead and tried to rearrange things.

"My money was obtained by false pretences … that's clear. It's a clear case of entrapment."

He nodded his head at me blankly.

"There are many other victims, hundreds, even more, who don't even know they're victims of this scam yet. Can you imagine that?"

"Did they also give him money without checking his details first?" He looked up from his notebook after jotting down a word and drawing a circle round it. No guessing what the word was.

We have circled back to my 'stupidity'.

I gave up further explanation with a hopeless gesture.

He crossed his arms, pinched his chin like a pensive professor, and said quietly, but not unkindly, "there is nothing wrong with somebody earning a commission".

I took a moment to marshal my arguments. I tried to explain it another way. "You are right, sir. But when you set it against his motives, it's a different picture. My overriding specification was that my capital remained safe. He agreed. I opted for stable, long-term investments. He picked high-risk, unregulated, illiquid funds, and some identical funds. This, sir, is the practice of mis-selling investment packages."

I paused, just a little, to check he was following what I was saying. He gave a slow nod, the sort that acknowledges the information and lets the conversation continue.

"Combine that with the fake company he set up and misuse of his other business licence," I reached over the desk to point out the two separate companies on the piece of paper in front of him. "This then becomes a con – a fraud. He was not helping me. He was helping himself to my money and putting up smoke and mirrors when I asked questions about my investments and charges."

Now could he take in what I had shown him – and truly see how it was fraud? The file was opened again, and he put on his reading glasses while asking, "and do you have evidence, any slips to show he was paid commission?"

And with that question, he killed the argument. No, I had no evidence of what he was paid or by who. I explained I didn't have any because he was paid directly from the financial institutions, and I went on to explain how.

He listened to me politely, smiling and shaking his head, as he slowly closed my file again, before repeating himself, "Ya'ani ... you gave him money, yourself". He paused, then said, "yourself" looking pointedly at me over his glasses, pushing his point.

He leaned back in his chair as he shared something else Grant had told him that was going to hurt my argument. "He said you approved every investment and he has proof of this."

"Yes, I did." I could see he was actually a bit taken aback by this admission, taking off his glasses sharply, "Oh?". But that is missing the point. I rubbed my forehead again as I thought how I was going to explain this to him. "I made my decisions based on his recommendations as the expert in this field, in investing. Just as we pay a lawyer based on his opinion."

He gazed at me while he considered this information; before he shook his head, as though he didn't know what to do with me, and then let out a big sigh that prompted me to say, "A statement from the DED will make everything clear, I promise". I was determined to keep his thoughts on the licence issue.

"Ya'ani, you should have checked all of this first, not now," indicating at all the paperwork in front of him that I had laid out on his desk. "There is no contract between you, you gave the money yourself, you approved all the investments ... I cannot just ask them for a statement ... there are procedures here." The file was open again; his glasses back on.

"I know it's no ordinary fraud case." Admittedly, at this moment in time, Grant had more evidence that he was innocent than I had he was guilty.

Then a thought just crossed his mind.

"Tell me one thing," he asked. And he looked me straight in the eye and said, "would you have come if you were making money?".

He looked at me as if he already knew the answer.

I wasn't caught off guard. I like it best when people are direct and put into words what many of us are thinking.

"No ... I wouldn't," I replied, truthfully, "but I would have changed my financial advisor."

"Really?" He was looking at me with great curiosity now.

"Yes, I'm sure."

"Sure?" This was getting strange.

I had rented a car recently only to be told that the company was scammers. They did not carry out frequent maintenance checks on the cars, and some people hadn't received their deposit back. Even though I had not yet suffered at their hands, I took the car back the very next day, as I drove to Abu Dhabi frequently, and I didn't want to be stuck on the highway with a faulty car.

I shared the story with the police officer, who simply nodded his head.

His face then cleared like: okay, enough of this.

"Ya'ani, I helped you, I called him to me, I asked him questions myself just as you asked … Khalass … there is no case." And with that, he took of his glasses and he shut the file again signalling the end of – everything. His legendary patience has run out.

He was polite, courteous and to the point. Never raised his voice. And to have still the willingness to have a conversation with me showed his inner calm.

"I simply cannot arrest someone based on nothing. In that case, I should arrest you for being stupid."

"I … what?!" He really did mean it.

I didn't know why it was so funny, because it was quite sad really, but it must have been because we both fell about laughing.

Known for their entertaining tongues, and indomitable belief in free speech against pathetic victims of crime such as myself, the police officer was not mincing his words. It was so easy to switch from misery to hilarity with them.

I gave him a few seconds to swell with pride at his own comic genius.

He was right. An objective observer, witnessing this dialogue, without knowing the background, would probably agree. There were red flags. Many of them. We make mistakes, of course. We all do. But perhaps in this case the real mistake was, ultimately, trusting someone too much. I should have been far more responsible and aware.

The most stupid thing I had done to date was going through the car wash with the sunroof open and some of the windows down – that had now been firmly relegated to the second most stupid thing I had ever done.

Either way, I promised the officer to keep my head down and not do anything stupid for a bit.

He softened a little. He was still clearly annoyed at me for the situation I had put myself in, "you have to be smarter than this".

I couldn't think of anything to say by response other than, "He was a friend". He didn't respond for a few seconds. Then he nodded: "I hear you. I do ..." For his part, he was very understanding and I was certainly not the first person to make a misjudgment over a friendship.

"Do you know how many crimes are between friends?" he asked me, as if I might be able to provide an intelligent guess. I just shook my head.

He referenced a statistic published in the local newspaper which claimed 72 percent of fraud cases that landed on police stations desk are between long-time friendships. That was truly mind blowing.

There was a silence as we both pondered on this fact.

At this point, another officer came into the room to talk to him and he was distracted for a while with what looked like a lot of extremely amusing mutual aggravation. What was fascinating about police officers in general was how they could switch to a totally different mood and tone of voice, seemingly at the drop of a hat.

I sighed heavily. This was it. This was as far as it goes. Without the DED statement my case was holed below the waterline.

I'd have to admit defeat and accept I'd taken it as far as I could and what was meant to be was meant to be. I had already written off the money, and in the scheme of things, yes it was a lot of money but not the end of the world. I was just after a little bit of something – answers. It was frightening the level of deceit Grant had gone to. I couldn't blame anyone else; it was my call and I got it terribly wrong. He was going to get away scot-free, and keep doing it – that I couldn't live with. Money comes and goes, but that was different. I was getting to the point where I was tired of seeing expats in Dubai leaving their moral compass back home.

I got up from my chair, picked up my bag, and slung the strap over my shoulder, preparing to leave the office, and waited for them to finish their conversation so that I could thank him. He did at least call Grant down for questioning for me.

I was just stepping away from his desk when he suddenly turned to me and surprised me by adding: "Go to the director, tell him we are not taking your case ... give him the information". And with that, he collected all the paperwork that I had spread out on his desk and handed them back to me.

The director was the head of police. The ultimate decision-maker. It seems an opportunity too good to miss. A sliver of sympathy.

"Where is he?" I asked.

He ripped a small piece of paper from a larger sheet and wrote on it before handing it to me.

"I just go and ... walk into his office?" I asked slightly unsure.

Apparently so.

The officer had thrown me a lifeline and I sprinted out of his room on my last legs before he changed his mind. I walked down a series of narrow corridors, full of offices, some of which were empty, or the doors were closed. Some had a window where private meetings were in full swing, and many were busy with officers at desks conducting interviews with various people.

"Ma'am, where are you going?" called out one of the

janitors as I walked up an empty corridor. I told him. "Come back this way," he said signalling the opposite direction, "that's to the jail".

I stopped dead in my tracks. A heavy aroma of sweat reached my nostrils, and I felt my stomach turn over. The smell was deeply unpleasant. The jail was along the same corridor as the offices I asked the janitor incredulously. He nodded. I definitely didn't want to stumble on that. Not one of the Dubai sites I wanted to take in, and so far had managed to avoid. For some reason I expected the jails to be located somewhere in the heart of the desert rather than within a popping champagne cork's distance of Burj Khalifa, the iconic and tallest building in the world.

I clutched the small, white piece of paper the police officer had given me and went along the opposite direction.

The formal high offices of the police was located on the other side of the building at the end of a long corridor and a very, very long walk – at least five minutes. At the end of it was a large reception area, where two doors led to a maze of small rooms and offices. The place was silent with empty desks. The secretary's office was empty as well.

I found myself walking directly to the director's office, which was the first room behind the reception. He was alone, sitting relaxed at his desk reading the newspaper. He was immaculate in his attire, in a uniform that judging by the medals and his cap was very high-ranking, indicating years of experience as part of the police's top team.

I drifted into his office like a ghost, creeping up on him without any warning.

"Salam' alaikom, sir," I said, totally unsure of what to call him. He looked up as I lightly knocked on his open door. "Officer Salah asked me to come and see you about my case".

"Alaikom salam," he replied and beckoned me forward.

"Your team is really helping me but it's such a difficult case," I said as I stepped further into his office, and approached his desk. Now, I had a good view of him. He had elf-like facial features and wore wire-rimmed glasses and a black beard.

"Sit," he indicated the cream-coloured sofa adjacent to this desk whilst he picked up his phone.

"Ah, Salah," and then he switched to Arabic. I couldn't understand what he was saying to the officer but I'm sure it was along the lines of "who is this sad pathetic looking person you have sent to me?".

After a minute or so he put the receiver down and turned to speak to me.

"Wait, your file is coming," before turning back to his newspaper.

If he had any problems with my presence in his room or my just turning up he didn't show them in his non-verbal signals. In fact, he has a serene aura about him, and despite the unusual, uncertain circumstances I was in, I felt comfortable.

His office was tidy but minimal with a large window which the director had his back to. The walls were a naturel beige, there were closed cabinets and shelves weighed down with books on the law, thick volumes of Islamic Jurisprudence and some Islamic religious books. In a prominent spot on the shelf was a picture of the Dubai ruler.

After ten minutes of complete silence on our own, which neither of us felt an obligation to break, the first officer who had taken my statement on the first day came into the room carrying my file, nervously tiptoeing through the open door. He greeted the director with a high level of ostentatious respect and sat in a chair opposite him.

The director put down his newspaper and then read my

file, rubbing his forehead in light repetitive movements. It was a bit surreal. I was getting a private audience with the head of police. I knew my elevation to his level was a big leap. I knew the stages and time it takes for a file to reach him and that I had bypassed stage two and I had somehow managed to book a face-to-face meeting with the most powerful police officer in the station, and he was reading my file in front of me. A stroke of pure luck.

Now and then he asked the officer a question and he would either answer or pull out the relevant documentation from the file, then they conferred.

He retrieved the Code of Conduct paper with the 'Prosperity Offshore Investment Consultants' letterhead that I had signed.

"This is a contract?" he asked me and before I could reply he had reverted back to the officer who seemed to agree with him, and was nodding along.

The Code of Conduct paper was clearly now rather significant. Was he accepting it as a contract between Grant and myself? The lack of a contract was the biggest problem. If he was happy to use that as a contract then so be it.

He turned back to me to explain that although Prosperity Offshore Investment Consultants did not exist, if the letterhead seeks to mislead in relation to the nature of the business, and that misrepresentation induces me to conclude a contract with them, then I can claim against them for misrepresentation. But the letterhead in itself usually does not get you anywhere. It was Grant's overall conduct which sought to defraud or misrepresent me that mattered for successful conviction and recovery in a claim. I nodded to show I understood.

They continued to go through the file, now and then looking over at me whilst they poured over various documents.

There was definitely an air of waiting to be spoken to – there was no discussion, there was not going to be a discussion. It was going to be a yes or no and that was it. This was not a time to start playing hardball with the police management. I'd never survive it. I had heard about the 10 by 6 ft cell with pale yellow walls. Now I had smelt it.

The glass coffee table in front of me was full of chocolates and dates and wonderful treats. Maybe it was because it was Eid. Seasons of goodwill and religious occasions and festivities are huge priorities in Dubai.

"Please," he raised his hand to offer me. I helped myself to them whilst my fate was being decided.

At that moment, I received a text from my friend: "Where are you?".

I replied back, "Eating paatchi chocolates at the pleasure of the police station".

I expected a worried message back asking, "What the hell are you doing at the police station?".

Instead, her bewilderment was, "There are paatchi chocolates at the police station?!".

Actually, the whole experience at the police station had been extremely pleasant. My second surprise was the general standard of service, in all parts of the station. It was faster, better and more consistently reliable than I had been led to believe.

"Okay," the director was ready to give me his decision. I sensed a tiny opening. Then more silence, more mutterings that I couldn't quite hear properly. Then the pronouncement, which was very direct and very determined: "We will send a request to DED. If he can manage money, there is no case. The file is closed". He peered at me sombrely over his spectacles wanting agreement to what he had said.

"Okay. Thank you," I readily agreed. To say I was

mildly excited by this news was the understatement of the year. It was the sort of breakthrough moment that most of us can only dream about. He nodded his head at me as I accepted his deal and drew the first and only very small smile from him, before he went back to his newspaper. He was brief, devastatingly sharp.

I already knew what the DED's statement was going to say, thanks to Nathan. I was elated. In less than one hour, my mood has gone from abject despair to one of bounteous joy.

Me and my case were now transferred to the head of police's private secretary, a tall clean-shaven officer in the olive green shirt and trousers uniform.

I asked him how he was going to go about getting a statement from the DED.

"I will first find out who to send the request to," he said to give him some time. He told me that they would be taking prompt action, as per the director's instruction.

But what was their definition of 'prompt'?

The problem was, I knew that at the end of the week Grant was going for his annual one-month family vacation. I did not have time to wait. If he got wind of this he was not going to return to Dubai. So far only Nathan and I knew what was happening but Grant was aware I had a meeting with the Insurance Authority, and it was fairly clear that he knew I suspected something as he had been called to the police station. So he knew we were closing in, albeit confident that we had no evidence to make something stick against him.

"I'll go to the DED and I'll find out exactly who deals with requests from the police regarding company licences and I'll get their details for you," I offered. I explained why I was on a timeline. "I really don't mind." The officer agreed.

On my way out of the station, I went back to Officer

Salah who was sat at his desk with a line of people waiting to speak to him in the corridor. Even though he had been a roadblock he had been well-meaning. He helped me by persuading the director to talk to me and I was still in the game because of him so I owed him a thank you.

His head cocked sideways as if he didn't catch what I said at first, and with a quick nod of a head he said a simple "okay"; a flicker of surprise sweeping his face. He'd probably thought I'd pulled some rabbit out of the hat but had no idea what it was.

After a dramatic start, we had managed to pull off an extraordinary day, and no doubt hoped to see the back of any further roadblocks.

I called Nathan, "We're still in it!" as I filled him in.

"Really, how have you wrangled this one?"

"To be honest, I have no idea, but let's see where it takes us." I felt the net was swiftly closing in on Grant.

The criminal court requires proof 'beyond a reasonable doubt' whereas a civil court requires 'a preponderance of the evidence'. I'm sure it's a bit like OJ Simpson being acquitted in criminal court but found responsible later in civil. That's why the DED statement was significant. Grant would need a damn good lawyer to overturn that piece of evidence issued from a government body in either court.

The next day, I arrive at the DED's offices situated in the heart of Dubai. I found my way to customer services on level one in the open plan call centre, just off the main corridor. The city's bright yellow 'Happiness Centre' smiling logo was everywhere brightening up the entire area. The staff wore the obligatory dark suit, a rather bold gold tie and the standard white shirt. I waited for my number to be called and I was directed to – ironically – an unsmiling, unhappy and ice-cold Haniff sitting on counter four. After listening to my request, he fussed around his desk, found the simple piece of paper he was looking for, and gave me a generic email address from it, in hardly legible handwriting on a teeny tiny Post-it Note.

No that won't do. I needed a name, I told him.

He didn't know and he was clearly irritated that it was not one of his questions and answers on the script that he was clearly reading from. He couldn't have looked less keen on prolonging our encounter and lost the ability to speak more than a syllable at a time. Finally, after an embarrassing long silence, he told me to go to Mr Sami on the ninth floor. "He has the answer to everything. He can help you". And with that, he moved on, and called the next number to the counter.

As soon as I came out of the elevators onto the ninth floor I knew I was somewhere I wasn't supposed to be. Thick carpets, high-quality artworks, marble walls, beautiful wooden furniture and top-end fixtures and fittings – those were key giveaways.

I approached the desk where sat an Emirati in a Swarovski crystal encrusted abaya and a very dramatic silver and black eyeshadow on her eyelids.

"I've come to meet with Mr Sami, I was told his office is on the ninth floor." An indignant face of horror looked back at me.

"Habibti, you can't just walk in here and ask to speak to him," the receptionist replied. She literally didn't know what to do, and kept rearranging her sheyla on her head. In an attempt to explain further she said Mr Sami was booked months in advance and even then my meeting needed to be approved.

Really?

"Mr Sami is who exactly?" I now asked, with uncertainty.

"The CEO of DED."

I giggled instinctively at her blunt reply, then stopped myself. Okay. Someone was having a joke at my expense.

"I understand perfectly well," I said to the lady. "I don't actually need to see him but maybe you can point me in the right direction". I then explained what information I was looking for.

Clearly relieved about my backing down, she then seemed highly admiring of my shameful conduct of asking to speak to the CEO unannounced. After hitting a few keys on her keyboard with her perfectly manicured hands, some letters appeared on the screen in front of her and she sent me back down to the first floor.

It meant I had to walk past the customer services open plan call centre.

"Did you meet him?" sang out the little joker, with a big smile on his face. The glint in his eye was almost satanic.

"Yes, all okay, thanks," I called out with an equally big smile. "In fact, they were very concerned why I was sent to Mr Sami, so I gave them your name and said it was Haniff on counter four and you were very helpful."

His smile dropped like a lead balloon. He looked utterly horrified.

On my way back I saw the joker had moved to counter nine.

With government houses, you'll find, you get through to someone and have to tell the whole story again. And then they pass you on. It's like the staff are following a script. And you feel you're going around in circles. After speaking to four different people, I finally had the name of the person who could help me.

The licensing office is on the first floor headed up by a local Emirati lady, a petite woman of fifty-five, dressed in a black plain abaya. She was at her desk, neatly arranging piles of paperwork, when I knocked on her door and introduced myself. I gave her a precise summary of my case and explained that the police needed a statement from the DED, and could I please ask them to send the request to her to speed it up for them.

"I'm working very closely with them on this matter," I explained.

She was very sympathetic about my plight. Yes, no problem, was her answer. She gave me her direct email address and mobile number so the police could coordinate with her directly on What's App in case the email was missed from either side.

I was listening with rapture, like a Royal Festival Hall-goer savouring a Schoenberg piano concerto.

I then went back to the police station with all the details and handed the gold over to the officer who then got to work compiling the request.

The lady from the DED replied to him the very next day officially confirming marvellously that the DED provided a licence for Prosperity Management Consultancy to trade as 'management consultancies' under the licence number 559536. Grant and Prosperity Management Consultancy did not hold the appropriate legal licence to offer financial advice or advice on money or be an advisory company.

The officer translated the DED statement slowly back to me in English, as I surreptitiously examined it and then concluded with a simple summary: "He's not supposed to do what he's doing".

In other words, his self-positioned halo was in fact completely fraudulent.

The reality is that he didn't meet the government's criteria to be an advisory company, and one (who has lost £60,000) could argue he wasn't issued a license to protect the public.

The findings were submitted into evidence. This statement, now, turned this whole case around and supported our claim that Grant had fraudulently acted as a financial advisor under Prosperity Management Consultancy with clear intent to deceive and for personal gain. He had put one activity and was very clearly doing another.

This was the starting point.

Roll on a few days. The head of police signed the necessary paperwork to open a case against Grant and then the station's administration team sent me a text message to confirm they had opened an investigation into Neil Ramsay Pringle Grant, along with the case number.

Grant's passport was immediately blocked in the immigration system as he had the motive and opportunity to flee before his investigation, and then they called him to come down to the prosecution office in the police station and asked him to bring his original passport.

Imagine getting that phone call, as you're packing your speedos ready for your summer vacation. I think it is safe to presume that Grant had no clue that this case was gathering momentum, or he would have left the country for sure.

As soon as he arrived at the police station, he was sequestered. He was in an interview room for most of the day and questioned at the prosecution's discretion for that time period. Again, he chose to be unaccompanied and not be represented by a lawyer. He was either oblivious to what was engulfing him, or in denial, or, my best guess was, overly confident. It doesn't surprise me from someone who simply knows how to avoid charges and probably thought he could talk his way out of it again using the no-contract angle. However, this time round, he did not know the evidence that had been gathered against him, and of the DED statement taking a prime seat in his police file.

After the interrogation, a determination was made that the state should open their own investigation and the file was then passed to the Dubai Public Prosecution unit on suspicion of fraud by false representation. The crime carried both criminal and civil penalties.

It was a massive step forward. I was tremendously pleased that our efforts seemed about to bear fruit. Grant had described the charge as "ridiculous" and said he had "no inkling this was going to happen".

Public prosecution is the only authority in Dubai to initiate the criminal cases and it is part of the judicial body as it undertakes the authority of investigation and imposing charges as well as referring the accused person to the competent court if involvement in the crime was proven. Public prosecution also supervises the stages of the case in the criminal courts. Therefore, at this point I didn't need a lawyer, as the state was, in effect, representing me.

I was never to see the director and head of the station again. I wanted to personally thank him for his help with my case, but whenever I tried, he always had a queue of people waiting to see him in the corridor with pre-arranged meetings and his receptionist never let me past. I realised I was never going to get near him again. It was only through sheer luck that day that I casually walked straight into his office.

What a fortuitous opportunity that turned out to be, and opened a gateway that had now taken me down a path I wasn't even intending to go.

The seed of the idea that had started during that phone call talking to Nathan had taken four weeks to take root but now everything was in place for battle.

Sometimes, fighting is futile. But it wasn't fighting about money. It was about principle, which is a more powerful drive.

I was not just in, but all in – fully committed. I needed to be. My fight was to make sure Grant was off the streets. That was the goal.

Friends unite

It was at this time Rupert contacted me. We had avoided the subject of Grant whenever we spoke but now he was contacting me directly about him. Just like Nathan, Rupert had just remarried, and just like Nathan's wife, she wasn't bowled over by Grant either. When she queried why I hadn't come over for some time, Rupert had shared with her our 'disagreement' over Grant and that I was probably keeping my distance. It was obviously playing on his wife's mind and she had taken it upon herself to do some private digging, and she had convinced him that he should listen to me properly and check his finances as I had suggested. He had eventually, reluctantly agreed and looked into his whole portfolio, and come to a terrible conclusion that I may be on to something. Finally.

It was interesting that whoever new came into our group of friends, saw right through Grant.

Whist I was running around town, Rupert was doing a parallel investigation. He had figured out he had given Grant to date some £25,000 in advisory fees alone since the Trust inception with Guardian Trust Company Ltd. Things went from bad to worse. There were some issues regarding consent that he had not given Grant which Grant seemed to have actioned anyway, somehow. One can only imagine the tensions between Grant and himself after Rupert had written a strongly worded letter.

To give him some comfort that something was being done about it, I discussed with Rupert the startling new developments that the past few weeks had brought. Now that we had filed an official case, and Grant was not disappearing anywhere, Nathan and I thought we could spread the word within our respective circles.

"They're setting up a proper criminal investigation?" Rupert sounded shocked, almost in disbelief.

"Yes."

"Against Neil?"

"Yes."

In the pause that followed, I braced myself for I knew what was to follow. Then he went all British in his deep melodious voice: "Are you out of your mind?" and "How can you take such radical steps without telling us?" and "Are you sure?" and "Oh my God ... Oh well done ... Oh, I knew you were up to something" and finally, "I wonder what will happen to him?".

Another pause. The idea hadn't really occurred to me until now. My only thought was to stop him, prevent him from fleeing like a cowardly brute with his tail between his legs.

Rupert was giving me a preview of the gourmet of emotions I would be facing in the future from Grant's victims. To anyone who really knows Grant, the idea this was all part of some grand plan would be utterly ridiculous – until they checked their portfolios.

As a way of conveying their distance to him as a 'friend', the men stopped referring to Grant by his first name. Bemused, I was told "it's a man thing".

Now I had Rupert and Nathan in my corner, together we compiled all the information together. When it comes to doing research, oversights can happen to anyone. If we looked through the files together, maybe we'd see something that the other person missed the first time. Unbeknown to us earlier, Rupert held the second key piece of evidence against Grant – a copy of the Terms of Business agreement between Grant and Guardian Trust Company Ltd, which crucially bought Grant's partner, Philip Van Neste into the picture.

This jigsaw puzzle really had been a collaboration that had made a way forward.

And having them onboard created the perfect sounding board. It was going to be a long, difficult journey of discovery. The case was so complicated, and patience was limited. There was going to be so many twists and turns with this prosecution. At times I was ready to throw in the towel but I met the mental challenge by getting their help and support, and their humour, as we were laughing at how we got ourselves caught up in a strange new world into which we had been plunged.

And none of it had been planned. When I explained to people that I "kind of fell into a court case" I received the most baffling looks. But it was true. This was so totally not my original plan.

"Initiating a court case is like getting a tattoo on your face," I was told, "You really need to be certain it's what you want before you commit ... you don't just fall into it". But that is what happens when you head into the unknown and discover things along the way. You just power through, follow the dots.

And as I said, I had no idea what to expect.

Maybe that was for the best.

Because if I had known from the start the complex problems I was going to face and the pitfalls that could trip me up, and the mountain I would have to climb to get a little drop of justice, I may never have put my best foot forward. I would have followed the same path as many others before me who think of embarking on a legal case, and just freeze into doing nothing.

What followed remains one of the most surreal experiences of my life.

CHAPTER 4

THE PUBLIC PROSECUTION ROLLERCOASTER

What happens when two people perceive the same thing differently?

This was the question: How do I explain this case to a prosecutor, and what went on with Grant?

Finding the answer to that question was the next part of my journey.

I naively thought the case would take one week with the public prosecution office. It took nine months. Nine long months. The investigation was riddled with delays; Grant asked for two extensions, I asked for one and the senior public prosecutor was off sick for a couple of months. Add to that the public and religious holidays that are generously allocated to government houses.

The file had been transferred from the police station to the state office in July 2016. I was told Grant was permanently posted outside the prosecution office for the first two months, pushing for the case to begin. After ten weeks of not hearing from the prosecution, I decided to find out for myself what was going on.

The public prosecution building was mentioned to me only a couple of months ago. Until then I didn't know it existed, or even where it was. Geographically, it was an extraordinary isolated place, stuck out off a major highway. Getting there was the easy part. Finding parking once I arrived there proved almost impossible.

From the moment I entered the main hall, there seemed to be armed security guards everywhere, inside and outside the building. It seemed a bit excessive, but then the prosecutors don't have me at the top of their wanted-list, so who am I to quibble?

The probe was being led by a senior prosecutor and I personally met with him, genuinely liking the guy. He had been a public prosecutor in Dubai for over seven years and 80 percent of his job was interviewing people and finding information.

"Oh, *Miss* Amber," were his first words to me as he welcomed me into his office. It was the usual response I get from the locals when they see my name in full. They assume I'm a male, thinking the surname is the first name. It doesn't bother me at all; although worrisome when they continue to call me 'Mr' after they've met me.

The senior prosecutor was a local, dressed in the traditional Emirati white robe, the candoura. Good natured, smiling easily with a wisecracking sense of humour, giggling at times at my own sarcastic comments. He carried his tall, broad build extremely gracefully. His large dark eyes set in his plump face glowed with a real love of life. He understood the difference between being a prosecutor and being a human being, and could have relationships with both parties wearing both hats. Hardworking, and well known for shutting himself inside his office for hours at a time mulling over a case file.

The great news was that the prosecution office fully

supported an open and transparent justice system that helped demonstrate their determination to ensure that Dubai is not seen as a soft target for fraud and investment of illicit finance. Therefore, they now sought to move further cases to the High Court.

The senior prosecutor had a team with him and their job was to determine whether Grant and any organisations associated with him have violated any laws within their jurisdiction. I was told that the prosecution staff, many of whom had been there for a long time, took great pride in their work and their enthusiasm for new cases was infectious.

Hooray, I thought.

Only, my case was one they had never come across before. The senior prosecutor added: "This is a very, very unusual case, and presents for any prosecutor a difficult investigation".

In other words, he was used to dealing with anything. But not financial advisory fraud.

Nothing like opening up about your lack of experience on the subject matter to set the mood for the investigation.

There were many fraud cases, of course. The stuff that hit their desk was grand and dramatic and of a multi-million dollar nature, but not of the advisory nature and certainly not of the kind where I have voluntarily given the money and there is no contract in place between the victim and the accused.

The victim and the accused. Those were our new labels.

I had already learnt that my type of case almost never gets past the police station. They were either difficult to understand or prove, or – what most likely happens – the accused has taken the first flight out of the sandpit never to be heard of again. None had been convicted. None had been settled. Not one penny had ever been paid to a plaintiff in a financial advisory case.

Fortunately, the senior prosecutor was up for the challenge.

I told him that I would like to know from them when they thought an investigation was going to happen. As ever, the senior prosecutor was polite, engaging, charming, and endearing. And as ever, he said nothing that he did not want to. Pressed on a date, he pushed back gently, telling me all would be revealed in due course. He only confirmed that this was an active case. All we could do was wait.

It was disappointing to realise that Grant was cleaning up his house during that time. There were a lot of things that had been removed such as the company website and media profiles. But there was still plenty of evidence that was left, thanks to Google. I think the most useful thing that we gathered was that the other victims' accounts, detailed descriptions of the mis-management of our investment funds the configuration of his businesses validated what I had told the authorities.

The allegations

The case against Grant was that he misused his professional licence of 'management consultancy' and worked as a financial consultant and advisor under Prosperity Management Consultancy. That was the licence fraud part of the case. Here we also included the fact that he had set up a fake financial advisory company, that was unregistered, unlicensed and unregulated called Prosperity Offshore Investment Consultants and he ran the business under Prosperity Management Consultancy's licence.

The actual fraud element where he benefited financially from his deceit, was always going to be more difficult to prove. We focused on how he mis-sold investments to me which were not what we had agreed or suited to my investment profile, and he hid the reality of their poor performance from me, along with the fake company documentation and contracts to mislead and misrepresent himself and his companies to me, to conclude a contract with him, with the intention to deceive me, for personal financial gain and profit.

And there were new, excruciating details. Before the prosecution investigation commenced, new evidence came to light. Forged signature. Perhaps this is the most scurrilous of all the accusations against Grant. I was on the fence with this one because I couldn't understand why Grant would forge my signature, as I freely signed everything he put before me. But the signature on a consent form from Grant to Guardian Trust Company Ltd to indicate my acceptance for my Trust to be moved from Jersey to Switzerland was definitely not mine.

When Grant learnt of the additional signature forgery allegation, his new employer's sudden interest in the investigation was baffling. They'd done nothing and shown no interest up until that point. Now they were on the phone to me straight away.

"He's still working at your company?" I asked the managing director who had personally called me from his private mobile number. "Not even on garden leave?" It was hugely disappointing to learn that Grant was being allowed to work directly with clients throughout the entire investigation. By now he had moved on to a new batch of investors – Pharmaceuticals. God knows how many unsuspecting clients he now had on his books.

"He's a suspect in a fraud case," I reminded him.

"Has he been charged?" he asks. The words were the flat, monotone of a busy man who doesn't have much time for nonsense.

"Well, no."

"Then, he's still working."

His matter-of-fact attitude was the theme throughout our entire conversation. It was clear, he had arrived at the belief that I would probably drop the investigation for money. A deal. Money for all charges to be dropped. The purpose of his call was therefore to facilitate a settlement offering me more money than the initial investment I had given Grant, and to exert pressure to take it.

"What do you want out of a lawsuit?"

"What do I want?" I ask back. "He's not a financial advisor. Somebody has to get mad; somebody has to say something."

"You don't want to do this," he said, in terms of pursing Grant. Whatever the truth, he wanted to draw a line under this matter on the call itself. Not only for Grant's sake; he didn't want the company to be dragged into the investigation itself. A verdict for Grant means he's out of work and his employer picks up the can. The settlement would be a tiny sum compared to the ultimate cost of a verdict.

"I'm not going to drop the case," I told him. "I have a duty to put the matter before the court."

"There's just a lot that I want to tell you, and I know your heart's in the right place." He was efficient with words. "I know a little about the system."

"And how's that?" I asked, only mildly curious. I was sure he knew plenty.

He then recounted his own experience of taking a case through the Dubai courts, a veiled warning to me that you could be left beaten and destroyed and with no answers. I listened as I weighed this engaging bit of background. "I'm not afraid of the risks," I told him. And I wasn't.

"What would really be upsetting, is for you to end up

with nothing." He went over it again slowly, explaining the advantages of settling, and the consequences of not. He spoke in tones of concern and understanding, sensing that establishing a friendship was the only way to reach me just then.

He then dropped into the conversation that he had already spoken to "their friends" at the Insurance Authority and clarified everything with them after my meeting with the manager. Admittedly, I was a bit taken aback by this news, but at the same time, I knew he was trying to subtly intimidate me into just abandoning the case.

"I told you – I'm not going to do that," I repeated to him.

The conversation moved to Grant himself and how he'd lost his energy; that he did not have the financial capabilities to pay the rent on his lavish villa and he'd had to borrow money from his mother, and will inevitably downsize to a smaller villa.

Very unlikely, I thought to myself.

From the stylish £1 million country home that he rented back in Scotland, Grant earned on average £2,500 per week. It was safe to say he was well able to ride out any economic turmoil that Dubai's current legal paralysis may spawn.

If I knew that then he knew that.

But that didn't stop his boss getting some drama out of it, and distracting me and using it as a tactic of sympathy. What he probably didn't know was that his wife was posting pictures of a swanky new £50,000 kitchen on Facebook and her seasonal extravagant parties. All in all, it was a bit difficult to believe they had endured a tumultuous last few month. Little appeared to have troubled their gilded life.

I played along and genuinely sympathised: "Yes, it must have been nerve-racking for him … the whole experience … and the fact his passport has been taken from him." I was still not inclined to settle, though. And he was still not inclined to give up. He continued to exert more pressure to drop the investigation, switching to personal tactics.

By now he had spent an hour on the phone to me. He was able to read me. Discover my weak spots. He made subtle references to my faith, Islam: "we pray that the Almighty bless every second of your life". And then he gave it his last shot. It was the reference to Grant's children and, for a very brief nano-second, I relented, which of course he knew I would. And I was convinced that this was a genuine invitation to settle the matter for their sake. I was told, the "four boys" were personally thanking me for considering it because they "really wanted to stay in Dubai" and were "grateful" to me.

Reluctantly and badgered, I found myself saying, "Okay, send me your terms." But it didn't feel right.

Only then came the conditions, heavily weighted in Grant's favour, and there were fundamental problems with their proposal. The first was I withdraw all allegations and "help" clear his record at the police station and the second was that I was to receive 12 post-dated cheques. The alarm bells that should have rung ten years ago when I first met Grant, started ringing now. I was not going to be fooled a single time. Grant was so sure that I was going to seal the deal that he personally met with the senior prosecutor and told him to halt proceedings because the matter was being settled.

Needless to say the offer was instantly knocked back.

Grant's boss immediately came back to me. "Neil and his wife agree to a lump sum." His tone was strident. He seemed eager to get it agreed and finish this ordeal. "You'll have it by the end of the week." It was blindingly obvious

Grant was been dragged by his feet to settle by his employer.

Now I was faced with the marshmallow test: delayed gratification. I could either take the money now or I could pursue a verdict and get the money later. It brings up so many emotions, in the sense that it was very personal. Nathan urged me to take the money: "I'm smiling Amber, take it." Likewise, the Irishman managed a guttural discharge whilst hammering his advice into me, mawkishly: "You're joking right? I've never heard of anyone settling like this," adding hastily "Hit him where it really hurts". However, I was inclined to pursue the second option.

After a few days mulling over the dilemma, I came up with my own Terms and Conditions, one of which included Grant was to inform all his clients that he no longer works as a financial advisor and hand their Trusts and policies back to them.

"It's non-negotiable," I wrote to Grant's boss.

"I don't think he will do that," was the reply.

"When I win what happens then? Best he quits now."

"He won't. You'll end up with nothing,"

But I was not prepared to compromise on this fact. Neither was I prepared for their prompt reaction to it. Grant immediately canned the deal. He wasn't prepared to compromise on that fact either. His boss ghosted me – he stopped picking up when I called and didn't return my messages. I never heard from any one of them again on the matter.

It hadn't bothered me. I wanted Grant off the financial advisory streets. I wanted him to not be able to dig his way out of the investigation with money. And this fact simply pushed me further to keep digging. Perhaps even more so.

Sometimes the long game victory really is better for a great story than a quick easy win.

The prosecution investigation

"I thought I had some understanding that this was going to be resolved in a satisfactory way. Why hasn't this happened?" asked the senior prosecutor. The settlement game had wasted a significant amount of time and he wasn't impressed with both parties.

I replayed my conversations with Grant's boss. "The settlement was designed to delay criminal prosecution," was my formal matter-of-fact summary.

The delay had meant investigations didn't start until late November, 2016, when I was eventually called to the public prosecution interview room.

Someone had made a half-hearted attempt to add some cosy touches to the very plain, relatively small room, but without entirely succeeding. A potted plant stood on the window sill, and a poster of some sort hung on the wall. There was a white small rectangular table with a computer and monitor on it with black chairs haphazardly placed around it. Wires to printers and phones ran over the floor in no apparent design. The sofa was brown leather, and in front of it stood the obligatory glass coffee table.

The interpreter, a local Emirati dressed in a dish dash, motioned for me to sit there.

The administrator was sitting in front of a computer and took my details, asking me questions about my life: "So, who are you? Where do you work? Tell me about yourself." He was later tasked with taking the minutes of the interview.

Our voices echoed in the room. The temperature was stuck at the freezing mark.

I was only there for maybe a minute or two and then the senior prosecutor walked in. A seating arrangement was developed. He sat down in a chair opposite me on the other side of the coffee table, next to the interpreter.

"Okay," he said, "let's begin." The mood was vastly different now.

He interviewed me first with the interpreter who I noticed had picked up a number of Britishisms from living in the UK. He explained that the prosecutor had a few questions which would require responses under oath. As I nodded, he picked up the small Bible from the table.

"It would be the Quran," I said. He looked at me confused, then apologised, put the Bible down and picked up the Quran. After I was sworn in, the interview began.

"In your own words, tell me how exactly you were introduced to this gentlemen, Neil Ramsay."

"The person that introduced Neil Grant to me was a good friend. He said, 'I know this guy' ..." I began. Everyone listened as I unravelled my story.

Generally, the interview, as they called it, was relaxed but challenging.

The senior prosecutor then asked me to talk through the chronology of the case. Fortunately, prior to the interview, I had sorted out a clear timeline detailing everything that had happened and when it happened. I had to sift through the information that really mattered and information that was great to have but not necessarily something you need to talk about. So you have to decide what is priority and what is not priority. It meant swathes of evidence were dismissed or considered irrelevant to the criminal case, and was to be reserved for civil. The police prosecutor had given them all of the background information and what they found in the DED system and what was written between the lines that didn't appear in a report.

I spent about an hour giving testimony so the senior prosecutor could understand how Grant's operation worked.

I kept the financial jargon on a level reachable by the average layman. With the prosecutor's prompting, I managed to replay the entire conversations with Grant about the type of products I wanted to invest in.

He nodded his head throughout, taking notes on his yellow legal pad, in between taking sips of coffee. To add to the light mood, I discovered he was ambidextrous, which I found fascinating.

Then he asked specific questions where the meetings were held, what name was on the business card Grant gave me, how and where he presented his business card to me. I noticed he asked me the same questions just in a different way. And sometimes he said two things at once, and I didn't know which one I was supposed to be aiming at.

He was kind but firm with me.

Why didn't I find have a contract? What was the link between me and Grant? Where are the money transfer receipts? He shook his head in amazement when I replied I had no answer to each one of his questions. I had checked and rechecked, but there was no paperwork whatsoever to link Grant to me as my financial advisor. Grant had gone to such lengths to leave no trail, I had nothing.

He suddenly enlivened the interview by announcing: "I don't understand ... how you can give somebody money like that ... without something, anything written?" before shaking his head again, and then the translator would shake his head at me, and then they would look at each other and shake their head.

This fact was seriously denting my credibility. But he was right.

"Don't mind ... but really ... this is all your fault." If he had something momentous to say to me the senior prosecutor spoke directly to me, bypassing the translator. I let the remark roll right off me. It wouldn't do any good to try to explain. I knew from experience exactly how this discussion was going to proceed.

"Yes," I conceded. "That was a horrifically stupid thing to do," I offered before he did; a statement I seemed destined to repeat many times and which seems to incite in him a shiver of giggles. I offered some further clarity on my stupidity. I was actually afraid he may decide to dismiss the investigation on this fact alone.

"I was wrong for being so trusting. It's genuinely as simple as that," I added. Why are the victims ridiculed and made to feel guilty? Because we trust?

He wasn't going to let me off that easily.

His was the best reaction I've had so far to my 'I was stupid' declaration. He first frowned at me, studying me with a quizzical look, and then pronounced with some good natured, gentle ribbing, "The British … are meant to be clever".

That's certainly one way of putting it.

My humiliation complete.

I had ruined the reputation of the whole British kingdom.

No wonder the other victims wanted to remain anonymous. And after enlivening the company by that punchline, the investigation swiftly continued.

The senior prosecutor was very surprised to learn that these alleged criminal activities had gone on for a fairly long period of time prior to the investigation – almost two decades. On the fact of it, it seemed very odd and unusual and compelling to him.

"That's the type of guy we are dealing with," I warned him. "He's clever." He agreed with this sentiment.

After I presented my side to the senior prosecutor, he then investigated what I shared with him and the evidence I submitted, and then the public prosecution had to take this account to Grant to essentially fact-check it and get his perspective. The story of a case is depicted from a victim's and accused's perspectives respectively, complete with memory bias which often results in vastly different scenarios. It was absolutely right that they asked probing questions to both of us to uncover the truth. I had no problem with the system. And so, to go into a case like this, you had to walk gingerly, you had to make sure that you held your information closely and you had to be absolutely sure that you were right.

And that's why I struggled on the signatory forgery claim.

"It's definitely not my signature," I said.

"Do you think it's his?"

"I'm not sure."

"Shuw yaniy?" he expressed to no one in particular and which in Arabic means 'What do you mean?'. He raised his hand, palm out, and turned and spoke to the administrator in Arabic, who immediately stopped typing. Then he turned back to me, clasped his hands in front of him and stared me straight in the eye.

"Miss Amber let me explain to you how this works. You have to convince me that he forged your signature. It's not my job to convince you."

The interpreter thought it was hilarious, as did his aide.

He tried explaining it again, "you have to tell me it's his signature, yaniy ... that he forged your signature".

"It's definitely not my signature," I repeated slowly, letting each word sink in. "It's definitely forged, and it's possible that he forged it."

He stared at me intensely. "You're not convincing me, because you are not convinced yourself. Why?"

"Because I was signing everything. Whatever he put in front of me, I signed. There was no need for him to forge my signature so I don't understand why he would do that. That's the only reason why I am not sure."

He tilted his head as if to get the measure of this remark. "And you didn't sign this yourself?" He already knew the answer, but still felt that he had to ask the question to remove any doubt. I shook my head. I gave specifics showing that I could not have signed the consent form on the date the form said I did.

Had Grant ever forged my signature before, he wanted to know?

"I don't know," I admitted. But so what? That was not the point here. This form in front of him was what we were questioning.

"Okay, let's take it for analysis," he said turning to the administrator, who nodded his head acknowledging the instruction, and then he added, "both of them". It meant both Grant and I had to get our signature tested. I was okay with that. At least we'd know for sure. If Grant was guilty of forging my signature on the consent form, then he deserved to be duly punished.

The senior prosecutor then turned back to me, and asked if there was anything I wished to add before he concluded the interview. I shook my head. I couldn't think of anything else except to ask if this case should proceed to the courts.

He tilted is head side to side, "we'll see ..."

I knew not to push it too much. It's whatever they want it to be.

He then said I needed to sign my statement. The administrator came over to the sofa and presented me with a computer printout of my 10-page statement, all in Arabic of course. I was asked to initial the bottom of every sheet and sign and date the last page.

"Thank you, Miss Amber. First, we'll get the results

from Forensics and then we'll call Neil Ramsay. If I need you, I will call you." He was suddenly ready for me to leave, "Anything else?" he asked again.

Not a word.

"Good." He got up from his chair and held the door open for me, as I left the room.

The following week, both Grant and I were sent to a special laboratory in another government building in another part of the city to have our signatures tested. The building was new and enormous, a one-storey brick with lots of glass and dripping with the UAE flag at every turn. As far as government houses went, it was ultra-posh. The hallways were wide and tiled, and the floors gleamed with new wax. All the rooms were white, sterile and ice-cold. The guards were heavily weighed down with weapons of all kind, immaculately dressed, immaculately groomed, their red and cream uniforms beautifully tailored.

After the security and the metal detector, came the identification checks, a rather routine matter but nonetheless an important one, that confirmed that it was in fact me that showed up, and not an imposter.

I was led by one of the guards into a tiny, square room with no windows, and placed at a school-like table with bottled water before me. I was given several loose pages of plain white A4 paper and was told how I was expected to write my signature on them. I was then handed a black Bic disposable ballpoint. The guard disappeared, and was replaced by a forensic officer, wearing a white lab coat.

"It only takes an hour," he said. And it did. The procedure was utterly ghastly. I wrote my signature non-stop for an entire hour, under his careful supervision, until I literally could not write any more, and could only manage a squiggle. I am sure, rather dramatically, my wrist had become dislocated or something in the process.

"We will send this to the lab," I was told. "It'll be a few days before we have a report."

Our signatures were sent to the lab for analysis for any likeness to the signature on the consent form.

"We've taken a few samples beforehand that the lab should be able to match with the signature on the form also." Unbeknown to me, from the minute I had arrived in the building they had also taken my signature from the signing in book, the profile form and the short questionnaire I was asked to fill in at reception.

Gosh, it really was like a crime movie.

"Sneaky," I said to the forensic officer. He smiled and nodded his head, pleased with himself.

"Anything else I need to do?" I was all ready to be hooked up to a lie detector.

"No. That's all for now." There was little to do but wait.

The whole experience had been surreal.

"What's the case?" he went on to ask me. I was surprised at how loquacious he was and genuinely interested. I served up a sound bite, although I soon realised he'd already been briefed. Grant had been in before me, and prompted by the officer, he had been very nonchalant about the case, putting the matter down to the simple fact that investments go up and they go down. He had gone into negative 'victim' mode, and had been very put out about even having to have his signature tested. He was feeling that he had already talked to the police, and he had already told them what happened.

Curious, I asked the officer, from his experience of dealing with 'alleged' criminals, what he thought of Grant; did he fit into that description? Was he enthralled by him? I was asking myself for the hundredth time how Nathan and I, amongst countless others, had missed this now seemingly obvious character trait.

He shook his head side to side, and said although Grant had arrived impeccably dressed in a suit and tie with a white shirt, "I can tell". Which of course made me feel even more stupid, if that was possible.

"Did he try to sell you something?" I wouldn't put it past him.

"No," he answered; my little dig at Grant lost on him.

I really hoped the senior prosecutor shared the same thoughts, because Grant is a very engaging person. He can be very convincing, quick-witted. That was my worry. When something arose that he might not have been able to predict he dealt with it in an impressive fashion; case in point, Officer Salah, who deals with criminals on a minute-by-minute basis. That's a trait of an effective salesperson. I was in no doubt that he would find a way to persuade and convince the senior prosecutor that he hadn't done anything wrong. And this is where his sales skills really resonated. He disarmed them.

The forensic officer's evaluation of Grant soothed my concerns for the time being.

The public prosecution office broke for the National Day holidays and then subsequently for the New Year, so it would be in February 2017 when Grant was finally called to be interviewed, and the allegations laid in front of him. Grant decided to confront the allegations head on. That was his level of confidence. And so he sat down the with senior prosecutor without any legal representation.

"I have done nothing improper," he had insisted.

When asked if he had the right qualifications to be a financial advisor or if he had misrepresented himself to me he referred to the fact there was no law in Dubai which states there is a minimum requirement to practice financial advisory. Unfortunately, he was right. No qualifications required at all in Dubai. No wonder he was confident.

Then he was presented with the DED statement. And now he started to squirm in his seat, "like a lizard," was the prosecution's description to me.

He skirted questions when he was asked outright about it by the senior prosecutor, before finally refusing to answer any more questions and wanted more time to study the case and requested an extension.

It was his right and he was granted one, otherwise it would have been grounds for a complaint against the senior prosecutor and his team. Under the rules of the state public prosecution, the accused cannot appeal against the prosecutor's decision on the outcome of the investigation. Only I could, as the victim, if I did not agree with it.

That meant there was to be another delay in the investigation.

Intrigued, I asked the senior prosecutor what his first impression was of Grant, wording the question as casually as I could.

"D-r-a-m-a," came the quick reply, with the word drawn out long. I already knew what he thought of me. He'd told me often enough. But, if he's dishing out characteristics and those are the only two options, I suppose 'stupid' is marginally better than 'drama'. 'Drama' was more sinister indicating that it was a red light when people behave like that, in an odd 'acting' manner.

Drama indeed. Everyone acts. Like the Japanese saying, you have a face you show to the world, a face you show to your family and friends, and a face no one sees – unless you're trained to, like the prosecutors. After years of pretrial warfare, they knew how to read every victim, defendant, witness and lawyer; and they knew virtually everything that they would say beforehand. This was never to be underestimated.

Neither the forensic officer or the senior prosecutor seemed impressed by him. None of them could understand how I had been, and it seems incredible to them that he conned so many of us. There must be some sort of common denominator. There was – stupidity. I turned to the Urban Dictionary to determine the official street definition of 'stupid' and it read 'foolish'. The senior prosecutor didn't need to spell out the meaning.

After each interaction with the prosecution team, I left thinking that the case would reach the criminal courts comfortably.

And then ... the whole other fiasco occurred.

Goliath's army

We soon realised why Grant cut short his interview with the senior prosecutor.

Grant left to organise a defence. In fact he left to organise an offense.

He came back – but this time with a human shield to weaponise his defence in a bid to dazzle the senior prosecutor.

Yes, he came back with Goliath. A lawyer.

In other words, Grant was finally coming to realise the situation he was in at the time. And they were going to drown me in litigation. It was now a David and Goliath legal battle: Goliath's army of trained soldiers against David's farmer, aka, me.

It changed everything. And then the real drama began. Now, Grant learned what all the evidence was against him. The senior prosecutor and his team met with Grant's lawyers, behind closed doors. It was a very hush-hush meeting and this time nothing was shared with me.

For the first time I was feeling nervous and uneasy at

this sudden change of mood. I hoped I was wrong but I could sense only a slap on Grant's wrist was being negotiated with the prosecution. This was compounded by the fact that I immediately noticed an alarming difference in the senior prosecutor's attitude towards me and most significantly towards the case. He was not as friendly, open.

The senior prosecutor had all but said to me that I had a really solid case and that it was going to go to criminal court. And now suddenly the teeth seems to go out of the investigation, at least on the side of the senior prosecutor. I had been speaking with him along the way, and now he started saying that I should look to settle the case as it wasn't strong enough to get to court on the charge of fraud – he thought the charges brought against Grant didn't go far enough. A line that sounded a lot like a defence lawyer chipping away in his ear.

Prosecutors follow the evidence and the law. But you have to guide them on it. And a lawyer is someone who bends the laws of the people for those few who can afford it. It was not supposed to be that way but it's very profitable and so it stands.

Grant's lawyer coached him through his second interview with the senior prosecutor. Very successfully. Because in the span of the next few days, he again managed to change the senior prosecutor's view of the case and therefore his mind. The senior prosecutor now told me that at the minimum he could get the case to the criminal courts on licence fraud, supported by the DED.

This must be a joke. This had to be a joke.

It's like ordering a juicy Big Mac via UberEats and watching the delivery rider waltz his way around Dubai, with each passing minute moving further away from your home.

"I don't think this is right," I said. It was disappointing.

But at the same time I was trying not to push too hard. The senior prosecutor was being extremely economical with information. At this point, I was indeed labouring under the massive misapprehension that we were heading to court on licence fraud. It would still be a criminal conviction, I consoled myself.

Grant was called back for a third interview with the senior prosecutor and his team, after which I was told he was going to submit into evidence a statement from "somebody".

Two days passed.

The senior prosecutor casually called me the following morning. I could sense a pause.

I took the call in my office at my desk, with the door closed, and I took the news calmly because I was too shocked to react. There were two pieces of bad news which he was passing along. One was that he told me, unofficially, he could find no case against Grant. Things then got worse for me with the second bit of news, which hit much closer to home.

I gripped my phone as he dropped the bombshell that the investigation was over and he was withdrawing all allegations against Grant. Not only were all the allegations withdrawn, the case was stopped. Closed. I was confused. What just happened?

The information about finding Grant not guilty of any wrongdoing spun me one way and the information about the investigation being closed spun me completely the other way.

I. Literally. Could. Not. Believe. It.

Everything?

All the allegations? He's withdrawing all the allegations. Just like that.

Oh, for Christ's sake, I thought, he can't be serious.

The move to hire a lawyer had saved Grant. He had even convinced the senior prosecutor – the mind boggles how, as it was once thought to be impossible – to throw out the charge of license fraud that was supported by the statement from the DED and which was the foundation of the whole case. Although they were not an official partner to the investigation, this was a cooperative investigation between the DED and the public prosecution. It's highly unusual for the prosecutor or indeed anybody, to sidestep the DED. I didn't think I had ever heard of that and that was one of the many odd things about the decision.

The outcome of a prosecutional investigation has to be approved by different levels of authority within the public prosecution itself. This decision went through various levels. There was no way that anybody could look at this and think this decision was okay – *surely?*

It didn't make sense. None of it made sense. It was the most empty, nasty feeling.

It was incredible, and extremely frustrating because I had all this evidence and the prosecutors had a plethora of information at their fingertips. They had different victims that were willing to give testimony. They had information showing Grant managing money in Dubai under different licences. More importantly, and more significantly, they had evidence he had set up a fake company. Now that's a pretty significant offence. At this point, he had clearly implicated himself in a crime.

So why didn't the senior prosecutor see that?

"You read the DED statement?" I asked him, putting him on speaker phone.

"Yes."

"How did he explain that?"

"He can." I tried not to imagine the number of ways a clever lawyer would find to challenge this sort of evidence.

"You know that's not my signature on the consent form?"

"Yes."

"How did he explain that?"

"He has absolutely no memory of seeing that form. He is sure."

"So he can't explain it?"

I studied the phone, and suppressed a thousand other questions. I didn't know why the prosecutor shut this case down. But it was clear he was not going to share how he had come to his decision with me, and I knew I was never going to be able to convince him that there was a case here. As far as he was concerned, Grant's lawyer had done his job and constructed arguments that made enough sense to prove to the prosecutor that specific incidents did not rise to the level of criminal conduct – it was therefore a civil matter. Grant walked free.

This couldn't be the answer.

They sky was falling, the case collapsing like a house of cards. The entire process had already taken too long and had now become farcical. The senior prosecutor who had previously not been enthralled by Grant was now leading the parade to set him free. I felt so bad for the victims who had supported me to this point because I told these victims Grant would get convicted and there would be justice.

I had to think fast. The difficulty was where to go from there.

The focus now had to be whether I could have a fair investigation. The introduction of a defence lawyer at the eleventh hour constituted a distraction to that. But I also conceded that the senior prosecutor's change of mind was not unusual. It was not rocket science, Grant had a lawyer and I didn't. They had no opponents worth a light to fight. We really had a situation where what the senior prosecutor heard was only the defence's evidence, and I had no idea what was being fed to the senior prosecutor, and so I wasn't able to challenge any of it.

Part of me felt like we should all have the same legal representation. How is it fair that money can essentially buy you a much better chance of being found not guilty?

And this light bulb went on over my head and I thought I could make a point of this. I could throw money at this problem. I could now solve this problem.

And so, before the hammer hit its mark, or in this case, before he put the receiver down, I told the senior prosecutor I was coming to his office – with my very own lawyer. I had a right to legal representation and he knew he could not deny me that. I didn't have to demand it. And it was never a case I had to.

"I am not going to change my mind," he replied, clearly annoyed, and clearly seeing it as some sort of theatrical stunt; and no doubt kicking himself for giving me a courtesy call about his decision beforehand.

It didn't hold me back. The best thing I could do right now was to enforce my rights, which ensure that victims, in criminal cases, have certain basic rights, which include the right to legal representation, and the right to confer with the prosecutor on the case before it's resolved.

But now I had an irate prosecutor who was not happy with me. At all. The case had dragged on for almost a year, and he was tired of it – we all were. Progress had, at best, been slow. And here I was asking to delay the investigation yet again, costing the state time and money.

Ringing off, he gave me only one week to bring my lawyer to him and present our case, which indicated how annoyed he was. I didn't have a choice now. He was the judge, and I had to shake hands with this fact and be constructive with him over the next week.

The only thing was ... well, I didn't actually have a lawyer – yet. I had to find one. And that was not something I looked forward to doing.

It meant I had to move fast, and somehow turn it into success by the end of the week.

"What would happen if Grant walks?" asked Nathan, who was on a business trip in Singapore at the time, adding that he found the situation frankly absurd.

Losing now would be an unbearable blow and the sense of loss was immense.

It would be a disaster, no question about it. We would be back to square one. He would have got away with it. That, above anything else, was the bitterest pill to swallow.

I started feeling anxious, but then calmed down. "He's not going to get away with it."

The search for the right lawyer

I needed to hire a lawyer. Sounds simple.

There is, however, just one problem: the search for a good lawyer turned into a major task. The search for a good lawyer who was the right lawyer for my case was, unarguably, a distressing scenario – more of which later.

Fortunately, I knew how the legal landscape worked in Dubai with regards to representation before the public prosecution and the local courts, so I could narrow my search in finding a lawyer. Essentially how it works is that only a local law firm and a local advocate could represent me in court before the judge. Yes, I could hire any one of the 75 international law firms in the city who practise English law, but they are just going to hire any one of the 300 Dubai-based law firms who practise local law to do the work. I would essentially be hiring a 'middle man' so at the very minimum a referral fee will be built in the costs, and at the very maximum I could end up paying double fees – to the local firm and to the international law firm.

Therefore, I needed to find a good local law firm – and reasonable.

Most of the firms I spoke to wanted fees up front, even before I was to set foot in their office, even before they knew I had a case or not.

Some offered a free consultation, with discreet clock-watching, as they aimlessly riffled through the pile of documents I put in front of them. Something I have never understood. A free consultation is when a lawyer spends an hour or so with you and you explain your overall story to them and based on what they hear they will give you their legal opinion – without reading any material. I never understand it because 99 percent of the time their opinion changes after you hire them and they have read through your documents and material. It's a complete waste of time.

I met with many lawyers, some recommended, some I googled myself, virtually all with the word Doctor somewhere in their names, and all with solid credentials.

I listened to what they had to say, but was not convinced by it, or swayed by it. In my view, the verdict of any case is always with the judge. For so many people their happiness and emotional state depends on their lawyers and their view of their case. My hope was not going to be pegged on another human being. I knew there was a case to be heard. And at this point I just needed a good lawyer who could present the information in the best way to the senior prosecutor.

"So, what do you think?"

They focused solely on the facts; and their response to my question was not very encouraging. Something I had prepared myself for.

Well versed in working in the legal sphere, I believe

there are two clear facts about lawyers. Their job, unfortunately, absolutely revels in other people's misfortune. And they are incredibly pessimistic.

What many people don't realise is that they are trained to behave and act this way – to be in a perpetual state of pessimism. If anything good happens, they think of what could possibly go wrong with this – in other words they highlight things that are not even there. And they are like that in their non-legal world. During a conversation I once had with a lawyer I said: "So many people have come to your conference". His reply was, "But what about all the people who didn't come?". They are constitutionally programmed to downplay reward, to kill the buzz, you might say and scan for problems.

During any discussion on the probability of a successful outcome in my case, lawyers broke into non-committal smiles in a way that suggested they didn't want to communicate their true feelings on the question.

"You know this case is not easy. There is no contract and you gave him the money." The vaguest suggestion of hope instantly eliminated.

"I know." It had become a reflective response.

"And you transferred the money out of the country – yourself."

"I know."

I had one lawyer who got a little excited and then put the brakes on and suddenly thought about peripheral issues that may be more important. It was as if he was afraid to wander into the 'unknown' and the 'possibilities'.

Another food for thought offered by another lawyer: "There's a risk that we're dealing with someone who is careful to erase their tracks".

"That's most likely, but we might also get a lucky break," I replied.

"So far that hasn't happened."

"No, it hasn't ..." agreed his colleague, sinking back on his chair, and they both pondered the case in silence. And we had circled back to pessimism again.

It was immediately obvious from early meetings and conversations that no one thought I had a case, by any stretch of the imagination, with little concrete evidence. Even with the DED's statement. I needed proof of what Grant was paid and as those arrangements were direct with the Fund Managers, Product Providers and the Financial Service Providers that was never going to materialise. The signature forgery was something worth pursuing, I was told, although the evidence had to be tight and beyond a reasonable doubt. And that was just some of the many matters they considered.

Every single one of them advised me not to waste time, money and effort fighting a battle I couldn't ever win, gently persuading me to Let It Go. They had in their own way so much experience of these type of cases and they were also wise to the hazards of the court process. And they understood, more clearly than most, the need to separate the facts from the emotion to take the risks seriously, and to compartmentalise those aspects of the case that might, were they to become too intertwined, eventually damage them. A mental financial calculation showed that the risks of losing everything were at that point greater than the potential benefits of continuing with the case. But again, as I explained to them, it wasn't about the money for me.

To which they would look at me, sadly, shaking their heads.

It was baffling to them why any sane person would involve themselves with this headache and put a down payment for a house collapsing down a cliff.

I suffered through the arguments of all the lawyers. It

was clear they were seeing 'What is' whilst I was focused on and asking 'What if?'. Bereft of any ideas on the case, it was taking an extra effort to get any of them to look at things even remotely positively.

Everything they said was factually true, but I was simply baffled that they were all missing the seemingly obvious key license breach, and the supporting statement from the DED – surely it was worth its weight in gold if used effectively? At the very least, because it points to character. We needed to build on that. And I remember feeling really irritated by the lack of creativity; they made it all look absolutely hopeless.

And to be honest many of them didn't want this case – this headache.

But some lawyers wanted my case, even, if, in their view, I didn't have one. Unfortunately, their natural craving to make some easy money marginally outweighed their concern for my winability rate, or at least it did for the ones I met with. That was incredibly baffling.

Another lawyer who had been recommended to me, wanted £20,000 to fight my case just for his fees alone. For what exactly I asked incredulously. A criminal and civil case against Grant and he would throw in a complimentary criminal case against Guardian Trust Company Ltd for breach of trust. But we were at prosecution stage, and he was already telling me the likelihood of proceeding to criminal was virtually unrealistic. And Guardian Trust Company Ltd was based in Jersey and I was fully aware that we couldn't prosecute them in Dubai. 'We' would have to hire a lawyer in Jersey if I chose to pursue them, through him, no doubt doubling fees. Did he even know the laws of Jersey? Did he even know where it was?

It's all or nothing I was told.

That would be a hard "NO". With a double underline.

"Well, if you change your mind …"

I coughed. "I'll let you know."

I could hardly believe what I was hearing. Suck all hope out of you. And still, try and find a way to make some money out of you.

There was no doubt in my mind, if I hired them Grant was surely going to get away with everything. Obviously, that was a huge If. In fact, it was an If so immense that it would take an astonishing amount of convoluted irrational thinking to see it as anything other than completely insurmountable.

I don't subscribe to the theory that lawyers are all dodgy, but this particular experience severely tested my faith. It's not very pleasant being on the other side of the business of law, as a client. Bleak and confusing; forget innovation, creativity and all those other marketing buzzwords. My experience as a client was a flood of razor-smart people with razor-smart legal antenna, but no substance.

To take Grant and his lawyers on, I needed a winning new message and someone who could deliver it in a clear and hugely effective way. My search was narrowed down to a visionary lawyer that could see an opportunity. They had to have the right vision, fire in their belly. They could not be afraid of the risk.

I needed somebody that not only believed in me, but somebody who would fight for me.

And I didn't see any sign of that in any of the lawyers I had met so far. Nobody seemed to click and I was getting quite despondent.

"You're afraid that they will not be able to fill Grant's lawyers' shoes?" asked Nathan.

"No, I'm afraid they will not be able to make my argument as well as they did."

"I was going for the metaphor."

"Yes, and I was saying the actual words."

My white knight

Just when I had almost given up hope, a light bulb went on over my head, and I remembered a person I had met at the police station. As I had waited for the officer, a local Arab gentleman in the room struck up conversation with me. He had recently hired a lawyer to represent him and he had said he was very pleased with him. He was an ex-policeman who understood how prosecutors work. By some luck, I found that I had saved the Arab's number on my phone. Maybe a non-lawyer recommendation would be better than a lawyer-recommendation. I may be better served by a more nurturing and less 'alpha' atmosphere. I took the plunge and I rang him and got the details, and promptly gave the lawyer's office a call, determined to find a way to see him.

The lawyer could meet me on Thursday when he was back from vacation, I was told. That left me three days to prepare something for the senior prosecutor on the coming Sunday. It was cutting it really fine. But he was now my best chance to lead the charge.

A fact confirmed within three minutes of meeting with him. Ironically, his white candoura was gleaming in some divine way, like he was the 'chosen one'.

Early Thursday morning, I made my way to Jumeirah, a coastal residential area of Dubai, mainly comprising of low-rise private dwellings built in a variety of architectural styles. The lawyer had renovated one of the large detached villas into a law practice. I saw faces behind the front window as I came up the walk. A young assistant of some variety answered the door before I had time to ring, "Hello there," she said, inviting me in. The villa was cool inside.

The front hall floor was white and black squares with a graceful central staircase. A flower arrangement with gladioli sat on a polished table beside it. There was a soft smell of oud perfume everywhere. I walked through the hall and was led up the staircase to the lawyer's office. I looked around. There were photographs everywhere of important local people. I could tell that this guy has some friends in high places.

"Salam," the lawyer greeted me before I entered his large office, and politely thanked his assistant. His office was beautiful, perfectly arranged, pale-coloured and peaceful. All the furniture was white, perfectly blending with his white candoura covering his 6 ft slim frame. Except now, my focus was on his moustache. Whoever designed his moustache knew what he was doing. A curled, flowing moustache, like a cavalier's, with a graceful goatee to match. It went with his hair.

Sitting across from each other at his desk, we exchanged small talk for several minutes and he seemed, on the face of it, to be a softly spoken, articulate, intelligent and rational man. His name, which was easy to remember as he shared it with 95 percent of the local Emirati population, was Mohamed.

This lawyer was characteristically matter-of-fact when discussing my case and actually interested in my story. We chatted for much of the next two hours about everything from his time and experience as a police officer to my situation, and he was very open, down-to-earth and funny. He listened patiently, as he probably had to with hundreds of people haranguing him about their cases, all the while tugging at the tip of his goatee. He didn't ask for money; he didn't discuss fees. He discussed only my case. And that's precisely why he struck such a chord.

"What's your opinion?" I asked at last. "Is it all as

hopeless as it seems?"

After I had shared all my financial information with him, and a long laundry list of other potential charges, he looked me directly in the eyes and said simply, "We need to scale it back". I had to drop some elements of the case at that point in time. It was too intense for the prosecutor to understand and I had to go for simple misrepresentation of licence to get the case through the first part of the process.

"When you get flooded with information what do you remember?" he asked.

"Nothing."

Sometimes, the answer really is simple. The opinions of trained and hideously expensive lawyers were not needed to know that the prosecutor was inundated, that we were engaging in a practice called overkill.

The lawyer came across as unstuffy and genuine.

And sensible. "I need to speak to the prosecutor and I need to see what the other party submitted. We cannot go in blind." I agreed. He was the only lawyer I had met and spoken to in the last few days, who had come up with this strategy.

"We will talk to him and get copies of all the documents relating to the case." That seemed mighty ambitious to me.

In his mind, the senior prosecutor had been running the investigation for nine months when he could have closed the file earlier. He had called me to inform me that there was no case before he closed it. These are positive points, he said.

He saw my quizzical eyebrow and tried to explain. "I think he was really trying to help. You either have not enough evidence or have not presented it in a way he can use." Ever-astute, he pinpointed a small but significant issue: the prosecutor doesn't know if Grant is guilty or innocent of all the offences. But licence fraud? Licence fraud alone: is it really a productive use of a court's time? The licence fraud was too small a case to warrant time and energy to go to a full-length trial and have a judge presiding over it. The maximum penalty would be a very small fine. And if the prosecutor did transfer the file to the court, the judge himself may eliminate the need for a criminal trial and refer the matter to civil on the grounds that the case was too small for the High Court. It was like preparing an operation theatre for a heart surgery operation and then someone walks in with a cut and just needs a plaster. It was certainly a lot more than licence fraud warranted, however notorious.

It was another possible science behind the senior prosecutor's thought-process for dismissing the case.

In any event, the lawyer didn't seem worried at all.

Myself, I felt totally confident with him, and it made all the difference feeling my case was safe with him; even more so when he offered his biography. His speciality was in prosecution investigation: he prevented cases getting to court. I had found the perfect lawyer for my case who already had an idea what the prosecutor was thinking. In turn, I was thinking the lawyer was an answer to my prayers, my White Knight.

The only thing he had asked me to sign was the Power of Attorney that gave him privileges to represent me on Sunday when we would meet the senior prosecutor.

That's when it hit me. We were instructed to present our case on Sunday at eight-thirty in the morning, and we were going to arrive to ask for yet a further extension and for a copy of the other party's memorandum; no mean feat.

Well, this IS going to be awkward!

There was no doubt in my mind. The senior prosecutor was going to flip his lid on Sunday. Absolutely Flip Out. He was going to throw that gavel at my face. He already thought I had pulled a fast one on him by getting a lawyer at the final hour and this was just putting the shawl on my casket.

I had no idea where we were heading, but the lawyer had a calmness about him. "Khalass, you don't need to worry, let me worry about how to handle him," that was after all his skill. And with a cheery smile he bid me farewell, "have a nice weekend, and see you at eight sharp Sunday morning".

The lawyer was not a guy who worries about a lot of stuff. His mere presence became my great and amusing sense of security and hope.

Even so, I spent the next two days, worrying about Sunday, worrying about a lot of things, until the day finally crept up. Sunday morning, I arrived right on time for the meeting with the prosecutor.

My lawyer had arrived before me. There he was – wearing a beige candoura, everything resting on him, casually sitting on one of the nondescript seats in the main lobby area.

"How are you feeling, this morning?" he wondered as I sat next to him.

"He's going to flip his lid," I reminded him, a word that had recently regularly entered my mainstream vocabulary during the investigation. The weekend break had done nothing to alleviate my concerns as to how this would now play out. My nerves were ragged from the stress of what the senior prosecutor was going to think when I turned up empty-handed.

In an attempt to lighten the mood and distract me, he showed me a picture on his mobile.

"Is that Mike Tyson with you?" I asked.

He was, apparently, one of his acquaintances. I was impressed.

He then said that he was in the process of moving offices as he needed a private elevator to take some of his clients directly to his office as they didn't wish to be seen.

I stared at him. "Who ARE you!?" I asked incredulously. I think I had found my very own Matthew McConaughey in the Lincoln Lawyer after all.

He chuckled. I knew he was an ex-policeman and he had hinted more than once that his brother worked for the government in some mysterious capacity, so he probably had lucrative ultra-high-net-worth clients. I suddenly had this picture of Grant salivating at the prospect of getting his manicured hands on them.

"So you're like Richard Flud from the Lehman Brothers," I told him. In the New York head office of the US Investment Bank, Flud, as CEO, had his own private elevator that took him straight to his office on the 31st floor, so he didn't have to interact with anybody. In 2008, he was widely responsible for triggering the global financial crisis – maybe he wasn't a good example to use, I thought. He was the only one I could think of with such a perk. Even Anna Wintour, the Editor of Vogue, didn't have her own elevator. The rule at Vogue was if she entered the elevator you were meant to vacate it so she could ride it alone.

"Well if things don't go well here, maybe I'll be hiring Mike Tyson," I said, straight-faced.

He laughed – a really earthy, infectious cackle.

The receptionist announced the prosecutor would see us now and we followed her as she led the way, her high heels clacking down the long white corridor, into the senior prosecutor's spacious square corner office where he was sat at the big desk with his aides sitting on either side. The office was tidy and pleasant but impersonal. No photographs of family members or framed certificates or odd little knick-knacks. Just piles and piles of case files in blue folders dotted everywhere – on the floor, on the window ledge, neatly stacked on shelves. White wardrobes lined one entire wall of the office. A gigantic UAE flag on the wall attested to his loyalties.

It was a change from my previous visits there. The atmosphere was formal for a start. It was our first encounter since I dropped the bombshell about coming to see him with my lawyer, and he was not exactly brimming with the camaraderie we enjoyed before.

My lawyer greeted the senior prosecutor and introduced himself while I was offered a drink. I declined the offer but was presented with a traditional cup of cardamom qahwa anyway.

Everything was spoken in Arabic – absolutely nothing was in English. But for some reason, I was completely calm. The senior prosecutor was understandably annoyed at the inconvenience I had thrown at him but, thankfully, my lawyer was handling it. I could tell by the body language between them, a wonderful form of easy communication. The reason was very simple: the senior prosecutor liked my lawyer. I could see from his demeanour that he had the utmost respect for him. My lawyer was after all an ex-policeman, able to find the right words to soothe the senior prosecutor's irritation, who understands how they work and organise themselves, how they think.

The senior prosecutor pointed to various entries on the file, probably highlighting the number of extension requests made by both parties since the investigation began. He handed a paper to my lawyer, who quickly read through it, showing an eagerness to hear more from the prosecutor.

Rather divinely, the light streamed in through the windows, creating a golden patch effect on the entire room.

At any rate, I could sense the atmosphere slowly thawing – who knew, maybe he was bargaining with him using a signed copy of Mike Tyson's new book as bait? Whatever he was saying was working. His points found its mark repeatedly.

Relief flooded over me when I suddenly saw the senior prosecutor open his diary that was on the desk in front of him – rather theatrically, as if to suggest it was rather irritating of us to bother him like this. I realised they were discussing a date. I felt a surge of hope.

And in a flash, everything was back on track.

One of the next things that my lawyer did was ask for the prosecution records, the other party's memorandum, Forensic report and other relevant documents. The list of requests was quickly acceded to by the senior prosecutor.

We left the meeting with a one-week extension to submit our memorandum and a copy of all the documents requested. My lawyer had managed to smoothly convert an irate prosecutor to personally giving him what he wanted. It was like watching the ballet.

I could hardly believe it.

"He's not a happy man." My lawyer confirmed what I had already suspected; the prosecutor was upset with me and wasn't happy about any of it.

"Well, neither am I." I did feel really bad, and it was not a great thing to do, but a necessary one if I was to save this case, and the meeting itself went well and that's what really matters – I tried to convince myself.

When we stand for something, we're unhinged. If we show emotion, we're called dramatic. If we want to take on an industry, we are nuts; and if we get angry, we're hysterical, irrational, or just being crazy. It's the modern disease.

We also learned that, during the investigation, Grant had made a complaint directly to the prosecution office that the investigation had taken too long.

"Interesting," I said, finally understanding the change in the mood of the investigation when lawyers suddenly appeared on the scene. "Interesting tactic?" I asked. My lawyer simply smiled.

"That's not fair on the prosecutor," I said. "They should focus on fighting the merits of the case, not target people or the system." It was simply a preview of more tactics to come from the defence team.

That wasn't the only surprise the senior prosecutor shared.

The name of Grant's lawyers.

When Grant came back with his lawyer, he didn't come back with just any lawyer.

He assembled a team of criminal defence lawyers from a top local law firm opting for starry advocates in terms of legal directories rankings and industry recognition. The appointment of aggressive local Emirati lawyers, who specialised in fraud, added to the speculation that Grant was very worried and had done some flipping out of his own after his first meeting with the prosecution team.

Even the senior prosecutor had been impressed by the name – impressed that Grant hired them. Whether he was impressed by them was a different matter.

"What defines a 'Top lawyer' from any other lawyer?" Nathan asked me out of curiosity.

"Outrageous fees I imagine."

To the untrained eye, on paper the odds were I was going to get trounced by the intimidating resume. But I was not worried.

Lawyers – love them or loathe them – you do need them. But you need the right lawyer. Grant's lawyers had already shown how a very rich person with a powerful legal representative, can snaffle the case away from even the most experienced prosecutor. My lawyer had shown how a specialist lawyer in a particular area of law, can swing the case alive again. Such is the killing power of a great lawyer. Essentially, it's what separates the lawyers from the great lawyers.

And that's why I was neither worried or impressed by Grant's choice of lawyers. I had a good hand, meaning I was never going to lose because I was not represented equally.

"Hello…"
Click – the phone went dead.
I looked at the time on my phone.
3 AM it screamed. I know, I know, I say to it.
I turned my side over and went back to sleep.

Walking through minefields

The quote by the fictional Violet Crawley, Dowager Countess of Grantham in Downton Abbey perfectly sums up the next part: "The truth is neither here nor there, it's the look of the thing that matters".

The next day, I made my way to my lawyer's office.

Dubai, early morning, is stunning. The temperature is in the low twenties, the air clear and fresh, and the green is greener than any green I've ever seen, other than Northern Ireland.

The law office it seemed was always open, and usually occupied with any one of a half-dozen subordinates. The receptionist greeted me and guided me to my lawyer's office.

"Morning," he said with a happy voice, as I entered, rising to his feet from behind his desk. A well-dressed errand boy was already pouring the coffee at the large table near the window.

"Good morning. How are you?" I took a seat across from him.

"Alhumdulilah." Sitting back down.

"You start very early." More of a statement than a question.

"Early mornings, late nights," he said waving at his cluttered desk of caseload files. I literally could not see the surface of his desk.

"Did you get a chance to read the memo yet?"

He passed me a copy of Grant's memorandum, a sheaf of some ten papers, that one of his colleagues had translated into English for me.

"He's defending all the allegations you made against him and relying on what is called 'a defence of truth'," he explained.

Truth? He doesn't know the meaning of the word.

"Remember, it is for Grant to prove that the allegations are untrue and "completely ridiculous" as he states, as well as the allegation he has fraudulently made money off you."

I nodded my head, to acknowledge I understood.

My lawyer then gave me a quick summary of the memorandum, whilst I studied the pages. "Grant's defence is that Guardian paid his fees; he physically didn't handle any money; his role is consulting and management and Guardian controls the investment part of the Trust and that there is no contract between you and him." The lack of any real expression of regret told me that Grant still believed that his actions had been justified.

"And the signature on the consent form?"

"He insists that he does not know anything about the signature on the consent form or who signed it." He paused. "I've gone through the Forensic report and I'm afraid his signature doesn't match the signature on the consent form."

"No way." It was an instant hammer-blow in the case against Grant. "And me?"

"No match."

Even though I knew I hadn't signed it, I was relieved that the tests proved I hadn't.

"More of that later, but let's go through this first," he said, nodding towards the papers in my hand.

For the next ten minutes I went through the memorandum, my lawyer watching my face as I read it, line by line.

The first argument, Grant's lawyer asked for the case to be dismissed on the grounds that it was over the time limit. Statutes of limitations are laws passed by legislative bodies in systems to set the maximum time after an event within which legal proceedings may be initiated. They had tried to exploit that. Then followed a slew of other technical reasons why the case should be thrown out.

"Pretty standard stuff," my lawyer explained, waving it aside. As with most cases, the sub-defence of technicalities often consumed as much time as the real issues.

And then came the first surprise. And not a pleasant one.

The defence had a witness.

"Philip Van Neste." Instinctively, I bolted upright. My reaction was one of total disbelief. My face contorted in confusion: Come again? Did I read that correctly?

"Philip Van Neste is the key witness for the defence?" I repeated his name to let it sink in, as I looked at it on the white sheet of paper. "You're kidding? Why?"

There was a pause as I looked up from the papers, "Is there any possibility that your colleague translated this name incorrectly?"

My lawyer thinks I'm joking.

In an extraordinary move, Guardian and Van Neste had acted as a witness to Grant during his investigation. And their defence had largely rested on his statement. He was now in the picture, only not in a positive way for me, or even a fair way.

"I had requested from him a factual statement regarding my Trust," I explained to my lawyer. "Only a factual statement, and he ignored all my emails for months."

It was incredible. In a conflict of loyalties between Grant, his loyalties to Grant on one hand, and any loyalty he might have to his client, he was clear on who would take priority. He obviously considered his loyalties were more with Grant than with me.

"Yes? And what were you requesting from him?"

"Just general questions," I said, waving my hand in the air, "you know, for example, when he had received the signed consent form from Grant ... he said the form had been sent to him from Grant's office and I asked him for evidence of that."

Addressing the forged signature claim, we learnt, in the memorandum, Van Neste stated to the prosecution that they had no way of knowing who had sent the signed consent form to their offices in Jersey, and that they could only confirm they had received the consent form by post.

I was lost for words.

Van Neste went on to state they were happy with the signature on the consent form and had verified it at their end. As far as they were concerned it "resembled my signature" and "found to be a true likeness".

"Oh, this guy," I grunted with disgust, "what's his sudden obsession with this investigation in Dubai?" That was the great and troubling question. Van Neste was emerging as this Svengali figure who seemed to have some unexplainable grip over this investigation.

He was showing that he did not take the issue around the signature seriously – at all. He described the forgery claim dismissively as if I was crazy or something, because, in his view, the signature was at least similar to the example he had on file.

"He's protecting Grant all the way." That was the bottom line.

"Certainly is." My lawyer agreed.

And the worst thing about it was, he wasn't even trying to look impartial. My blood pressure was raising.

"You received the golden silence, he instead submitted a statement to support Grant against the allegations against him, setting out a version of events that was favourable to him." My lawyer was wearing his trial hat.

I swivelled around in my chair as I slowly realised some of that blame rested with me.

As per DFSA's advice, I had contacted Guardian and was introduced to Van Neste. I made him fully aware of our suspicions regarding Grant's conduct and subsequent charges against him.

And unbeknown to me all this time, Van Neste was keeping Grant in the loop of everything I was asking and requesting on behalf of the senior prosecutor.

I had been slightly disconcerted with Grant knowing some facts regarding my Trust. I had removed Grant as the investment manager from my Trust yet he relayed information that he would only have known if he had gone onto the online portal itself or if Guardian had provided the information to him.

When I had enquired with Guardian how this was possible, they said it took time to remove someone from the system due to all the internal processes.

But it had been two months!

And how does he know such exact details?

"Who's talking to him?" I had wondered.

Now, I found the answer. The answer became crystal clear. It had Van Neste stamped all over it.

"This is just great," I mumbled.

Now, I found Van Neste had gone on to support Grant openly, it was obvious it was him who was continuing to provide Grant with access to my Trust and its details.

And there's more. He's only getting started.

I turned another page.

Grant's lawyers dealt with the statement by the DED by ignoring it. They never mentioned it in the whole of the memorandum – not even a passing reference. They simply ignored the evidence. Instead, they focused on Van Neste's statement which directly contradicted it.

The statement from the DED confirmed that they didn't issue a licence for Grant to perform a financial advisory role. And yet, Van Neste, unequivocally praised Grant and stated they completed due diligence on Grant and his company, and were satisfied that he could perform a financial advisory role in Dubai.

"Why did they think that a statement from Van Neste, some unknown person sitting in a place called 'Jersey', was going to be more credible than a statement from the DED who issues company license in Dubai?"

Who was Van Neste to say, over the DED, that Grant did have the correct licence because they had done due diligence?

That didn't even make sense. None of it did. Van Neste was in no position to say that. How did they even get his statement admitted into evidence? I would thus literally see my case being turned into a nightmare right before my tormented eye by Van Neste as he trespassed dangerously on the DED's authority.

My lawyer nodded. "Well," he said, "you have a solid statement which they have to find a way to counter." Van Neste's statement was not to prove anything, just to contradict the DED, and to muddy the waters so there would be some doubt in the mind of the senior prosecutor about whether or not Grant was operating illegally. My lawyer agreed it was a poor attempt.

"Forget Mike Tyson," I looked directly at him. "Do you have the number for the Sopranos?"

He thinks it's funny – I'm only half joking.

Grant's lawyer knew a conviction, without the DED statement, was difficult to obtain. By choosing not to include any reference to the DED statement that might challenge the narrative that he was determined to sell to the senior prosecutor, he neglected facts so he could craft a narrative so blatantly one-sided that the senior prosecutor never got anything close to a balanced portrait.

My lawyer took a long drink of his black coffee. "We have to bring the prosecutor back to where the evidence is and follow the evidence," he explained. "And that will lead him back to the real truth, and dismiss anything this man has to say about Grant's licence."

I looked up at him. He seemed completely undeterred so far at the defence's punches.

"Why is that?" I wondered.

"It's textbook."

Intriguingly, despite the robustness of the statement which risked denting Van Neste's reputation as Grant's number one fraudulent cheerleader, it left one question about the statement unsaid: Why was Van Neste supporting Grant over me? Whatever the truth behind this baffling decision – and make no mistake there was some kind of motive – the contretemps did shine a spotlight on the remarkable relationship between the Financial Services Company and the Independent Financial Advisor. A very bright spotlight, I thought, but not one to be pursued right then.

"They really will resort to anything to get this investigation dropped, won't they?" I said to my lawyer. He nodded with a solemn grin as if this was unfortunate but expected.

A case in point was the next passage in the defence's memorandum.

They were less inclined to talk about Prosperity Offshore Investment Consultants – never once referring to the company throughout their memorandum. However, the next section read that I had agreed and signed a document acknowledging I understood the services Grant was providing through Prosperity Management Consultancy. Only they had taken a photocopy of that document and cut off the header at the top. Because the header at the top reads "Prosperity Offshore Investment Consultants" – the fake company Grant had set up, thereby deliberately misleading the impression it gave of the letter.

"Good Lord, I need a second to let the classiness walk over me." I know I said I was looking for 'creativity' in the lawyers of today, but they took 'creativity' to the extreme.

Taken aback, I asked my lawyer: "Isn't that illegal?" and he replied: "It's not not illegal." I frowned in disbelief whereas he had seen much dirtier tricks. Well, I thought, we knew what we were going to be up against with aggressive lawyers, we can hardly be surprised now they're behaving exactly to type and dancing around ethics.

These were all striking moves – dramatic even – partly because the defence saw that I was not represented at the time with a legal team, and they took this as an opportunity to throw everything at the senior prosecutor.

"They're treating this like a game." They are playing in the gutter.

"Actually, this is not unusual, especially in weak defences. We'll take the high road." He paused, and smiled adding humour, "we'll show them how it's played". His composure was a sharp contrast to my explosiveness.

My lawyer said we would hit back that this was only part of the story and was presented in a way that was very misleading without additional context – which is lawyer-speak for they were blatantly manipulating the evidence. In short, Grant's lawyers used an edited version of the document in their legal papers. My lawyer introduced the unedited version in our memorandum.

So far, all of this focused effort of the defence yielded evidence for us that proved Grant's lack of credibility. They had nothing substantial; they weren't tackling the subject matter head on.

People in the judicial system undoubtedly have a high level of intelligence and are some of the highest earners in the country. But some of them have expanded their defence into such a convoluted mess that they have lost sight of integrity and have befuddled their own abilities, determined to emerge as the winner in this one-sided war of attrition. Like everything else in the toxically tribal world we now endure, the truth doesn't matter – all that matters is that your side wins.

I read a little further. Just when you thought it couldn't get any goopier, anything that could be thrown was being thrown. Any court trial is expected to focus on the victim's character and credibility and part of the reason is to devalue them and portray them in a damaging light in front of a judge or a jury. They want to make this person look like someone who's not worthy of reasonable doubt in a fair trial. And so, from that point on the defence's memorandum heavily emphasised that they questioned the character and credibility of the victim, where they devoted the entire conclusion to a vituperative slating of the complainant, aka, me.

Clearly, Grant's lawyers were looking into who I was and what I was doing, what my past was and whether there were any peccadilloes that would make me vulnerable to attack – in lawyer-speak this means basically 'going through my trash'. And the reason that it happened to the degree that it did is because Grant had the resources to do that. He was paying for that.

Except they had nothing; not even a parking ticket. If I ever did get one it would be for going too slow along Sheikh Zayed Road, the busiest highway in the city. Banks hate me because I pay my credit cards on time, so they make no money out of me. I pay all my bills on time, mainly on direct debit. All declarations I have ever made on any form were proven to be legitimate. My paperwork and CV credentials checked out. I had a police clearance certificate. By all accounts, I was the perfect expat living in Dubai. They couldn't find a single lie, misrepresentation to question my credibility.

So they had to change their tactic. My character and credibility was subject to question because of my investments to convince the senior prosecutor of the likelihood of probability that I was making up my claims and not telling the truth – about anything – she knew about the risks related to investing, the investments fell and now she wants to blame someone, and was trying to recoup the money from Grant. I shook my head at it: Disappointing defence from a high-powered legal team. Unoriginal. Uncreative. Usual defence.

The penultimate part of their legal papers veered off into an extraordinary rant, reading like a sour litany of complaints against me and the case I had bought against Grant. Again perfectly normal, nonetheless, they were unashamedly brutal, and floated: "I was only after the money", "I've made Grant's life a nightmare" and "Grant has put up with her for seven long years". Not to mention the heart-rending factoid that Grant worries about his children and that "I'm an awful human being for putting him and his family through this". They were hitting their laptops faster than Usain Bolt hitting his stride.

"Really, they wheeled his children out?" I froze in mid-sentence, "Again?". I read the passage once more.

"Always garners sympathy." My lawyer nodded his head as though he approved of the tactic.

"Tell me about it," I said, recalling my conversation with Grant's boss. "Especially when they're so young and innocent."

Shaking my head, I pressed on to the next subject: which in fact was the settlement Grant had reached out to me on. Only Grant and his lawyer both appeared to be confused on this matter.

Although the lawyers for Grant did not oppose the extension I requested, citing it as a matter for the prosecutor, they labelled me "obstructive and acting in bad faith" who purposely stretched the investigation hoping Grant will settle – an allegation that was demonstrably untrue – deliberately structuring the story to falsely claim that I tried to settle with him, missing out the part that Grant was the one to approach me (and the prosecutor) and tried to offer me a settlement. But then who cares about accuracy?

They were truly maddening.

"The only thing they refrained from calling me was a bunny boiler," I said, almost mocking, which drew a couple of chuckles from my lawyer. "Seriously. I always knew the other side was going to throw a lot of mud, but look at all the names they're calling me, the things they are twisting, and even fabricating."

"Well, you are calling him a fraudster," he gives me dutiful smile, "that kind of trumps all the other names".

That was true. In that one statement, I was obviously

not sugar-coating anything either.

He added that legal responses to lawsuits are infamous for invective and hyperbole. It's the law of the legal jungle, that it was nothing more than a schoolyard spat on paper that no judge took seriously. Incredible. If the defence knew from the outset that their insults were not accepted to be statements of fact, and legally pointless, what exactly was the point?

"It's ridiculous," I said, to myself. My outrage relented a little, but I wasn't quite ready to abandon my sense of injury.

Grant was fortunate that he could afford a large defence team to challenge a prosecutional system not really familiar of financial advisory fraud, and who were more concerned with winning than with winning with facts. And who were unable to debate the substance without attacking the person.

In their conclusion Grant's lawyers wanted to leave no room for any doubt. They reached peak anger: "We demand she pays Grant's legal fees for wasting everyone's time on a nonsense investigation".

No, it's not. It's a legitimate investigation that just saw a lot of smoke turn into furious fire.

It turns out a rather boastful Grant was privately messaging friends that his lawyer, bizarrely, was working on his case pro bono, and the whole affair was entirely gratis. Therefore, there weren't any legal fees to pay. It was a ludicrous suggestion peddled by him anyway.

"He's filthy rich," I stated.

Again my lawyer said it's not unusual. "We see it all the time."

"Then what do you do?"

"It's a small point, but we'll use it. We'll hit back to suggest that Grant appeared to be confused regarding the payment of his legal bills and attach copies of those messages. Enough to bring into question his credibility."

However much his lawyers charged, it was plainly ridiculous to suggest that the law firm picked up the bill for representing him.

The final section read to remind the senior prosecutor of more weightier matters: their client's high moral plinth, he was the very beacon of honesty, decency and fairness in a world increasingly blighted by Waheed-related lies, indecency and unfairness.

I mean, God almighty, it was almost poetic. The language too sugary. I could become a diabetic just by reading it. I came out of their memorandum so badly, but Grant came out like Persil.

Grant wanted us to believe he was a British gentleman who could never do what he's being accused of. But little of his behaviour appeared even remotely gentlemanly. Anybody who secretly frauds their self-described friend is by definition, dishonest.

My lawyer said there was more but nothing of any value. I dreaded to think what 'more' was.

But that was their story – their defence. And I thought: "Oh ... well ... thank God", because their story didn't match any physical evidence. It didn't make any sense. And the fact is they were offering conclusions not found in any evidence. Their memorandum was absolutely impeccably produced, written, executed, and edited on fancy letterhead paper but not a shred of evidence was presented to back up their claims. Totally entertaining and readable if you were not the centre of it.

"The perfect memorandum, of course, is not one that will be fair, but one that will deliver the verdict they want," said my lawyer. He was right, of course. Even if it meant coming close to crossing the line.

"Well, now it's clear why the prosecutor was going to

drop the case." At least the sun had set on that question.

As they made no reference to the DED statement and the Prosperity Offshore Investment Consultants company altogether, I saw that as rather encouraging because in many ways their memorandum raised more questions than it answered.

"So what do we do? What do you normally do in situations like this?" I was done with their memorandum and put it down on the desk.

"Well, I think our first step is to focus on the key points only, reassemble the case like a 'jigsaw'," he said, pointedly borrowing my word of the moment. "We need to work with the prosecutor and lay it out clean and professional. He'll like that." Prosecutors, on the whole, hated the natural lawyerly compulsion of overkill. They prefer cases that are black and white and show clear wrongdoing.

Our response would therefore be simple and subtle. Bringing the prosecution back on track to the core complaint, we would argue strenuously that there were two elements to our case. Firstly, the funds were invested contrary to my requirements as the investor, who wanted a more conservative approach. The second was that Grant was not licensed and did not have the experience to provide the service. As Grant was not licensed this provided a clear route for prosecution. If he had been licensed and experienced there may well have been a different outcome. Then we could drive the fact that he purposely misguided me for personal financial benefit to bury him for fraud.

"And the forged signature?" I circled back to the consent form.

"Well, the allegation was proven by Forensic testing. The signature had been forged, but not by Grant himself. We can't escape that fact."

Well, it is what it is. For this reason, I accepted it. I was never sure about it and I was not going to bet on someone's freedom if I was in doubt myself. Grant would have had to create an entirely new style of writing that could not be linked to his own style to fool the forensic experts.

We could argue he had directed someone else to sign the document, but my lawyer advised me that there wasn't enough evidence to back up the claims. For a criminal conviction you need to prove beyond a reasonable doubt. And that's why, he anticipated, the senior prosecutor would withdraw the allegation. It meant Grant would avoid jail for sure if the case did get to trial on the other charges. The signature forgery carried weight and it was the one that Grant was afraid of as there is no way of dealing with this matter other than by a period of imprisonment.

But if he didn't do the crime, then it was the right result.

"And Van Neste's statement?"

"Oh that's easy. We'll be able to throw out Van Neste's statement altogether."

Unbeknown to both men, I had a copy of their Terms of Business, which Rupert miraculously got hold of. Van Neste's big mistake was to admit he had conducted the due diligence because the Terms of Business document between Grant and Guardian clearly showed he hadn't. If he had conducted any form of due diligence he would have known that the information Grant has written in the document was incorrect.

In the legal document Grant had written against the category 'Nature of Business Activities', "Offshore Investment Consultants" (the DED provided a licence for Prosperity Management Consultancy to trade only as a management consultancy).

To rub salt into those gaping wounds, in the category

'Regulator Authority' he wrote "Department of Economic Development, Dubai" (the DED only registers a company and are not regulators) and in the category 'Business for which regulated' Grant again wrote "Offshore Investment Consulting".

Really, those two. What a pair. It told you really how bad this was.

We would use this document to undermine Van Neste's statement and credibility before the prosecution and show that Van Neste had 'tailored' his statement to meet Grant's memorandum, which is lawyer-speak that it shows he's a slimy worm, and has no bearing on the investigation whatsoever. If the case was transferred to the criminal courts, we would file a motion to prohibit his testimony on that basis.

You couldn't grasp the magnitude of this man's meddling effect in the investigation. He withheld evidence to protect Grant. He turned evidence against me to protect Grant. He worked with Grant and his lawyers to discredit me and my case against Grant. He tried to control and manipulate the case without ever setting foot in Dubai.

The question of why he was so loyal to Grant hinged on a simple question: What did he have to lose if Grant is prosecuted?

That was now for me to investigate.

My lawyer had also made the decision to ignore the personal attacks in the other party's memorandum. It had no legal standing. It was that simple.

Only now did my lawyer hand me an engagement letter with his fee for preparing our memorandum which he had discounted for me. And he never charged me for our initial meeting or his time at the prosecutor's office.

Moreover, he gave me the name of his legal translator, to help reduce the cost further. He told me which documents I needed to have translated as part of our memorandum and after our meeting I sped across town to arrange for them to be urgently translated.

Somewhere in the old part of the city, squashed between a car maintenance garage and a guy making chapatis, was the legal translator's office. A square boxlike building of yellow brick and painted windows, the type of structure that could be used for anything, and probably had been since it was hastily constructed. Let's put it this way; whoever built it had been pressed for time and saw no need for involving the architects.

I entered the office from the street and stopped at a makeshift tall front desk laden with envelopes stuffed with documents waiting to be picked up. It was certainly busy, and I understood why.

If I sent the documents for translation through the law firm, the law firm, generally, takes a cut, which can be up to 50 percent top up on the fee. If I went directly to the translators as a private client, it was a hell of a lot cheaper. And they provide a further discount on top of that if you give them quite a few documents to translate at a time. Considering how many documents I had translated into Arabic, I saved a fortune on costs.

Two days later the translated documents were cycled over to my lawyer's office and he got to work on our memorandum.

I was elated with our success so far. My case was dead in the water a week ago. Thanks to my lawyer it had a fighting chance once again. After we submitted our memorandum, I felt upbeat, hopeful, confident that a miracle was on the way. For the first time I felt a glimmer of excitement about this part of the journey.

But for the moment at least, we had to wait for the decision.

The senior prosecutor said he was not going to make any predictions as to when that would be, but that he would deliver his ruling as soon as he can.

What happens next? That, frankly, was anybody's guess.

"Hello…"

Click – the phone went dead.

I looked at my time on my phone.

5 AM it beamed. God, again.

I lay back down and tried to go back to sleep.

The pay-off

A whole day went by.

Then another.

Every time the phone rang, I was fully alarmed and certain I was about to hear some dreadful news.

"And on top of that, I was getting some nuisance calls …" My mom was on speaker phone from the UK, telling me about her day. We had a tacit understanding that it was necessary to keep busy, that this was the best way to get through the days, to take my mind of the imminent verdict.

"Sales people?"

"Oh, people dialling and then realising they've got the wrong number when I speak."

"I know mom, I get them too. Everyone does. Just ignore them."

Finally, more than one week later, on a quiet morning, with nothing much happening, my lawyer came back to me with news that the senior prosecutor has sprang heroically to my defence and rejected Grant's bid to have charges dismissed.

I raised my eyes heavenward and gave an exaggerated

sigh of relief. "Well thank the Lord for that." It was hard not to be moved by the sheer happiness of the result. It was a tremendous relief. There was always a faint worry about the chances of winning. But my lawyer had done it. He completely turned the tables around. We were back in the game. We had clawed our way through the prosecution system, after nine long, long months.

I read every word of the email he sent to me. "We are pleased to inform you that on April 17, 2017, the public prosecutor has decided to refer the accused and criminal file to the criminal court. consequently, the court will fix the first hearing for the attendance of the accused later on."

I gave another sigh. What wonderful news to start the day.

Not so for Grant. His nightmare and potential disaster continued. He was now awaiting a trial date and to hear exactly the charges against him. In the meantime, the senior prosecutor agreed to keep Grant's passport as an indication that he presented an extreme risk of flight.

The group at a bar whooped and hollered, celebrating some good fortune in the case. Now, when Grant's victims found out that he was on trial, their reaction was: "Oh, my God! Finally ... He's going to pay for everything that he has done".

"Bloody unbelievable."

"I can't believe it."

I still couldn't believe it either.

We even raised a glass to Van Neste, after all, his statement had helped undermine the defence's case, as their key and only witness.

"What did he do again?" slurred one confused but merry drinker and victim of Grant.

"He screwed me at every turn." Simply put.

"I get that. But how?"

"Which football team do you support?" I asked him.

"Man Utd."

Well, that's a separate problem that needs addressing I thought to myself, as I threw him a mortifying look.

"Okay ... well, it's a bit like discovering Wayne Rooney was going over to Man City to score goals after skipping United games claiming unfitness ... I don't think you would like that very much, would you?"

He thought about it, I could see him digesting that information, and then the penny dropped. "Hell no," and raised his glass above his head in a salute to Van Neste.

"Why bring the kids into his fight?" asked Nathan, a father himself.

"My lawyer says, emotion."

"You think you know all there is to know of him and then you peel of another ring of the onion," he responded angrily. He was right to be angry.

And now that Philip Van Neste had surfaced, I refused to let him sink back to oblivion. Why did he attempt to inveigle his way into the prosecution investigation? This question pushed me to start digging.

"We need to find the connection between Guardian and what happened here," I said to Rupert as he held a similar Trust to me in Jersey. It's even more important now that we've determined that fraud really did occur. It might be something that we haven't thought about before, some tiny detail that could help us understand the bigger picture.

I parted company with my lawyer with the usual promises to keep in touch and to share the updates. He was a very genuine guy. Most lawyers only see the money, he saw the moral obligation and acted upon it and really wanted to help me. That is the kind of lawyer most of us can only dream of representing us.

I would have loved him to work with me but it was just

too small a case for him and he had far bigger deals going on. And his speciality was preventing cases getting to court, nipping them in the bud. He had barely charged me anything and apparently, he had written my memorandum the night before.

If every legal case tells a story, then these two opposing lawyers during the prosecution investigation told an epic tale of ongoing imperial divergence; of home front versus starry-eyed rankings, of old school versus new perspectives, of substance over style.

"They may call you before the judge to give evidence," he warned me. "However," he offered some insight, "the other side should avoid doing so if they're smart, and focus on him, not you".

He claimed that I had managed to get the case through the police and to the prosecution office so I had made them think there was something here they needed to look at. A trial is not won by popular vote – well unless it's OJ Simpson's trial – it's won on evidence and the law but your character is important. Just how someone comes across in the witness box can decide it. You can possibly lose the judge or jury at the very first question. Combine that with visual effects; if you're pleasant to look at you're easy to believe. Your testimony then makes perfect sense, and you've connected to a judge or jury. The defence's focus should therefore be on Grant, and put him before the judge so he could give the best and most important sales pitch ever.

"Let me know when you get to civil," were my lawyer's confident parting words. We had decided to push back the civil trial until after the completion of Grant's criminal trial. The findings of the criminal court would count as evidence in the subsequent civil trial.

The goal-posts kept moving. First it was to get Grant to

the police station, then it was to get his passport blocked, then to get the file to prosecution, and then to get through prosecution to the criminal courts. There was still some road to travel. We were literally crawling along it. Every goal was just a stepping stone to the next and the next and my ultimate goal. The biggest goal. A conviction.

A couple of weeks later, a trial date had been set for May 10th, 2017. The senior prosecutor had put together a case against Grant and transferred the file to the Dubai criminal court.

There are three primary sources of UAE law, namely federal laws and decrees (applicable in all the seven emirates and heard before the Abu Dhabi courts in the capital), Sharia'h (Islamic law) and local laws (laws and regulations enacted by the individual emirates). Dubai has its own judicial system, independent of the other emirates. Grant's case fell within the local law, not federal, so the file remained in Dubai and case was to be heard at the Criminal Court of First Instance: The first degree of litigation in the Dubai court before HH Sheikh Mohammed Bin Rashid Al Maktoum, in front of a judge only with no jury.

In typed, single-spaced letters at the top of the page, the charge is one word, with a capital F, with plenty of space around it.

Fraud.

I let that word sink in.

Then I read the order. Grant was charged with fraud; a crime under the UAE law (Article 399 of UAE Federal Law No. 3 of 1987, as amended, (the 'Penal Code') that involves any cheating of a client to procure their money or allow someone to procure their money. The prosecution's case against Grant was to punish him for his fraudulent activities that on paper was going to put him in prison for two years if he just gets convicted.

145

Gosh. I was beginning to wonder where it would all lead.

Right now – Neil Ramsay Pringle Grant could be the first person to be convicted of financial advisory fraud in Dubai that goes to the grubby heart of the industry. A victory over Grant would lift a huge barricade to future advisory litigation. It might very well open the industry up.

Even though I didn't want to see him, I was going to see him in a courtroom. Being treated like every criminal would be treated. This had got to be it. This is when it was going to happen.

Trials are a rollercoaster ride because when you go to court, you lose control of the case, of your life. Your own future relies on the decisions of others.

As I quietly pondered the great question: What happens when two people, perceive the same thing differently? The answer is clear: the judge's perception of reality is the one that truly matters. And not even the lawyers know what that is.

The stage was set for a historic trial.

The ring of my mobile phone wakes me up, sharply.
I snatched it up and looked at the time.
1.30 am.
I looked in the display. Withheld number.
I let it ring three times before I picked up.
There's silence on the other end.
Click – the phone went dead.
I lay back down and couldn't get back to sleep.

CHAPTER 5

THE PEOPLE V NEIL RAMSAY PRINGLE GRANT

∽ Even if it's one dirham ... it's a verdict ∽

My lawyer advised me to come prepared with a legal team to help and guide me through the court process and ensure everything went smoothly. Someone had recommended a new law firm to me. The managing partner had been an associate at a large firm with international exposure and had now branched out on his own.

"He's good enough to get you through the courts ... that's all you really need at this point," I was told by the person who referred him to me.

So I relied on this trusted choice to take care of me during the trial. But for me, the choice wasn't controversial – the lawyers themselves had been in the legal profession for years, even though the new law firm was little-heard-of outside legal circles. They operated from a suite of offices which took the middle floors of a new building not far from the courthouse. And they marketed themselves as a local firm with international exposure and experience, which is lawyer-speak that they bill the same as international law firms.

That's one useful thing about having worked in the legal industry and with lawyers, at least: I have extensive experience of their internal dialogue.

In the UK, solicitors give legal advice, draft wills and represent clients in less serious matters. The actual argument in the higher courts is done by barristers, the senior branch of the legal profession.

Things are different in Dubai.

A lawyer in Dubai is classified as either an advocate or a legal consultant. The Federal Law on the Regulation of the Profession requires that advocates cannot practice unless they are registered on the Ministry of Justice's role of practicing lawyers if they are practicing in the UAE courts. In order to fulfil this requirement, the advocate must be a national of the UAE states. Additionally, they must be 20 years old or older. Additionally, they must be considered to have full civil capacity, including a good character and reputation and not have had any type of disciplinary or criminal sentence involving a breach of honour or trust.

The firm had two advocates who had privileges to represent me in the Dubai court before the judge. One of them was managing partner, the other I was to meet at the first hearing itself.

The charge

Grant was charged for fraud; and the criminal order noted a few examples of his fraudulent activities as follows:

- He alleged that he has a company called Prosperity Offshore Investment Consultants
- He alleged that his company Prosperity Management

148

Consultancy is authorised to provide financial consultancy and financial brokerage

- To strengthen the allegations he provided the victim with a business card including the company's name, website, and achievements
- He advised the victim to invest in funds with a foreign company called Guardian Trust Company Ltd

According to the documents provided in the case, all of the above led to me being cheated and transferred monies to Guardian. As anticipated, the signature forgery charge against Grant was dropped.

Nathan and Rupert thought the charges ought to be much more serious, because they believed a strong case had been made against Grant along with the volume of evidence and a number of potential victims. But trying to get it inside the law was a different matter, as I had learnt.

Before the first hearing, I received a blow. The associate assigned to my case had gone through everything and in his 'professional and considered' opinion my case tanked. In short, it could do with a lot of magic.

"I don't understand." I'm in my lawyer's office in their new age meeting room turned Arabic tent where I'm sitting on a red and white low-rise sofa, my knees almost touching the floor and my feet tucked under my legs. "How is the case over when it hasn't started?"

"I know it's not making much sense," he sympathised.

"Much?" I exclaimed. It didn't make any sense to me. Now that the case was continuing, with the DED statement it looked like there would be a guilty verdict, surely.

"It's not unusual," he replied, unlike me, sitting comfortably on the sofa adjacent to me having mastered the art of sitting gracefully on them. "Some criminal cases end before they really get going. Yes, the criminal order sounds heavy-hitting, but the reality is, this matter looks more of a civil case than a criminal case, and it is more likely that Grant would be declared innocent from the criminal charges."

He was very matter-of-fact about his predictions. It was the collective legal opinion of the senior lawyers within the firm, a group with a combined total of fifty years of criminal law experience, that this was the reality. Not one could recall a single trial in which a defendant was found guilty of such charges. They were unanimous in their belief that I would lose.

That's their game plan? Follow precedence? I thought.

"I see," I nodded. Clearly, I didn't. I was still confused. It just sounded like a cop-out all round to me. Simply passing the buck to the next court.

The associate was a young Egyptian, late-twenties-early thirties, I couldn't quite tell as his eyes were covered with dark prescription glasses. His hair was dark brown, almost, thick, and grey at the sides. He did not circle around topics, searching for right phases, or double back to restate a previous sentence. For that matter, he did not say um or ah, or use any form of conversational mitigation: his sentences came marching out, one after the other, polished and crisp, like soldiers on a parade ground as he continued giving me the devasting news. "This does not mean that you wouldn't get your money back, but it means that he does not go to jail for it and you need to claim your money through civil proceedings."

There was no 'protocol rule' that said I will lose at trial: just precedent and, well, according to these legal experts, common sense. With the current evidence, 'victory' was way beyond reach.

"After all," he reminded me, "it was a lawyer's job to know the law".

After a brief pause, he continued to say, "there have been several of these cases around the UAE, and the advisory industry has yet to get hit with a verdict". He paused, looking around, and straightened his tie. "A small fine may be possible," he said giving the conversation some hope, before quickly dimming it again, "but the administration will take longer and cost more man hours than that".

Received wisdom was that the statistics proved it – no one really won by suing a financial advisor. Moreover, if I do win in court, it is at best a pyrrhic victory.

But to me that administration would ensure Grant has a criminal record for life. Not something you want to have in your life, ideally. The punishment would outlast his fine for years to come. I definitely thought he wouldn't get a jail sentence, but a light fine. All I wanted was a verdict. Because that was enough to get him off the streets.

"A defence lawyer can easily get the charges tossed before trial with a motion to dismiss," he said, which now, among the legal team, was expected at the first hearing.

I held onto the fact that at the very core Grant had shown a clear refusal to follow the law. That blatant disrespect to the law surely had to count for something. There was no way the judge was not going to make him accountable for that. I mean, that really solidified the whole case, as far as I was concerned.

"We, after all, have the inside track," the associate said confidently. It's true they did.

"Well, let's just wait and see, shall we?" I replied.

I felt differently. Very differently.

By now, I was tunnel visioned. When I go for something, I truly go for it. And hearing negativity had become regular music to my ears – and not the Hills are Alive with the Sound of Music kind. All I had learnt was to just push through it and see what happens.

Perhaps this, then, was how it should be.

But I thought, perhaps I could even win.

Anything can happen inside a courtroom, and even for an experienced legal eagle nothing was more unknown than this territory. It might even be that fraud was discovered. I knew Dubai's courts were not a pushover. Legal challenges need to have some evidence. And we needed to convince the judge that these allegations about fraud – all these 'theories' – actually amounted to something. That's what the lawyer was hired to argue.

"So, I'll take my chances," I said to the associate.

"Okay, well, you were very lucky to have the case reach this far," he said to me, "and even a fine of one dirham," holding up his index finger to my face, "is enough for a guilty verdict". He added, "we will do our best to keep this file alive". I wished I could take more comfort from this.

After a pause, he hesitated. "I'd like to discuss a settlement with them before the hearing." I point blank refused. We had come too far. Besides, if my lawyers had determined the risk to be minimal, the defence would be giving Grant the same advice, no doubt.

A conviction was the goal, I reminded him. Even if it was a one dirham fine.

"Yeah?" he said slowly, though obviously still confused.

Not for the first time, we were on different pages: my heart says get the rogue, and his head saying forget it.

Everyone was expecting an easy verdict for the defence. Life, however, was on a new page, and has a serendipitous way of making solutions appear when you need them. It seemed I had Grant himself to thank for my next stroke of luck.

Face-off: The trial begins

It's May 10th, 2017. The day of the hearing.

I spoke to Nathan before heading to the Dubai courts.

"Just look poor," he offered.

"Nathan, I am poor."

"And don't wear anything bright and don't be the focus." My bubble-gum pink suit was out then. Sigh.

"And if they ask you a question don't look down, they'll know you're lying, don't look up, they'll know you don't know the truth. Don't use eight words when four will do and don't shift your weight ..."

I knew Nathan travelled around the world and was away as often as he was at home but I had no idea what he actually did for a living. From the sounds of it, he could work for 'Experts in psychology, body language and speech' (who I generally find are brilliant at identifying the guilty party – usually after they've been found guilty).

His other pieces of advice continued flowing. "Be unfussy, unpretentious, it's okay to be slightly overwhelmed by all the circumstance," concluding with, "... just be ordinary."

"Nathan, I am ordinary."

Anyway, it was not going to be about me.

This was, emphatically, Grant's day. I prepared myself to leave my office, when my assistant popped her head around the door.

"Amber, there's a call for you."

"Yeah? So early? Go ahead, transfer it."

"Hello ..." A silence, no sound at all. Then a deep resonant voice, "Is that Amber?".

"Yes, it is, who's speaking please?"

Click – the phone went dead. I looked at the receiver in my hand.

Trials are very intense. Even for those bringing a case against someone. So I found myself feeling unusually nervous as I arrived, even more so for Grant.

Yes, he had behaved appallingly on innumerable occasions; but despite it all, I knew him. It would have been so much easier if I hadn't known him, that he was just a regular rogue financial advisor. As those with personal experiences of such a thing will know, your feelings alternate between being angry, being compassionate, being uncomfortable and being hurt. I didn't hate him enough for him to be locked up in a Dubai cell where prisons are what they should be – a deterrent and for punishment, not a holiday camp like in the UK – but I wanted a verdict against him to make him accountable and to stop him defrauding others.

If someone had said to me on 2016 New Year's Eve, that in the coming year I was going to embark on a complicated court case in Dubai I would have thought they were mad.

Sorry, What?

With who?

This was definitely not on my goals list.

When I started this journey of discovery, I had no idea what to expect. I had never seen the inside of a courtroom before or even filed a police report against anyone.

One year later, I was embroiled in the Dubai legal system, with my former financial advisor, of all people, in an unfamiliar and unpredictable legal process.

And now, today, I had the unappealing reality of facing Grant in a court of law.

I made my way to the Dubai courts which is a two-storey brown building adjacent to the public prosecution low, white building. The Dubai courts and the public prosecution building are symbols of two very different worlds, part of the legal sphere, but separate from it. Large swathes of the building and courts are actually open to the public all day and all year round.

The queue waiting to enter the building was long in the early morning. It was incredibly busy, full of people running in all sorts of directions – victims, defenders, witnesses, experts, and lawyers. People of every nationality jostled with advocates, carrying bulging briefcases of documents, about to fight for their rights. It was another reality.

All the courts are located on the first and second floors with multiple minimalist seated areas dotted around in the atrium. The walls bare and white, the floors plain and cream, and the desks dark and brown. I made my way to the courtroom on the second floor where my case was to be heard.

There was an electronic board outside the court with the list of cases running that day and Grant's name was listed as case number five. "Neil Ramsay Pringle Grant".

It was safe to say, he wasn't going to be taking a selfie with that board.

I loitered in the dark cold main hall, waiting for my lawyer, the advocate who had privileges to represent me before the judge. The court prosecutor was tasked with guiding the case through the system. My lawyers' task was to guide me through the criminal process. Whether the prosecutor and my lawyers worked together on the case remained to be seen but so far no one had mentioned such a collaboration to me.

By eight, a crowd was already gathering outside the large wooden doors leading to the courtroom. There were young men in dark non-descript suits, all of whom looked remarkably similar with their sleek black hair. They were paralegals sent from their respective law firms to follow the developments of various cases. Each member held a piece of paper, a court notice, or a black leather folder. No fewer than six security guards were assigned to keep things safe and smooth.

My lawyer was late but his colleague soon arrived assuring me he was on his way. Although not part of the official legal entourage he explained, he was there to help navigate up to three cases that morning and negotiate their jam-packed schedule. For lack of a better job description, he was known as a runner.

The security guards opened the courtroom door at exactly eight-thirty, which led to a flurry of movement, and each person was admitted in one by one through the metal detector.

My lawyer still hadn't arrived. The risk that the judge would decide to pass the case straightaway to civil was playing on my mind in repeat mode, as I sat patiently waiting for him. A minor crime played in a major key presented my lawyer with the dilemma of somehow finding the right tone without alienating the judge – turning up late was not going to set the right tone.

By now a load of expensively dressed lawyers have turned up in abundance alongside advocates in their traditional white or beige dish dash along with a small media presence. After a short while I decided to make my way into the courtroom, and wait for my lawyer inside. The courtroom itself was spacious and could seat around a hundred people, easily. I made my way to the back row and took a seat on the padded bench.

Just sitting in the courtroom was fascinating. The atmosphere was positively funereal. It had a pungent, leathery, underneath smell, like old rope or damp cloths. There seems to be only a few dim lights. The lamps cast a yellowish hue, not cold and greenish but buttery and dim with a tinge of brown. The effect was soulless.

It all reminded me of the type of courtrooms you see in American legal drama series; the interior all dark and brown and mushroom beige, and cold. The colours looked a little dirty, like the squares in a paint box when you forget to rinse the brush. The judge's bench was straight ahead running the full width of the room. The public seating was divided into two parts with a long aisle down the middle and off to the right a rectangular open gallery with a large, closed door inside it where the prisoners appear handcuffed in regulation blue jail uniform as their cases were called, one by one. Unlike the American legal dramas though, there were no counsel tables. The only decoration in the whole courtroom was an enormous, beautiful UAE flag standing in the centre behind the bench.

Most of the people appeared to be anxious and fidgety sitting in their pew seats, rocking about and fiddling with their tie and jackets. The women looked calmer and politely sociable, chatting in a much more demure way to the person either next to them or in the seat in front. Most of the lawyers stared fixedly at their phones, pounding out urgent messages into their tiny typewriters.

There were no cameras and no sketch writers. Security guards were everywhere, weighed down by the numerous weapons hanging off their bodies. It was a stunningly efficient and impressive set-up that was entrenched in history, tradition, protocol and timetables. A strict world, where the men seemed to outnumber the women by far.

"What's your case?" I asked the lady sitting next to me. She was a young, dramatically thin, Filipino girl who looks very uneasy. She had been working for a company and the directors had used her email address to place orders. Only it turned out the company was running a fraudulent business. The directors had run off leaving her to can it. I felt desperately, desperately sorry for her. Surely, no one will believe that this young, tiny, fragile looking woman, peering out from between two curtain folds of long black hair, was running a global multi-million fraud business. "I'm sure it's going to be alright," I tried to reassure her, "we have a good judge". I had no idea if we did or not but I wanted to say something to comfort her.

We had all been conned in some way or other, including me, and we had all been slotted in together.

Indeed, I had always heard stories from people who have undergone extraordinary experiences, triumphs and tragedies in these very courtrooms – along with people with tales to tell about maddening brushes with officialdom or the law.

Now, I couldn't believe I was here. In a bemused daze, reality hit me and I realised I was at a criminal trial I had initiated.

The wait gave me plenty of time to wonder what I had got myself into.

I took a brief look around the courtroom; it's the one place you actually hope there's no one you know.

Guilty or not guilty?

This was the first time I was going to see Grant. The last time was at a hotel lobby in December 2015, when I was questioning him on why my finances were in such a catastrophic mess and why was I trapped in them.

Hard to believe that eighteen months later here we were. In new, potentially incarcerated surroundings a world away from a luxurious five-star hotel lifestyle.

Just before the judge appeared, Grant arrived flanked by the stern-faced and immaculately suited male members of his entourage, appearing unrepentant in the face of a slew of allegations of fraud. The size of the entourage spoke to his relevance. Six, at my count. All occupying the front row.

He was fighting the case all the way. I knew he had

instructed a team of highly skilled lawyers, to argue his case during the public prosecution investigation, and now, in light of that outcome, and as the legal battle raged on in the courtroom, it looked like he was leaving nothing to chance.

If my lawyers had told me the high likelihood the case could be dropped at the first hearing, it was a safe bet that Grant got the same advice from his lawyers. I had a feeling they had sold the idea to Grant that the case was a slam dunk during the prosecution investigation. That it was in the bag. They were probably all scratching their heads as to how they were now here in this courtroom.

Criminal litigants are the scariest type of lawyers. Brimming with confidence. Virtually incapable of sympathy. Bending the rules, and the ones they can't they'll challenge. They are fighters. Needing a battle like we need air. I thought of this observation while I watched Grant in the courtroom interacting with his team. From what I could observe Grant was very close to his lawyers. All of them. They were huddled together like on the rugby pitch. The law firm had obviously put together a 'team of suits' for Grant which included several members who had immediately set out to comfort and protect him, including a local advocate wearing a pristine white candoura and a white guttra. Grant obviously felt the costs were necessary in order to protect his reputation and prevent any chance of him facing a conviction.

Either that or his lawyers thought they had found a golden goose.

A lot of back-slapping. Yeah, I could imagine a few people wanting to slap that back. And he wouldn't be smiling at the back-end of it.

I looked closely at the group. Noticeably his wife was not with him.

We avoided eye contact but were fully aware of each

other's presence.

He made me look like Billy-no-mates. Alone, unknown and unaccompanied on the other side of the room. Nathan's wife had offered to accompany me that morning, but I didn't know how long it was all going to take, and didn't want her to be hanging around when she had a family to look after. But, despite the unpredictability of the proceedings, I wanted to be present at the court hearings, myself. I was simply intrigued. It was either that or I subconsciously didn't trust my lawyers.

The pace now picked up.

Suddenly it went quiet and the guard tapped on the door with the immortal words "All Rise" in Arabic. The urgency of his voice brought everyone to their feet and all eyes watched the door behind the bench. The room fell silent as the judge, wearing a suit under his black robe and not the traditional dish dash, walked into the courtroom and sat down without a trace of a smile on his face.

It felt genuinely eerie.

We all dropped and sat back down.

Four cases were before us. As each case was called by the court clerk, various people got up from their seats; all larger than life, with the character to go with it. Everyone was jostling for position and attention. Everyone was unusually reverent. They all wanted to please the judge and get airtime with him. It was the one time that they could make an impression, speak into his ear and attempt to thaw his icy persona.

At one point a mobile phone was heard shrieking urgently in the stillness of the courtroom. The judge paused from reading a case file, scanned his audience and found its owner, a lady in the middle row. He met her reddened cheeks with a long hard pointed stare; it suddenly seemed imperative for everyone else to discreetly check that their own mobile phone was indeed switched off, not wanting to chance disfavour or show the slightest hint of disrespect.

I had to wait for our case number to be bellowed by the court clerk and then Grant's name was announced. We all got up. Well, when I say all – Grant, his glossy posse of well-bred lawyers, and me. We walked to the front of the courtroom, to the bench, and stood next to each other around a small square table, before the judge, who was perched higher than us – just like in the movies, with his two female assistants on either side of him. The court prosecutor, a small rounded man, wearing a black robe, with a beautifully sewn-in name tape, joined us at the table, gliding in from the side of the room where he had been sitting. He stood at one side of the table, directly across from Grant's lawyers on the other side, and Grant and I completed the tight huddle and stood facing the judge.

Sporting a clean shave, Grant donned a fetching three-piece suit paired with a light blue tie, which contrasted nicely with his deeply tanned face. In comparison, I appeared to have stepped from the pages of a Chandler novel in my blocky suit. Even our choices of outfit mirrored our contrasting approaches.

For the first time in eighteen months, Grant and I were breathing the same air without having apoplexy. No veil or lace was deployed to obscure the view. Not a flicker of recognition or guilt. Grant just stood and looked slightly amused by what was happening. Like when you're forced to stand next to someone you don't like, or has very poor personal hygiene.

I didn't know if I was meant to be at the table before the judge because I wasn't sure how it worked and no one had told me either way; and my lawyers were conspicuously absent. But I wanted somebody to be there to represent me, the victim, with the court prosecutor. If the judge had any problems with my presence at the table, he didn't show them.

I found it very humbling. The occasion, the interior, the formalities, standing in front of the judge, a few feet away from him. This powerful man. His power didn't require him to impress anyone. There was an instant respect there – for everything. It was like playing God with people's lives. He gets, ultimately, to decide everyday who lives and who dies by the legal sword. And that sword can be a ruthless highly destructive implement. It does not allow much room for sentiment. It was sure as hell an experience. I put myself for a moment in Grant's Mont Blanc shoes and felt glad that I was on this side of the case.

My lawyer just made it, a petite, young man – glided in with seconds to spare, eliciting not even a whisper of interest from the other side, and started rearranging his guttra wrapped around his head with one hand, clutching a sheaf of papers to his chest with the other.

The court clerk asked Grant to state his name and address, which Grant answered. His voice, thick with a Scottish accent, was raspy.

Reading from the court order, the court prosecutor gave a quick synopsis of the trial, but only for informational purposes.

The issue here was whether or not the public prosecution could make a case based on the evidence they had of the commission of a crime. The defence's job was to try to persuade the judge they could not make that case.

Now, the court announced the charges against Grant. His demeanour changed when the court prosecutor began outlining the allegations against him. Each charge was read out in Arabic and then translated into English to Grant – slowly and precisely. Between allegations, the court prosecutor would stop, look at Grant, then return to his list.

And with every allegation, Grant either scratched his face, jerked his shoulders or adjusted his tie.

"The charges carry with them a maximum of two years in jail," continued the court prosecutor. Upon hearing the punishment spoken aloud, my own heart flipped a few beats.

There was a point for me, somewhere within these first several minutes standing in front of the judge, where I felt complete and utter compassion for Grant and uncomfortable about bringing the case against him even though I felt it was the right thing to do.

That feeling, however, would not last too long.

"How do you plead to these charges?" The translator asked. All eyes on Grant.

One of the questions I had found myself asking different authorities – the police officers, the prosecution and even the forensic officer – was what did they think of him? And the response had been the same: "drama". I was now to learn exactly what they meant, and how they were frighteningly spot-on.

He was expected to speak briefly and only to enter his plea by saying: "Not guilty, Your Honour".

All he had to say was "not guilty".

But it couldn't be that simple could it? No. Grant added his own piece of theatrics.

He replied by scoffing at the notion that he could be guilty and of the question. With just five exquisitely chosen words, he launched his salvo, stating: "Not Guilty. Of Course Not. Absolutely. No". He looked positively defiant when responding to the accusations. As if the mere thought that he was guilty was ridiculous. The fact that he was standing in front of a judge was ludicrous and insulting to him. The crime itself was absurd. The whole thing was a circus. And to ram home the message, he shrugged in utter bewilderment as if his integrity had been questioned, exaggerated with his hands and then shook his head.

The courtroom was still.

At first, I was startled. I couldn't help but look at Grant, who must have felt it because he turned slightly and for a split second caught my eye with his own. I had never seen him with that much of an emotional outburst. Then, I was amused. Then I saw an equally amused court prosecutor, a stern-faced judge, and a completely baffled defence lawyer. I suddenly heard Nathan's advice to me in my head, "Don't use eight words when four will do". "Guilty" or "not guilty" was what Grant had been ordered to say – no theatrics.

The infamous line from the 80s classic UK television sitcom Only Fools and Horses suddenly came to me. Most people have never heard of Del Boy. But there is one fragment of his speaking everyone will be familiar with, namely the phrase "Rodney, you plonker". That was an old-fashioned way of referring to an idiot. And here I was now thinking: "Neil, you plonker".

I didn't expect him to put his hand up and say, "I'm guilty". But some form of polite manner would have been better. It was an ill-judged moment to showcase an irrepressible sense of his own self-importance.

I glanced at the courtroom behind me and saw nothing but open mouths and slack jaws. Few things can be more entertaining in a courtroom than the sight of a man in front of a judge putting on a show. The fact that the man was a tall white immaculately-dressed 'Englishman' with an 'exotic' accent took the courtroom show to box office status. The mere presence of one dressed so well could only mean serious crimes were being trialled.

Meandering off-script, his lead council, the local advocate, realised it wasn't the focus they wanted. He performed a subtle eye-dart to Grant, a bit like a mother whose kid is trying to interrupt her grown-up conversation, before turning away from him to speak to the judge in Arabic. My lawyer would later explain to me that he was justifying to the judge, ever so delicately, why Grant was feeling so "emotional".

Well, that was pretty obvious to everyone as he made it very clear. He shouldn't be standing here.

Grant's lawyer further elaborated: the fascinating question to them was how my case was ever allowed to see the light of day? Wasn't there a court officer or secretary with a red pen who could have sensibly intervened and saved us all some time? Using humour, emphasising the preposterousness of the matter, he was making statements in order to convince the judge to close the case without hearing it.

This was my introduction to Grant's local advocate.

An evidently strong-willed and obviously intelligent and indisputably highly opinionated defence lawyer. Whose job was to make my life hell.

I don't know if it was because of this knowledge, or because of his small, thin build, pointed face and lizard eyes, but I was thinking he could easily pass as the male version of the Wicked Witch in the Wizard of Oz.

Now the judge eyed us all until his eyes rested on me. Up close, for a judge, he was quite young, mid-fifties was my guess. He had black hair, a wide thick black moustache that covered most of his round face and big black eyes that kept staring at me devoid of expression.

I gave no reaction. I felt like he was waiting for a reaction.

Oh no, I thought. When I'm excited or nervous or lost, I look excited and nervous and lost. My face is a transparent transmitter of my every thought and the complete opposite of a poker face. And right now my face was saying "take my case" on repeat mode, as I eventually raised my eyebrows at the judge and gave him a rounded smile.

He looked around the courtroom to assess the reactions and, finally, his mind was made up.

He lifted his hammer – followed by some rapid instructions to no one in particular, and then the hammer went down.

On, what? Both our heads swivelled at once; Grant staring intently at his lead council while I bore my eyes into the interpreter, who flipped pages for a second so the drama wouldn't be rushed, before he matter-of-factly explained in sound bites that the judge has decided to move forward with the case. Proceedings were adjourned for Grant to prepare his defence, and the next hearing was May 17th.

I let out the breath I had been holding slowly through my nostrils. I kept my profound sense of relief very much under wraps, trying not to give the slightest hint of teeth, as I absorbed the news.

That meant the judge was going to hear the case in its entirety. That meant a full-length trial and that meant a verdict would be given. There had to be a winner. And there had to be a loser. The question of whether Grant was a fraud or not had to be answered right here.

Grant's lawyer was quick on his feet. "These charges have been bought based on no evidence against Mr Grant. And this is a very, very good thing that we can expose the untruths against Mr Grant."

And to reiterate his statement, he looked directly at me, pointedly.

It's quite unbelievable that Grant's legal team could get up there with a straight face and talk about the injustice happening against him. Strangely, Grant himself didn't seem to have much reaction. When I sneaked a look at him, he was in shock at what had just happened. It was like it wasn't registering with him. Then again, there's no standard of behaviour after something like that. I was left with no doubt; he had expected a slam dunk defence judgment that would have him walk out the front door. They all had.

Grant's loose tongue with the judge – never a good thing when pacifying any official – was very ill-advised and a gift to us. Here he was casually handing it to us like he was giving us a box of caviar.

Slowly we all stepped away from the bench. Grant's lawyers packed away their belongings and were filing out of the courtroom, directing Grant to follow them.

My lawyer and I followed, a few minutes after. The sudden flicker of hope for my case had swelled my heart, and I could finally let rip a beaming smile as I walked down the aisle and collected my bag from my seat.

"That is good isn't it ... for us?", I turned around to ask my lawyer as soon as we were outside the courtroom, "I think that kind of backfired on them".

"Yes" he replied, nodding his head, vigorously, "it's very good". I couldn't have hoped for better start.

Small victory and so the trial continued. This would go on for weeks. Grant, standing in the atrium, with his back to me, was deep in a hushed conference with his entourage.

Now, my attention was on my lawyer and his outlandish debut, bounding in at the last minute. "Really?" I asked him, not unreasonably I thought, given his job.

He loosely apologised, brushing aside my concern, with a tight smile just under a thick moustache.

He had just returned from vacation and come straight from the airport. An alarm bell rang.

"So you don't know the case?" I asked him. He did his best to bluff and act knowledgeable.

"So you don't know the case," I said again, this time as

a statement. After trying to avoid answering, he eventually replied no he didn't; but he would go straight back to the office and read my file in detail. I was not remotely convinced. He was just saying what he knew I wanted to hear so he could take leave from me and move onto his next hearing.

With lawyers by my side, I thought I will have one less thing to worry about, meaning, I could focus on other things.

But sending me a lawyer, arriving a little breathless to the argument who had not even read my file was as useless as a bodyguard wearing heels and a skirt. What if she needed to do Kung Fu?

I didn't want a 'fake-it-till-you-make-it' kind of lawyer, and there was no way I could hand my case over to someone if I could never trust a word they said.

"A dynamic backroom team is corralled for your case," he explained to me avoiding eye contact and glancing around as if others were listening. That was all very well, but there was no point someone sitting back in the law office conducting high-powered meetings and preparing crisp and empowering notes for the case if the one standing in front of the judge was not brought up to speed and unable to present it to the judge.

This was bonkers. Lawyers never cease to amaze me. "What if the judge asks you a question and you can't answer it?"

Words that would literally bite me at the next hearing. Exactly what I was afraid of happened.

The naysayers

No one was more surprised by the judge's decision to continue with a full-on trial than my own legal team. Their initial reaction was of total disbelief; it was certainly a twist they'd not predicted, nor had they ever heard of such a thing, and by now they thought they'd heard or seen it all.

However, they managed to work themselves back into their usual state of pessimism.

The associate back at the law office, leading my case, came back to me swiftly on email to dampen my spirits once again just in case I got carried away, reconfirming that my matter was a civil case and overall, of a civil nature. "You were lucky to have this case reach this far. We have confirmed this understanding during our initial meeting and we are reconfirming it again." I just shook my head at their email.

I was waging an inner battle with them.

They were bright, and they were good lawyers, capable of dealing with a case of this complexity and scale; but they were lazy lawyers. This associate in particular was someone who liked to talk and debate and share and tell you how he felt. Their strategy was a little loose, and I was a little annoyed at the lawyers for being so flippant about the whole case. Even though they honestly believed beforehand that it was a case doomed to failure, they took it on.

Were they the right lawyers for me? That remained to be seen. At the moment, they just worried me to no end.

Even though our case was weak there was no way to appeal the decision of the public prosecution or ask him to amend the decision by adding other facts. However, my lawyers said they would (since we claimed our civil rights) add facts and highlight points to the judge to strengthen my case and persuade the judge that there was a criminal case here.

With regard to the strategy going forward, they were going to strengthen the points that Grant tried to show a different company name than his company, fake affiliation, and that my signatures on documents were forged.

They said they expected what the defence would present but let's "wait and see". A court case is an unpredictable business at the best of times. I was just going to have to muddle through, feeling my way into the thrilling but tarrying adventure that is suing someone.

After almost one year of investigation, the Neil Ramsay Pringle Grant trial finally kicked off.

"Hello …"

"Is this Amber?" She asked, quite pleasantly.

"It is. And who is this, please?"

A soft pause, then there was a click, and she was gone.

"Can you describe her voice?" I ask my mom later that evening.

"Not really." She hadn't noticed.

I absorbed this, thought a second, and ask, "what did she say to you?".

"Not much. Just asked to speak to you."

"Then she put the phone down?"

"Yes."

"Anything unusual about the way she talked?"

"No. Is she a friend of yours?"

A private audience with the judge

Today was a big day; a massive humungous day, in fact, and for many reasons.

Today was the first day of the trial, a day that most people, including me, never thought would come.

Today, I was to bag the big prize, the managing partner of the firm, himself, was representing me in court, and by default I was to have my own entourage.

And today, I was to learn, the focus was going to switch to me.

All of this was unbeknown to me when I arrived at the Dubai courts that morning, ten minutes early, feeling decidedly calm.

The managing partner arrived, wearing a white candoura and white guttra messily wrapped around his head, with a five-person entourage in tow. This consisted of ushers and assistants, who seemed to be racing around in a terrible hurry, without, it seemed to me, knowing where they were hurrying to.

We had a brief conversation in the atrium before he turned to speak to his aides about their morning schedule.

I had met the head of the law firm once before, at the consultation stage, and he came across as a confident, modest young lawyer, seemingly well equipped to handle the pressure and the pitfalls of a criminal trial. He was short, and oblong in shape, so that his candoura fell straight from shoulder to hip with no pause in between for a waist. With dark big features and a goatee, he reminded me of Hardy from Laurel and Hardy; a fitting description for the dark comedy that was about to unfold.

At eight-thirty sharp the courtroom doors swung open and my lawyers beckoned me to follow them inside.

As I approached security, Grant was actually going through the metal detector with his team of lawyers at the same time. And they were rushing him through security to get him into the courtroom. I remember thinking that was a little odd.

The courtroom was again packed.

I got myself cleared through the metal detector and, once inside, I eased into the rear row on the right side of the courtroom, opposite to the defence team who were occupying the front two rows, on the left side of the room.

My lawyer and his entourage were occupying the front row on the right side of the room. I observed his team who were ready to spring forward with unabashed loyalty at the slightest hint the big boss might need something.

I switched my focus over to the Grant, huddled with his team. At one point I saw the local advocate whisper in Grant's ear, who then stood up and gazed into the sea of faces around the courtroom until his eyes rested on me for one very long second. He turned away, sat back down and whispered something back to his lawyer, who immediately sat upright, as if ready to act on something.

What are they up to?

Spotting a vacant seat, I moved forward to the third row from the front, on the aisle. I had a better view, although just outside the ear-range of Grant's local advocate, who at that moment was just sat two rows in front, on the aisle, on the opposite side.

A few minutes passed. I carefully watched the door behind the bench from where the judge would appear from.

"All Rise." Eight-forty-five, the judge entered the courtroom, his black robe floating around him, and proceedings commenced.

When the case number was called and Grant's name bellowed, everyone lurched forward and upward and made his or her way to the judge. As my lawyer was here and on time, I remained seated.

Grant's second performance in front of the judge seems to have been limited to a rather over-posed and rigid-looking smile and his hands were clasped in front with one holding onto two fingers of the other in a rather formal and tense way.

Grant's local advocate took centre stage, again.

After a few minutes of conversation, suddenly, all eyes turned to me.

And obviously, at that point, I started realising that something was happening here that was bigger than just a routine hearing.

My lawyer beckoned me to come forward, mouthing "Quick" at me. I approached the bench very curious as to why I had been summoned. First, to confirm my identity I was asked to produce either my original driving licence, passport or emirates ID. I went back to my seat to collect my handbag before returning to the bench. I started rummaging in it.

My lawyer leaned over to me. "The defence is asking permission to ask you some questions," I was told in my ear as I handed over my ID to the court clerk.

Caught completely off guard I whispered back naively, "ask me what? I haven't prepared anything".

"Just a couple of questions," he replied, as if this was perfectly normal. I felt uneasy. The courtroom was unusually attentive.

With a copy of my statement to the police in one hand, and a copy of our memorandum to the public prosecutor in the other, the defence lawyer insisted that they wanted to 'test' my evidence in cross-examination. It was obvious that it made no sense to Grant's lawyer how I had got the case to this point – unless I had lied. I was taken aback at how forcefully the lawyer pressed the issue.

To lawyers, the written statements which the court used as a main source of evidence were a poor substitute for evidence delivered in person from the witness box. The prospect of an unrehearsed testimony coming from a victim was a defence lawyer's dream.

I felt thoroughly ambushed.

From the start, Grant and his lawyers were determined to dance to their own tune. The latest chapter in the process was no different. It was designed to shake me up on the very first day, and to be perfectly honest it worked.

A cross-examination meant virtually anything relevant or even semi-relevant could be thrown at a witness. Of course, even without knowing what questions they had in mind for me, it goes without saying they would be designed to discredit me, my character and my entire case. A quiet word of warning in my ear from my legal team that they may spring this on me might have prepared me for what happened next – which irritated me in turn.

Right before my eyes, the judge, sitting elevated above us all, then nodded his head, as if he was agreeing to the defence's request, and turned to his assistant on his left to say something.

Barely breathing, my heart started to race. Was I going in the witness box, today? Now? I stared at everyone around the table in front of the bench and thought *Somebody damned well better start speaking some English soon.*

The judge then turned back to us and, after some polite Arabic exchanges between all the men around the table, I was told by my lawyer: "The judge himself wants to ask you some questions".

Can this get any worse? Hopelessly ill-equipped, with no prepping or role-play, I had to give my testimony before the judge? Everyone dreads going into a witness stand, but to go unprepared in front of a judge? The risk of a spectacularly destructive own goal remained high.

Needless to say, there was nothing I could do. I couldn't refuse. You don't say no to the judge.

I watched, still dazed, as the judge now turned to his assistant on his right, and they fell into a brief hushed conversation, before turning back to us again.

Then, after some further Arabic exchanges, my lawyer said the judge would allow me to be heard outside the public courtroom proceedings and had decided to move the hearing to the judge's chambers, with an English translator.

Well, that was a little relief. I had time to adjust and collect myself. The courtroom was very intimidating and the judge's chambers were, no doubt, more informal. I was fully aware my relief had been observed by the steely-eyed defence lawyer, while Grant looked on in silence. They knew I had been blindsided. They knew they had rattled me.

The hammer slammed down on the decision. The banging sound effect, ominous of the fact we have arrived at a perilous moment in the trial – on the very first day.

All parties turned and immediately left the courtroom and the judge was going to join us after he had finished running through his caseload.

"Come with me." My lawyer motioned for me to follow. It was a long walk to the judge's chambers, which was down one flight of stairs, not only in distance, but in what you're thinking as you go.

You have one chance in front of the judge to make a credible impression and to ensure that you get all your points across and are consistent in what you say. The judge will make a decision, not on the balance of probability, but proven beyond a reasonable doubt, which means he has to consider what scenario is the actual truth in light of hard evidence. The judge has to decide whether I am being truthful or lying. Not fifty-fifty. And it would depend on how I come across to the judge in the next hour or so.

Simultaneously, you're bracing yourself for a grilling and once you take the stand, the defence lawyers are going to pick holes in your testimony.

"I think this is a mistake," I said more to myself, as I followed my lawyer. Being cross-examined by a defence lawyer paid handsomely to hate you will never end well. Thinking the judge would like me was delusional. This would all backfire spectacularly.

I knew immediately that I should not have worn the powder-blue dress. Powder-blue is lightweight, happy. I was supposed to be suffering. I should have worn nun black, Dracula-black, like a proper female victim. In fact, I should have worn an abaya, to show some respect in front of the judge. I should have some vampire lipstick instead of wimping out with Rose Perfection. In fact, I should have worn no lipstick at all. All these thoughts were running in my mind as I walked to the judge's chambers.

You could argue that I was not the one on trial. Neil Grant was the one on trial. But my evidence was at the heart of the case and my credibility as a witness was what the whole case largely rested on. This is why people spend several hours each day preparing for this moment, ensuring they had all the right comebacks to all the possible questions. And trials always come with risk and how someone comes across can decide it.

My lawyer's entourage continued to lead the way through a maze of narrow hallways until we finally came to the door of the judge's chambers within a large empty reception area. There was a row of red folding chairs next to the door on which my lawyer and I sat down. I now turned towards him.

"Did you know they could do this … call me unannounced … why wasn't I told this? … why wasn't I coached in anticipation?" My questions were thick and fast. I was knocked for six. I hate being unprepared for anything, and I hadn't even prepared any soundbites to fall back on. I was overwhelmed by how truly unprepared I was to handle the next hour or so.

At that kind of moment, you need support; stronger, wise, more experienced heads backing you. Only to make things worse, my lawyer decided that was the appropriate moment to remind me that I didn't have a case. And as always, it fell to me to pluck a positive from the debris. "I got it this far," I reminded him right back, quite stunned. I wondered if he gave all his clients the same confidence 'boost'.

"That's correct," he replied, still a bit miffed. "To be quite honest, it was a small miracle that you got the result that you did." He went into a crisp, dispassionate lawyer mode.

I'd become very accustomed to people saying things about the merit of the case that weren't that positive. Like him or loathe him, he was generally saying what the silent majority were thinking. Sitting outside the judge's chambers, just before I was to give my testimony, was probably not the appropriate time to share it though.

"Why have you got so little faith?" I simply asked him.

"If you win, it will be a miracle," he responded levelly, making it perfectly clear that was not going to happen. Nothing will come of it. Nothing will happen.

For a second, I wish he also had my staunch faith. Perhaps things would be easier if we were on the same page, the same side. A stray ribbon of bad taste fluttered between us. This rang alarm bells. It's troubling language to use when speaking to anyone, but especially a client. Which begged the question, why did he agree to take my case then, if he, in part, ridiculed it?

This was not the time; I stopped myself. Right now, a cool head was needed.

I had to focus on centring myself, and not lock horns with my own lawyer. I was just going to have to pull myself together and get on with it and focus on delivering a confident testimony before the judge. By now, I had my story committed to memory because, up until now, I had always made a point of sticking as rigidly as I could to the truth. Therefore my story was consistent, so I just had to focus on saying it as it was, without worrying about matching it with previous statements I had made.

Yes, I understood the temptation to embellish a story in order to make it more convincing or support the case. But the fact is that the truth is so much easier to remember than a falsehood. And though I'd like to claim it was pure piety that kept me on the straight and narrow, it was also the terror of telling a lie and then forgetting all about it, only to be caught out in an inconsistency later and your credibility goes right out of the window. And what I had learnt from the prosecution investigation is that they ask you the same question many times in a different way to test if your story is consistent and true.

While I focused on compiling a mental testimony in my head, my lawyer then surprised me by asking casually, "They tried to settle with you right?".

I eyed him suspiciously. Why did he not know the answer to that?

"Yes," I reminded him, as I tried to imagine where this was leading to, "but that was all a game to them," referring to both Grant and his employer. He nodded his head at me, as though deep in thought. The fact he couldn't remember this point, when sitting outside the judge's chambers when we were about to give evidence, speaks volumes. It was as if he was trying to remember the facts of the case from our very first conversation a few months ago. What else was he trying to remember? What else had he missed? Has he even read my file? Or has it been collecting dust since day one?

My lawyer's entourage, meanwhile, was milling around us awkwardly while in an anxious state. This unexpected turn of events meant they were going to finish late, and their schedule for the rest of the morning would be thrown out.

Grant and his lawyers soon arrived looking like they had been confidantes since infancy, co-conspirators and fellow mischief-makers on the legal circuit. Except for the Emirati lead council, the pack of them wore harsh blacks and navys.

They hung loosely together in the centre of the reception, as we were huddled on the row of folding chairs. I suspected that this was just the kind of razzmatazz Grant's lead council enjoyed. After all, defence lawyers are masters of spin and oratory. In front of them I managed to look perfectly relaxed, though my heart was pounding from nerves.

The waiting began.

Some thirty minutes later the judge arrived in a rush, his robe floating all around him as he walked straight through the group casting wary glances all around and went to his chambers. Two female assistants soon followed.

The sudden movements meant they were almost ready for me and this did little to calm my nerves.

After a short while, the judge's assistant called us all into his chambers.

"Just be yourself," my lawyer said to me was we trooped into a sleek room with expansive windows and elevated ceilings.

This helped, for approximately five seconds.

I was instantly hit by a smoky aroma that emanated from the room. The judge was sat at his desk facing the door, robe off, with his back to the window, a translator on one side and the assistant, who was tasked with taking the minutes, on the other, ready with her stenographic machine. In the centre of the desk was a nameplate that announced the presence of Judge Ahmad Khalid al Hamdan.

The overall impression was of a powerful, intimidating man, but this was softened instantly when he spoke in a slow low-pitched tone. Judges are dealing with incredibly hard decisions on a daily basis, the kind that would make most of us never want to leave our rooms, so I sympathised with the rather large ash-tray with several stubs already in it, next to his nameplate.

I took the measure of the room, small and modern and much less intimidating than the majestic courtroom; the atmosphere was remarkably different. Formulaic, yet informal. The thing I liked about it was that it was light. I have this thing about light. Light and sunshine can make everything seem better if you're feeling a bit anxious. A beige leather sofa along one wall, floor-to-ceiling bookshelves on another and two leather armchairs in front of the judge's desk. The most striking thing was that there were no personal possessions in the room. No photographs of anything. The only sound in the room was the ticking of the ceiling fan and the faint murmur of traffic from the main road outside that only served to emphasise the silence of the room.

We all remained standing.

Stood in front of the judge like naughty school children hauled in front of the headmaster there was a large spatial gap between me and the defence lawyer who was on my left, and I realised I was taller than him. My lawyer stood a few steps behind me looked positively glum and reflective, standing almost to attention, while Grant stood to the side of the room, on my right, facing us.

The rest of our entourages were left outside in the corridor.

I glanced at Grant, impeccably dressed again in a smart pinstripe suit and patterned tie.

Does this trivia matter?

Actually yes.

These are hardly the mistakes of a male ingenue. Grant is a skilled salesman who understands the value of appearance: dress, accent, education, ethnicity, class and profession and how signals can be sent to those who know how to read them. And he was clearly sending them.

His defence lawyer was primed and sharp. He would not suffer small talk; one look at him and he was ready to waltz his way through the next hour or so.

I was told by the interpreter that I was to give my testimony under oath. I nodded my agreement. I was then told that lying under oath in a Dubai court is a criminal offence called perjury for which on conviction I could receive a custodial sentence. He allowed this grievous warning to float around the room. I felt guilty just for receiving it. I could have been an Oxbridge-educated intellectual, but the law has relegated my status to a mere decimal point in their view.

There was a silence as all eyes rested on me, prompting me to nod my head again to register agreement.

"Raise your right hand please," requested the assistant in Arabic.

"Do you swear your testimony will be the truth, the whole truth and nothing but the truth so help you God?"

With my right hand on the Quran, I was asked the same question again, through the interpreter. "Yes," I simply responded, prompting everyone to turn to look at the judge to follow his direction.

In his chambers the judge adopted a gentler style. I instantly liked him. I had prepared myself for being treated like some convict on day release, but now I relaxed a bit. I had been told he was one of Dubai's most experienced, respected judges and considered to be someone of total integrity. Standing before him, I was getting that vibe.

My first exercise was simple. All I had to do was answer a few questions that the judge asked via the translator. Where do you live? What do you do for a living? What is your date of birth?

I answered slowly, although I could tell the judge, who was listening closely to the answers, understood every word I was saying.

I learnt from the first time I had my interview with the prosecutor, how truly different the translation is in that it's not always translated in the exact way, in particular when it came to long questions and answers. They blank out the question. It's like an interpretation of the question and sometimes it's worse and sometimes it's better which is why it receives different answers at times. And there were some references that I knew they wouldn't get as some words and things are very British-centric. As all the questions were through the interpreter, I kept my answers short, generic and direct, and easily translatable. Nathan's advice: don't use eight words when four will do, resurfaced in my mind.

After the routine housekeeping questions were out of the way, I found myself completely relaxed, and after a couple of more questions, I found my feet and felt I could have stood there and talked all day.

The judge began. "Please tell us your case." He was flipping the pages of some computer printouts.

For the first ten minutes I recounted what had happened to me, starting with how I had been introduced to Grant. He allowed me to tell the story at my own pace. I spoke directly to him without the benefit of any papers, and each word drilled into his eyes. His eyes stayed on me and then moved around the room, taking in their curious glances one at a time.

And he listened. He was letting me have my day in court. When I realised that, I found myself getting stronger. And that's all I ever wanted, to get Grant in a courtroom in front of a judge. I was laying out all the facts and it was up to the judge to reach his own conclusions. Throw myself on the mercy of the court and reserve emotional sentiments.

And I really wanted him to believe me.

However, the defence lawyer was not happy. "We just have a few questions on cross-examination," he said politely, standing upright, interrupting my flow. He didn't want me to be given a platform to tell my whole story. He opened his mouth to object further, but the judge held up one hand. Brushing aside his objection, the judge let me continue. This was his courtroom.

One look at the defence lawyer, and it was clear that he knew he has lost control of challenging my testimony. As I resumed my story, I knew he was going to pull out whatever he can to try to unstable me further.

When I was in front of the judge, I laid it out very specifically. By now I had learned the right approach when it came to expressing myself and telling my story: keep it punchy, factual and honest. All that experience with the police and the prosecutor was now helping me in my presentation in front of the judge. Out of respect I kept my language polite and referred to the evil villain standing across from me as simply "Mr Grant".

Indeed, throughout my recitation, "Mr Grant" remained emotionless, his face revealed nothing. The only indication of Grant's true feelings was his glacial demeanour as he ignored everyone in the room except for his lawyer.

His lawyer on the other hand, had to earn his fee; his gaze never averted, ready to pounce if I stepped over the barrier, in his mind, between fact and fiction. It was another intimidating tactic. As was his head cocking suspiciously to one side when I made my heart-felt statements. As a double-act, we had a few moments of mirroring and more moments of contrasting body language rituals. Whilst I spoke with minimum movement, he gesticulated heavily throughout the entire time. When he was not in speak mode, he performed a stream of fidgets, ranging from eye-stutters, sucking and chewing his lips, fiddling with his papers, forehead-scratching, and pulling at his dish dash. It was incredibly distracting to me. It was, of course, meant to be.

After I finished recounting my story, the judge quietly said, "thank you". He nodded with great assurance.

Now he picked up steam as he went along, pumping out completely unambiguous statements, making it clear that he had reviewed the court file, had a copy of it on his desk, and knew every detail of my case. But he gave me the confidence that, unlike everyone else, he came into this trial without a fixed opinion.

For the next two hours, I answered questions again through the interpreter. And throughout it all, the judge simply acknowledged Grant as 'he' without ever mentioning his name.

"Was he managing your portfolio, or managing your money?"

"Did he correspond with you on blank pieces of paper or on letterhead?"

"What was the letterhead on the correspondence?"

"Have you signed any type of contract with him?"

Then came the more strategic, deeper questions.

"When did you realise the alleged fraud?" He had taken out a large legal pad, and pen. "June 2016," I replied, and the judge wrote down the date without hesitation.

"And you gave the money, voluntarily?" he wanted me to reconfirm this fact, without sounding unkind. And without turning the question into an accusation.

I hesitated and didn't respond immediately. "I did what I was directed to do by Mr Grant, thinking it was normal."

The judge said something to the translator, who in turn asked me the question again.

"Yes," I answered, simply.

The judge nodded and made a note.

At this point, the defence lawyer invited himself to join the questioning and his thornier questions came thick and fast via the judge who he asked to ask me this and ask me that, before the judge stepped in and politely, and with utter bemusement, ticked him off: "I'm asking the questions here". A small, yet extremely pleasant moment.

"Afwan," clutching his chest, he offered his apologies. He wasn't sorry about a damned thing. If you want to be a defence lawyer you can't be concerned about what people think of you. Similarly, if you want to bring a case to court you can't be concerned about what the defence lawyer thinks of you. And so commenced a tug-of-war: he was determined to have his questions to me answered, and I was determined only to answer the judge's questions.

The defence lawyer's interrogation centred around two questions: who is my contract with, and who sent my money to Guardian? This was what their whole defence was based on. And I understood why.

Typically, a judge refuses to refund scam victims on the grounds that the customers authorised the payment. When a judge receives a complaint about fraud, they first consider whether the customer authorised the money transaction. This means transferring money out of your bank account yourself to the funds, policies or Trusts. If the judge thinks you did not do this, they will then consider if the individual or companies acted fraudulently. However, all the financial advisors are too smart for this and they get around this loophole by asking the client to make the transfer themselves. The key is to show you were tricked into doing the transfer and that the financial advisor directed you to move your money.

I repeated my testimony that my contract was with Guardian – a fact Grant's lawyer seized on with glee, looking directly at the judge. I don't know why; I had been open and upfront about this from the beginning with the police and with the senior prosecutor in various statements and testimony many times before.

I then repeated my testimony that I had sent the money directly to Guardian, upon the direction of Grant.

There was no visual reaction from the defence lawyer, but he quickly glazed over my answer with an off the mark comment. He put on a pantomime of weariness, a slumping of his shoulders, a blowing out of his lips, as he argued that I was a "professional and educated woman" who had worked for the likes of "Clyde & Co" in a senior position and that I did understand what I was entering into and the agreements that would govern the financial consequences of the investment funds if they fell.

Well, that was an interesting take.

Did I hear that right?

Baffled, I looked back at my lawyer, hoping for a clue. He didn't look back at me or he was deliberating avoiding my eye. Wonderful.

It took me a few moments to process fully the implications of what the defence lawyer was saying. In other words, in lawyer-speak – she's not naive and clueless and she knew exactly what she was getting herself into, and this is more a case of her own greed, rather than his client's malfeasance; an accusation the lawyer cynically alluded to, on at least one other occasion.

Fortunately, the judge was suitably unimpressed.

Before I could reply that all the risks had not been explained to me, the judge interjected. In a welcome spark of common sense, the judge refused his reference to Clyde & Co, "one has nothing to do with the other," he simply commented, gesturing with his hand for the lawyer to move on from this argument.

I glanced at the defence lawyer, whose face was caught

halfway between a polite smile and a grimace, as he stroked his meticulously trimmed black and grey goatee and looked down at the papers in his hands. I couldn't help but wonder if exposing him to an empty script nullified his power; like Superman exposed to green kryptonite.

I sneaked a look at the clock on the wall next the defence lawyer. My testimony had eased into the second hour.

The next set of questions came from the judge directly and many of these same questions had been used in the prosecution's investigation. I felt it was all going quite well until the subject of the settlement came up. Asked whether Grant had offered to give me my money back, I answered no.

The way that it was worded to me, or the judge's question translated to me, was confusing. I took it to mean "did he offer to settle with me before I went to the police station and filed a complaint?". In which case my answer was correct.

However, one look at the defence lawyer showed that he was satisfied with my response – almost happy.

It doesn't take a genius to know, that it is not a good sign when the other party's lawyer is pleased with the answer you have given to a judge, and is even nodding his head in agreement.

I knew I was in trouble. Something got lost in translation.

I glanced at my lawyer for guidance, who didn't lock eyes with me. The lack of attention from him was so blazingly obvious that I felt embarrassed.

I thought if I had answered incorrectly he would have jumped in with clarification – or so I thought. But I couldn't help feeling that we should have clarified that the settlement offer was made to me after I filed a criminal complaint and during the prosecution investigation, even if the judge's direction was to know if Grant offered anything before then.

This picture of Grant's eccentric lawyer invested in the case, quite magnificently fighting for his client, spewing a stupendously pompous tone of faux moral outrage at some of my answers was far removed from the out-of-sight shot of my lawyer.

Of course, the lawyer for Grant was paid handsomely to do that. That was clear from his expensive white candoura and the immaculately dressed entourage waiting outside. Fair point. But so is my lawyer. Whereas my lawyer was somewhere in the background, with his hand on the door handle as if ready to exit at any time. The two lawyers could not have adopted a more different approach.

The judge went on asking more questions, bringing up my first statement the officer had taken at the police station. Grant's lawyer now changed his demeanour and couldn't suppress a smile as he latched onto the only inconsistency in my story; that the initial complaint and statement I had given to the police was related to non-compliance of a contract and not once explicitly stating that I believed Grant had defrauded me. He waved my statement like a burning flag. Inevitably, he went on to argue the statement and fact was evidence that I had made the allegations up and my statement seemed to acknowledge that the matter was civil rather than criminal.

There was a pause, in which both the judge and the defence lawyer turned to look at me at the same time, waiting for my answer.

I had to explain the circumstances behind the statement and my answer was so pathetic that no one could have made it up or admitted to it unless it was the truth and the truth is the only thing that would make it believable. I recounted the moment I went to the police station and admitted that at that time I was not aware it was fraud, that my statement was taken prior to any investigation. What I actually said, reflecting on the meeting with the officers, is that I knew something was wrong and I wanted the police to investigate the case. Whilst they investigated, I did my own investigation and found the information on the DED website which I later presented to the police.

At this point, there was little doubt in the room that I could not only explain this, but had explained it without much trouble. In reality it didn't seem to matter to the judge and he glanced at his watch as a signal to move this dialogue on, devaluing the defence's argument. It was Grant's lawyers trying to make something out of it, and as I proceeded to elaborate, I noted the lawyer's expression of satisfaction faded. His spine stiffened noticeably as he pinched the bridge of his nose. The judge was giving me too much space to answer and he wasn't liking it.

The judge rolled on. He now pursued details of the type of investments Grant had sold me.

And then, on an impulse, he suddenly looked up at me as though a thought had crossed his mind and he asked in English, rather bemused, "Where is Jersey?". The question prompted the interpreter to shake his head in wonderment too. I had to smile because both men were genuinely bewildered that they had never heard of a place that was at the centre of and the setting for the whole case.

I looked at both of them and it was obvious it was my turn to say something.

"It's an island in the Channel Islands," I offered which did nothing to clarify their geographical understanding and two confused faces kept staring back at me. Both the defence lawyer and my lawyer remained quiet, prompting me to speculate they didn't know where Jersey was either.

"Near the UK," I finally said. "Oh," they nodded their head in perfect unison to acknowledge they understood. The mood around the room lightened for a fleeting moment and there was a pause for everyone to gather their thoughts and get back on track. During which I felt a little nostalgia. It was the kind of scenario that once would have had Grant and I chuckling in his office during one of our catch-ups. Instinctively I looked across at Grant who darted his eyes away quickly.

The judge's next question, however, reminded me why I was standing in front of him.

"What is the current value of your investments?"

"Nil." One word. And after a silence, just to reinforce the point I elaborated, "they are worthless". My emotions were firmly back on track. I had to keep reminding myself that whilst I had seen "Mr Grant" as a friend, he had not.

"Do you have evidence of the current value of your investments?"

"Yes." I pointed to the case file on the desk, in front of the judge. "It's in there." I could see where this was leading. For the purpose of a lawsuit, the judge had to determine what my investments were worth at that moment. Anything above red would have to be discounted from the total amount awarded. In this instance, the maths was simple.

"In your testimony was he responsible in any way for your decision to invest in these funds?"

"Yes," I stated with unwavering certainty.

"How?"

"He encouraged me to invest in them whilst hiding the risks from me."

"In your testimony was he responsible in any way for the loss of your total investment?"

"Yes, absolutely."

I sneaked a quick look at how the defence lawyer was

reacting to my answer; chewing on a thumbnail. For a rare moment he didn't say anything or visibly react. Why had he let that point slide? When he didn't pipe up with his objections, interceptions and distractions I worried about him even more.

The judge flipped his notes and quickly changed direction. "How did he profit from you?"

I explained in three ways: an introductory fee, quarterly advisory fees paid to him directly from my Trust, and commission that was earned on every investment fund he recommended to me.

Then came the question that stung, "Do you have any evidence, receipts, slips ...?" His voice trailed away as I shook my head to show that I hadn't.

"Do you know how much in fees and commission he was paid?"

"No."

"Can you venture a guess?"

"No. It's impossible to guess. I don't know how much money he was making off me." After a few seconds I offered, "I have a rough idea of percentages". The judge didn't show any interest.

"Do you have any documents that show he was paid in fees and commission?"

"No." Guardian and Philip Van Neste had ignored my countless requests to provide me with any such documents. And the rules of evidence prevent verbal descriptions of no supporting documents, for obvious reasons. The best evidence is the document itself. I had a collection of valuation statements but nothing supporting them that might turn a verdict.

The question was a hint that the link between the licence fraud and proof that Grant benefitted financially was weak in that we hadn't done enough to prove it. Or he was going to refer that part of the criminal case to civil – which was most likely. I instantly felt deflated at both conjectures.

In an attempt to salvage the point, I added that I was not privy to anything related to Grant's fees, and that I had requested the information many times to no avail.

"From whom?"

"From Mr Grant and from Guardian."

"Did he comment on anything related to his fees and commission he earned?"

"No. He wouldn't tell me anything."

My attempts were futile. I knew it wouldn't make a difference in the judge's mind. I had lost the argument.

Not to miss an opportunity to score big, the defence lawyer scoffed at my whole answer, denying that his client benefited in any way financially from me. I looked at him pointedly, with first genuine bemusement, and then serious eyebrow-raised concern; and it hadn't gone unnoticed by the judge. For God's sake – a financial advisor not benefiting financially from a client? That's like saying Hannibal Lecter is a vegan.

He didn't care. He knew they'd won that point.

And there was no doubt the judge found this all rather amusing. He was already nodding, as if to discourage him from overstating his case.

He flipped a page and then looked at something on his legal pad, glanced at me, and asked, "So he was acting as a managing consultant?". It was a deliberate attempt by the judge to provoke me into clarifying what I thought Grant's role was. The defence lawyer suddenly looked alert, nodding his head, agreeing with the judge.

"No." I knew the answer, and I delivered it with convincing authority, holding the judge's gaze unblinkingly. "He was a financial advisor." There was a heavy pause, a stillness broken only by the defence lawyer shuffling his papers, until finally the judge nodded indicating this point hit home with him, and it would not be forgotten.

"Did you continue to take advice from him after you realised you were losing money?"

"Yes."

"Why?"

"He always had a plausible reason for the fall in investments."

"Have you been a victim of fraud before?"

"Luckily, I've never had any connection with fraud."

"Did you continue to work with him, after you were convinced he was deceiving you?"

"No."

"What did you do?"

"I filed a complaint with the police."

There was a long pause as the judge studied his legal pad, and then he turned to speak to his assistant who checked the monitor at her typed notes. She looked back at him and nodded her head.

The silence stretched out so long that I thought the judge had spotted a contradiction in what I had said, causing an anxiety bump against my chest. Only, suddenly, the judge was wrapping up things on his side. "Is there anything else you would like to add to your testimony?"

"No," I say, and as I uttered the words, I felt a surreal moment of peace. Finally, they finished questioning me. The pressure was momentarily off. My expression, always a mirror of my thoughts, registered the fact with a small gleam of relief. The punch I'd been bracing myself for had finally been delivered. The plaster ripped clean off.

Grant gave no visible reaction throughout my entire testimony which was unusual for him. I wondered if he had been told by his lawyers not to. There was definitely some tactic behind it. Or maybe because out of every single person in that room, he knew I was telling the truth.

Another stolen glance at the clock on the wall confirmed we were just entering the third hour of my testimony. I had spoken nonstop for two hours, yet it passed by as if it were only a matter of minutes.

Was the judge moved by my testimony?

No.

Did he believe my testimony?

I could tell that he believed me, and it now fell to the defence lawyer to predict how the judge absorbed my testimony.

"Could we have a few minutes, Your Honour?" he asked. Of course he did. My moment was indeed quickly hijacked by the searingly ambitious lawyer who asked the judge if he could read their memorandum to him that they had prepared and would submit into evidence. The judge nodded without saying a word.

Determined to have the last word, now without a doubt was his 'Moment'.

There was a pause as he cleared his throat loudly.

Defence lawyers can go on a rampage like a human King Kong, lashing out at the victim and any evidence that gets in their way. It's how they win their legal cases. But that brash, bombastic, abusive style, can, at times, grate with some independent judges. And therein lies the big question for lawyers in their campaigning: do they unleash the furious beast, or the more reasonable creature?

The answer depends on how they read the judge. In this instance, it was clear the defence lawyer shared the same belief as I did that the judge believed my testimony.

And so, revealing a sheaf of speaking notes, for the next twenty minutes – too long for my liking – the defence lawyer swayed his way reading through his memorandum displaying spontaneous exuberance, every word thumped out with a punch of defiance, exuding an air of someone who thought he was delivering the State of the Union address to an expectant nation. I remember at one point taking a step back to allow him to sashay in front of the judge's desk as he delivered his presentation. A complete whirlwind of energy. He was a man of many legal opinions and he was anxious to share them with the judge in a desire to persuade him.

I had no idea if he was sharp, innovative, witty or eloquent, or a legal genius at the top of his game, inspiring justice – it was all in Arabic, almost classical Arabic. So understandably, it was impossible to take in his words as his monologue made no sense to me.

Maybe it was good it was in Arabic, and I couldn't understand it, and nor was I sure I wanted to know, otherwise I think I would have been provoked into a confrontation if it was anything like their first memorandum. It would have been handbags galore.

Instead, I forced myself to listen, forced my brain to giving meaning to his tones that were aggressive and persistent, and to the syllables he was saying, trying to keep my face poker.

There's something quite surreal about standing next to someone who is literally saying the worst things about you in an unknown language, while it was all you could do to maintain a neutral expression. I wasn't worried. In fact, I was remarkably calm at the moment. I was just so relieved that my part was over, and I had survived it.

Twenty minutes is a long time to pretend to be fixated with your Marks and Spencer's stiletto shoes. Understandably, I lost my struggle to stay tuned and I found myself looking around the room.

At the judge, who started fiddling about with paperwork on his desk, and smiled and nodded along approvingly as the defence lawyer spoke.

At my lawyer, who had become adept at fading into the background and was still standing at the back with his door on the handle, looking fixated by what Grant's lawyer was arguing.

At Grant. I can safely guess at the moment he would rather have me hurled from the top of the Burj Khalifa into a pool of hungry crocodiles.

And back at the defence lawyer. There's no doubt that his fire-breathing energy and showmanship give him a massive performative advantage over my lawyer who looked like a timid and beaten man. As much as I disliked his work, I could admit, only to myself, that Grant had picked a far better lawyer over mine.

Suddenly he fell silent. I looked up. Has he finally finished? He had. For a few moments silence descended over the room as he handed out copies of his memorandum to the judge, his assistant and to my lawyer; all were exchanging looks and not exchanging words as they cautiously leafed through the papers.

At this point, the judge invited my lawyer to respond and asked if there were any questions he wanted to ask, to which he replied, "No".

Come again?

I looked back at him. No rebuttal?

After a long silent pause, the judge then asked him if there was anything he wished to add to my testimony. My lawyer shook his head. I looked back at him again.

He was oblivious to the disapproval being beamed his way. He had just heard the other party's defence – what did he mean he had nothing to ask or say? The judge was giving him the opportunity to close on a strong point, and to emphasise our key points as the session was obviously coming to a close. And yet he offered nothing. No closing arguments. Had he logged off?

When my lawyer said nothing, I turned back to the defence lawyer. He had a look of satisfaction on his face that was slightly unnerving, demonic.

"Anybody else?" The judge asked, and looked carefully at each of the three of us, except for Grant. There was another long silent pause where no one moved.

"No?" At this point the judge looked at his assistant. "Then I conclude this hearing," he declared. His tone of voice indicated there no room for discussion. He cast a glance at his watch, signalling an end to proceedings.

I could not believe it. We had an opportunity here, a really amazing opportunity – and my lawyer said nothing.

Furious was not the word.

It was the single most bizarre performance from a lawyer I'd ever seen, which when you think of all the stuff that had gone on so far was quite an achievement.

He just didn't say anything.

But, why?

I glanced at the defence lawyer, oozing self-assurance as he started to gather his papers, a sign that he knew it was all over and who clearly couldn't believe his luck that his presentation wasn't being challenged. I glanced back at my lawyer. The answer slowly dawned on me. Maybe he had never logged on. He looked like someone fortunately saved from having to mumble words he barely remembered. He was clearly not prepared and he didn't know the details of the case well enough to discuss it or highlight the key points, especially after the defence lawyer's polished performance. He had turned up expecting just to submit a piece of paper, take his fee, and be done. I was not the only one that had been blindsided by the defence.

Okay, so he was lost without his autocue and could not answer unscripted, unprepared for questions, but if he got caught out he could have at least requested time to respond to the defence's memorandum.

He didn't even do that.

The judge wrapped up the hearing, working in a little dig of his own by suggesting he'd heard enough. Three bizarre hours that had flashed by like some high-octane fireworks display.

"Thank you," I say and I let out an inconspicuous sigh glad the game of chess is over, only I wasn't sure who had been checked-mated. It all ended quite badly as far as I was concerned and felt it still didn't get down to the meat and potatoes of the case. It wasn't the judge's fault; we simply hadn't guided him to it.

I was told by the judge to wait for a copy of my statement that required my signature. A few minutes later, the assistant handed me a clipboard with several sheets of computer printout in Arabic which I flicked through, then signed whilst standing.

Both parties left the chambers. Grant and his posse left very pleased with themselves and their performance – it was as if they had hoisted the defence lawyer into the air and carried him towards the make-believe crowd. I, on the other hand, was furious at the manager partner at what had happened.

He didn't present my case and offered no substance to the judge, giving the opposition the advantage of influencing the judge with no objection from our side. As I had no one advocating for me the judge was left with the other party's memorandum, only. I was clearly at a disadvantage.

"Don't worry," he said as we stood in the hallway, where his aides had been loitering all this time, waiting for us to finish. "You did very well, actually."

Me? What about you?

It was a cute answer, and I suspect he knew I was furious with him.

"You didn't say anything," I said stating the obvious. "You didn't DO anything," emphasising the word "Do". "This was IT, this was the opportunity ... and you didn't DO anything."

He hadn't, and he knew he hadn't.

But he chose not to take this as a question. He tried to bluff himself out of it by repeatedly saying he didn't need to "step in" as the judge was satisfied with my testimony, and I delivered a confident testimony during judge's questioning, and the other party hadn't landed any punches.

It was clear he would brook absolutely no criticism of himself.

"Well, I, you know ..." I started to stammer, before he interrupted me.

"You've got a good judge. He asked all the right questions. You're lucky." There was that word again. The judge, it turned out, did in fact care about the case. Many would not have so readily engaged with the case, or been so hands-on.

Still, I was not consoled. I had never felt worse at this point in the entire prosecution investigation and the trial.

"You'll have to excuse me, but I need to go to another appointment. You can find your way out can't you?" Then he rushed off without another word with his entourage, and I had the distinct impression that he was glad to escape.

By the end of the exchange with my lawyer, I felt pretty much defeated. I felt he had let me down. I had worked so hard on getting the case this far, and I had handed it over to lawyers, so I thought, it would be safe and better – and in fact they had almost blown it. They had been notoriously unhelpful.

"They didn't DO anything," I kept telling myself. But

I do know they are actually making things more complicated. On advice, I had taken on a lawyer in the criminal case to basically hold my hand and deal with everything for me but they hadn't done anything, and, in part, ridiculed my case.

I ended a terrible day thinking I had blown it.

I replayed what happened in court that morning to Nathan, who was equally shocked, at everything, but particularly at the lawyers. "That's ridiculous. Representation is what you're paying them for".

"I'm relying on the fact that the judge realised how badly I was represented today and cuts me some slack. Otherwise, I am doomed, Nathan."

"What is the point of having them, then?" It was a fair question. The maid of honour is one of the people the bride relies on most during her big day. Similarly, at a court case, people rely on their lawyers. But at today's hearing it seemed that my maid of honour was rather absent from his important role.

"Do you think he was bribed?" he said as if he were only joking. I burst out laughing, a proper belly laugh.

"Believe me, Nathan if we were talking about 60 million quid, I'll be inclined to agree with you, but it's only 60 thousand, remember."

"Oh, yes." He started laughing at himself. This is what happens in a trial; your mind wanders off to try and make sense of something that just happened in the courtroom that is completely inexplicable and so utterly bizarre.

"Can you imagine Grant behind some Shawarma joint in some old part of town, purchasing a verdict?"

"Not with those short arms." Nathan knew his former friend only too well.

To round off the evening, a phone message from Grant to a mutual friend is sent on to me: "We got her!"

You're fired

Indeed, why did I have them? The next morning, my stomach felt dull and heavy, as if full of earth, and I was still asking myself the same niggly question. One thing was for sure, I had not hired the lawyers to be mere passive observers.

The court prosecutor was supportive. "I think it's smart of the judge to do the testimony knowing you're unprepared. Answering these questions, this way, might be strategic." The argument, he offered, was that lawyers are known to prepare crib sheets for their clients to learn before a hearing. "And the judge can see right through it," he said. He spoke from years of experience. The problem for victims and defendants – who rely on these crib sheets and lawyer coaching – is that judges can uncover who is honest and who is not.

Then he added, "but, yes, your lawyer should have prepared you that you may be called to give your testimony". He gave my shoulder a sympathetic pat. "I think people need to think they are prepared to take the stand. But I think that nothing can prepare you for being in the witness box. It's something very different."

He was right about that. It was indeed something very different.

Suffice to say, I was still furious.

Every part of this case was an uphill battle. Yesterday, in the worst example so far, my lawyer even forgot what his role was in this case. The next morning, and after learning of Grant's gloating message to people, I still felt it was an ignominious blow to our case.

By the sounds of it, my legal team knew I was going to lose and didn't spend any time on my case. Inevitably, this woefully complacent attitude resulted in delivering a poor service as they treated the whole thing with shocking flippancy: two court hearings and two advocates showed up not knowing the case. Their assistants were with them too – to do what, I don't know to be quite frank. To lead them to their next case?

In comparison, my prosecution lawyer did a splendid job during the prosecution investigation. He seemed to take the role extremely seriously. Whatever his personal views on the case and its chances, he had remained a consummate professional and had been very supportive. With this law firm, I was waiting for them to finally realise their duties and why they'd been appointed.

I wrote to them about the way the case was being trialled. It would be interesting to see what they have to say for themselves.

They responded in typical lawyer fashion.

"It is unfortunate that you had to do this on the spot without preparation and without having a chance to read Neil's defence," wrote the associate. "Your presence in court allowed Neil's lawyer to question you unprepared." Hang on, were they indirectly blaming me?

"We have explained to you how weak your criminal claim against Neil is." Here we go again.

"Anyways, let us stop crying over the spilled milk; we trust that we have done our best."

You can almost hear the wind whistling through his ears.

Matters went from bad to worse when the managing partner himself popped up in my email box and wrote a masterpiece, "I had topped up a few of the statements (in front of the judge) that you made in order to keep him on the right track".

Come again?

So far, I had dealt with lawyers manipulating evidence,

obscuring the facts or using 'deliberate, careful and sophisticated language', but this breathtaking professionalism of lawyers shone through brightest.

Well, now, I thought, I'm royally pissed off. That was it. I didn't think it could get any worse but it just had.

I conceded that hiring the firm was a mistake. I had simply picked the wrong lawyers. It just wasn't working for me, and I didn't feel from their side that there was a commitment, so why drag it out?

My mind was made up. It was the logical next step.

The next day I fired them.

It was over, done, kaput.

"You fired your lawyer midtrial?" was the incredulous reaction from Nathan.

I didn't think the lawyers would be receptive to the decision either.

My now ex-lawyers, of course came out fighting with their boxing gloves.

An email arrived at 8 am the next morning demanding payment with a copy of their bill attached. Otherwise, wrote the keyboard legal warriors, we will pursue our rights through the Dubai courts. I stared at the size of their bill.

AED 20,000!

For WHAT!?

I thought for a minute. There had been two hearings so far, we had submitted nothing but a Writ Notice and they hadn't done anything that they said they were going to do. How had it come to this?

There were no notes attached to the bill, so I asked them to send me a detailed invoice.

I was immediately offered a discount of AED 4,400. The bill was now reduced to AED 15,600.

I was suspicious at the speed of the reducing bill, and even more so when the invoice arrived.

It was the most complex invoice I had ever seen. I couldn't work out what it was on about. Upon closer examination, I could see that it was actually manually put together, and not displayed in a systematic date order. Instead, it was a random selection of dates and actions. As though they were deliberately trying to muddy the waters. Billing systems are able to print out time sheets and actions in a systematic date order. This is standard in any law firm. You don't need to manually put an invoice together like they had done here which can confuse the client. For every action you take on a case file a code and a fee is attached to it automatically.

I had to go through each 'correspondence with client' as that was the only label in the invoice. They appeared to be charging me for an email they wrote to me, informing me that they cannot complete a piece of work before the date they had promised. There was a lot of duplication of work and charges. I was charged three times for one email on separate parts of the invoice. They charged me for two emails on a certain date, one of which was mistakenly sent to me that was meant for the managing partner.

They were billing me for compiling the engagement letter. And at this point I had not even hired them. And they charged me for visiting their office to leave them a copy of the Power of Attorney certificate that was rejected at the Notary Public.

There are charges for case briefings, and discussions on the case between the team and the managing partner. Yet none of the information they reviewed and supposedly discussed with the managing partner was used in court, in the actual argument before the judge.

The real icing on the cake was that the managing partner was charging me AED 1,900 for simply turning up at the hearing. And to really lace the deliciously sugary icing on the top, they were billing me for the managing partner debriefing the team back in the office after my testimony before the judge – where he hadn't said anything.

I laughed out loud. The sheer audacity.

Whoever conjured up this invoice made a numpty of himself.

I obviously had a massive stamp on my forehead that read 'Come, rob me blind'.

The invoice was clearly an attempt on their part to generate work for the sake of generating fees, and to expand the work to try and match it against the bill. They had panned it out as much as they could and couldn't get to the AED 20,000 mark. That explained the AED 4,400 reduction.

What depths will some lawyers sink to next?

One thing's for sure: it's greed. Insatiable greed.

After receiving such an invoice, I completely understood a client's plea for rejecting the billable hour standard. The industry's finger was truly on the billing pulse.

"You have to pay something," said the person who referred me to them, and who was prominent in legal circles. "They must have done some work on it."

"No – absolutely no way," I replied, defiantly. Payment was out of the question. Any work they did on the case was irrelevant if they didn't use it. It's like preparing for a job interview and conducting all the research on the company, and yet you remain completely silent during the interview itself, and refer to none of the information you gathered. What was the point of doing the legwork?

He went on to tell me that law firms have taken clients to court for as less as AED 5,000 in non-payment of fees; simply out of principle.

Well, I was also acting out of principle.

I was insatiably curious to hear how they were going to explain that invoice to a court. And if they had a modicum of sense they wouldn't try to.

I had not worked so hard to get the case to this point for it to crash around my ears by my own lawyers. They had no passion for the case, they didn't believe in it and they actually ridiculed the thought of a conviction. They had taken the case purely to milk it, knowing they would have to do very little work and charge a large fee. It was a dream case for them. Easy money. A temptation like this was too much to resist.

I already had so many stab wounds on my back. More of the same was madness.

But then it became intimidation. I started receiving emails that had threatening undertones which were still within the legal lines. I refused to entertain them with a response other than "You can take any action you deem appropriate".

No doubt that these were unsettling times for me and I had no idea how I was going to manage moving forward. But then no one said powering a case through the court system was easy.

Yet in some crazy way, I actually felt relieved – and free. Liberated from their negativity.

The defence strikes back

I read through Grant's memorandum, which his lawyer had presented the day before to the judge. The defence's responses, I was learning fast, were like being in a choppy ocean: you just got hit by wave after wave until you realised it was always like that and you learn to ride them.

It was the same approach the defence team used in their first response to the senior prosecutor a few months before. The lawyer didn't supply new arguments for the trial. It simply parrots what's said in the first memorandum.

"Grant is innocent," was their opening line.

It read, in summary: he has not committed fraud or any fraudulent activities. At no time had Grant taken any money from me. He was just performing the company's activities as it is licensed to do – completely missing the point that his licence was not actually to advise individuals on how to invest money. The memorandum then went on to plead that in the event that this crime was true, the money was transferred in June 2010, and according to the law fraud crime is time lapsed and should be dismissed (without acknowledging that the crime was ever committed). It ended that I had acted in bad faith by dragging the file for a long time – which apparently was a reference to the one-week extension I requested to hire a lawyer during the prosecution investigation – to "abuse" Grant and take advantage over him forcing him to pay me undue money; again claiming that I tried to settle with him, intentionally misrepresenting this issue in an attempt to discredit me in the judge's eye.

The prosecution, they argued, had provided no independent evidence and absolutely no proof in support of their accusations, which meant the entire case hinged solely on the "alleged" victim's word. Because, they further argued, there was clearly not enough evidence to pass the threshold test for a criminal prosecution (beyond all reasonable doubt) all charges should be dropped.

There was no fresh evidence. There was no evidence to begin with.

Still, I'd certainly ruled nothing in or out at the moment given the closeness of the final verdict and the vast army of lawyers on Grant's side engaged in this ferocious battle to deliver victory for their client. Especially a slam duck court battle that no good lawyer should ever lose for him.

Saying that, it confirmed to me that the managing partner could have addressed and answered a lot of those points in front of the judge as they were the same points raised in their first memorandum. My lawyer at the time had already replied to most of it in our response. In particular, the defence's point on the "time-lapse" should have been immediately shut down by the managing partner, as we had evidenced that I had only learnt of the fraud in 2016.

That is, of course, had the managing partner read my file. A last shake of the head, a last twinge of annoyance towards my former lawyers.

"… and somebody called for you today," said the receptionist.

"Really, who?"

"I didn't get that far, because the line went dead."

"What do you mean?"

"They asked if Amber is there, and when I said you were in a meeting, they put the phone down."

"Man or woman?"

"Man."

"Can you describe his voice?"

"British … very quiet voice, I could barely hear him."

Pleading

"Is he in jail yet?" Rupert called for a quick update on what was happening. His humour as dry as my toast first thing in the morning.

"Grant is never going to jail," I adamantly reminded him. Drama indeed. There had been a lot of speculation and drama peddled by Grant's camp, and I was quashing the rumours once and for all.

The purported possibility of a two-year jail sentence was a ludicrous exaggeration. Jail sentence for licence fraud? The purported pro bono work by his lawyers for all parts of the proceedings was another ludicrous fabrication.

Court documents revealed Grant was a man of substantial means. Lawyers were smart with figures and with money. The idea that the work they did for Grant was free was so ridiculous it had to be a joke. He was a multi-millionaire financial advisor – since when do they become eligible for pro bono work?

There was enough drama in the courtroom to contend with, without Grant creating more on the outside.

The trial moved to its third day; the next hearing was for July 12th, 2017, for pleadings.

Grant was due to give his pleading in court as part of his defence against me. This is usually just before the judgment is heard. It was an opportunity for Grant to speak and plead his case to the judge directly, almost like a last plea for mercy – only I thought he was going to plea for common sense, and treat it as though he had made some minor transgression such as forgetting the house keys or spilling his tea.

His lawyer could do the pleading for him, but as any lawyer will advise, it's more powerful coming from you, whether you're the accused or the victim. And it's known to sway the judge if he's still sitting on the fence. It's the perfect opportunity to close strongly on a case, because you have the last word with the judge.

I did hope it would be him pleading so I could hear what he said. But at the same time Grant giving evidence was going to be challenging for me, as I would be up and down in my seat like a jack-in-a-box protesting against every statement he made.

And what was he going to say? I was intrigued. I remembered his call with the Insurance Authority and how that had been an eye-opener for me. Was he prepared to say anything under oath, and be untruthful, in order to win this case?

It was to be another sensational day in court. This was a guy who manipulated his way in and out of trouble. Anything could happen and he could very well walk out the front door.

I turned up by myself on the morning of the hearing soon after eight and made a quick inspection of the noticeboard. Today we were third on the caseload. Grant was already there outside the courtroom, surrounded by his team huddled over a table and I could see they were going through his pleading, guiding him through it one final time, steadying his nerves. No doubt, Grant had spent the past days being prepped by his team, rehearsing his lines, getting grilled in a mock courtroom setting in preparation for the judge's questions.

At precisely eight-thirty the doors opened and I went straight into the courtroom and just waited until proceedings started.

Grant walked in with his entourage, all strutting their stuff and went straight to the front pews. It was just like high school when the cool kids walk in last and grab the best seats in the classroom. A 'Men in Black' parade. As usual, we waited for the case number and name to be called out and we all got up. I stood next to the court prosecutor. Of course, as I had no legal representation, this prompted speculation amongst the defence team that I'd fallen out with my lawyers.

You may think Grant would have been feeling nervous with the pressure of the eyes of the courtroom on him. But he was confident as ever, bounding up to stand before the judge. He embraced the moment, straightening his sleeves as if to say "Right, let's stop this nonsense once and for all", and with a relentless determination to tell his part of the story. All set to impress the Boss. Tall, as striking and well dressed as ever. I braced myself for a thumping tirade and Grant spinning fairy tales worthy of Hans Christian Andersen. I was anticipating his pleading to be a full denial in every way and so gut-wrenchingly emotive I could see no way of surviving this if the judge falls for it.

Now, it was his moment in the trial.

Well, it was meant to be.

Only it wasn't to be.

If there's one thing everyone surely can agree about a judge, it's that nothing about them can ever be safely predicted, and this trial was turning out to be as unpredictable and sensational as any American legal television drama.

The judge was a man on a mission this morning, and took less than a split second to decide that, no, he didn't feel like hearing Grant's pleading – despite extending the invitation to him, himself, in writing.

"There will be no pleading today," he announced to the horde of surprised lawyers watching him intently.

The judge suddenly rapped his gavel. Next case. Just like that. The whole thing was over in less time than it takes for Lionel Messi to take a free kick. On at 9.00 am and over by 9.01 am. Just like someone opting not to have milk in their coffee.

We all stood rooted to our spots, looking hesitant. Grant stared at the judge, stunned. His lawyers prepared him for his pleading, no doubt; but didn't prepare him in the event the judge decided to cancel it – in his face.

By this point, even the court was stunned into

temporary silence. Did we hear the translator correctly? The judge was handed the next case file from one his assistants to show we had.

The lawyers bolted from the courtroom herding Grant with them, expressing the surprise we all felt, and I could see them through the small glass window huddled outside the doors as I went back to my seat. Was it adjourned to after all the cases have been heard or what? Or was it simply the case the judge was not in the mood for any pleadings today? Or was the memory of the outraged Grant meandering off script at the first hearing not lost on the man in charge today?

This seemed manifestly unfair and I couldn't work out if it was a good or bad thing for me. I decided to wait in the courtroom to speak to the court prosecutor after the caseload had finished.

Only, the drama wasn't over.

Minutes later Grant and his lawyers all came marching back into the courtroom and sat on the first two benches again. I was incredibly curious, and felt uneasy as I observed them. Something very odd was going on.

While his lead counsel, the local advocate, was his usual animated self, Grant was rather more subdued with the rest of the entourage and the group looked very stiff as they sat beside each other in the pews. Grant was placed front row in full view of the judge. His entourage seated one row behind. And his lead counsel sat directly in front of the judge as if signalling to him he wanted to speak to him.

Eventually, the judge called him up. The local advocate took a sidebar and went up and talked to the judge, who leaned downward so that he could hear something that the rest of the courtroom couldn't hear, nodding mutely from time to time. Grant was then ushered to the sidebar but didn't speak to the judge. It looked like they were working out a deal with the judge to have his pleading heard. By now, they were a matter of avid fascination to the audience in the courtroom. Every person was either staring at or straining to see Grant or his group of lawyers.

Now the local advocate seems to be having a slightly firmer conversation with the judge, raising his hands and then bringing them together and using a small head-baton gesture for emphasis.

There was a moment when he pointed to me. I spontaneously ducked my head.

The audience were curious, and heads turned to look at me. I sank further in my seat.

"What is going on? Why is he pointing at me?" I stammered as I leant over to the lady sitting next to me who spoke Arabic.

"They want the judge to hear their pleading. They say you are still in the courtroom so it is possible to hear their pleading."

I flashed a look at the judge, who seemed totally uninterested in whether they had something to say or not, and paid the minimum amount of attention to Grant's presence.

The Arabic lady leaned over to me and whispered, "now, they say it's not fair to his client not to hear his pleading".

Then I could see the judge knocking that argument back politely, confidently and with his hand drew a line as if to say no.

Defeated, the local advocate walked back down the aisle and seemed to gesture to Grant and his entourage out of the courtroom with a rather impassive-looking hand-tilt. I watched with great interest as they walked past my row in single file, and out of the courtroom, as did everyone else. Aside from brightening up a drab packed courtroom, the parade of defeated lawyers had put on quite a show.

Again, through the small glass window, I could see they were huddled outside the courtroom.

I am totally bemused. Why? Contemplating their next move? The lawyers knew they couldn't allow the opportunity to pass.

Good God, the drama of it all.

Grant's lawyers looked like a train of money, power, and influence that was barrelling down in the courtroom, just trying to get their way. I felt that they eventually would get their way. Their presence was that overpowering in the courtroom. They were actually reminding the judge, a distinguished judge no less, that his job at this point was to guarantee a fair trial. And the judge was reminding them that the most important person in this trial was him; not the lawyers and most certainly not the defendant.

It slowly dawned on me that the more I stayed in the courtroom the more they were going to try and get Grant's pleading heard. And if the judge sees I am still in the courtroom he might be persuaded to let Grant plead. I needed to leave by working out a way to remove myself tactfully from the room. But they were right outside the courtroom door and I would have to walk through them. They would have to part from their huddle in order for me to pass and I really did not want to interact with them.

It gave me a barmy idea. It's old and very childish, I know, but it works all the same.

I got up and pretended to be on the phone and walked out of the courtroom. Looking totally absorbed in my make-believe conversation with the make-believe person on the phone, covering my free ear with my other hand, I managed to walk through them without glancing at them. I could feel every pair of eyes boring into me. With me no longer in the courtroom, they couldn't use that to plead their case in any event. They saw their opportunity slip away as I slipped through them.

I, meanwhile, walked on with a backward glance.

They were no longer grinning. The grinning that would frequently annoy me because to me it was a clear indication that they were removed from their actions; they still had not made the connection between their actions and the effect.

I found a vacant meeting room on the same floor and parked myself in there for the next twenty minutes after which I made my way back to the courtroom as I still needed to speak to the court prosecutor on what exactly had happened. I knew he was able to read the mood and texture of the trial.

"Well," I said to him, after the security guards cleared the courtroom, "that was quite something."

Nothing to worry about he told me. The judge probably had all the information he needed to now make a decision and felt he didn't need to hear from Grant, which is entirely his prerogative.

Yes it was. But still – Grant had a right for his pleading to be heard. I said I was worried that they would use it as grounds of appeal. Yes, it's possible was the prosecutor's response. This is what I now feared might happen. Appeals become retrials, something I did not want in this case.

At this very moment though, this trial was over, he told me. There are no further submissions as the judge held further litigation to issue a judgment. The decision now belonged to the judge. I've done all I can, I can do no more. I should let it go now, leave it with the judge.

What another extraordinary day. As if courts aren't already fun enough. Prior to the public prosecution investigation, I read up about the prosecution and the court process, a decision intended to better my understanding of the litigation processes that I was to routinely sit through over the next few months, as well as broaden my knowledge of the legal industry. Let me warn you – nothing prepares you for the reality. It's not always predictable.

There was nothing to do now but to wait, whilst flipping a coin on the verdict. The prospect of another miracle was that slim. For certain, both Grant and I would sweat bullets until we heard the verdict.

From the depths of sleep the phone shrieks angrily.

It's 4 am.

A long pause as I look at the blinking red light on the phone.

I don't pick up.

The verdict – on a wing and a prayer

None of us knew how it would end. And I was almost afraid to be optimistic. I had learnt over the past months that it was virtually impossible to predict what any judge would do.

The verdict was delayed twice. Each time, Grant prepared himself to hear his fate and to stand before the judge only to be told he needed more time to pass judgment. The intensity of those final months for Grant must have felt like a pressure cooker waiting to let off steam. By the summer news spread that his wife had taken the four children and settled them back in Scotland having enrolled them into new schools, as she couldn't cope with it all, leaving Grant to face his fate alone.

Meanwhile, I had developed the habit of keeping myself busy during the day whilst staring at the phone. My eyes seldom left it.

Until finally we received notice that the judge was ready to announce the verdict against Neil Grant.

Panic settled. Now the time had come I didn't want to go to the court to hear the judgment. A verdict sounded much different in open court, with lawyers and the public watching, than it did in the comfort of your home with people that you actually knew. Fortunately, it turned out, I didn't need to. The judgment was filed on the court system immediately after the hearing so I got my friend in the legal service with access to the court system to look it up.

Then came the magic words.

It read the judge deliberated for three months before returning with his verdict – in favour of me.

Me!? Blimey!

Now, 'blimey' is a word I can categorically state I have never used in everyday conversation, so even I'm amazed that's the first word that came to mind when I heard the verdict. It goes to the strangeness of a court case. The thrill of a victory.

In the first emotions of the moment no real sense could be made. I let the verdict sink in for a few minutes, until the realisation slowly dawned on me of the magnitude of what I was hearing. I won. I actually won. I had actually won a case. A trial. In a courtroom. With a judge and everything. There was a flood of happy emotions. Strangely, even though it was never one of my goals in this thing called life, it felt like it was the biggest thing I had ever achieved. It felt monumental. I knew it was a fantastic victory. Small, but significant. Given our odds, our meagre resources compared to the opposition, the concealing, withholding of evidence and personnel dramas along the way, I was grateful for the result.

On one side, there was Grant, with his high-powered lawyers, who had every ounce of legal expertise working for him. And on the other side, there I was unprepared, being messed around by my own lawyers and after having every obstacle being thrown at me before I even got to court.

And I won. Well, my goal was to win. I wanted to win. I was not planning on losing. I was hungry to win and defeat him. There was a fierceness in me that losing was not an option. That's why I put in the work; that's why I put in the effort. I was focused on winning. When you have that kind of focus, it doesn't matter about the odds. When you have that kind of focus you will be empowered to snatch victory from the jaws of defeat.

Details were, as ever, sketchy, but, it read, by a judgment dated August 2nd, 2017, Neil Ramsay Pringle Grant was found guilty by the Dubai Court of First Instance of running an unlicensed business, and unrightfully taking my movable assets, comprised of money and commissions, on the basis that he unlawfully acted as a financial advisory without the required licence. He was ultimately fined.

"Enough to get you over the line," Mohamed, my prosecution lawyer said when I rang him with the news.

"Enough to get him off the streets," I responded. I breathed an enormous sigh of relief. I had stopped him.

When the eight-page full copy of the judgment finally arrived a week later, in summary, it stated that in May 2010, I had engaged Neil Grant of Prosperity Offshore Investment Consultants to act as my financial advisor. Grant introduced me to a company called Guardian Trust Company Ltd and through Grant, I invested money into Guardian. The funds were subsequently placed in high-risk investments and lost. Grant earnt commission and fees for this introduction, and Guardian also benefitted from fees payable by me as part of my investments. I came to learn that Grant was operating without the necessary licence and was not properly registered with the authorities. The Dubai public prosecutor's office made the decision to pursue criminal charges against Grant. A criminal judgment against Grant evidences that Prosperity Management Consultancy was licensed by the Dubai Economic Development (DED) for management consulting through which it provided "consultancies and management studies for the public organisation and companies". Prosperity Management Consultancy was not licensed nor did it have competence in investment or financial advisory, or any fiduciary role.

There was no direct evidence of signature forgery which we had reintroduced in the trial. In light of 'beyond a reasonable doubt', in my view, the judge had made the right call, especially concerning the penalty of incarceration if Grant had nothing to do with it.

The mystery of the forged signature, therefore, remained unsolved.

The verdict shocked Grant's camp beyond reason. But procedurally there was nothing his lawyers could do. But I knew they weren't finished.

Immediately, after the verdict was announced, Grant was getting out of Dubai as fast as he could. He took the very next flight out of the emirate, presumably to join his wife and family in Scotland. No one was sure. But to be frank, at the time, there wasn't any reason not to let him go. He was free to go wherever he wanted. But he was just gone. I think it was a very cowardly thing for him to do. He escaped everyone, and their questions.

Meanwhile, Grant's lawyers asked a three-judge panel of the Chief Justice Appeal Court: The second degree of litigation to overturn the criminal conviction from August 2017. It was still enough to fill me with worry. First trial – you think yes, they gave it their best shot. They will now sell this to Grant as a tactical miscalculation. At the retrial, the defence will go in much harder. The lawyers are pissed now and they will go through those memorandums with a fine-tooth comb for Grant. They are going to be more focused this time, they're going to be strategic. And as predicted, Grant's lawyer argued that the judge in the case had not permitted to hear Grant's pleading that they say would have corroborated their claims of a not guilty verdict.

However, on a plus point, the fact that Grant had not been present in court, leaving his lawyers to handle matters, was generally, according to chatter around the courthouse, frowned upon by judges. In judge's speak: if you can't be bothered to attend your own hearing, why should I bother to read your case?

I didn't go back to court for the verdict. I opened the email containing the judgment like a condemned woman on death row waiting to see if she'd received a last-second pardon.

However, it turned out, I had nothing to worry about.

Upon appeal, the original verdict was upheld on November 27th, 2017 and again by the Court of Cassation: The Highest and final level of litigation on February 19th, 2018. All three courts found Grant guilty.

And the findings of the court would count as evidence in the subsequent civil trial. The guilty verdict and file were approved for me to claim my civil rights and seek through civil proceedings compensation including and above my investment. So, if I wanted my money back, there was still some road to travel. That's another day in another courtroom. But this little moment here was happiness. To stop him was worth it. It wasn't about the money; it was about the principle.

Yes, the single fine was pathetic – the old rogue was only fined AED 2,000 (try defrauding a police, judge or prosecutor and watch the sentence miraculously fit the crime) but the feeling was, so what? It was a guilty verdict and that was what I wanted. It was enough to prevent this happening again to others. I felt triumphant. He never, ever thought that he would be held accountable. He thought he was invincible. We proved otherwise.

We had nimbly avoided the traditional fate of rogue financial advisors down the ages. For years, Grant's predecessors have been solidly saved and rarely saw the inside of a police station never mind a courtroom. Today, the lawyers were hailing this case as a significant landmark because for the first time a financial advisor had been taken to criminal court and judgment was ruled in the victim's favour. The line was drawn of what is right and what is wrong, and intolerance. It will start the process of making rogues in the financial advisory space accountable for cheating people and for other victims not to be afraid to take them on.

In comparison to other judicial systems, it's the same penalty as in the UK for operating without a licence but a much higher financial penalty. In a recent High Court case a doctor was fined £14,000 for running an unlicensed transgender clinic where she prescribed sex-change hormones for children as young as 12. She was ordered to pay £11,307 in costs. It was still a criminal conviction, despite no jail sentence, much to the public dismay.

Here, Grant is somebody who is not ever going to work with money again. And that was a huge relief. Like I had done my bit. That I had taken one rogue off the streets.

He will never work as a financial advisor again. He will never cheat clients again. The court verdict made sure of that. It was written on paper in ink. By a judge in a criminal court of law.

Or so I thought.

What followed was, well … nothing.

"Hello." I said into the receiver.

"Hello, Amber?"

His line went dead.

His first call of the day was at 6 am.

Her second call of the day went to my office at 12 pm, the third call to my home address in the UK.

And so the pattern continued for almost two years.

CHAPTER 6

THE SOUND OF SILENCE

ᴕ The pen is always mightier than the sword ᴕ

Nothing happened, in a very weird and rather uncomfortable way.

It first occurred to me that Grant's business partners may not know about the conviction. So I contacted them and asked, "Haven't you been informed?".

The echoing silence from them was even louder.

Grant continued working and acted as though nothing had happened – as did his employer and Guardian and the like, all of whom had received a copy of the judge's verdict.

I let that sink in.

Did they read the judgment right?

Did everyone understand what the man just got convicted for?

After the criminal conviction, nothing changed. It barely caused a ripple in financial circles.

Everybody looked the other way.

And that's what makes this story all the more remarkable and I think that is one of the tragedies of the case, that Grant was allowed to just resume business as usual. It was troubling to find out that Grant's partners kept the victims in the dark intentionally and they continued working with Grant and allowed him to sell their products to current investors and to new investors, all of whom had no idea they were signing their savings away.

No one seemed apprehensive about the consequences of his conviction or concerned with the fact that Prosperity Offshore Investment Consultants was an illegal set up and that the Prosperity Management Consultancy licence had expired in 2016.

To share one example: In November 2017, I held a meeting with insurance giants, Friends Provident International, also known as FPI within the industry. They are one of the biggest providers of expensive fixed-term investment plans, and, like most insurers, pays advisors high commissions on the sale of fixed-term products. In light of Grant's conviction, I told them that they needed to look out for their clients. As the managers nodded their heads unanimously they said that they were all deeply concerned about this news and the potential impact on their clients and that they were determined to understand the full details of what has happened and would communicate these to investors and stakeholders as soon as possible. Although I didn't expect them to discuss the practicalities in detail with me, I left the meeting with a pretty good inkling that something was going to happen.

I followed up with them three times.

Nothing had happened.

They had a criminal verdict in their hands. What was there to think about? A superficial investigation into the matter would yield proof of the conviction.

I once again followed up with them, where I said I was worried about the effect of keeping this development from their clients. "When we last spoke you assured me that, although you cannot inform me what action you will be taking, you will be taking some action to safeguard the victims of Grant and their interests, and at the very minimum, you will be informing the clients of the verdict so they can make the decision if they wanted to continue to work with Neil Grant or not."

No response. My vocal disapproval at the lack of action from the company had started seeping upwards. Finally, months after my first meeting with them, I received an email from their managing director, in the UK.

"You are not a policyholder of Friends Provident International and have no connection with our business, we are unable to comment on this matter any further and will not engage in any future correspondence with you with respect to the same."

Like a fly, I was squatted.

I came to learn from Grant's victims that they haven't heard anything from Friends Provident International at all. They certainly hadn't written to all the investors to say what was happening. In fact, they continued to work with him.

I had thought maybe their reason for the delay in actioning anything was that Friends Provident International wanted to try to 'manage' the message, and part of managing that message was engaging with the agencies, such as PR companies or regulators. I didn't expect them to manage the message by not messaging anything at all to their clients.

What this meant in practice is that they took the third way – to do nothing about it. They had gone into steely negative 'no action required' mode. Why, why, why?

"Was that a consensus decision in your office?" I asked the senior manager.

Hesitant.

"It was a broadly held decision," was the response.

Did they think what their silence would mean to other people? The other victims? Or were they so cavalier they didn't care?

How many investors will Grant have come into contact with? Advising them? Why did they not allow considerations of public interest and client interest to be paramount?

It's pivotal because it raises important questions about how some financial companies treat their investors, their practices and policies, and how they exercise their dominant position in the market.

My fear was that some of them had a natural inclination, a predisposition in favour of protecting and defending rogue financial advisors, and a prejudice against the rights of the clients and what is in the public interest. This is a disturbing thought. There has always been a shockingly complacent attitude to morality in the financial services world, where the bar for acceptable behaviour seems entirely conditional on an advisor's success and ability to make others successful.

For as one advisor told me: "We all feed from the same trough".

And he's right.

My guess? They were too busy counting.

It had nothing to do with loyalty. Grant was a great connector for all the big companies. The common people are nothing but pawns in a game for greed and power by a selective few.

The whole purpose of obtaining a court verdict was to stop him. And yet the reality was, the court verdict was doing nothing to stop Grant, people were still getting fleeced because the industry was still supporting him. Yes, the victims were conned by Grant but they were re-victimised by his partners whose main job was to protect their interests. They muted their voices.

On top of that, Grant was giving contradictory accounts to everyone on the criminal conviction. Turning everything around, leading everyone to believe, black was white and white was black. In fact, he was saying that all the charges had been dropped, and that he had to pay AED 2,000 administration fee to receive his passport back from the Dubai courts. He tried to play if off like that. The very fact that he felt no shame about what he had done or not recognising the judge's ruling of his conviction tells you all you need to know about how serious this issue had become.

With all these contradictory accounts buzzing around, friends had no idea which direction to follow. This tipped me over the edge. Someone had to put their hand up and say, "He can't just get away with this and resume business as usual".

But how do you clear a hurdle like that? How do you hold them all accountable?

There are moments in your life where you just have to take everything a notch higher and go for it. I had no choice. I had to bring the crime back into focus.

Winning a court case gives you back a piece of yourself. To stand up and say this is wrong, it shouldn't have happened to me, and I don't want it to happen to anybody else.

In high profile cases, there are two trials: outside the courtroom and inside. The court of public opinion is very important and often overlooked. That's the real trial. People may say you need a "good lawyer" to get a result, but I was to learn you need a "good journalist" to actually stop ruthless people.

All hail *The National*

The National, a private English-language daily newspaper

published in Abu Dhabi, was steadfast in a review on the story following a few meetings with the newspaper's key journalist, British National, Nick Webster. They were interviewing numerous people over the last few years as financial advisory fraud was quietly escalating. But this particular story stood out for them; not least because it was elaborately planned and premeditated – but because Grant had got away with it for so long. An additional celebratory point for me was that *The National* has one of the most diverse readerships across all the Gulf newspapers and I knew the story would get across, as well as the message. The story was more complicated, far more complicated, because the regulation system varies from country to country, and I didn't want to get the message tangled up with that and for Grant to use that as a technical acceptable reason why he did what he did. Financial advisors were already suggesting to me that he was "probably a good advisor but got caught up in the technicalities of the law".

Sorry, No.

This really wasn't a case about regulatory systems and loopholes. The point of this case is that there was no consent here to defraud investors.

The journalists from *The National* got to work on the article. They contacted Grant's victims and they told them they had this investigation going on in Dubai and they wanted to get as much information as they could. If they had three people on the record willing to stand by me, with the victim's experience being used to compose the article, they would run it, even if Grant threatened to sue on the grounds that the article was completely inaccurate.

Nathan wanted to be interviewed for the newspaper, and many other victims agreed to be interviewed alongside him. Understandably, they spoke anonymously to the newspaper, not wanting their name to be known, apprehensive that they would be judged if their peers knew they were one of the 'duped' ones. Being taken advantage of by someone who was so cunning, so depraved, is something that most people are embarrassed to admit. "They wouldn't trust me or my advice after knowing this," was a comment routinely shared with me. And fair enough.

I, on the other hand, was not afraid of looking naive and stupid; I had passed that line months ago.

Grant was, of course, entitled to a right of reply.

With every article, *The National* had continued to give Grant and his employer the chance to comment. Which meant that Grant knew we were running the story and he was offered the chance to comment on the specific content of the article, and for *The National* to interview him. He chose not to respond to the invitations and equally his employer declined to comment. But Grant's employer in Dubai wanted this to go away.

There were calls to reporters and notices to make the story disappear. Financial companies have always avoided trouble by having lawyers on hand to aggressively silence any person or media body who might be tempted to point the finger.

Supported by their editor, the journalists were not deterred. Great, I thought that would have been the biggest hurdle that we cleared. I was wrong.

The story then had to go through for legal review and sign-off. "We have a very, very experienced legal team. This has to be vetted." I entirely understood, and agreed with the newspaper.

The entire Gulf had strict reporting restrictions. Every newspaper follows a protocol that checks every story before it's sent out into the world. It's signed off by an internal media lawyer before an outside law firm is hired to review the final article before it's published. Every comment has to be substantiated; every word is checked for mistakes. There is no room for error, especially in Dubai.

Top media lawyers were parachuted in to help get the story within the legal guidelines, and to sign the story off; big names that has previously been stamped on approval documents in legal offices of media organisations across the country. They were described as "the safest pair of hands you'll get". As time went on, however, none of these big names were raising their marigold hands to approve the story.

Eventually one of them would put their hand up and sign this story off, surely?

Nope.

"You know what they always say?" Nathan reminded me. "When in doubt do nothing."

There were just so many layers. I felt the lawyers were acting a little cautiously because they knew there could be blowback from Grant's lawyers, which ultimately would come back on them. They wanted guarantees on every single point as if it were a contractual negotiation. Even though the article was written while Grant was living elsewhere, presumably in Scotland, the UAE cyber-crime laws meant that a prosecution could be brought. The journalists and I had no concerns as the story was backed up by comprehensive evidence.

One of the lawyers actually came back with a checklist, asking the newspaper to check they had followed the guidelines, implying they could sign it off themselves. 'Make sure you've stated this correctly' and 'Make sure you've checked this correctly'.

Meanwhile, another lawyer just wanted to prove the myth that 'lawyers can make things complicated' and also hellishly hard work to sign anything off: "Although lots of these plans are dodgy and mis-sold, many of the people who take them out do sign papers in advance acknowledging the high-risk nature of the investments so they can be risky but not necessarily illegal."

Had he even bothered to read the judgment or know what the story is about?

He went on to share another observation which showed that he clearly had not.

"What does the fact that Grant was British have to do with anything in terms of trustworthiness? Just my opinion but that kind of reduces my sympathy for her plight."

Which led me to spill: who was actually going to have the balls to sign this off?

The editorial team kept pushing on; we were all extremely frustrated at the pace of it.

Another lawyer, eventually, just said it, "Does AW know all of this will be used under her name?".

After feeling myself drowning under a tsunami of competing media legal advice from the big branded named lawyers, I put my own marigold hand up. It's okay. Just get the story out.

Finally, three months into the approval process, we went to print, and the official line was Grant's name could be published after it was agreed that it was in the public interest for his identity to be known.

The night before the story broke, I thought of the impact this was going to have on many people. Tomorrow, Grant's friends would discover that he had been operating illegally as a financial advisor and they would check their policies and whatever he had sold to them, which they were still paying money into. Many of them would discover their investment had plummeted in value and was worthless.

That was quite scary. Tomorrow was going to be complete mayhem. And an appalling day for many people. It was a bad, bad feeling. But at least they could stop pouring money into worthless investments.

It would also no doubt elicit a few yelps of nautical language up in say, Scotland.

If you're going to do it, do it with a bang

Is anyone surprised?

Appalled, yes.

Horrified, yes.

Sickened, yes.

But surprised?

I doubt anyone was genuinely surprised by the breaking all too familiar news that yet another rogue inexperienced financial advisor has done it again – fleeced his non-experienced cautious investor clients. That yet another British foreigner caught making a mockery of Dubai's rules.

Except by the name.

January 29th, 2018 and Neil Grant is named in *The National,* as the convicted financial advisor at the centre of a criminal case.

Imagine the scene. You're casually opening up the newspaper and a familiar face peers back at you and the headline "Rogue" in type so large you'd think he'd been assassinated. And then the penny drops.

The morning had passed peacefully. I had seen a draft of the article but hadn't yet read it online. Just before midday my phone began to buzz and ping incessantly from friends and acquaintances who had spotted my name in the paper. And then all hell broke loose. Grant's clients had started bombarding *The National* news desk with calls asking for more information, clarification, any form of assistance, and asking if they could reach me. Texts, emails, phone calls and alerts were arriving in a torrent so fast I had no time to reply.

"Hi there! How are you?" they began. "I saw your name in the newspaper regarding Neil Grant!"; routinely followed by "OMG all my investments were through Prosperity Offshore Investment Consultants".

The effect was instant and impactful.

"The shit has hit the fan," warned Nathan's simple text message to me when his colleagues learned the news in his office.

It was clear that nobody outside my 'circle' knew anything about the trial until that day. And Grant and his employer were still keeping the conviction a closely guarded secret.

Meanwhile, emails to Grant went unanswered. Text messages had gone unanswered and calls had been ignored. He had vanished from all modes of communications, and there followed a surreal period during which he seemed to have disappeared entirely, offering neither explanations nor apologies to his many clients. Where was Grant? Why hadn't he called? Why couldn't they get hold of him? The questions were coming to me thick and fast. Some didn't bother to even mince their words: "Where is he? I'll have him". I think he was Irish. And then it just exploded with panic as investors pondered about the only question that mattered: "Have I lost everything?".

Had Grant lied to them? Had he pitched them a vison of their dream life, but sold them their worst nightmare? Are their Trusts and policies empty? Understandably, they went absolutely nuts. No one bays for the blood of a human more than a raging victim of money-related crime.

Wouldn't anyone in that situation?

The National was quickly on the follow up with this exclusive, and did a range of heavyweight articles and commentary. Lawyers were now commenting on the case from a legal standpoint and personal finance experts – a mix of Fund Managers and leading Independent Financial Advisors were being interviewed calling Grant nothing more than a "failed salesman".

"Expats are putting their financial futures in the hands of unregulated advisors who have little experience or qualifications," said one expert. "These people are not financial advisors; they are salespeople."

Lawyers operating in the world of the white-collar crime said the criminal verdict was important and a "landmark" because, "Grant's judgment is the first of hundreds of similar cases that have previously failed. This particular case has set out a roadmap for other prosecutions in this area. It will give a number of people hope".

After *The National*'s articles, and realising that it was newsworthy material, the rest of the media duly followed, with the story becoming front-page news. You can never underestimate the level of people's curiosity when it comes to a scandal. And financial advisory fraud always gets people going. Bit of intrigue. Bit of mystery. Who did it this time? And to whom? And all set here in a gilded city silhouetted against a golden setting sun. What more do you want in a story? All you're missing is a gruesome murder.

A photo of Grant grinning in his office against a backdrop of Dubai had become the defining image of the scandal.

"That picture should really come with graphic warning," Nathan was full of great humour. "Seeing him grinning like a Cheshire Cat put me off my Coco pops this morning." Nathan is really quick. Like when I told him Grant appeared in court sporting a deep tan after sunbathing, he said, "Did he melt?".

An article written in *The Times* newspaper in London generated extremely high visibility for the case in the UK. Though interestingly, the Scottish paper, *The Scotsman* wouldn't run the story. I later found out the reason through one of the victims. Grant's whereabouts had largely been unknown since he left Dubai. However, five months later, after purchasing a one-way ticket out of the sandpit, he resurfaced in the Scottish newspaper, of all places. Ironically, the editor had just done a piece on Grant and his wife celebrating settling back in Scotland after twenty successful years in Dubai and showcasing their wonderful new six-bedroom house in the Scottish borders. The supreme irony didn't go unnoticed by those whipping up the fervour who were quite enjoying it. One publication splashed a headline "He's on the Run" – yeah, in Scotland!

Gathering momentum, the story was getting picked up everywhere, including internationally. I counted fourteen different publications with all the papers deliberately choosing pictures of Grant looking suitably smug and jowly to go with it.

"I'm Dave am I," joked Nathan.

We all have a mate called Dave.

The victims come forward

Grant's story is as big as it gets in a small city. So when the news broke, we started realising the gravity of a British Dubai based millionaire and the stories from other victims that we were starting to hear, revealing the appalling scale of Grant's actions.

He targeted expats – something that most financial advisors do, of course. I think when you are an expat in any country, we instantly look for someone who we can relate to at some level. The first step in the grooming process is spotting a vulnerable victim, someone who is financially uneducated or already have some financial trauma in their past. Rogue financial advisors like Grant have an eye for picking out someone who is in need of something, and they identify that need and then they exploit it. When you're pairing a financially uneducated person with a brilliant sales conman, our untrained brain is not equipped to understand or react to what was happening.

All of the victims emphasised the same basic theme: they were manipulated in a unique way. They were made to feel responsible. And they were offered opportunities that could get them out of their life circumstances. And the added bonus that they didn't have to do anything themselves, or spend time on it. They could focus on other priorities. He offered them something that he knew they wanted, and needed. And he made them feel that, basically, they were lucky to be in his presence and had avoided being conned by other rogue advisors. It was just a glorified manipulation thing he had going on and that worked. On all of us.

Victim after victim, the names differed but the denouement was the same: they were introduced to him through a friend, they invested with him expecting good returns from long-term funds, and he had promised them they will be able to see good financial return on the Trusts, funds and policies. They had all made it clear to him that they didn't want to gamble on financial investments with money they couldn't afford to lose. At some point, Grant requested they all provide him a Power of Attorney over their financial affairs. I was astonished at the volume of men who did this. His victims were not the type of guys who give up control over anything, let alone their own money. But, again, it was all part of the manipulation.

And for those clients still sitting on the 'should I, shouldn't I invest?' fence, Grant had a different approach. "I said no, a lot of ways, a lot of times, and he always came back at me, returning for second or third meetings, with some new ask," one victim said. "It was all this bargaining, this coercive bargaining routine", until she eventually relented and purchased something.

The experiences were identical. They were all literally in the same select few policies and the same funds. Very interesting modalities of partnerships. Grant had been hugely successful at selling Bamboo (Eco Planet) investment fund in South America to his clients that, unknown to them, was a start-up and classed as extremely risky. Investors now discovered it was not only suspended, legally they should never have been allowed to invest in the fund as they did not qualify in terms of what the Isle of Man regulator calls a "Qualified Investor". Now we learned an eco-friendly investment scheme would be unprofitable. Eco-friendly and return on investment are incompatible. In fact, anything with green or eco in front of it will send you broke. Ask the government and local councils how much they've wasted.

For many, Grant put most of their money into New Earth, a waste recycling firm he said was an "up and coming" green earth fund and was sure to take off. It had plummeted spectacularly. News was shared of a fund called Forsyth. Grant ploughed investors' money into this fund which two partners had bought to him. After several meetings, Grant spent the next two nights and day using his Power of Attorney privileges and invested his clients' money into the fund. Two days later the fund crashed. Grant still picked up his commission.

There were many stories of how he talked trusting clients into moving their cash out of relatively safe pensions and investment funds to instead put their money into these type of start-up companies. Other such funds included Lucent (Land Purchase and Planning); Brandeaux student accommodation; Centurion (Life Insurance Settlement); Prime (Burj) India; Aliquot Precious Metals – all high-risk funds but giving a false impression that the fund was low-risk and offered higher returns. He was simply gambling his clients' futures on the spin of a roulette wheel.

There's a big difference between people who invest because they believe in a project and people who invest due to a good return. I suspect none of Grant's clients were talked through the plans and designs of these funds; they simply heard how much money they could save for their future. It goes without saying that if they had known they were investing in these illiquid alternative investments – which provide no opportunity for capital appreciation, and an extremely modest projected absolute return for the risk involved – they would point-blankly have refused. Usually, you only put money into illiquid alternative investments chasing the chance of massive upside. This sort of thing is gambling. If we cannot afford to lose, we should not be playing. It's a finger in the air job.

As far as people were concerned Grant was still running 'Prosperity' and were unaware that his 'licence' had expired in June 2016. Sure enough, post 2016, their valuation statements still read Prosperity Offshore Investment Consultants on them. Others were unaware he was an employee of an insurance broker, working under their residence Visa.

I found that the victims ran the entire gamut from those that were thankful that they now knew the truth, others who said that they were happy with the services Grant had provided them, and that their investments were "okay".

To which I would reply – have you actually had them checked out?

I glanced at one investor's valuation statement. He held the same type of Trust in Jersey with Philip Van Neste as I did, and overall, it was showing impressive returns.

However, upon closer inspection I noticed that one of the funds he held in his Trust, New Earth (Waste Recycling), was showing a healthy profit.

Hmmm.

It's 2017. New Earth (Waste Recycling) was suspended, crashed and burned in 2014.

He hadn't even realised that the New Earth (Waste Recycling) fund was suspended, a fact Grant had neglected to mention to him. In a further twist, he didn't even know that his Trust had moved from Jersey to Switzerland and hadn't received Guardian's letter let alone signed authorisation of it. Well, it doesn't get much more hopeless than this. He was one of many to have now received confirmation to dash their hopes of any percentage yield, or even of seeing their original investment again. He was a sitting duck and didn't know it, just like me.

I soon learnt my loss was not big compared to most people. People had lost hundreds and thousands, one had lost an eye-watering million, selling his house to invest, whilst another guy lost all his savings plus his Dad's full pension.

It's amazing looking back at it from the outside – you're like, "Woah, that was hit after hit after hit!". As suspected, many had taken a hands-off approach to managing their money and let Grant handle it, explaining why they didn't notice anything untoward until now.

Investors whose funds hadn't withered away or were not suspended, didn't know whether to abandon their investments that were underperforming or to keep going, and try to stick it out, which would require resilience. It was a terrible predicament. Grant had advised them they had a better chance of not losing it if they kept up their monthly instalments, saying it was their only hope, however remote. But selling and locking in losses is the worst thing investors can do.

I had dropped a call to a friend working for a Chartered Financial Service Provider in the highly-regulated DIFC free zone, asking him if he could do some pro bono work and review clients' investment portfolios. He was eager to help, and was soon inundated with requests but constantly giving investors bad news was starting to wear him down. "Is there anything that could be done to save them?" was the repeated plea.

As all this additional news of losses sunk in, clients went further bonkers on Grant's deceit, affording him the same sort of public tributes as the Yorkshire Ripper.

Other investors were completely honest with themselves about their experience with their financial advisor and shared a different perspective, admitting that their financial advisor made a lot more money for them out of their not very huge capital than they could ever have managed on their own.

Fair enough.

Was your financial advisor a friend? No, was the answer. They had hired a fee-only qualified and highly regulated financial advisor.

We can easily see how we made that mistake.

Partners blow with the wind

The court of public opinion instantly delivered another verdict and declared that Grant's financial partners were equally to blame for Grant's deception. Anticipating this, and a torrent of threatening lawsuits, Grant's partners were ready with their carefully crafted responses and loopholes.

It was interesting that after *The National's* article was published, everyone who had a relationship with Grant, suddenly ... no one really knew him.

Suddenly, "Oh, well, we really weren't partners, I knew him in an ancillary way" or "More like business networking way" or "I haven't worked or spoken to him for decades" and "I am not a big fan. Never was".

It was understandable. Amid the furore over the media articles Grant was now a monumental liability for them. Big corporations usually have knee-jerk reactions to adverse news in the media. They don't want anyone, even Grant, spoiling the party unnecessarily.

It led to the instant high-profile withdrawal of so many financial institutions who sent notifications to their clients that they had now dissociated themselves with Grant, drawing a discreet veil over the reasons for their parting. The manner and speed in which they all ditched him was like watching dominos falling one by one.

Funny that.

It would be funny if it weren't so tragic. They had a physical copy of the judge's verdict five months before the story hit the media – and they had done nothing.

It never ceases to amaze me how being named and shamed brings people back to their senses and suddenly the difference between right and wrong becomes crystal clear. Some trustees said it had launched a review: "We are now learning of serious irregularities, that are deeply concerning, and which we are investigating,". Others said: "We expect to investigate how this criminal was able to register as a financial advisor and put measures in place to make sure it can't happen again".

As insurers and advisors battled it out over who is to blame for poor financial advice in the UAE, Friends Provident International, publicly blamed "the quality of financial advice" for "discontent among customers", making it clear they shared no liability.

As so many victims came forward, the financial

companies collectively wheeled out high-powered lawyers to rely on the throwaway clause deeply embedded somewhere in the Terms and Conditions, that you have agreed to appoint Grant as your investment manager, as per the Prescribed Direction document Grant had got you to sign at the very first meeting. This clause meant that these companies are legally protected, making any lawsuit against them thrown out from the very beginning. They made this very clear to all the victims when approached. A typical response was as follows:

"The Company does not provide investment advice, nor does it recommend any specific assets to link to a policy, as these are matters for your duly appointed Independent Financial Advisor. This Contract was taken out upon advice from your Independent Financial Advisor, who is in no way associated with the Company. As the Company played no part in the sale of the Contract, we am unable to comment on the advice received prior to submitting your Application."

Some companies even argued that the investors make the final decision. The advisors were just expressing their opinions, and their opinions and recommendations were merely advisory and you shouldn't "rely on it".

Interesting tactic.

Their response, without the slightest trace of apology, did little to deter the resentment that has been boiling harder than a pan of rasp jam within the expat community.

Where is he?

"So you don't know where he is right now?" I was frequently asked.

"Not absolutely sure."

Grant himself answered the question.

Scotland as we suspected.

Eventually, seven days after the news broke, Grant surfaces and emailed his clients with a litany of bombshell claims in response to *The National's* story:

"I was found to have fallen foul of a technicality on my license and was asked to pay a fine of 2000 AED. In reality, therefore, you may see little change, and you can be assured that you will continue to hear from me on a regular basis as your appointed advisor."

Come again?

It read as an update about stock that had dipped a pound at the opening bell, but by noon had found itself sufficiently corrected and adjusted and was now weathering the brief storm; or a doctor saying to you, "Listen, I don't have a licence that technically says I am a doctor, but, hey, don't worry, I'm still going to perform your kidney transplant next week".

I wondered if he'd been misquoted, or misleadingly paraphrased.

One read of his email confirmed he hadn't.

And there was more. He went on to write he actively worked for his employer and his associates and referenced his active UAE residence Visa. Essentially, he'd been planning to set up a new life with his family back home, whilst still working for his Dubai employer, using their licence to place business.

He had a horrifying ability to talk about his criminal conviction in a detached, almost casual manner. He was acting as if it were a mere trifle. As a victim, I think one thing we ask for is some acknowledgement and some remorse. Grant had not shown a scintilla of remorse.

Privately to his clients, Grant came out fighting with his boxing gloves, slamming the anonymous clients for their "disgraceful lies" in the newspaper article and on "THAT

WOMAN".

To one particular client-friend he spouted biting commentary about the whole case and wrote that he had written to "ALL" of his partners and provided them with a copy of the judge's verdict which was a fine "purely based upon a missing activity on our 'old' 2004 licence", before adding "FACT".

With the two words "missing activity", Grant reduced his illegal activity to a casual, dismissive punchline. They were actually important "missing activities" because it meant he was not legally allowed to manage money under his licence. The emails made clear he was spinning the narrative to confused investors who were on the fence, torn between loyalty for a long-time friend and the very real possibility that they may be one of the 'duped' ones.

It turns out nobody had received a copy of the verdict nor did he share a copy with his clients.

He had right to sue for defamation – if it was untrue. Only if *The National* was sloppy and wrote critical things about Grant that are not true. In order to sue and win a claim of defamation, he would have to prove that the newspaper was intentional or reckless in their claims, and that he was harmed by their untruths.

He wouldn't sue, of course, because he couldn't. It was all true. In 2004, Neil Ramsay Pringle Grant faced his own decision and moral choice: whether or not to start cheating his friends for money to boost his own income and lifestyle. Grant chose to start the deception. And it was to run for fourteen years.

Of all the unanswered questions about Grant's deception, perhaps the most intriguing choruses all is: Did the wife know? Was the woman who shared Grant's life really unaware of his true persona?

I always wondered: at first, I thought not.

"Really, no inkling of his crimes?" It was a staple of everyday conversation in Grant's circle.

I gave her the benefit of the doubt.

Until I learned from one of the victims who, a few years back, had worked with the family, that all the commission cheques were sent to her. One cheque she had seen was for the sum of £95,000, earned from one client alone. It's unclear, however, how much involvement his wife actually had in the selling aspect of the business.

There has been a general shock that we've all been duped by her, too. Believing there might be grounds for charging her as an accessory.

As far as I was concerned, the media did its job and shone a much-needed spotlight on the couple. One week after Grant's email to his clients, under mounting pressure and client outrage, Grant's employer terminated him.

Now he changed his email and phone number and, the ultimate smack in the face – he blocked clients from Facebook. Ouch! He totally disappeared.

Now, Grant's victims were gunning.

Some wrote to the local council from where he hailed from to let them know what he was up to. Others wrote on Social Media, one resourceful victim contemplated hiring a private investigator to track him down.

One of the victims was a member of British Dads Dubai Group, and posted a message "Does the name Neil Grant mean anything to anyone?". The question naturally inspired some parody posts from parents at the same school his children attended. Conman, fraud, arrogant … were some of the nicer tame terms, as they made reference to how he had built up his multi-million pound income.

They hadn't just caught a financial advisor cheating on them, they'd caught a family friend cheating on them whom they had spent the past decades socialising with, attending charity balls, kids parties, play dates you name it they shared it – someone they had provided with their intimate details. In turn, he has spent his time conning everyone.

It's hard to imagine a worse betrayal, isn't it?

Well …

Victim's stories: the other side of the money

Take for instance the story of Sarah, that encapsulated the betrayal.

I think I was much more sympathetic with this particular victim at the time. It was very personal, the betrayal that she suffered, and it came at a heavy price.

Incredibly, while the prosecution was investigating his crime, and the trial was going on, Grant and his wife ploughed on with their deceit on more unsuspecting friends. Sarah, a family friend of ten years, was sold a plan where Grant would make $115,000 in commission in just one year from her alone. Throughout the court case, lonely and left to his own devices, he had leaned on her when his own wife couldn't cope and fled the country. And how did Grant reward this act of apparent kindness? He had been fleecing her during the whole time – whilst her investments had deteriorated for its own multi-complicated plethora of reasons to the tune of £475,000.

Grant had told her that he was being prosecuted by the criminal court on the charges of fraud. He had even shared my name with her and despite having a surprising amount of knowledge on the case, she hadn't once thought of questioning him or asking me, or even check her investments. At the beginning I found her story crazily ludicrous. It was very hard for me to wrap my head around the fact that she didn't check his story.

"He was a friend," she simply said. And I immediately

resonated with her. She really was in this 'friend' bubble and certainly could not have foreseen she would be the friend he would one day fleece. It's what I had said to the police officer when he had incredulously questioned me on why I hadn't seen any warning signs about Grant's operation and had just handed over my money to him.

And I would have done exactly the same myself. It was like Rupert telling me that someone was accusing him of fraud. I would have gone absolutely mental at the person. I would never have questioned him.

Fleecing her whilst she had been a pillar of support, listening to his endless fears was a particularly cruel twist. He knew she had earmarked part of the money to pay for her children's education.

"That's why I have all the lines on my face," she joked. But no doubt Grant's behaviour had accounted for more than a few grey hairs over the years.

She helped him emotionally as he was leaving Dubai. He was so nervous going through immigration, detailing his fears to her on What's App as he walked through passport control, scared that he was going to get stopped at any moment. He didn't rest until the plane was in the air. In hindsight he had indeed been incredibly lucky because just four days later his passport was stamped as 'Wanted' in the immigration system, meaning he was wanted for questioning over a case Nathan had now opened with the police.

Her letter to Grant summed up what every victim was now feeling and makes uneasy reading.

Dear Neil,

I was very uneasy about the conversations we were having on mail and particularly with your lack of communication since the last one and therefore thought I would take matters into my own hands and seek advice from another Financial Advisory firm.

(Name removed) and I have been subjected to huge upset, disappointment and misery from our findings. It has been calculated that you have received over our 3 FPI plans $115,000 in commission not including any management fees over the past 7 years!

You encouraged me to keep opening new funds and warned me NOT to touch them within the first 18 months otherwise there would be a huge penalty to us in doing so. This was a complete lie and was all for your personal gain so that you could get 3 x commissions it was not enough for you to just get the management fee for the funds. You could have advised us to pay more into one fund but no that would have been no money to you! I have been informed that this is not legal to do in the UK so you took advantage here in Dubai. When I discussed the funds with you and showed concern you reassured me that the funds were up so nothing to worry about so we continued and ploughed more money into the schemes feeling proud we were doing the right thing. Of course when selling these plans to me you cleverly omitted a very important fact about your commission basis with FPI, what fool would ever take on these plans if this was clearly explained to them before signing a contract that the first 18 months would be paid out to the Financial Advisor for commission?

I am beyond words, I thought you were more than our Financial Advisor you became a friend over the 10 plus years yet all the time it was fake, it was you just trying to win me over to trust you as I did so you could get your hands on our money.

I have one question – WHY? where is this ethical, honest or fair. You know our circumstances, you know how upset I have been over the years that my family, rarely see their Dad because he is always working to pay for schooling, invest in what we thought were worthwhile funds for school fees and a pension for (name removed) and I in the future. You also know that I work full time to manage our money and try and do the right thing, sacrificing time with my children. You don't give a damn about us!

Lastly and most importantly I was a huge support to you with this case that you have been going through. I felt so desperately sad for you and Abi and the kids that you were going through such a horrific time. I was supportive and generous with my time, listening to your desperation but all the time you were screwing us over too.

I dread to think what has happened to others, we have lost a huge amount of our life savings and our dreams are shattered we need to start all over again ......

I hope you manage to sleep at night Neil Grant.

(signed)

When people ask me why I pursued Grant and the like with such tenacity, it was against this backdrop; hearing these kinds of deeply upsetting stories on an almost daily basis.

That time in my life was crazy.

The media articles and the victim's stories were

something that I had never dealt with before. Once I started talking, it freed the others to say the same.

I was a regular at Starbucks, meeting investors who needed to "talk" and get some "help". "Are you interviewing for something?" asked the coffee guy at one point as I ordered yet another chocolate chip frappe. Only a few words into their story, I recognised it. I knew this story, start to finish. It's my story. They're saying my story back to me.

I was an advisor, consultant, coach, motivator – all in one to victims who were terrified at the consequence of learning that they had lost their life savings. It was a bolt out of the blue to them. They had never experienced something like this. And they wanted someone to hold their hand and they needed to feel some comfort right at this moment. But there's power in more than one person. There's definitely strength in numbers. I think people feel more comfortable to come forward when they know they're not alone, and finding support from each other is a huge way towards healing.

I think Grant's victims in particular, have an unspoken bond that many people won't ever understand. This is not someone who went rogue because they were seduced by the trappings of money and success and the Dubai lifestyle. This is someone who started as rogue. Who met me and others, with the intention to deceive us, by forging a relationship with us, and robbing us.

And I'm not just talking about robbing us in terms of money, only. I'm talking about peace of mind, energy, self-confidence, trust in others. He was making money whilst thousands of us had lost everything. It's humiliating and embarrassing. You're the man of the household, your job is to protect your family and your future financial security has just disappeared. That's rough. When you're suddenly no longer the family financial security guard anymore – when you've lost that label, you don't know who you are for a while. For years I think a lot of them struggled and probably still struggling to this day.

There has been, of course, a general shock that we've all been duped. Questions were being asked as to whether it is credible that Grant could have misused his licence so blatantly without anyone knowing. "Why did no one challenge him sooner?" the question was on repeat mode. To which I reflected; it is strange that there has never been a whisper of him being suspicious before. Actually, I was wrong.

Some of Grant's acquaintances came forward to say they had suspected he was fraud; his long-time friend had even named him in a letter to the Central Bank of the UAE. Stories came out that people had raised concerns with Grant in the past but that he had got them to go away and had each time managed to escape any kind of accountability. They had shared too much with their financial advisor – I'm guessing they had shared some skeletons in the closet with him and if they ever did take him to court, those skeletons would turn up – probably at Inland Revenue, or their wife's email inbox. It was very clear to me that was Grant's MO; to hold things over people. After speaking to so many victims of Grant's, there was a pattern developing. He had a lot of information on a lot of people. Case in point, when Grant replied to Sarah's email, he subtly referred to helping her out with "a problem"; a thinly veiled warning should she pursue anything against him.

One client in particular spoke candidly about how he had made some noise about Grant back in 2010 and had made some headway in his investigations before he was slapped with a legal notice. Grant got a lawyer onto him and threatened him with defamation following an acrimonious email war between the two former friends. To the vast majority there's something about the word 'lawyer' that shrivels the organs and fills the soul with foreboding. Everyone fears lawyers and having the 'full force of the law' thrown at them. If you are not used to the legal world, receiving such threats can be intimidating. Fear was their greatest asset. That's what gave them their power. And up until that moment it had worked. Clients had backed down.

He showed me the legal notice. The name on the stationery was impressive. An international law firm. The notice read, basically, your accusations are baseless and deeply offensive, unpleasant and a hurtful attack on Grant.

Surprisingly, at the time, even his own lawyer hadn't checked him out or checked his license or credentials.

However, the legal notice was too threatening and almost juvenile: "We put an advocate on watch at the Dubai Courts if you try anything". It was not the language of someone acquainted with the legal world. From my experience lawyers would not make such threats, and if they make a point they back it up with reference to a law. The notice wasn't signed by anyone which was not unusual as most firms sign off with the Firm's signature, so we couldn't see who sent it.

I was pretty sure the legal notice had been written by one of Grant's friends who worked for the firm in some sort of support capacity – like business development or human resources. But it had done the job. The investor had backed off too scared to take things further against Grant. He had been silenced.

To the old clients that emerged with their experiences following the newspaper article, in the Facebook of his mind Grant unfriended all of them years ago. That's why I think the number of victims could be much higher because it is thought some victims may be too ashamed to come forward, or have their hands tied behind their backs.

To think that Grant could have been stopped years ago. But, unfortunately, he wasn't.

There was a huge gratitude towards *The National*, and in particular, Nick Webster who despite a high-level risk of threats with this article, still went ahead with the publication. He could face direct legal action personally, and trusted the contents of the story. He helped stop Grant in his tracks and prevent other investors from losing their savings. What the likes of Grant had not counted on was the crazed world of social and mainstream media whose pen is always mightier than the sword and is really the only life-line you may have. In our case, it finally stopped the fraudster in his tracks – a fortunate man who rode his luck until his luck finally ran out.

The wider circle

With news stories, there will be a bit of initial novelty value and then it will be obscurity. This story was different. It went beyond just Grant's victims. I was to quickly learn, what had affected me so profoundly was experiencing something that affects, at some point, almost half of the expats in the Middle East: financial advisory fraud.

Since *The National's* article about Grant's conviction, our revelations caused unease amongst other investors who decided to check out their financial advisors and their investment practices, and many realised they too had been stung. After checking the true value of their pensions and portfolios they had lost most or all of their money in high-risk schemes that yielded their advisors high commissions.

As I found additional victims, one victim would tell me about others who would then tell me about others, and it began to multiply exponentially.

After two or three months I feared financial advisors

were a universal problem – it's the same everywhere. The victims who weighed in against Grant dispelled any notion that it's simply disgruntled investors trying to blame their financial advisor for their lost investment. The problem is not confined to Grant. Far from it. And, as we shall see, the sheer number of mis-selling complaints, and ugly lawsuits making their way into the public domain suggests an industry-wide problem only just starting to come to light.

And every single right-minded person within the industry knows this is going on, and yet nothing has been done about it.

After such media articles, you will hear any number of wild-eyed commentators on the news channels speculating grandly about what will happen next. But most decent investors will be sitting at home, subdued, not holding their breath.

They've heard it all before. Nothing will happen. Nothing will change.

'You have been served'

I've announced the publication of this book and, as I predicted when I started writing it, the instant hysterical reaction perfectly exemplifies why I needed to write it. A legal notice popped up in my email box from Friends Provident International, about my decision to mention their company name in my story. The law firm they hired is no stranger to me as they served as counsel for Grant in his defence claim against me. And, so I was no stranger to their approach.

They did not mince their words: 'Make sure, that my client is not in it' was their message otherwise they will come after me – and not under English law, but under Dubai law, quoting Federal Decree by Law No. 5 of 2012, as amended,

Article 20 under Criminal Defamation. Once the book comes out, they've threatened to recover damages in the Dubai civil courts.

This is like the shark from Jaws writing a notice about how the beaches are not safe.

Like slander, libel refers to making a false statement that is harmful to a person's reputation.

The difference lies in how that statement is expressed. Slanderous remarks are spoken while libellous remarks are written and published (which means defamatory tweets could be considered libellous, not slanderous).

Keep in mind what makes a statement libellous or slanderous is its inaccuracy, not its harshness. No matter how nasty a tweet, as long as it's factually correct it cannot be libellous. Truth is an absolute defence to defamation: you might wish a customer hadn't said something derogatory about your business but if what that customer said is true then you have no legal recourse.

I think this is common for some financial institutions: to use fear rather than reason and logic. And they always have more money than the plaintiff. In fact, they have unlimited funds to fight these cases. And their legal notices are designed to hammer that message to the one that has been served creating an intimidating image of a little person against a large powerful corporation. With the latter always coming through.

I will hazard a couple of guesses about their choice of lawyers.

I think it was a coincidence that they hired the same law firm that Grant did during the prosecution investigation and criminal trial. In other words, they opted for criminal lawyers, not media lawyers. Which meant they wanted the story to vanish – just disappear. Media lawyers would have asked to see the book before publication, or at the very least extracts of the book where their client was mentioned to negotiate favourable changes in the narrative.

Or, it's possible, most probably, they just hired 'a lawyer' not aware of the different specialisations.

But why now? It's not like Friends Provident International had only now got wind of the book. Before the book was finalised, I sent an email to everyone named in the book saying, "This book is coming out. By the way, you're named in the book". Although I would never allow my subjects to veto my work, by allowing them to see 'parts' in advance is courteous and allows those involved to challenge key points, if necessary. It allows debate. If they don't agree with something, we can argue it out.

Friends Provident International had taken no action. Until now.

Why now? What was their thinking behind this legal move?

Then the news broke.

Friends Provident International is now back in the headlines as attention turns to other victims filing lawsuits against the powerhouse. A massive class action was being organised. A multi-million pound lawsuit. More than a dozen victims came forward to accuse Friends Provident International of misconduct and of consistently failing these investors "from structuring the products to conceal the true risk of the investments, through to failing to carry out enough due diligence on the high-risk funds which they made available to the investors."

Again the same story. It never changes.

Three funds, including New Earth (Recycling Waste) are at the centre of the scandal – all of which collapsed and rendered the investments worthless. The funds were picked for the investors by their financial advisors, and their money was then invested by the insurers. Investors say they were told their money was safe and believed that because the firms were registered in Britain their investments would be protected by our laws.

But because the investments were not made in Britain, the Financial Conduct Authority, and the Financial Ombudsman Service have no power to act – and victims are not entitled to any of their money back.

Lawyers say the insurers should never have made such risky funds available to novice investors outside of British regulations. Yet the insurers say the blame lies with the investment decisions made by financial advisors.

It's a game of pass-the-parcel.

Hardly surprising, then, Friends Provident International denies wrong-doing or liability. They state: "FPI is exclusively a provider of insurance products and does not provide investment advice. All investments are selected by the policyholder themselves, often with the assistance of an Independent Financial Advisor chosen and appointed by the policyholder to provide personalised advice. FPI does not approve any asset as a suitable investment and is not responsible for investment management or performance."

That big black umbrella, again.

So, their timing may be subject to question because of their motives.

At this point, I felt it's worth reminding them exactly what they did in light of receiving a copy of Grant's criminal conviction: Nothing.

I thought the associate at the law firm did not like my reminder to his aggressive legal notice to me, or the inference that I would continue making my opinion known on issues that matter to me.

I was wrong.

In short, he didn't like the fact that I replied. Period.

Another email promptly landed in my inbox.

"Despite the points of law we outlined to you in our Legal Notice dated 29 April 2020, you still proceeded with issuing the Reply."

I well and truly got my knuckles wrapped as their 'message' was hammered home to me once again.

As George Orwell said: "If liberty means anything at all, it means the right to tell people what they do not want to hear".

So why do I persevere? Did I not hear them? Did I think they didn't mean it?

No, I knew they did.

But wheeling out a legal notice against people to scare them from publicly expressing an honestly held concern for fear of retribution is not the answer. If they know they are in the right, there are questions they need to answer to their clients and they need to focus on that notice.

An unwelcome penny crashes the party

The media attention also caught my former criminal lawyer's revolving eye and they circled back into my life:

"If our due professional fees are not paid within the specified timeframe, we shall have no other option but to file a case against you claiming our unpaid invoices."

Sigh.

I am still living rent-free in their deluded heads, I see.

A positive verdict did not mean they had won the case for me. "You can take any action you deem appropriate," was my boomerang response. They are never going to accept they are wrong.

Six months later, another email arrived. Rather than threaten me with the law courts, they chose a more direct and powerful approach: "If payment is not received within 5 working days other avenues will be taken to recover this debt owed".

Other avenues? Besides the courts what other avenues were left?

I had been suffering from terrible flu – not the ideal physical conditions for a mental tussle with lawyers – and right now every part of my body ached. The thought of being dismembered with a bone saw, or being put through the mincer was rather welcoming.

Oddly, as I amused myself by pondering exactly what they meant, I was in no way worried about it – in fact, I relished the prospect of asking them in court about that invoice in front of a judge. "You can take any action you deem appropriate," continued to be my only response.

Bizarre. Utterly bizarre.

The way things were going, if anyone actually took responsibility for their actions instead of threatening me, that was going to be the miracle of my story.

CHAPTER 7

THE CIVIL TRIAL

⟆ When nothing is certain, everything is possible ⟆

Following the criminal judgment in August 2017, I asked myself the radical new question: "What do I want to do now?".

The answer: I stay the course. I have to see it through. Get back on the rollercoaster, and see if I can win my money back from Grant. Of course, it's still technically possible that we could pull off another miracle like we did in the criminal court.

Come September 2017, my focus was now on the Dubai civil courts.

"What type of representation did you have in mind?" my friends would ask.

"I need a good, but gentle lawyer."

"Gentle?"

"Yes, someone who's not going to rip me off."

"You mean someone cheap?"

"I mean, well, someone reasonable who's actually going to put in the work."

A good friend of mine, who worked in the local legal industry, called me and said he knew of the right lawyer. He had his own law firm dedicated to representing crime victims in civil cases; a small yet successful practice that was well regarded in town.

The only thing was he was based outside the city in Sharjah – one of the smallest and most conservative of the emirates. No alcohol can be drunk anywhere and the only beach where Emirati women can bathe in a swimsuit is overseen by a female lifeguard. Sharjah is about an hour from where I live in Dubai and given the famous horrendous traffic snaking between the two emirates, and unexpected road accidents on the busy highways caused by Michael Schumacher wannabees, it's simply too far away to be a practical option.

I was sceptical, and I had no idea which direction I wanted to go with the case, so I decided to check the referral out.

The building was in no way like the starry buildings of Dubai where all the elite law firms have their regional head offices. In this non-elegant, multi-coloured-brick townhouse building, I had to take an elevator that rattled and mumbled to the fifth floor and then walk down to the fourth floor where the law firm was based. Unfortunately, it didn't give an air of mystique – it simply emphasised how run down the building was and poorly maintained. But as I had learnt during this past year, in my experience, all the best lawyers were not necessarily in the posh elegant buildings or in the tier-ranking legal directories.

There seemed to be only four rooms in the entire office, indescribably messy, piled high with lawyers' papers and a ballooning caseload on desks. Everything looked haphazardly jumbled together. And in the reception a rather large fish tank – maybe they thought it would be particularly stimulating to their creative process. They probably could have afforded to rent a nicer and bigger office, but this suited them just fine.

The lawyer was Egyptian – a round, 50-year-old, grey-haired, bespectacled man of many words and from what I could see a very fiery temper if you got on the wrong side of him – like his assistant, who that morning had no need of a blow dry. Once he relaxed, though, he was thoroughly good company, and did not disappoint: he was fizzing with raw energy, brilliance, and mischievous delight. There was just a touch of French intonation in his speech, which added to his allure. His name, which is easy to remember as he shares it with 95 percent of the Egyptian population, was Ahmed.

The strategy

"Interesting case," he said to me indicating he had never come across one like this before. I was learning fast that this was actually advantageous. It meant they didn't simply tick boxes and it forced them to think outside the box and be innovative. He had reviewed the criminal file, and knew every detail of the case. What was clear, he said, to any legal eye, was that Grant had taken "a scattergun approach" to criticising my overall complaint and their evidence was argumentative and often inconsistent.

I had to smile. I have never, to this day, found a lawyer agree with another lawyer's approach to their legal work.

I took a seat at the small round table in his office and began discussing strategy with him. In his view, our civil case would be centred on the fact that Grant took advantage of me and a number of investors with low financial literacy, and suggested large and risky trades that led to heavy losses for me and profits for him. We would show there were clear parameters about what we would be investing in and what we would not, which he did not follow. Our case would be built around the fact that Grant was not licensed and did not have the experience to provide the service as proven in the criminal courts.

A civil case requires a less stringent test of guilt. Criminal cases require proof the defendant is guilty 'beyond reasonable doubt', whereas civil cases only have to prove that 'on the balance of probability' the defendant is guilty.

But the lawyer wanted me to wait. Wait for what? I'd already spent a year pursing Grant.

No, he wanted me to wait a few months before filing a civil claim – and I needed to trust him.

By now, of course, Grant had already left the country. And it was safe to assume he had no plans coming back to Dubai, not in the immediate future anyway. So filing a civil case against him, without him defending it, was pretty meaningless. But the lawyer didn't want to go after Grant – well, we would of course but he had one ace up his sleeve. He wanted to go after his employer, who were in Dubai and not going anywhere, and whom Grant had officially joined in 2016, but had unofficially been working with for many months prior. It would put pressure on them to bring Grant back into the fold. To make the lawsuit against them legitimate, we needed to wait and gather up more evidence, which he said would take three months. Why? To prove that he was still working for them and employed on their residence Visa, despite relocating to Scotland, and therefore they remained liable for him. We had to build a case against the employer and put it in front of a judge, and these things took time.

The proposition was deliciously intriguing, albeit morally questionable.

There was no way his employer would take the punishment for a criminal practice Grant orchestrated; they would definitely put pressure on him and I was assuming that kind of action must be hard for Grant to live with or ignore. He would have no choice but to surrender and face a trial.

I sat back in my chair pondering on the thought.

The lawyer's strategy was a real possibility, and we could not entirely rule it out. And it was really the only option available to me at this time. I had no contractual arrangement with his employer and it would be a challenge to legally connect them to the case against Grant. The Visa angle was the only way to put pressure on them.

After some discussion, we suspected what must have happened is that Grant approached his new employer and said, "I run Prosperity, and I generate money in the market. I have some rather silly gullible investors that I regularly skin, and we can skin them together. I'm not currently regulated, so I will work with you and I can sell your products and I can sell my products, and you give me a Visa and your licence to place business. If I sell your products, you pay me a commission, and if I sell my products, I'll pay you a commission." That's potentially the arrangement. His employer would, therefore, be allowing a non-regulated financial advisory business to use their license to sell non-insurance products.

That's the theory anyway, and I thought it was bang on the money.

I liked the lawyer, and the strategy was good. In fact, it was a great idea. I liked the fact the lawyer was thinking outside the box and he seemed very dedicated to seeking justice for his clients. I appreciated the fact that he didn't try to discourage me with the unpredictability business of a court case or the slow pace the justice system in the Dubai civil courts.

But if I hired him, I would have to hit 'pause' on the

crusade, and on *The National*'s article (which hadn't been published at this point). We didn't want Grant's employer to fire him before the civil trial commenced, which my lawyer predicted would happen as soon as the article was published.

Three months was a long time. It meant that I was not in touch with my lawyer for weeks or even months. And I had to weigh up the long commute I would now face coming into Sharjah for meetings when the case did begin.

But then again, he was the best lawyer to lead the way.

I hired the lawyer at the meeting; the travel to his offices suddenly became manageable.

"Good," he nodded his head in approval.

"And it won't hurt to find out as many facts about his finances as possible," he advised, "I'm sure he's got plenty but has a good accountant that hides it well. Not everything is visible on the outside."

"I have no idea." It was too early to speculate about that.

And the question mark over his employer, of the morality of the proposition? "It happens all the time in my line of work," he admitted airily. "And if that means bending the rules a little ... well ..."

"It's really bending the rules!" I regarded him thoughtfully. The codes of conduct don't always cover every eventuality. Sometimes you have to make a decision that satisfies the needs of natural justice. I gave a light shrug before giving in. "D'you know what? I'm completely okay with it." I liked the idea of putting these guys on the ropes. If we were going to send them a message, then let's not be shy about it.

For now, though, I faced three more months in limbo.

Something I've noticed: when good things happen, they spread like butter on hot toast. No sooner had my lawyer come into my life, in the next coming months important bits of evidence started falling into my lap.

By now Grant and his employer must have thought it was all over. He'd left Dubai so I couldn't pursue him. I'd given up. Grant thought he had escaped civil justice and relaxed and when you're relaxed and in off-duty mode you tend to slip up. When his guard was down and he was intent on letting off a bit of steam, Grant, himself was to provide key evidence to support the case against him and his employer. This was all the result of emails and texts uncovered by Grant's victims and the dogged work of former clients in learning what was happening behind the scenes in the case, and in getting Grant to open up.

"All the calls are coming from unknown numbers, Nathan. The same man and the same woman. Calling me on all my numbers … UK, mobile, office."

"Any idea how they got the UK number?"

"No. I can't think of anyone in Dubai who would have my UK landline number."

"That means they are calling you from the UK. Picked up your address on a form or something and found your home number through that … easily done."

"Can we trace it?"

"No. Well, I don't think so, maybe it's possible. Let me check it out."

"What would they gain by these calls?"

"Intimidation maybe, I don't know."

Another day another court

By December 2017, a civil action against both Grant and his employer seeking the return of my money was underway and being heard by a Dubai civil court.

Grant had months to anticipate this, but still they must have had a shock when three months later a lawsuit landed on the employer's desk and, in Grant's case, email box.

Things kicked off as usual with the other party's response. "What the hell is this?" Grant's employer demanded at my lawyer during an intense phone call, "We have nothing to do with this". My lawyer simply responded with, "It's our client's case". They were quick to threaten a counter suit if litigation proceedings against them were not instantly retracted. We stood firm.

His employer denied all allegations and maintained that they had no involvement in or knowledge of Grant's alleged misconduct.

"Alleged?" I picked up. It's been proven. I didn't like the word and I certainly didn't like the casual way it had been thrown back at us.

They said they believed that I didn't act earlier because I knew I didn't have a copper-bottomed case against them. We didn't react. They then said they believed that we blindsided them into forcing a trial upon them by not serving them with the appropriate legal notice beforehand. Again, we didn't react.

The judge was equally unperturbed.

With shocking predictability, Grant hadn't arrived at the first hearing nor was he represented. It put all the pressure on his employer, who would inevitably now put pressure on Grant to attend the next hearing.

We hoped.

We had to sit back and wait.

My lawyer's double-stamp masterplan worked superbly.

At the second hearing, Grant's shiny new representatives arrived. He thought he'd slipped through the net but crumbled under the pressure from his employer. And that's the only reason we ever got Grant back in court.

It was clear to Grant that if he refused his company would find a reason to fire him in the immediate future.

Relieved; it had been a clever move from my lawyer. A shot in the dark but he had outsmarted them all. Now we had a meaningful trial.

It seemed the criminal verdict was a catalyst for a dramatic overhaul of Grant's legal team. My lawyer said it could be any one of a number of reasons: it may be the criminal lawyers were too expensive to hire for another full-on court trial, or it may be Grant didn't hire them because they lost him the criminal case they had sold to him was a slam dunk, or maybe the lawyers themselves rejected the case, although this seemed unlikely.

His employer, labelled as the second defendant, were being represented by a different law firm. It was a usual tactic on the defence's part to show that each party was being represented by different law firms to show the two of them were totally unconnected to the alleged crime.

Unlike criminal, civil courts are different and all paperwork, so neither I nor Grant needed to attend the hearings and neither did the lawyers. The paralegals would submit the documents via the local advocates and receive the instructions for the next hearing. And it continues on like this until the judge decides he is ready to order a judgment. The judge never sees our faces.

Yes, it was strange, because they don't offer a fair assessment of the characters involved. Instead, they reduce them to one-dimensional puppets, defined by fleeting snapshots that fail to capture the real them.

My concern with this court process was that it was a time-consuming affair and that the case was so intricate I worried the judge would be left confused. The other party's job is, of course, to confuse the judge.

Grant's defence focused on getting the case thrown out

on technicalities, using the same language and arguments Grant's previous legal team tried in their criminal response to the suit, in which they stated that the "Plaintiff's own pleading on its face shows that the claims are all based on conduct that occurred more than five years ago, and therefore the limitation periods for all of the Plaintiffs' claims expired years ago".

The employer's defence focused on not being party to any of this as Grant joined them in 2016 and they were not responsible for anything prior to that. My case was based on the criminal verdict. Suffice to say I was right; all three lawyers successfully bewildered the judge who couldn't see the wood from the trees.

After months of back-and-forth, I could not see any way out of this and I couldn't see how we could show the judge Grant actually committed the fraud, as the case needed to go deeper into the details. The key to winning this case lay in the details.

Then, a stroke of luck, and a glimmer of hope. As the hearing entered its ninth day, the judge decided to refer the whole case to a court-appointed expert to see the investigation fully from all sides and evaluate it, considering every detail.

Based on the expert's opinion the judge was to make his final judgment on the matter. The expert's opinion was final, and should the case go to appeal, their decision would be carried over.

The judge was very matter-of-fact about what the expert does.

The expert was to sit with all three parties and go through everything in detail. The sessions were to be focused on the law and on evidence led by the expert. They had unlimited powers to investigate this case, and unlimited time. They had the freedom to request and ask the financial industry, government and all the other relevant authorities, anything they liked. There were five specific areas the expert had to comment on: the relationship between the plaintiff and the defendants; the reality of the money that is being requested by the plaintiff and the link to the first defendant to the money; how did the plaintiff give the money to the first defendant and the purpose of giving this money, and if the first defendant fulfilled his promises against what the plaintiff paid; and if the first defendant returned what he took from the plaintiff and how much was it? And finally, what was the relationship between the second defendant and the link with the money?

Based on these questions that the expert's report was to determine, it was clear that for months all three lawyers had indeed confused the hell out of the judge, and the case was as clear as mud to him; which is why this development was the ideal solution for me, and I was very happy about it.

All court documents are traditionally submitted in the Arabic language. The Arabic legal terminology was so difficult to translate into English that most of my Arabic speaking friends and colleagues struggled, eventually giving up. I only got a summary of what was submitted. Furthermore, translating English documents into the Arabic language was challenging as there was the possibility that you lose the essence of the message in those documents and emails. Appointing an expert meant that I could submit all the evidence in its original format and language.

My lawyer was equally happy with this new development and fresh outlook in the case. He had a new approach in mind.

He decided this was the perfect opportunity for me to write and piece together my own witness statement so the expert would hear 'my voice' – it was more impactful and less technical and simpler, and complementary to the evidence. It would be a complete story of what had taken place, with no clever legal drafting or obscuring the facts or using 'deliberate, careful and sophisticated language'.

"Are you willing to do that?" he asked looking directly at me, his glasses perched on the end of his nose.

"Absolutely."

This was the best approach as it meant I could tell my story from the beginning and, the bonus, I could explain it in English to the expert.

By now, I was tired of legal tactics. I was tired of lawyers complicating things, and muddying waters. In my view, you don't need to do that if you're telling the truth, if you're confident with the truth. If it doesn't make sense, then it's not true.

Court memorandums, I found, are like looking at your figure in the mirror and saying, "Right, I like this about me, and this is what I want to draw attention to", and then it's about playing up the good bits and forgetting about anything else. In this instance, the one thing I was deadly serious about was total transparency when it came to evidence. Yes, there were parts that would go against me, like admitting there is no contract between myself and Grant, and myself and his employer, and that I transferred the money myself, and out of the country. But in light of the evidence seen altogether I believed it would prove the allegations against them. And I could prove that this was by no means an isolated example of Grant's crime. I had a list of witnesses I could call upon to give testimonials to add to my witness statement – they didn't want their name in the media but here they had my back.

My lawyer would handle the points of law written in Arabic and with these two documents, our legal papers would be extremely powerful. And I had a mountain of evidence to present including financial valuation statements to support our allegations. Together, it all sort of worked.

"Then we'll go through all the material together before the expert meeting, to see whether there's anything else we can use." My lawyer was confident with this strategy.

However, he said, I needed to go deeper in the fees paid to Grant. We have bits and pieces that sort of came up in an unstructured way but what we're trying to do is get a complete inventory. I needed to evidence exactly how much Grant was making in financial advisory fees, in wrap fees and in commission. Any evidence or proof that supports the claim that he financially benefited from his deceit. Without some kind of evidence, it's just words. And words alone do not get you a verdict in a court of law.

I didn't want to alert Philip Van Neste, who in turn would alert Grant of what I was requesting, so I asked a local financial advisory expert to access the Guardian web portal with my passwords to see if he could make some sense out of them. The portal contains pertinent information in respect of the Trust and these included valuations of the Trust funds and the historical fees I had paid out over the years.

However, my access to the online account to the Trust was denied. In fact, the message stated I was no longer an active client. Not a coincidence, I'm sure. It had Van Neste stamped all over it.

Begrudgingly, I had no choice but to contact the man himself, who would have already known by now, through Grant, that the case was transferred to a court-appointed expert who would want to look into historical financial information. Which he knew was in the online web portal.

When approached, his silence was deafening. He didn't respond to any of my emails for over three weeks. When he finally did respond, he wrote that they were experiencing technical problems with the online portal and I should have access "relatively soon". Can I direct all inquiries to him and he will email me the information "as soon as practical?".

The situation was impossible.

To me, suppressing actual information was tantamount to him colluding with Grant.

I had no choice but to rely on past valuation statements issued by Grant and, without Van Neste knowing, I managed to get one of his colleagues to explain in writing to me Grant's fee structure and how Grant's fees were calculated from the Trust from inception in 2010 to 2016. And I just hoped that it would be sufficient evidence to satisfy the expert.

After completing the statement I realised that someone partially colour-blind can even see the red flags. It took less time than expected to compile. Partly because I was just regurgitating what was on repeat mode in my brain, and partly because my lawyer's 'Egyptian energy' – which included 7 am starts and text message bombardments – drove me to complete it.

As predicted, there were parts of my statement that would not help me, but if I started to take parts out, it would leave holes. And when there are holes in a story, it leads to suspicion – that someone is hiding something. And your credibility takes a hit. And the court feels disrespected. And if I wanted to avoid numerous expert meetings, I had to tell the whole story from the start and put pressure on the other parties to respond.

"The corroborating evidence around your account is very strong, I've looked at that," said my lawyer. He was excited. And as he had advised, I had written the statement in very simple and basic English. This was not the time to show off any literacy skills, he had joked.

He had spent some time ploughing through Grant's narrative descriptions of some of the valuation statements:

the complicated Excel charts showing a breakdown of my investments; and I saw that he already had the same thought as I did. "It's designed to be complicated, that's all we will say about it," he concluded.

My witness statement[1] tallied up everything that had happened in the past seven years, as if it were a mathematical problem that was finally solved. But in reality, it showed a tragedy. It laid bare we had known a lot more about what Grant has been up to than he probably realised. And if nothing else, Grant had a lot of explaining to do with regard to his financial dealings.

By now, Grant was no longer an employee of the company. Three months into the trial they had suddenly terminated his contract, following *The National's* article in January 2018, and a day after Grant had messaged his clients to reassure them he was still employed by them. This fact was likely to be seen by many as suggesting their relationship was fractured in the extreme. Grant now needed to use this trial to clear his name, especially now after he was everyone's front-page news.

To compound his troubles, some of Grant's former clients had already come forward with fresh allegations and filed new criminal cases at the police station many of whom accused him of fraud, mis-selling and signature forgery. His name ran, like letters in a stick of rock, through a dozen or so claims pending against him, and a dwindling number of financial institutions willing to settle these cases. Because Grant's passport was stamped as 'Wanted' in the immigration system it meant that if he tried to enter Dubai he would be detained. An even bigger surprise, which also suggests more paper for Grant in the future, was the revelation that an additional two victims had filed pre-

---

[1] A copy of the witness statement can be found in the Appendix

claims, in the form of legal notices, that could become civil lawsuits in the near future.

It was safe to assume Grant had no plans coming back to Dubai.

But his employer, albeit now his former employer, was in Dubai and not going anywhere. And the decision to include them in my lawsuit has raised eyebrows amongst the chatter in financial advisory circles and a little unease amongst the Financial Service Companies, Fund Managers and the like, all of whom started to follow the trial closely.

"I'm getting calls," I said to my lawyer. "The unusual type. Unknown voices, and always calling when least expected."

"Really. Since when?"

"Since the criminal trial began."

"Why don't you tell the police?"

"Because it's harmless ... just scaring me."

"How do you know that?"

"They are annoying calls not menacing or threatening. Amateur-like."

Pause.

"They will end after the verdict."

"I think so too."

A pause while he thinks what to say. "Next time ... just say Allahu Akbar." No one could miss the mischievous glint in his eyes.

The expert meeting

I'd been told expert meetings always builds to a climactic episode in a civil trial, worth its every entertainment value, as my case is not so much dissected as eviscerated.

Others broke it down more simply: it's like going to a

dentist for a root canal.

I'd been prepared that things may get quite 'loud' with a lot of 'shouting' and the meeting can last up to a number of hours, and can go on for a number of meetings, over a sustained period of time.

My plan was to have only one meeting.

I headed off early morning in August 2018, to the first meeting with the expert where I met my lawyer outside the building.

"Good morning," he said with an abundance of confidence. His smile was even wider than usual.

This was a moment we had spent weeks preparing for in painstaking detail: the case hinged on detailing Grant's catalogue of deceit. Today was the day that all of our hard work, since we first discovered the scam in the summer of 2016, would become real and our quarry seized.

"Ready?" he asked me, "Let's go." He looked fit and pumped up. I laughed, shaking my head. I couldn't think of anything worse in the entire world than spending the next few hours locked in a closed off intense legal meeting with a bunch of defence lawyers ready to slaughter me.

But for lawyers, this is what they love. Legal cases are a passionate business. It inflames people. Which is why my lawyer was in high spirits today. For most lawyers, I find they get to release their own inner feelings through their cases. I remember thinking Grant's defence lawyer during the criminal trial seemed to have a lot of pent-up anger.

My lawyer was dressed to impress, wearing a dark suit with a blue shirt and tie. Meanwhile I kept it casual in a black-and-white trouser look as we headed into the building. We walked up a flight of stairs to the office and once in reception we were ushered by a large jovial local lady straight to the meeting room – a plain room, with no windows and with some books neatly stacked on a shelf on one side of the room. On the other side was a large whiteboard, with erasers and different colour pens. Before taking our seats, my lawyer put his hands on his hips as he surveyed the long ten-seater table, which was in the centre of the room. He nodded his head indicating he approved of the meeting set up. His perfectionist trait might be weary were it not for the fact that he was kind, down to earth and damn good fun.

"You sit here," he said pointing to the end of the table, and then he sat beside me.

Grant's former employer and their lawyer arrived soon after and sat on the opposite side of the table.

They were blatantly suspicious of me at first – *this is her?*

The polished looking representative from the company introduced herself as their in-house lawyer. Dressed in a brown pencil suit with a low-scoop vest peeping underneath, she looked a few inches taller than me, slim – probably mid-forties. Her black hair was short and cut into a trendy sweeping bob. The external counsel for the company was of medium height and bigger build, dressed in a snappy dark blue suit. He had a wide, square face and very fine black hair and big hooded eyes. He looked very uptight, like he had a mountain of workload that follows him around in his mind like a big bully. Both were Egyptians.

Our choices of lawyers were strikingly different.

Grant's former employer chose to go the conventional route – big shot, nationally prominent defence lawyers. I chose a less marketed lawyer – in fact he wasn't marketed at all. He's a different type of lawyer, altogether.

The mood turned sombre but professional, as we waited for the expert to appear, each party talking amongst themselves, throwing glances to the other side of the table now and then. At some point, we embarked on a peaceful dialogue, one of those ridiculous, empty conversations that people have in surreal situations such as these, before returning to each other. My lawyer reached over to the middle of the table and picked up a couple of mineral water bottles that had been placed there, and handed one to me.

Suddenly we heard the sound of heels clacking along the hall and then the expert walked into the room. She was a petite and fine-boned local Emirati, wearing the traditional abaya scattered with black crystals, who spoke in fluent English in a pleasant steady voice; her demeanour composed. As my lawyer had predicted, she seated herself next to me, at the head of the table, and greeted everyone very friendly.

There was an aura of expectation in the air, and also authority. I was intrigued to see how she was going to control the meeting in light of such characters sitting around the table, where all three lawyers were Egyptians, and known to be quite fiery. I soon learned her apparent fragility belied a spine of steel.

A tall lean male assistant, dressed in simple white shirt and brown trousers, soon followed her in the room with a laptop and took his seat at the table next to her, and directly opposite me. He was tasked with taking charge of all the administration duties and the taking of minutes, and several other duties, and was generally content to be ignored. He was not unfriendly, just preoccupied. The expert herself preferred not to engage in small talk with anyone, and no one was about to entertain her.

Grant's lawyers hadn't yet turned up and, in fact, didn't turn up at all for the meeting. It led to speculation of what reasons may have been behind it.

I turned nervously to my lawyer, concerned that their no-show was a ploy by Grant's legal team to delay the trial by another month or so. Fortunately, the expert was not in the mood to postpone matters.

Seeing that the meeting was going to go ahead without Grant and his representatives, his former employer immediately wanted to distance themselves from him and made it clear that they were not representing Grant and they had nothing to do with his representation.

"Noted," said the expert.

In fact, the persistent distancing from Grant, it seemed, was becoming something of a theme of the meeting.

And so, the meeting commenced with some smooth easy dialogue during the administration part, which, because I was sitting next to her, the expert personally guided me through, almost mothered me through it – until we began to discuss the case. The expert was literally going to start from the very beginning. She had been given no notes on the case, no briefings. Just a piece of paper with the case details and the party details, with some notes she had scrawled on the top. Grant was referred to as the first defendant and his former employer, the second defendant.

My lawyer glanced at the expert, who motioned for him to start.

He started proceedings by announcing that we would be submitting a statement and a substantial amount of evidence whilst patting the Dracula black lever arch folder in front of him – to which the other lawyer's eyes bulged by the sheer volume of the stuff we had. Admittedly, it was a huge folder. My witness statement alone was some twenty-five pages and all the pieces of evidence amounted to almost four hundred pages in total. It was going to be an expensive (if they were being paid by the hour) and a time-consuming affair for both defence parties. If the lawyers were not being billed by the hour and were accepting a flat fee for their legal services, no doubt their eyes were bulging at the missed financial opportunity.

I felt I needed to go all British and offer an apology for

the work we were asking them to do and for them having to wade their way through it all.

"This is nothing ... don't worry," the expert reassured me, whilst the other lawyers, didn't offer anything. She went on to explain that they were used to going through bundles of paperwork. "We follow the evidence and the law," she explained to me, "and establish a pattern of behaviour, no matter how long that takes". Her words instantly gave me a lot of confidence in her.

The pace now picked up, with both opposing lawyers ready to box with a bitter volley of direct questions, occasionally contorting their features into expressions of disbelief or disgust.

"Why didn't you bring a criminal case against my client?" Without asking the expert's permission to question me, the external lawyer leaned over the table and asked his first question directly to me, pointing his finger at me. "Why is our name not on the settlement offer with Mr Grant?" The in-house lawyer, herself, started to chime in with a nasal twang, and asked me her question with an ice-cold stare – that stare women reserve for women they don't like. Her indignation matched her fiery red manicured hands as she tapped the table with her index finger.

They weren't methodical and it all seemed random and I didn't know which question to answer first. So I didn't answer any. Because I remained quiet, they fired further question after question, first to my lawyer in Arabic, and then repeated them to me in English. If the expert asked me a question they would also jump in with their own question on the subject.

Talk about being between a rock and a hard place.

They then seemed content to fire questions not waiting for the answers, so the questions became statements, sound bites, leading my lawyer to counter with a few soft words in

Arabic. The external lawyer looks amused and wrote something down in his notebook. The in-house lawyer equally bemused, like someone who has been told off by the school master, leaned back in her chair, and looked directly at the expert. An intense quiet had settled over the room.

And this was just five minutes into the meeting.

Sitting across from them, both opposing lawyers reminded me of the old properties you find back in the UK; aesthetically pleasing, but not constructed to a high standard. I knew I had to watch the external counsel in particular. You never knew which way he was going to turn, so you had to be careful what you said to him.

My lawyer was half smiling half grimacing, but his eyes were dancing, mischievously. He had a special way about him in situations like this, no question. The differences between all three of them was clear. My lawyer's approach looks calmer and his calm confidence is in contrast to the opposing lawyers more active confidence. Their only similarity was their 'say it as you see it' mentality that is a common trait with all Arab lawyers. You either find it refreshing or aggressive.

For the next half hour, I kept out of it as the three lawyers went toe-to-toe with each other, their voices rising a little above the comfort zone. You could watch them vacillate all day long trying to outdo one another.

If these were people in your workplace behaving like this, you'd think they were bitter and avoid them like the plague. If they're lawyers, they're seen as marvellously eccentric.

Right now, though, they were all giving me a blinding headache.

I glanced at the expert, sitting at the head of the table, to see how she was taking this amusing clash of gigantic egos. She looked engaged yet relaxed and kept a pen in hand as she jotted down notes in her notebook. This was not her first expert meeting, I could tell.

The external counsel then tackled the thorny issue of frivolous lawsuits, and things quickly became a little more heated as he questioned our motives for bringing his client into the claim. Bristling with indignation, he began making some big points trying to expose the whole case as nonsense, using large, high and very emphatic illustrative gesticulation as he spoke. They clearly felt they were being railroaded into this by us for reasons that were not logical, and waxed lyrical of the lawsuit.

He told a string of rambling woes about the rights of his client and the fees they have to pay for lawyers to fight against such cases forced upon them. For the record, they wanted it noted that severe financial penalties would be placed on the plaintiff if the case was deemed to be frivolous. The expert listened with reams of patience, and showed no commitment on anything. Meanwhile, my lawyer scratched his chin whilst looking at the ceiling, as if waiting for the moment to pass.

My mood fluctuated during his monologue between disquiet, utter bemusement and annoyance. Initially, I thought frivolous lawsuits are absolutely wrong. What we were doing was sneaky, and I was a little uncomfortable about it. But now I was in the presence of these numpties, I had a complete change of mind. No – I have not been vituperative on this issue.

To me, their attacks on the merit of our case beggared the question: What the hell was his client doing while all this mayhem was going on? Now, I was having none of it. His client had benefited from supporting Grant throughout the criminal trial. They knew what he had been up to, and they had continued taking a very generous cut from his commission, not once thinking about their clients and allowing Grant to advise them on money matters. As Grant's employer, they did not follow through on complaints and it was pushed under a rug. Greed motivated their silence and lack of responsibility, with no regard for the consequences. I, therefore, had not even a molecule of sympathy for them. My sympathy had been completely vacuumed out of me. A verdict for them would be messy and far-reaching. In my case, yes admittedly, they may not be liable, but they were aware they may be liable for any victims of Grant's who did business with him after 2016. And I knew they knew that, and that's why they needed to fight this and distance themselves from Grant. A not guilty verdict would help them tremendously should any further lawsuits land on their desk. They were not innocent of any wrongdoing. Mentally, I placed the guilt where it belonged – at the other side of the table.

Eventually, after a few minutes of intense non-stop tug of war with words on the subject, the expert interjected saying something in Arabic and both opposing lawyers then changed their whole demeanour in a nano-second and backed off again. It was time for the cosy gloves to come back on. All questions were to go through her she politely reminded everyone. Despite the lawyers having a very intense delivery style she did not appear fazed by any of the heated exchanges or intimidated by any personality.

The meeting continued going slowly; progress painfully slow. Like words collecting in your head but without forming into sentences.

My lawyer had told me not to say too much, and not to volunteer any information. So throughout the meeting, I either didn't say anything or at the very minimum gave monosyllabic answers to everything I was asked from the other party.

After almost forty-five minutes of really not achieving

anything, as the in-house lawyer was banging on about all sorts of things that had nothing to do with the question at hand, the tedium had set in. I felt emboldened enough to ask if I could make a suggestion, feeling almost grateful for the chance to end the meeting. Without waiting for a response I said all the answers to everyone's questions are in my statement. I proposed that we all read through it and reconvene at another meeting. I did a quick summary for them and pointed out the headings on each page to prove what I was saying, and to show them how I had organised the information in the folder.

I paused for effect, as the room has now been rendered virtually silent through intrigue.

"A very good idea." The expert follows this compliment with a very small bow. She seemed happy with what she'd heard which meant the other party had no choice but to agree. My lawyer then enlivened the company by suggesting to the expert that maybe she wanted to hear me read through my statement first. It was something we had agreed before the meeting that I would do if she agreed. However, now I had second thoughts. Sensing the tone of the meeting had turned a tad confrontational, it was actually a bad idea. In fact, a shockingly bad abomination of an idea.

I cleared my throat. "It's okay," I quickly said, "the statement is very detailed. Everything is very straightforward. It should answer all the questions you may have". While speaking, I handed a folder to the expert that contained all the original certified documents, a second folder to the opposing lawyers that was a copy, and a third copy to the assistant to be held with him for Grant's lawyers. If I read through my statement now, I knew that the opposing lawyers were inevitably going to interject, interrupt the flow, and question everything and every paragraph, and attack it, argue that I was obscuring the facts and we would be sitting here for hours, needlessly. And I didn't think I could endure another hour in the meeting.

Two troubled faces stared back at me, as though they had read my mind.

Fortunately, the expert was with me on this one, and concurred. She did some fast, staccato nodding to signal I should let her take over and started to offer some advice to the other party on how they should respond to my statement. She recommended they go through every paragraph and respond if they either agree or deny the point being made, and challenge the evidence with proof.

The other party nodded their head in unison; the in-house lawyer drumming her nails on the table while scanning the contents of the folder given to her. There is little much they had to say, which was not much of a surprise given how the expert had directed them to respond.

It was going well, until near the end, when, in a shockingly bold move, my lawyer then asked if everyone was okay with the fact that the statement was written in English and the evidence was being submitted in English. At this point, I tugged on his suit jacket under the table. I didn't want to translate the whole folder into Arabic – it was almost four hundred pages!

The in-house lawyer lifted the folder and made an event of flipping pages, before passing it to the external counsel who did exactly the same thing.

Thankfully, the expert said she didn't have a problem at all and, taking her lead, the other party had no choice but to mirror her words. I couldn't help casting a glance in my lawyers' direction. His eyes were mischievous again. He was enjoying himself. I was later told that my lawyer, feigning politeness, needed to ask that question so the other party didn't attempt to throw out the evidence all together in their responding memorandum or appeal on the basis that the evidence was submitted in English.

"But what if the other lawyers had said they object and they wanted it translated in Arabic?" I asked, surely that had been a gamble.

My lawyer scoffed, to show that he didn't think much of my concern. "Nah ... he's not going to admit to a room full of people his English is not good." Then he laughed, "but he will translate it into Arabic," he said. "They all do."

It's a bit childish, but bloody funny. Especially if he sent his client the translation bill.

I was happy because my lawyer was able to engineer an opportunity for the other party to agree to how we were submitting our case, although a non-verbal heads up would have saved me a few skips of the heartbeat.

I thanked everyone for allowing me to submit all the papers in English, sensing my own voice sharp and anxious to move on now that an on-the-spot interrogation of my statement had been averted.

The expert then wrapped up the meeting, sharing strict timelines and deadlines, which everyone noted down in their various notebooks. She had given the opposing lawyers two weeks to submit their response to our statement. She hammered them on this point for a good five minutes. "And then we will go on from there." It was only the start.

She thanked everyone for their attention, smiled and then left the room, closely followed by her assistant. My lawyer and I filed out of the meeting room after the opposing lawyers had gathered their belongings and left.

Now we would just have to sit back and wait for each of the defence's responses. The ball was now bouncing between their courts. It would be fascinating to see just how the parties respond and what or who they unearth.

It's strange. Sometimes I felt I had more proof than I could ever need that Grant deceived me and other times I worried I had nothing. Nothing concrete.

We were out of the door in less than an hour. But that was rather a long hour, I can tell you.

"How do you think it went?" I asked my lawyer for the traditional post mortem on the meeting. According to him, that was, by all accounts, a pretty, tame meeting.

"Really?" I was shocked. I have never experienced anything like it.

"And …What do you think …?" I asked him his thoughts on the outcome. After a pause he said it was too early to tell.

"But everything turned out for the best," he exclaimed, looking as if he truly meant it. "The expert really has a big heart, she agreed to everything we asked. It's in very good hands," before adding, "you're very lucky".

There's that word again.

Second defendant's response

Grant's former employer chose not to follow the expert's guidelines on how to respond to my witness statement.

Their reply was what we had anticipated. When their memorandum was read, the vast majority of what they had said had been disguised to obscure their involvement. At the same time they protected Grant of the 'alleged' crimes.

In short, their two-page response to our statement was to deny everything and reject everything I had said as a load of nonsense. They did not challenge any piece of evidence, or of its originality, or validity nor did they submit any evidence supporting their denials, and against the evidence of colluding with Grant to avoid liability. They adopted the 'less is more' legal tactic.

They did, however, admit to negotiating a financial settlement along with Grant but, they argued that didn't make them liable. They pleaded for some common sense and to focus on the fact that there was no contractual arrangement with me, and Grant joined the company in September 2016. They could not possibly be held liable for anything he had got up to before then.

"What do you think?" I asked my lawyer.

His response was short: "They won't be worried".

First defendant's response

Immediately after the meeting with the expert, Grant's lawyers had filed a complaint to the court claiming they hadn't received notification of the expert meeting, and expressed their surprise that the meeting had gone ahead in their absence. "How was this even possible?" they queried.

The expert was undeterred and explained to an irate defence lawyer that both sides in the case have a duty to disclose relevant documents such as statements, messages and emails to the other side, and that was the stage we were at in the trial.

They were given the same deadline as the second defendant and, sure enough, two weeks later Grant's lawyers filed their memorandum to the expert. And just like the second defendant, they blatantly ignored the expert's guidelines on how to respond to my witness statement. In fact they ignored the statement altogether. Their response was so abrupt, so devoid of information that I felt a beat of alarm.

"No people are more frequently wrong than those who will not admit they are wrong." A quote from the 17th century French writer Francois de la Rochefoucauld suitably summed up Grant's response to our statement.

'What happened?' should have been the title of Grant's new five-page defence.

And one thing was absolutely clear: Grant revealed an extraordinary degree of resentment towards the criminal court's judgment. At times it seemed Grant was blind to reality with a list of complaints that read like those of a sullen child who cannot understand why he got a guilty verdict. What shone through in their legal papers was that Grant wanted a sympathetic ear for his tale of perceived woe at the hands of a Shakespearean villain Lady Macbeth, aka me and the press.

This was a man right on the edge, exploding before our very eyes at what he perceived to be the horrific injustice of what has befallen him. This was the work of a man who never thought he could possibly lose the criminal case to me, a woman it seems he considered his inferior opponent in every possible way imaginable from intellect and legal representation, financial experience to credibility.

Such was Grant's self-confidence he would win at the criminal trial.

Yet he lost. And he lost all the appeals.

Not wanting to lose is a good thing. Refusing to admit you've lost, however, is an absurd thing. No one can change the result.

What I resented most about his defence was that they had attempted to shift the issues away from the civil case, and turn the trial into an emotional debate on the criminal verdict. What did that have to do with this court? Grant's lawyers basically boiled down to this mantra: the case is ridiculous, the verdict is ridiculous, and the truth is that nobody is accepting the criminal verdict.

Who is drawing these conclusions?

Oh, they are. And so it went on, with increasing ferocity.

Surely, they should have focused on actually trying to win the civil case and not engaging in petty point scoring over a previous hurricane.

Grant still appeared in complete denial about the real reason he lost, so let me help him with that because I could pinpoint the exact moment. It's when you set up a fake company, and used a fake licence. No surprise that in their legal papers, Prosperity Offshore Investment Consultants was never mentioned or alluded to.

More worryingly his lawyer challenged the judge's ruling in the criminal case by claiming he 'made crucial errors of law' when he rejected their initial proposal that the case was heard in the wrong court and jurisdiction, especially as I, the plaintiff, have admitted in my testimony that I had transferred the money out of Dubai. He argued the judge misunderstood financial law and as a result misdirected himself to that effect, despite there being a non-existent contract. He argued he found the decision to be wrong and, as a result, there being a real danger the wrong judgment be made here.

Attacking the verdict is one thing – but attacking the judge itself is quite admirable.

When the memorandum did eventually get round to discussing the civil case at hand, the lawyer argued that the civil case must be dealt with in the UK, not Dubai. He also asked for the case to be dismissed on the grounds that it was over the time limit.

No new evidence had emerged. And they had brought no evidence of errors in our statement. So, they tried to throw the evidence in another way. His lawyer went on to say his client denied everything and every piece of evidence, arguing photocopies are not evidence and argued for them to be rejected. Considering the majority of our evidence consisted of email correspondence, this argument was mortifying.

It was an interesting tactic, of course. They couldn't

argue the point that my statement had been submitted in English, and try and throw the evidence for that reason, because my lawyer had obtained the expert's approval at the meeting beforehand. The defence choose instead to blow smoke at it.

Of the 80 exhibits submitted to the court, 58 consisted of email correspondences between myself and Grant and between myself and his former employer, of which both parties, unquestionably, had copies of the exhibits themselves. Eleven exhibits related to financial statements and company documents issued and sent to me from Grant himself. Six exhibits consisted of documents from government bodies including the criminal court judgment, the statement from the DED, a statement from the SCA, and documents from the Insurance Authority outlining the legal clauses relating to the case.

In order words, what were Grant and his lawyer moaning about?

They were maddening.

They were unable to challenge any piece of evidence for they knew them to be true and unshakeable, they therefore beat us up with insignificant details.

'They're trying to cheat, they're trying to cheat,' the legal papers implied, but produced no evidence to explain how.

They then ranted for several paragraphs implying fake emails – but produced no evidence either to back their claim.

My lawyer voiced his resentment at them for throwing mud and trying to tarnish his integrity. "This is beyond anything I have ever seen before," he snarled. "Do they think we're stupid? Do they think we're fools to submit fake emails?"

I held my breath. The ploy could work. Technically, of

course, it was still a defence that needed to be considered by the expert – and giving us all a dramatic finale that could yet produce a twist ending and shock result.

We pleaded that their defence on the subject of photocopies was nonsensical, explaining their ploy. Fortunately, the expert was firmly in our corner, and said she would allow all the photocopies, and the motion was denied.

Relief flooded over me, but not for too long.

There were more surprises.

This time, however, after he provided 'substantial' assistance during the prosecution investigation and criminal court, the memorandum intentionally avoided mentioning their previous star witness – Philip Van Neste, or even added his statement to counter the DED's statement.

No – they had bigger guns this time.

"Guess." My lawyer leaned closer, enjoying the moment.

I was too stunned and confused to offer an intelligent guess. "Who?"

He paused for effect.

"Clyde & Co." He clarified, slowly and emphatically, and then reared back to let it sink in. And I duly fell off my chair. That's right. The defence have taken their argument one step further.

I quickly flipped through the memorandum, and sure enough there it was.

Nestled between his personal statements, Grant's latest salvo included an explosive documented evidence of a partnership agreement that had been drawn up by none other than Clyde & Co – one of the biggest UK law firms in the Middle East – and, as Grant wrote "highly respected in the field of financial services regulation and the advisor for the UAE government, DIFC, Insurance Authority and SCA in the Middle East". I recognised that marketing description. It was from the law firm's website.

I assumed this was some kind of wind-up.

But no, sure enough, the firm's brand and logo were all over the document.

"Well, this just got interesting," I said. But what exactly was their point?

Referring to Clyde and Co, Grant added that in 2004 he had been informed that a professional licence was acceptable to set up a company in Dubai, and that's what he applied for with the DED with a copy of his UK qualifications, and he had discussed with the law firm what his intended business activities would be. He claimed the firm had "witnessed" his professional Diplomas in financial advice, and his professional licence from the DED. Sure enough, it was written within the partnership agreement that the business of the civil company was "conducting the business of consulting in personal financial planning and project finance".

But again, the point was being missed.

Just because Clyde & Co had 'approved' his business activity, it didn't mean it was legitimate. Clyde & Co is not a government body, and such claims offend common sense; the implications don't really bear thinking about. It was the same argument behind Philip Van Neste's statement.

The statement by the DED clarified all the activities Prosperity Management Consultancy was allowed to provide. The company was not permitted to manage people's money as it was not part of their activities. It makes that point very clearly. No one can override the DED who issues company licences. That, surely, was the point? You can always look at other outside things. But it always comes back to the statement from the DED. How can that then be challenged, even by legal geniuses?

"Why did they not present this defence during the criminal trial?" I asked my lawyer. Any backtracking attempt Grant now made would be a hollow, pointless one.

Post-criminal judgment, the madness apparently continued.

"It's all very, very silly," agreed my lawyer, but their half-baked attempts to hatch together another argument to challenge the DED's statement were particularly difficult to understand. Grant had become so seduced by Clyde & Co's marketing spiel that he thought it had a chance to get him off the hook. Their decision to include them now on the matter has only served to add to the intrigue, even more so as the firm was not called upon to give evidence in the court, leaving Grant's statement with no merit at all.

Can it get any worse? Yes, in fact, it could.

Piling irony on top of irony, it turned out Clyde & Co didn't seem to have any recollection that Grant and Prosperity Management Consultancy was a former client of theirs – or, perhaps extraordinarily – they didn't check.

Sure enough, in one of the media articles on the story of Grant's criminal conviction, Clyde & Co wrestled in for a moment in the spotlight with a quote saying it was important people "do their own due diligence, including asking to see their registration and paperwork or licence".

This trial was full of surprises.

Clyde & Co, not content with just a car crash moment, went for a full Sheikh Zayed Road pile-up.

It also emerged that they were one of the law firms *The National* newspaper had asked to check and approve the contents of the story before its publication.

Unless you're suffering a chronic sense of humour failure, what a spectacular own goal.

After rereading all the detail, though, it struck me, rather worryingly, that if Grant managed to fool the mighty

Clyde & Co – and it's quite an achievement – it proves, rather disturbingly, what an excellent operator Grant is. Extremely clever, tremendously powerful. A man with a slick sales patter had outsmarted every single person along his way. He could sell life insurance to a 99-year-old.

The lawyer's parting words in their memorandum to the expert was to think carefully about the precedent they will be setting if they found Grant guilty. Our parting words of their memorandum was that Grant was now a professional victim who wouldn't take responsibility for his choices and blamed everyone else instead.

We had to wait to hear from the expert on what was going to happen next following the defence's filings.

The answer was nothing.

The expert had no further questions on my witness statement either, and declared that there was to be no more meetings or submissions. The case now belonged to them. It was now left in their hands to decide our fate.

It was all rather anti-climactic after that. None of us really knowing which way it was going to go.

"What do you think?" I asked my lawyer of Grant's reply to our statement. He looked as if he were considering how to put his next thought into words. "Fifty-fifty," he finally said, which is lawyer-speak for he had no idea. It was impossible to predict how the expert might rule.

"How long do you think it'll be before we hear?"

"One month," he said with no hesitation, as if he answered that question many times a day. But this external waiting was going to drive us both crazy.

But my lawyer saw it as a good sign. "It's a complicated case, it's good that they're not rushing things without careful deliberation."

He was of course right, and there were hundreds of papers – exhibits and documents – to comb through, not to mention financial reports.

One month had gone by. "We're so sorry it's taken so long," the expert's office said, "but these investigations are always time-consuming. Apparently writing the report was the time-consuming part. They had made up their mind weeks ago.

I was ringing my lawyer's office every other week, "No news, we'll call you, it will be fine, don't worry".

Until finally, almost three months after the meeting, we were told the expert was ready to submit their report of their opinion to the judge.

The expert's opinion

"Congratulations," was his first word, when I was given the news by my lawyer in an early morning phone call. His news was nothing short of magnificent.

"What? For real? That's amazing." I over excitedly spat out the usual garbled idiotic reply from someone grappling with the sheer enormity of such extraordinary news. Once again, we had pulled off what almost everyone said was impossible.

Court cases are the most emotional, all-consuming, energy sucking experiences you can put yourself through, mostly because of the incessant uncertainty – and I had put myself through two, in under two years. This wasn't easy, and I couldn't stop. I don't think you can when you've been that involved in a case for so long. It's all in you, it's in your head. It hangs around your mind all day, every day like a heavy raincloud.

Awaiting the final judgment was even worse. This was it. The last two years had come to this moment, waiting for this one piece of paper – well actually it was a 15-page report. The ramifications of losing now wouldn't bear thinking about.

But when you win – that moment when you know that you have won, there is really no feeling like it. It's an instant shock, followed by disbelief, and you need that reconfirmation from another human being if you heard right, and then a powerful relief floods through you, from head to toe.

On October 31st, 2018, the expert ruled entirely in my favour – against Grant. The report, which was formally submitted in court to the judge by the expert, found that after studying all the evidence and reading all the emails, in their opinion, Grant had indeed taken advantage of me.

However, in the expert's opinion, there was no connection with Grant's former employer. Details were scant, but what I already knew was enough.

The odds against Grant were always better, but we had tried our best with his former employer and shook them up a little. Time will tell if the win against Grant has a knock-on effect on Grant's former employer and Guardian and the like who Grant was working with.

In summary, the expert concluded in her report that there had been a clear mis-selling and described Grant's actions as "a gross breach of trust" which had a "profound financial and emotional impact" on his victim. The report stated that Grant had provided no sufficient credible defence and that his statement of case was unclear and lacking in the essential particulars.

My lawyer replied that we accepted the expert's opinion and asked to move to judgment which was set for November 14th, 2018 in two weeks' time. Grant's former employer replied through their lawyers, that they also accepted the expert's opinion that they were not to be held financially liable for my losses. Well, that was expected. Grant's lawyer, however, didn't submit a response in an attempt to sway the judge in one final effort. That was somewhat unusual.

Oddly, now it felt rather anti-climactic. Judgment in the case has been reserved.

"You can relax, and wait on your verdict." My lawyer was unshakably confident.

Meanwhile, *The National*, scenting Grant's blood again, wanted to run the story. If I won this case and there was a big verdict, it would open the floodgates of financial advisory litigation in Dubai. However, I was not in favour of just lobbing it in. I asked them to wait until the judgment because, to me, there was no point banging on too much before I've even got the verdict but they were determined to run it especially as they had received statements from Grant and his lawyer as they wanted a proper chance to put across both parties' side of the story.

However, both Grant and his lawyer used the situation to try to manipulate the journalist in convincing him that there was no criminal verdict against Grant and he had been cleared of all charges. It worked. The journalist was temporarily confused and halted the story until I reminded him, he had seen court documents which showed proof of the criminal conviction and that's all that mattered.

Grant's statement to *The National* referenced Clyde & Co, pleading with the newspaper to give, on balance, a full backdrop to the story. He believed this would clear his name in the public eye.

The newspaper was keen to interview my lawyer, who was not remotely interested. He waved his hand at me. It was refreshing. Any other 'marketed' law firm would be on the phone. He just wasn't interested in any of it.

"Neil Grant liable for client's six-figure losses" screamed the front-page headline the next morning. A watered-down headline to what I personally would have gone with. The experts' opinion sent shockwaves through the expat community, more so than the criminal verdict had, because now an independent person had confirmed something all the victims knew – fraud. It was a salutary read.

The article brought renewed attention to the case. There were still swarms of victims still milling around looking for some sort of direction, closure or answers. Financial experts popped up again, everywhere.

For me, there was too much hype before the actual judgment and even though I knew there was nothing to worry about, until that hammer went down, nothing was guaranteed. The UK papers were covering a story at that time where a mother who suffered years of abuse from her partner had criticised a woman judge who said she was too "strong and capable" to be a victim. Incredibly the judge said the victim coped too well with the abuse for him to be convicted under domestic violence legislation, "It is to her credit that I cannot find the defendant's behaviour had a serious effect on her in the context of the guidelines for this offence".

Bizarre, utterly bizarre.

And that's under English law.

What next? If a rich person is robbed, "Oh well, you can afford it" from the judge?

One can understand my apprehension. There had already been too many surprises in this case and the final judgment could yet be merciless.

However, in a welcome spark of justice, the judge's verdict hit the perfect note in my case.

CHAPTER 8

THE JUDGMENT

✧ *The ink has dried* ✧

I had won again!

My shoulders jerked upward and I exhaled mightily. "Are you serious?" I asked into the receiver to my lawyer.

"Yes, I'm serious. I told you not to worry."

Snatched another victory against all odds.

After just over a year, on November 14th, 2018, we finally had a conclusion in the civil case. The judgment, which was formally published that day, and twelve pages long, found that I was induced to enter my contract with Grant by "false" representation, and ordered Grant to return all of my initial investment entrusted upon him – £60,000, along with all court costs and expenses, and the legal interest by nine percent from the date of the claim until the full payment.

What sweet words.

In his ruling, the judge agreed with the expert that "there is no relationship between the Second Defendant and the Plaintiff" and "the court sees that the Second Defendant has no capacity in the case and the pleading is valid and in its place. Accordingly, the court rules to not accept the case filed against it as it was filed without capacity".

With regard to the pleading made by Grant that the Dubai court does not have jurisdiction to hear the case, it was rejected, and quoted the text in the articles of the Civil Transactions Law, 19/1, 20, 21, 24 of the same Civil Procedure Law. The judge stated: "the international jurisdiction of the courts is of public order and that the state courts have jurisdiction to hear cases brought against a foreigner who does not have a home or residence in it if the case relates to an obligation entered into or executed or conditional on its implementation in the state".

Concerning the pleading of not hearing the case due to the passage of time, it was also rejected according to the Article 82 of the Civil Transactions Law which states that the ageing is interrupted by the judicial claim or by any judicial action taken by the person holding it. If the ageing is interrupted, a new ageing shall start as from the date of expiry of the effect resulting from the reason of interruption. The period shall be the same as the previous ageing period according to Article 485 of the Civil Transactions Law. The judge went on to state: "It is established for the court from the papers and documents of the case that the Plaintiff had filed the criminal case against the First Defendant, and the subject of the criminal case was related to the claim in the current case, which the court considers to be a judicial procedure with which the ageing period is interrupted. Hence, the court considers that the pleading is inappropriate and unfounded from reality and the law and rejects it".

With regard to re-examining Grant's criminal conviction, quoting 269 of the Criminal Procedure Law, the judge stated: "that the final criminal ruling shall have force probative towards all parties in terms of its final decision concerning the occurrence of the action constituting the common ground between civil and criminal cases and in the legal description and its attribution to the perpetrator".

The judge went on to state: "If the criminal court decides a final ruling and becomes final in these matters, the civil court must adhere to it in related cases and refrain from re-examining it, because this authenticity is connected to the public order, and that this authenticity applies towards all".

And to leave no doubt, the judge concluded: "Accordingly and based on the above, and since it is established for the court from the papers and documents of the case, and as it is evident that the First Defendant was convicted in the criminal judgment issued with the penalty outlined in the judgment, and that judgment became final for the lack of appeal, which he did not argue with despite his presence at the pleading hearings, the court concludes that the action of harming (fault) act was committed by the Defendant, wherein he is liable for the same".

In conclusion, the judge agreed with the expert that "an amount of (60,000) pounds is payable by the First Defendant, as he deluded the Plaintiff that he is a financial advisor, contrary to the reality, which led to the loss of her money".

Well, there we have it.

For Grant it has become a tragedy of epic proportions.

And I hope that's the end of all his denials.

The fact of the matter was, according to those well versed with the chatter in legal circles, Grant was incredibly lucky. You only need to skim through the voluminous report drily entitled Independent Expert, to wonder if the judge in the criminal court had appointed an expert, Grant's fate may have been a bit different. At the time my case hadn't gone deep enough into the details and hadn't proven the link between the misuse of the licence and the allegation of fraud enough to justify the judge using up the court's resources to appoint such an expert.

Grant had thirty days to appeal. If he did appeal, as seemed very likely, and is the norm, then we had to go through the whole process again. However, my lawyer shared a different view: "If his lawyer is giving him advice, he would be as well to listen and to take it". Upon appeal, the expert's opinion carries through to the next round. In other words, another expert cannot be brought in. The expert spent three months trawling through documents, witness statements and testimonies to piece together what happened from 2010 to 2016. It means Grant was subjected to a thorough investigation, which is why my lawyer didn't believe they could win an appeal. But, as I have learnt, nothing is predictable, and everything is possible.

Grant must have thought so to.

As the family geared up to spend their second Christmas in Scotland after relocating following the criminal conviction, Grant appealed against the civil decision in the eleventh hour, with his lawyer saying the court made a mistake and they were disappointed with the ruling but remained confident that Grant would be "completely exonerated" at the Appeal Court.

His request was accepted by the Dubai court, and Grant was asked to pay the court fees within the next five working days.

Then, just before the case entered the New Year, in 2019 things took a rather dramatic turn and we were told via the court system that the appeal had been withdrawn. Very strange. We were thinking did Grant's decision not to appeal have anything to do with the fact that Grant knew he wouldn't win?

Whatever the reason, I was elated. It was finally all

over.

The withdrawal saw the judgment upheld. The judge upheld the damages order, which would continue to increase at a rate of nine percent per annum until full payment was received.

Immediately, my lawyer filed for the execution judgment and opened an execution file, the last stretch of the case. This is where we investigated Grant's financial background to pay off his debt to me. This is the part where the guilty party starts selling or transferring things around before it's frozen. Because of the way the execution process is set up, they have at least two months to do this because the process takes that long. Assets cannot be frozen before a judgment is awarded.

Are there any assets? This was now the pertinent question. At the start of the civil trial, my lawyer had previously advised me to find out as many facts about Grant's finances as possible, and had continued to emphasise the advice throughout the trial. The very fact that I hadn't even explored this up until this moment, made me realise that, subconsciously, I really hadn't expected to win.

My lawyer was undeniably right about one thing. Time was of the essence when it came to this part of the case, particularly as we knew there was never going to be an easy, genial transfer of money from Grant to myself.

I mean, seriously who are we kidding, right?

Is his New Year resolution: Man up! Pay up, especially in defeat?

Nope – the unpredictability of this case continued to be "seriously unbelievable".

Along came another twist.

Somewhat surprisingly Grant's lawyer appealed again on January 8th, 2019 against the civil verdict. It had everyone scratching their heads. The appeal was now out of its time limit. Way out. His lawyer would know this. But that is, of course, what makes lawyers manoeuvres so very maddening.

What is his lawyer playing at?

Underneath the smiles, the poise and the professional, there seems always to be a tacit purpose and underlying motive in all they say and do.

I said to my lawyer plaintively, "I don't get it".

"Don't worry," he told me, in a tone of reassurance. "The case is over, there's not much to be done about it now." Still, this case had so many twists and turns, the demands on your energy are immense and you can't relax for a moment. I had programmed my mind that it was all over. I could see the white winning line. To now go through all this again for the next few months at least, had me on edge. All I wanted was to get this whole thing over with.

"It's just a formality by the court to throw out the appeal." Sometimes the constraints of the process taxed my patience.

To me, it was obvious what's really going on here.

"Do you think they ..." I paused, then asked, "Do you think the lawyer forgot to pay the Appeal Court's fees on time?". Surely, they hadn't forgotten to pay the court fees within the five-day window?

That was a much simpler question to answer. I knew my lawyer had no fear of being blunt. "It is very tempting to suggest it ... it's most likely," he replied.

"And that's why ..." I hesitated, but I had to ask, "his lawyer is now desperately trying to get another appeal?".

"Possibly." And with a shrug of the shoulders, he added cheekily: "It happens ... We always appeal well within the 30-day rule ... just in case."

"So, it's not totally unheard of?"

"I think you're right," he finally conceded. Of course

I'm right; it's the only explanation. And if that was so, what a complete and utter cock-up. Arguably the most aesthetically pleasing legal own goal.

They had employed stalling tactics and appealed at the last minute within the 30-day period, and had got caught in their own games by failing to pay the court fees in time. If you don't pay the court fees in time, the court's system automatically withdraws the appeal. They can appeal again, but by then of course, they are out of 30-day time limit.

But will the lawyer blame the court system for the appeal being rejected rather than shouldering any blame himself? It was getting interesting. He couldn't very well just come right out and say they forgot to pay the courts fees in time; he needed to take a more circuitous approach.

But, as with every area of the law, there are exceptions and exceptions to the exceptions, and soon, it was clear what his strategy was – in order to thwart the result of the first hearing, he went after the one thing that makes all the courts nervous: the judge of the case.

In legal documents filed with the Court of Appeal, Grant's lawyers claimed he did not receive a fair trial and said the ruling was "plainly wrong", and they would ask the court to "set aside the judgment and order a new trial".

In simple terms, they didn't like the judge and how he had conducted his civil case.

Never a smart move.

Especially as they had already gone after the judge in the criminal case, for exactly the same reason.

But I do know this: if the defence lawyer persisted in trying to delegitimise the civil judgment by claiming it was wrong, sparked by Grant's assertion he's been unfairly robbed of justice by a poor judge, then that was not going to bode well. It was a poor defence, but the only one they really had that could get them over the out-of-time-limit line. On the plus side, such a strategy could simply play into our hands and turn these attempts into a massive legal asset for us.

On January 8th, 2019, we immediately submitted a motion to dismiss the action filed, simply because it was out of its time limit. The appeal judge set the review for January 27th, 2019, which was extended to February 27th, 2019, then to March 17th, 2019, and then again to March 31st, 2019.

The delays didn't matter to us. Parallel to the extensions, we were continuing with the execution process, and during that time, unbeknown to Grant, the court has executed the judgment against his property.

The execution of assets

I knew Grant was 'sophisticated' at hiding his financial resources, so I didn't hold much hope on discovering where his treasures were residing.

Indeed, we found Grant had moved his money out of Dubai to various safe places. He probably knew he was going to be taken to court by many people, not just me. And it made it much more difficult for the victims to get restitution. It basically showed that he had no remorse whatsoever. He had done nothing wrong. He would never accept the verdicts against him. His lack of empathy was a constant fault-line throughout both his trials, in the courtroom and the media public court of opinion.

And he probably knew if I was seeking to enforce a Dubai court judgment in Scotland it would be very complicated.

I spoke with a partner and disputes specialist at a local law firm in Edinburgh who confirmed that a Dubai judgment can be recognised by the Scottish court. However, there is currently no treaty in place between Scotland and the UAE to streamline this procedure. Therefore, the procedure is relatively slow and would require a fresh court action in Scotland known as seeking 'Decree Conform'. This would not be a rerun of the action in Dubai. However, it was possible for Grant to defend the action by arguing that my court order in Dubai was obtained irregularly and improperly, or in such circumstances as would make it against justice to give effect to it.

In other words, it can be done, but it wouldn't be a quick administrative process. A court action would be required.

It seemed utterly hopeless; until one random day over a random coffee, a mutual friend of Grant's discussed how the property market in Dubai was taking a dramatic nose dive.

"I'm so glad I never bought Grant's property off him. It would be half the price now," he casually dropped into the conversation.

My chocolate chip frappe was instantly abandoned. "I'm sorry, what did you say?" Grant had property in Dubai?

"Well, yes, well, he had, not sure now."

And apparently, I had regularly visited it.

"I assure you I have never been to his home, or even know where it is," I had said. That's true. Only it wasn't his home he had bought, but the office where he had conducted his businesses. Unbeknown to most of us, he owned the office. He had told no one about it except this particular person, and only because he had wanted to rent out half of his unit to him, offering residential Visas along with the offer.

"Have you found out anything more about his financial background?" My lawyer now asked me, again.

I hesitated. "Possibly, but I'd like to double-check a few

things first."

"Do that," he said. "Try and get the exact details."

I had the details, but I needed to reconfirm that the property was still in Grant's name and not his wife's or had been transferred at any time during the last two years. We could request information on whether or not Grant owned any property in the UAE through the Dubai courts as part of the execution process, but that would take far too much time. Considering how things were starting to escalate, we couldn't afford to waste any more time.

Had Grant rented out his property?

I found myself in the reception hall of Grant's building in Business Bay that very afternoon. I knew the floor number and office number, both of which I scribbled on a Post-it Note and handed to the receptionist.

"Yes," she confirmed peering at it, "that office is occupied".

"Do you know who the owner is?"

"Who are you?"

I gave an alias and said I was working for a real estate company.

"Let me check," she started searching her system with a flurry of keypunching under my unwavering gaze; paused dramatically causing me to hold my breath, and then nodded at her monitor.

"Mr Grant."

This splendid woman, had caused my heart to stutter and had no idea how happy she has just made me. And rich

The property was still solely in Grant's name.

That's how confident he had been in winning the civil case. In any event, he will have thought if the case ever does get to execution stage, he had a two-month window of opportunity where he could either sell the property, or transfer it to anyone, even from Scotland. Even from jail.

My lawyer was utterly delighted for me. He immediately got to work and asked the judge to impose an asset-freezing order. We said Grant had not complied with earlier orders and suggested that he would not pay the debt.

"It was rejected?" I exclaimed to my lawyer, when we followed up on the request.

"Well, no, not exactly."

The court requires a copy of the title deed for the property, we were told. They cannot freeze any property without it. Usually the court requests this from the Land Department as part of the execution process, but again that takes months because of the maze of approvals for the procedure, and by then Grant could sell or transfer his property, even within one working day.

"Why do they need the title deed, when we have given them the address of the property?" I asked my lawyer. "They can see it's under his name." He explained that they needed the exact project details of Grant's property as per the Land Department system so the court system could find a match. Sometimes the way the property is marketed in terms of the commercial space is different to the details in a title deed. And the court only matches the details on the title deeds.

There was nothing we could do except wait for the process to play out.

It was a devastating blow. I had been so close, so very close. I knew the opportunity would never again be mine. Throughout these two trials I had programmed myself that I may not get my money back. But now that it had been 'possible', the candy had been snatched from me. I felt truly dejected.

"Try and get a copy of the title deed," said my lawyer, anxious for me to speed things along.

"From where?" Where on earth can I get a copy of the title deed? "Only Grant will have it."

"Try, just try." This was a new challenge. My options were limited, and the more I pondered the situation the fewer choices I had.

There was DEWA – but this was a government body, and there was no way they would hand private details over to someone without conducting any verification on the person requesting it.

The developers? A quick call to Nathan, said that would be unlikely, and the project details would have changed so many times in the last ten years; it was not going to match the original title deed.

Bereft of any other ideas, it looked damning. The only thing left was to try the Dubai court itself. A formidable idea, I knew, and a long shot. But I'd given up hope of getting help elsewhere. This was my only chance. And I knew that despite emails, phone calls, and apps, the quickest and only truly effective mode of communication with government officials remained face-to-face contact. So early the next day I made my way to the other side of town.

The execution department has its own court and wing within the Dubai court. I approached the desk and asked to speak to someone who blocks properties as part of the execution process.

The receptionist asks me for a copy of my judgment, court order, and the execution file number, which I handed over to her. She checked it all, made copies and handed the original and the copies back once satisfied.

A few minutes later, I was told to go to a room down the corridor that opens up into several small rooms inside. There were lines of people waiting outside each room for their turn to speak to whoever is inside.

I was directed to the first room on the right, with four people waiting outside. I waited patiently until it was my turn to enter the room, rapping on the door as I entered it.

It was white. A white plain room with a local in a white dish dash sitting at a white desk in the corner of the room. And two huge white arm chairs across from his desk, with a white table in-between.

This man is The Blocker. He blocks properties as part of the execution process. Just blocks them all day. What a job. Well, judging by his demeanour, it looked to be a mundane job. There wasn't a flicker of life in his whole body language. It was like he'd just woken up from a self-induced coma.

I hand over the photocopies of my paperwork to him which he flipped through whilst leaning back in his big white arm chair, and dispensed with the chitchat. "Yes?"

I explain my story to him and that I didn't have a copy of the title deed in order to block the property.

He didn't seem surprised and shrugged as if this happened all the time.

"And, I'm sorry, but I have no idea where to get a copy for you," I continued to say. He looked blankly at me.

"Make a request to the judge and he'll send a request to the Land Department," he answered, in a robotlike voice, just loud enough to be heard, glancing at his right and then to his left as his words trailed off.

"Sir, I'm up against a clock," and then I explained why.

Again, no reaction. Again, he'd probably heard it all before.

"What is the plot number," he slowly sat upright in his chair, his fingers ready to pound in the numbers on the keyboard. It turned out he didn't actually need the title deed itself, just the original plot number of the property. Relief swept over me; however, my joy was short-lived.

"Well, I don't have it; it's on the title deed."

"Oh," he looked at me in realisation as he finally understood my predicament, and slowly reclined back in his chair. I could actually hear the dead bolt rattle from inside his head. "What to do." It's not a question.

"What do you mean 'Oh'?"

"I need the plot number to block the property in the system."

There was a pause.

"Where is the 'system', who has it?" I was thinking that I could at least try to speak and reason with that person. I started glancing around, ready to be directed.

"I have it here." He leaned forward in his chair and patted the computer in front of him.

I was expecting him to point me in the direction towards an esteemed panel of court officials. My eyebrows arched. It's just him, really? He was too cute and too young to be The Blocker. And he still had spots.

"You can find all the properties in Dubai in this computer?" I ask him, pointing to the monitor.

"Yes."

"Wow," I said, as I absorbed this unexpected revelation, and staring at the goldmine sitting on his desk. It was apparently directly linked to the property system in the Land Department.

"You ask a lot of questions." *You present a lot of questions.*

"But they're easy ones, aren't they?" Undeterred I pressed on. "So, you yourself can go into this very computer, into 'the system' and find a property, and block it?"

"Yes." He shrugged his shoulders.

I tried another way.

"So, if I give you this man's address, you yourself can go into this very computer, into 'the system' and find his property?"

"If you have the plot number, I can find it."

"But you can find the plot number in the system if I

give you the address of the property, right?"

"Yes, but it will take time, better for me if you have the plot number."

Better for you? I shot him a look of exaggerated incredulity.

"Sir, I told you I don't have the plot number. It's not practical for me to get it. But you have it, in this computer," I said tapping the top of the monitor, "right in front of you."

He checked his watch whilst arguing that he still needed the plot number. I argued back I couldn't get it and was up against a clock.

"There is nothing I can do." My goodness he was infuriating. He could do everything for me.

"It's a brief search in this very computer. The court knows about it. It's all right there in the papers," I said pointing to the paperwork in his hands.

"What is the execution number?"

"Here," I leaned forward and pointed to the unmissable large red-coloured box on the top sheet that was in his hands. He gave the appearance of looking at it. "So," I said with a happy voice, my best effort at pleasantness, "let's not waste time, and I suggest you read it, instead of asking me questions that are answered by the papers In Your Hand".

"Let me see what I can do." He froze his face into a mask of noncommitment while he put the paperwork down on his desk, indicating he needed to press on to the next person in the queue.

I looked back at him. That was it? I knew he had no intention of doing anything. Just like the gelled hair on his head, those papers were not going to move an inch.

It was impossible. He was horribly impossible. I worked hard at being patient. Now I was dangerously close to exasperation.

"You want me to run across town in this heat to get you a copy of a title deed, that is impossible – when the only information you need from that title deed, is the plot number, which you can get from this computer that is Right In Front Of You?"

My voice raising, I stare at him incredulously. There was a pause. And his face finally broke down into a big smile. He had perfect teeth, which now he delighted in permanently showing to me.

"Would you like to sit down?"

"No," I say, whilst I took a seat on one of the white arm chairs. "All I want you to do is find the plot number for me in your computer. I can go through the back story again if you like. I am not asking you to do anything that's going to take time, or wrong or illegal, or even sinful."

His smile beamed even brighter at the last word.

"There is a procedure, Miss," he insisted.

"I'm well aware there is a procedure. A procedure for everything. I have just explained to you my story and why I don't have much time to waste."

His smile just got bigger and bigger as I kept talking and repeating myself. "If we have the plot number we can block the property – it's all there in the paperwork by the judge."

A pause as he picked up the paperwork again, glanced at it, and then put it back down.

"Let me check what I can do for you when I have some time," he finally said. "I am very busy." I looked around his empty desk. He didn't even pretend to be preoccupied with other matters on his desk.

It was the end of the conversation. The slim prospect of any assistance was stamped out. The only person who would win the cut and thrust of a high-stake duel like this was the one who actually controlled 'the system'.

He most certainly was The Blocker.

"You sir," biting hard on my tongue to keep from calling him a few choice words. "You. Are. Not. A. Very. Nice. Man." And with that I got up from my chair in a huff, spun on my heels and clacked loudly out of his office, not before I caught his smile beam even brighter.

Clack, clack, clack. People are Impossible. Clack, clack, clack. People are so Unhelpful. Clack, clack, clack.

I clacked and muttered under my breath all the way during the long walk out of the courthouse, getting odd looks from everyone along my way. I got as far as the car park when my phone rang. Unknown mobile number.

"Miss Amber," came the familiar Arnold Schwarzenegger accent.

"Yes," I snapped. I could actually hear his wide toothy smile.

"I blocked the property."

I spun around, stunned into silence.

"Really?" I asked, almost to myself. Relief swept over me, as I was temporarily lost for words as I took in the magnitude of what he has done for me, and so fast.

And then a thought suddenly hit me. "You have blocked the Right Property, haven't you?" It wouldn't surprise me if in his self-induced semi-slumber he had gone ahead and searched under my own name and blocked my own property while enveloped in his cloudy mist.

He chuckled as he read out the property's name and indeed it looked like he had blocked Grant's property.

I needed to sit down, the shock, I couldn't believe it! I thanked him profusely and waffled on about how long this case had taken to get my money back.

"No problem, Miss Amber, anytime."

"See, you can help, why do you people make things so difficult?" Something that took two months, was done in virtually two minutes.

"Ma'am, there are procedures. I did this as a special only as you have the judge's approval."

"Well thank you. And you can go home today with the satisfaction that you really changed someone's luck today." And he had. My ship had finally come in, steered by The Blocker himself. He asked me to get my lawyer to call him on his mobile which I promptly did after I got off the phone with him. My lawyer duly fired off a second request to pursue proceedings to block Grant's property to obtain my dues with the plot number attached. The Blocker arranged for it to be immediately accepted, and my lawyer then sent me the official notice that Grant's property was blocked under my case number. All done within the day.

So, whilst Grant was busy with his appeals, we had managed to freeze his property in Dubai. It meant the property would have to eventually be auctioned. Whatever money was owed to me would be paid to me and the rest transfers to the court's 'bank' where it would be held. It meant, in time, another process.

Now, as far as we were concerned, Grant's lawyers could delay matters and stretch the appeals out as much as they wanted.

"Now, you have The Blocker's details," I teased my lawyer. "Don't lose it."

"Are you kidding? It's gold."

The judge's final ruling

I attended the review hearing on March 31st, 2019 at the Appeal Court.

The advocates for both parties had a frank exchange of views until the judge intervened and one look on the judge's face and I knew the defence had lost the argument.

They had not paid the fees in time. That, in hindsight, had been their monumental mistake. Nothing else needed to be heard or reviewed. Bang. The hammer went down. The case file was finally shut.

"Is it actually over now?" I asked my firm's court representative. "They can't appeal again?"

"Hmm ..." he seemed to be actually searching his memory. "No, even if they do, the decision has been made."

But they did.

Good grief, they were agonising.

After learning his fate, Grant, of course, got to work to either sell or transfer his property to his wife's name, only to discover his property was frozen. The wake of this realisation led to his lawyer filing a civil objection in June 2019 to the Dubai Execution Court arguing the execution process could only commence after final judgment had been given on March 31st, 2019 at the Appeal Court, and not before. Furthermore, they said they were amazed at the speed in which we had escalated the action through the execution process which led to the Execution Court seizing Grant's property, without their knowledge or notification.

Well, that's their story.

My lawyer was surprised that Grant's lawyer "really didn't know" the execution process was running alongside the appeal, especially as he knew that technically the appeal would never go ahead, no matter what he threw at the courts.

"I don't understand. Why didn't he tell Grant to sell his property if he knew or suspected we had started the execution file?"

Pause. My lawyer looked at me waiting for the penny to drop, as I searched his face. "Oh," I covered my mouth in mocked shock. What are the chances he didn't tell Grant he had missed the appeal deadline by not paying the fees on time?

"I didn't say anything." My lawyer drew his hand across his lips. In other words, the chances were excellent.

Now, Grant's lawyer's tactic was to try to get the civil judgment thrown out on procedure: that we didn't follow the proper execution procedure. There was a possibility, however slim, that his conviction could be thrown out on a technical basis, and his property unfrozen. The case was to be heard at the highest court level: The Cassation Court.

Un-be-live-able.

This was going a lot worse than I had expected.

"No, no," my lawyer hastened to reassure me, "it's the usual stuff".

The judge and the court was obliged to hear their argument.

A date was set. On August 1st, 2019, at a hearing into Grant's claims against the seizing of his property, the judge ruled in our favour, and refused the cassation. It meant we had won the cassation procedure and the property was allowed to remain frozen to pay off Grant's debt related to my case.

Legally, Grant has now exhausted all options available to him. The case, once carrying its own storm around it for years, has now sailed into a calm harbour.

After numerous battles stretching over almost two years, it was over; finally, it was over.

"Is it? It is, isn't it?" I was a child again, seeking reassurance from my lawyer who gave it wholeheartedly. I was almost afraid to believe it. Expecting yet another unexpected twist to emerge from over my shoulder. What next? Grant's evil twin surfaces?

What a moment it was. The two-year quest was now over. Everything had worked out to perfection. I had been convinced many, many times from many, many others that it could never happen.

And my lawyer was right about another thing. The mysterious phone calls I had been receiving over the past two years had been few and scattered over the last few weeks. Until they stopped entirely when the verdict was announced.

Whilst the property remained frozen, we did give Grant opportunities to unfreeze it by paying the debt. We also had the option of hiring a debt recovery team in Scotland. We explored all options and gave Grant and his wife plenty of opportunities to settle their debt, as per the court of law. They ignored every single request from us.

I hadn't pursued Grant for the money, but when it became a real possibility that I may get my money back, I was determined to have it. End of.

In hindsight, I realise, I was able to pursue Grant for that very reason, because I hadn't been focused on the money. In my mind, I had written off the £60,000. I had to move on from it. Worrying about it was not going to get my money back. I had to just put it down to a life experience and a valuable lesson.

"How can you just write off £60,000?" My brother asked me in complete wonderment. I had to – for my own sanity.

When you take money out of the equation and it's not used as a goal it's amazing what you can achieve. If you look at all the people who are successful, their driving force was the passion, not the money. The key to 'flow' is to pursue an activity for its own sake, not for the reward it brings. Achieving each goal post, however small, was a reward in itself for me. When you focus on something that you care about, you will find your energy is boundless. You have the power of persistence, tenacity and clear-sightedness – and belief. And that's when luck will find you, and appear in various ways be it a random email, a call, a stranger, even an admin error.

And I simply believed that something different could happen for me.

And I had a strong team behind me infused with basic honesty and the strength of character to stand up with me when I needed support. The support provided to the case by Grant's victims, friends and industry professionals who became friends, throughout this two-year long trial process, was invaluable in winning both cases, and was a great demonstration of how we work with each other across the community, and across international borders to fight crime. I hope the conclusion of this case offers some justice to them. And I hope my story sends a message and is proof that no case should be written off. In our round-up of ignoring expert predictions at the beginning of the case, we said there were grounds for optimism – and that had borne fruit.

To which we simply ask: Why?

What kind of an existence do you have when fraud is the centre of your life?

Is ANYTHING really worth that level of deceit?

To the likes of Grant, yes.

These sort of people's mindset and philosophy of life is very much 'Carpe Diem'.

It's dangling a big financial carrot in front of them. When you start to think you can create something out of nothing, it's very difficult to resist.

In the 1990 film Derailed Jennifer Anniston's character introduces herself. "I'm a financial advisor," and then she goes on to explain what that means. "I cheat clients."

There's no tongue in the cheek. It's a statement. She

knows what she does. And she knows why she does it.

Just like Grant.

For us to understand why the likes of her and Grant do what they do, and be comfortable with it, we need to turn to psychology: the psychology of fraudsters, the addiction, the application.

What we put at the centre of our existence is the thing that dictates our lives. It's the thing we love most. It's the thing that we live for, and we would die for. It's the thing that determines how we live and why we live. It's our centre.

Fraudsters take their own desires as the centre of their existence – anything they want, they take, regardless of the consequences, regardless of things like right and wrong, regardless of morality, regardless of whom it hurts. If they want it, they take it. If they think it, they do it.

This is worship of the desire: money.

And this is, unfortunately, the type of culture pushed on us; this is what advertisers sell.

Sprite: "Obey your thirst".

Nike: "Just do it".

Pepsi: "Live for now".

The theme here is to tell you to worship your desire if you feel a craving then obey it. Because this is how they get you to spend on things you don't need. So the idea here is a culture very much about the worship of self. What you feel must be right, obey it. If it feels good, do it, regardless of right and wrong.

This is the type of culture that is literally shoved down our throats and we're supposed to accept it. And if we say that we believe things are morally wrong, these types of people are called various types of names because you're not being tolerant of a person's desire. But if you obey your desire regardless of right and wrong and whom it's going to hurt and whom you're going to have to take from – that's a worship of the desires.

There are people who will take money because of worship. Where they are literally willing to do anything for money. Money is at the centre and whatever it takes they will do it for money. Same with power. The levels that people will go to for money – if it means betraying your friends, concealing documents – that is a worship of money. That's taking the money and worshipping it. That means you've taken the money and made it a God. It's an idol of the heart.

Internally, they have become slaves to money, at all costs.

Psychologists say money releases the pleasure hormone dopamine – the same one that gets people hooked on drugs. "Think of the pleasure as more akin to cocaine than sweeties," said one.

And this is the mentality that we are up against.

Neuro scientists have conducted experiments where they have noticed that when the subject of 'earn money' is brought up, the part of the brain that gets stimulated is the same part that cocaine stimulates.

This is how fraudsters are comfortable engaging in large-scale criminal activity.

They are type A personalities. It's part of their behaviour and personality. A blatant disregard on what their actions may have on society and on families. They have no problem with it.

They don't turn into this person in seconds. The person you thought you knew was never there in the first place. Like a phantom.

For every thousand financial advisors there is a man like Grant who would sell his soul for another high-net-worth individual that he can dig his manicured hands in, and line his pockets. It's fun, exciting and opens up all sorts of doors – to first class plane cabins, brand new cars, designer kitchens and the best restaurants in town.

The circle never ends. And it was never going to end.

When diving into the realm of individual crime, Grant is probably one of the first names you'll come across. Even by the opulent standards of Dubai, it was the most lavish one-man fraud the city had seen for many years. To any expat in Dubai who had the misfortune to come across Neil Ramsay Pringle Grant, the very name will remain highly emotive.

PART 2

CHAPTER 9

PLANDEMIC: THE PERFECT PLOT

Behind every rogue is an enabler

What had begun as a probe of Guardian Trust Company Ltd had turned into a much broader investigation into the financial advisory industry, and the magic words, 'perfect plot'. I didn't realise the scale of financial advisory fraud until Philip Van Neste came into the picture and emerged as a very central figure in the Grant story.

My thought was yes, we were conned by Grant, an Independent Financial Advisor. But the question I kept asking myself was: How did he con us? How had it been so easy for Grant to deceive and manipulate us? How did he orchestrate a clever plan, and lock us into these various Trusts and policies?

He can't have done it alone. Technically, it's not possible.

And so the question is: Who was helping him?

Rupert and I started digging into Grant's professional life and started pulling out all these people and loosely-connected entities that were linked to him. We knew that they fitted together somehow. It was just a matter of working out how.

And I started with a chart. First, I had to try and map out this pyramid scheme. We now know Guardian and Van Neste was one of the partners who Grant worked with. The other partners were identified as time went on. Product Managers, Fund Managers and Financial Service Providers. All powerful big branded names. And then from there we bridged down. This was something that we assembled for the prosecution investigation and realised that this chart could go off like a spider web – an international spider web that was part of the story.

At the top of the pyramid scheme was not Grant, but these big branded companies and Grant was really their right-hand person in Dubai who already had a portfolio of substantial long-term clients. They knew he could sell, and upsell these clients anything because of the trust he had built up with them over a sustained period of time. And he was in the position to help them target more individuals for selling investment schemes. In return, Grant understood he could deliver substantial results for them and be rewarded handsomely by them.

By this point, what we were beginning to realise was that Grant was not just a random case. This was an international investment ring, and Grant was a very small piece in a huge network.

Then you realise this story goes much further and murkier than just Grant. It goes right to the heart of the financial industry and some of the most trusted names in the industry.

Without the likes of Van Neste, Grant wouldn't have been able to make the money that he did, and investors would not have lost some or all of their money.

Blind eye

The key question I was constantly faced with was how did Grant manage to operate within the industry for so long without a financial advisory licence? Yes, he could get away with conning the naive trusting person on the street; but the industry itself? It's like a doctor operating without a medical licence or a lawyer without a legal licence: clients are none the wiser, but the hospitals and the law firms have to perform due diligence on those licences.

Grant, therefore, would have needed help with his set up in Dubai, that's for sure.

Grant's operation could not have been accomplished unless it was supported within the industry itself, by the Financial Service Providers, the Product Providers and the Fund Managers he had partnered up with.

The people at the top of these companies had agreed to simply look the other way and pretend that they did review the documentation and performed due-diligence to see whether Grant's business had been made with the proper paperwork, truly ensuring the duty of care with their clients. The very fact is, they never did. Had they performed the most basic of checks they would have realised Grant was not licensed, they would see his papers were a chock-full of irregularities, and they would never have entered Terms of Business with him. Instead they summarised the risks and saw the potential profits that Grant could bring them from unsuspecting investors, and they did nothing except happily take Grant's financial contributions and his introductions to new clients. It's this kind of risk-reward miscalculation that contributes to rogue financial advisors flooding the markets, everywhere.

One could even go as far as to say, they literally plotted together with Grant, as perfectly demonstrated with the

Grant-Van Neste partnership.

A bullet proof plan

Philip Van Neste.

There was something about him I had to know.

He meddled in my court cases, influencing the trials from the shadows. It was time to find out why.

I did not hear anything about Philip Van Neste nor was I suspicious of him until he involved himself into the picture at the prosecution investigation. That's when I started probing into his partnership with Grant.

It meant digging up information, combing through emails and researching small details that could be later connected to form a whole picture – a scheme.

And their scheme was simple – hoodwink expat investors out of their money, and provide a backdrop where neither party can be held legally responsible.

How did they do this? How did they hatch this plot? Financial advisory fraud looks to be extremely complex in makeup, and it can feel really overwhelming to try to understand all the nuance and how it happens. But when you break it down, you will find it's actually not. It's simply manipulation.

Grant recommends to his clients a long-term savings plan with Guardian Trust Company Ltd, a Financial Service Provider, domiciled in Jersey, in the Channel Islands. Van Neste is the chairman of the company.

Grant is the Independent Financial Advisor between you and Guardian, so you think Grant is dealing with everything in your best interests. And Grant convinces you, as his client and friend, into giving up hundreds and thousands of dollars in an incredibly well-honed script.

We're then shown pages and pages of the Guardian

Trust application form which is laid out like a contract. Grant offers to fill it in for you, to save you doing so and so he can ensure it's done correctly. At some point, Grant requests we provide him with what he 'says' is a Power of Attorney over our financial affairs, which he explains, as meaning, that he is authorised to make, move and control investments in your Trust on your behalf. He further explains to you that it is simply to let Guardian know, he is your financial advisor and is managing your investments by your authorisation. And he makes it all perfectly plausible, professional even. To the unknown eye, it is worded to look like an agreement between you and Grant.

In reality, this document is what is called a Prescribed Direction. It is written on a blank piece of paper with no letterhead. It is addressed to Guardian only. Grant is not copied in the letter nor required to sign it. You may notice that but don't enquire why. You are asked to sign and date this piece of paper and, once you do, the document is filed with Guardian. There is a short time-lapse between when you sign the Prescribed Direction and the formation of the Trust – a legal tactic to prove you appointed your advisor prior to the formation of the Trust.

After Grant completes the Guardian application form and arranges the signatures in Dubai for you; the Trust is then set up in Jersey by Van Neste.

And then the last piece is, at the direction of Grant, you transfer the money yourself to Guardian to activate the contract.

Grant has taken care of the delivery. Van Neste now takes care of the operation.

Grant's happy, Van Neste is happy. Because they're about to make a pot full of money and you are still none the wiser that you have just signed your money away and will continue to do so for years to come.

What this means in practice is that Grant is now legally protected in the event a lawsuit is lodged against him by several tactics. There is no contract between you and Grant. Your contract is directly with Guardian, as the trustee. You have transferred the money directly to Guardian yourself, and out of the country. Grant is paid his fees directly by Guardian from your money in your Trust. In short, there is no link between you and Grant, or a paper trail. No mud can stick to his hands.

Only after you signed the paperwork and you sent your money to Guardian, do you receive a copy of the Trust Deed, a legal document setting out various obligations placed upon the trustee, the beneficiaries, the settlor and any other associated parties. Guardian then slaps you with their Terms and Conditions in fine print – which Grant brushes over with you during a meeting – and don't require your signature of acceptance. They say the devil is in the details, the fine print. Here, he bypasses the devil altogether, though you'd have to have had a microscope to see it.

It later transpires that somewhere in the fine print, in the lengthy Trust Deed document, is a throwaway clause, that you have agreed to appoint Grant as your 'investment manager' via the Prescribed Direction form. In other words, Guardian has not appointed him for you, even though Grant introduced you to Guardian and is selling their products to you. This clause and the Prescribed Direction certificate mean that Guardian is now legally protected, making any lawsuit against Guardian thrown out from the very beginning.

So any legal recourse will be directed back to Grant – only there is no paper trail leading to Grant. There is nothing to suggest from Grant that he has 'agreed' to be your appointed investment manager. His signature is not on the Prescribed Direction. And the biggest part of my case against Grant was establishing a paper trail to him.

It had all been planned with military precision.

Our money was now firmly lodged in their hands, and unbeknown to us we had no legal protection or recourse in the event should something go wrong.

That's why many fraud victims cannot get their investment back because the Independent Financial Advisor and their financial partners both state the other party is responsible for your investments. And, because of some carefully drafted legal documents bearing your signature, both parties can appear bullet proof when it comes to the law.

These contracts have been systemically, proactively engineered by some clever lawyers to deceive victims. It's called a defeat contract. It's designed to defeat the investors.

"It's clever, it's so insidiously clever. It's genius," my lawyer's words – not mine.

My words were along the lines of vicious and duplicitous. Everybody is confusing an obvious fraudulent activity with 'creative genius'. An ingenious, devious plan with 'sheer brilliance'. It's not. To the layman, these words meant they had showed 'some serious capability' and could be 'clever' and a 'genius' with a PhD. In reality we're dealing with conmen with minimum financial qualifications. It was dark and dangerous and they were operating ruthlessly. When your own lawyer is impressed by the other lawyers' work, you know you're in trouble. 'Clever' and 'genius' is lawyer-speak meaning victims are unlikely to be able to claim compensation from them for any loss in investments.

Guardian now provided the platform where your various fund investments were going to be held, and together with Grant they had full access to, and control over your investments. All the incentives the financial institutions offered to their advisors were based on selling the most profitable products which were start-up firms carrying a high-risk. Another reason they preferred start-up companies is that Grant, operating without a licence, would go undetected.

In the midst of the Terms and Conditions of the Trust Deed are the fee arrangements, which your financial advisor never explained to you, and which are described in very generic terms that are difficult to understand. You discover that Guardian paid Grant's fees directly from your Trust. But you never know how much he is being paid from the Trust; the calculations and distribution of which you have no say in. It's like they've agreed between themselves how they are going to pay themselves with your money.

Industry professionals predict the formula for Guardian could be similar to the following: 3 percent of the total value of the Trust, plus, 45 percent marketing allowance, plus, 2.5 percent of each contribution outside the initial allocation period.

Together the duo provided investors with inflated valuation and performance metrics to dupe investors, allowing Van Neste and Grant to collect higher investor fees than they were actually entitled to receive. It was inflated, because the funds held within the Trust were suspended from redemption, performing poorly, or illiquid and their NAV (net asset value) was calculated at the point that redemptions were suspended.

Their response to this?

This was how it had to be shown.

But it was completely misleading. Smoke and mirrors.

Additional to the fees are the charges: initial unit charges, plan fees, fund administration charges, and external fund annual management charges, and many more. Bear in mind, these are the charges you've worked out; the 'known' charges.

The 'unknown' charges are embedded in the funds but they do not make these explicit as they are built into the fund price, and any gains are automatically swallowed by them. As a guide, life companies levy an additional fund charge, usually of 0.75 percent on top of the fund annual management charges.

The commissions are a devil in disguise that can eat up most of your future returns and literally halve your retirement pot. This happens because of the commission camouflage effect.

Let me give you an example. If you invest your money in a simple fund, you are paying a two percent annual fee. And this doesn't sound like much. When your financial advisor tells you that you are paying a two percent management fee, your brain says "Okay ... this is not a problem. They take two and I keep 98".

Right?

Well, no.

We are doing simple calculations: two percent out of $1,000: one percent of $1,000 equals $10, so two percent must be $20.

But, when you add a longer time period maybe 10, 20 or 30 years, our brain just can't process the math anymore.

If I ask you how much is two percent deducted annually for 30 years in a market that grows by eight percent on average, our brain is just not wired to calculate complex calculations like this.

And that is perfectly normal, and that is why we subconsciously make some assumptions: "If two percent of my invested money is a small number, then a two percent annual fee can't be a serious problem for me".

But unfortunately, the harsh reality is that, as a rule of thumb, a two percent annual fee halves your retirement pot in the long run. The financial industry knows this and takes full advantage of it. That is why they will never explain the effect of commissions over the long run to you. Even if you have the best financial advisor, it just doesn't happen.

What would you say if your financial advisor offered you a financial product where you got to keep only half of the future returns?

If you are like me, you would run away as fast as you could.

But most investors don't and think their advisor has provided them with great advice. Why? Because nobody told them about the commission camouflage effect.

The commission camouflage effect states that small annual commissions tend to eat a large part of our investing returns over the long run. It's one of the deadliest concepts in investing and for most investors, this amount can easily go into the six-figure range.

Coming back to Grant, in addition to Guardian, he would have set up contracts with each of the Fund Managers for New Earth (Waste Recycling), Centurion (Life Insurance Settlement) etc., and we cannot know the exact amount each of these companies paid him, except that he was picking up four to eight percent commission on each investment fund placed. The percentage is high because again, they were high-risk start-up companies.

And you never knew this. You never saw an invoice. You never saw a receipt. The money was collected from the Trust by Guardian and paid in full to Grant.

This is another legal tactic as it's difficult to prove how Grant benefitted financially from you if you can't provide evidence that he did indeed take commission and fees from you. Grant doesn't share details, Guardian doesn't share details and the online web portal is designed not to share details so it is impossible to tell what got paid and to whom.

They're helping themselves to your hard-earned cash

and putting up smoke and mirrors when asked pointed questions about charges, or in fact anything.

Together they were in absolute 'control' of your Trust, as well as its administration. In 2013, Van Neste wanted to move my Trust from Jersey to Guardian Global Capital (Suisse) SA in Switzerland. By law, such a move required the investors' consent and signature which were never received or granted. Either Grant's camp or Guardian's camp had taken care of the signature to indicate the acceptance of my Trust to be moved and Van Neste simply verified the signature as a 'true likeness'.

Another case in point: in 2018, I wrote to Van Neste to say as settlor I wanted to close my Trust and subsequently requested a full breakdown of the overall value of the Trust. For two years, he failed to take any action, all the while continuing to take fees from the Trust. When there was no money left in the Trust, only then did he close it, and without prior notification or need of authorisation from me, the settlor.

Another issue is the duration of the Trust, lasting 25 years. Yes, you can opt out, and you are sold that idea by Grant at the beginning. However, if you choose to get out before its lifetime you pay a swingeing financial penalty, a fact which he did not share with you. It's so clever that Grant warns you that abandoning a Trust before the end is "like ripping up a book manuscript in front of the author as he's on the final paragraph". And that's exactly how you feel. Trapped. From the moment you transferred the money to initiate the Trust, you lost your hold on your capital, and you were indeed trapped.

It's called rigging the game of investing.

And learning that the very people who brought us these Trusts and funds are shunning it in their own homes is galling beyond words. As so often in modern corporations, it's the malodorous stench of rank hypocrisy that is as outrageous as their bank balances.

Everything is meticulously mapped out, through to the very last detail, in order to ensure they – and no one else – own the agenda. Again, that's an example of the planning that went into the way these partnerships were entered into.

As an additional layer of protection, Grant and Guardian produced a Terms of Business document on the off chance that if they were ever caught out, that document protected the other party to avoid any liability. The document, drawn up by Grant and Van Neste, referred to various waivers that Van Neste has conducted the correct due diligence and security checks on Grant, thereby allowing Grant to sell their products in the market. In return, Grant agrees: "We hereby hold you harmless against any claim, damages, compensation or any loss which may be sustained by Guardian as a consequence of any transactions carried out or any advice given, by me, during the currency of this agreement". Simply put, Guardian waives their own responsibility, their own obligation.

It's like opening the doors and walking up a winding staircase into their ornate and bizarre world. They basically set up a fraudulent pyramid scheme in plain view. And had fine-tuned the practice and made it an art form. It's a perfect crime and partnership, all done under your very nose, with your consent and it's all legally acceptable.

With the odds in their favour, it explains why the financial reward was too hard to resist for both men.

And this extends to the chairman of the company – of all of Grant's partners, not just Guardian. They were all in on this. They knew what was happening and became enormously wealthy in the process. Philip Van Neste was just a reflection of all the others.

An honest comment from a financial advisor admitted I

was not wrong. "Everybody's doing it, everybody knows it's wrong, and everybody knows it's going on – and so no one should rely on these advisors anyway."

And after you place the last piece in the jigsaw, and you step back and look at the overall picture, what no one expected – and what repeatedly wrong-footed his novice clients – was that Grant deliberately involves you in non-standard entities, which were never required. You don't know that you can set up investment funds directly with the Fund Management companies and the Product Providers, and Grant sells you the idea to route it through Financial Service Providers and to hold them in a Trust or policy.

You agreed to his advice because the pitch sounded good and safe as it was part of a long-term savings plan. And this is where the boulder drops on your head. You never needed the Financial Service Providers in the first place. You are basically paying the 'middle man', in this case Guardian, for a transaction between two parties, and paying them a fortune for it.

It's like renting a storage space and keeping all your boxes in it, in one place. You didn't really need the storage space and you were handing them fees for no reason except to keep the boxes in them. These policies and Trusts that have been sold to you, via your financial advisor, only work in favour of their stakeholders – and you realise, you aren't one of them. It is the single deadliest product on the financial advisory market, nothing else comes close.

It has been an eye-opener. No, a shock to the system. This isn't okay. We're sold these Trusts and policies with the view that they are expertly managed and will gain wealth over their lifetime.

This will never happen.

What they said publicly was different from what they did privately.

Smoke and mirrors, gambling with other people's money, modern highway robbery from a desk. You're up against a system you can never beat because it is all a burdensome mystery rather than an exact science, which is why we don't know how to trace the misinformation back.

This is how Grant and the like created a rogue financial pyramid scheme. And this is why behind every rogue is an enabler. That's the secret sauce. Rogues cannot perpetrate without those close to them who enable it.

In 2016, Grant was on trial in a criminal court in Dubai for several charges of fraud, including licence fraud that carries a fine, and the more serious crime of signature forgery which includes a jail sentence. Now the partnership between the two confidants was tested. To turn a blind eye to Grant's illegal business affairs one may argue may be financially motivated, but to support Grant in a court of law was legally motivated. Their statement was intended to influence the prosecution investigation. The concealing of facts and withholding of evidence was intended to influence both trials.

At the time, a savvy observer might inquire: "Why would he do that?".

Now, we understood, it was in Van Neste's interest to personally help throw the case in Dubai against Grant and be directly involved in the efforts.

CHAPTER 10

PLANET GUARDIAN

ᴊᴄ The art of smoke and mirrors ᴊᴄ

What IS the story against the Guardian businesses? Guardian deny any wrongdoing, but in light of the criminal and civil verdict, that is now questioned.

For the sake of putting the Guardian businesses, into context, we have to journey back to Grant, and look at his conviction from a different legal standpoint. Did the Guardian businesses commit a crime through Philip Van Neste's participation in Grant's crimes?

Through another lens

At the beginning of May 2010, I was approached by Grant of Prosperity Offshore Investment Consultants, a financial advisory company based in Dubai. Grant proposed investment products to me to be held within a Trust declared by the Guardian Trust Company Ltd. Guardian Trust Company Ltd required due diligence documentation, information to identify the settlor (including bank account details, as well as a certified copy of a passport and second proof of residential address) from me before settling the Trust, which I provided through Grant.

Prosperity held itself out as an entity licensed by the DED for offshore investment consulting.

In his letter to potential investors, Van Neste wrote: "I would like to confirm that Prosperity Management Consultancy applied to Guardian Trust Company Limited for Terms of Business having completed an application form dated 5 October, 2005. Prosperity at that time was authorised by the Government of Dubai, Department of Economic Development, and held a Professional License issued on 18 July 2004."

Prosperity provided Guardian Trust Company Ltd with the paperwork, and Van Neste admitted in his letter they had seen this evidence of licences: "Evidence of this and copies of the constitutive documents for Prosperity, and the Financial Planning Certificates held by (Neil Grant) were provided to Guardian."

It is unclear what further steps Guardian Trust Company Ltd took, if any, to verify documents received from Prosperity, Prosperity's qualifications as an investment manager, or investigations that it made with the DED.

A later criminal judgment against Grant evidences that Prosperity was licenced by the DED for management consulting through which it provided "consultancies and management studies for the public organisation and companies". Prosperity was not licensed nor did it have competence in investment, financial advisory, or any fiduciary role.

The Trust was settled by a Trust Deed made by Guardian Trust Company Ltd. An application form annexed to the Trust Deed appointed Prosperity and Grant as investment manager to the Trust. The initial Trust property was £45,000 cash for investment, and £5,000 cash held on account of Guardian Trust Company Ltd's ongoing administration fees, to be deducted quarterly. I, however, never executed Guardian Trust Company Ltd's Terms and Conditions, and was never asked to do so by them.

Grant went on to instruct Guardian Trust Company Ltd (acting by its nominee Guardian Asset Management) to place investments on behalf of the Trust. These investments were extremely risky, unsuitable for a novice investor such as myself and each decreased in value until they were worthless.

Due to the poor performance of each investment proposed by Grant, he agreed to waive the majority of fees payable by the Trust to Prosperity in its capacity as investment manager of the Trust. It was discovered that this did not happen.

Guardian Trust Company Ltd maintained oversight of the Trust from a compliance perspective, and requested updated due diligence documents when those held on file were out of date. Guardian Trust Company Ltd (and later the Guardian Global Capital (Suisse) SA (the current trustee) took fees from the Trust for administration. The trustee acted in bad faith by failing to carry out its contractual and fiduciary obligations while charging fees.

Guardian Trust Company Ltd (and later the trustee) provided me through Grant with monthly valuation statements for investments held on Trust, which bore Guardian Trust Company Ltd's insignia from at least February 19th, 2013 (and the trustee's insignia following the transfer of trusteeship).

In 2013, Grant instructed Guardian Asset Management to invest the Trust's investment in the Burj India Fund, and invest in New Earth (Waste Recycling) Fund.

The market value of the Trust fund decreased from

£45,000 to £41,941.86 during the period from the settlement of the Trust to December 2013. However, this figure includes the Student Accommodation Fund's market value on the date when redemptions were suspended and so is inflated.

By December 2013 the Guardian Global Capital (Suisse) SA became trustee of the Trust. During this time Van Neste moved from chairman at Guardian Trust Company Ltd to his current role as chairman of Guardian Global Capital (Suisse) SA.

The change of trustee from Guardian Trust Company Ltd to the Guardian Global Capital (Suisse) SA occurred as a result of 'someone' forging my signature on a letter giving my consent to the transfer as evidenced in the criminal judgment. Van Neste, when alerted of the possibility that there was signature tampering on the consent form, had stated in an email to me that the signed consent form had been sent to him from Prosperity's office in Dubai. Despite my requests, Van Neste had failed to provide evidence or other support relating to this to the criminal prosecution against Grant in the Dubai criminal court.

Instead, Van Neste supported Grant and stated to the prosecution that they had no way of knowing who had sent the signed consent form to their offices in Jersey, and that they could only confirm they had received the consent form by post.

After taking in all the evidence, and the report from the forensic analyst, the judge accepted there was no evidence to suggest that the forged signature on the consent form had been signed or arranged by Grant. The charges against Grant were dropped.

Six months after the criminal verdict, as per his words, Van Neste confirmed that the signed consent form had been sent to them from Prosperity's office: "There can be no doubt that the transfer instruction was received by Guardian in Jersey from Prosperity by courier on 20 November 2013", and produced a copy of the Skynet tracking document as confirmation that the consent form was received by Guardian from Prosperity and he confirmed he had approved the signature as "it bears a verifiable likeness to the signature on the account opening documentation".

After the transfer of trustee, Van Neste wrote to me directly confirming that portfolio valuations of assets held on trust by Guardian Global Capital (Suisse) SA were "updated every Monday morning and reflect the price as at close of business the previous Friday... We thank you for entrusting your assets with Guardian and look forward to continuing our relationship".

He went on to confirm: "Guardian Asset Management Ltd (which provides various investment services and is a sister company to Guardian Trust Company) will continue to be regulated in the Island and provide a continuation of investment services from Jersey in relation to your Trust."

On Guardian Global Capital (Suisse) SA's appointment as trustee of the Trust, investments comprising the Trust fund were in a poor state of affairs. From July 1st, 2013 redemptions were suspended on the Student Accommodation fund, with no certainty that the fund could restructure and realise solvency or any value for shareholders. The Centurion (Life Insurance Settlement) 101 Growth Fund had been suspended since at least 2012, which Guardian Asset Management was aware of.

On June 9th, 2016, the High Court of Justice of the Isle of Man appointed Deloitte LLP as Joint Liquidators of the companies and funds underlying the New Earth Solutions. On June 16th, 2016 the company underlying the funds wrote to shareholders informing them that it "remains unlikely that the sale of these assets will generate a return".

On June 29th, 2016 the directors of the company underlying the Lucent (Land Purchase and Planning) Fund informed shareholders that the fund was suspended.

With an accelerating fall underway, all of the Trust's investments were and are worthless.

When Grant's questionable activities came to light and his case was transferred to the Dubai public prosecution, I contacted Guardian Global Capital (Suisse) SA informing it not to take instructions from Grant with immediate effect and I instructed Van Neste to remove Grant as investment manager to the Trust. The process took two months, all the while, Grant retained visibility and access to the Trust.

I subsequently commenced a criminal action against Grant, which was heard in the Dubai court on August 2nd, 2017. Grant was convicted of "unrightfully taking movable assets comprised of the money and commissions (under his licence) which belong to the victim" and orders were made for him to pay fines.

On November 14th, 2018, by the Dubai civil court, Grant was ordered to pay damages for deluding me "that he is a financial advisor, contrary to the reality", which led to the loss of my money.

To date, I had difficulty in engaging the Trustee. I had been denied access to the Trustee's web portal which contains pertinent information in respect of my Trust, including current valuations of the trust fund and the Trustee has failed to respond to my requests for access, while continuing to charge fees.

Meanwhile, I remain trapped in the Trust.

In an email to me, Matt Hill from Guardian Global Capital (Suisse) SA wrote: "The termination of the Trust is dependent on the investments, and in this case all investments are currently illiquid". In short, it seemed highly unlikely that Fund Managers will allow the transfer of the holding directly into my name to enable the Trust to close.

In reference to the Centurion (Life Insurance Settlement) investment fund he went on to write: "This can be transferred into your name, however you must meet Centurion's 'Eligible Investor' criteria. If you do not meet Centurion's criteria then they will be unable to transfer the holding into your personal name. If you do not meet Centurion's eligibility requirements, it is still possible to transfer the holding to another regulated custodian to hold on your behalf – but given the situation on this holding it seems unlikely that another third party would be willing to hold it."

And with regards to New Earth (Waste Recycling) he wrote, "The fund is an Isle of Man (IOM) regulated fund, and it is therefore the Fund's administrators/managers responsibility to ensure compliance with IOM regulations (particularly the requirement to sign disclaimers/acknowledgements relating to the fund's status). As the investment was made through a Trust advised by an IFA, the applicant (i.e., the Trust) is automatically a qualifying investor and therefore no disclaimers/acknowledgements were signed. For the avoidance of doubt, we (nor the former trustee – who were responsible for placing the investment under instruction) are subject to IOM regulation."

I was now trapped on Planet Guardian, a crazy place where Van Neste called all the shots, oblivious to the consequences.

Responsibility and accountability

Here's the harsh reality: the ruling in the Dubai criminal court confirms that Guardian's due diligence is wrong, it was in fact incorrect, because Grant and Prosperity did not have a licence to provide investment services and so on that basis, in accordance with their own regulations in Jersey, in relation to the regulations in the UAE, Guardian had no business allowing Prosperity to come into the market and sell their financial products. It just should not have happened and Guardian are in breach of its own regulations.

Surely, what the Guardian businesses as a regulated entity are not permitted to do directly, cannot do indirectly?

If Guardian were to sell their products directly into the UAE market, they would have to be regulated, they have to meet with investors, such as me, they would have to enter into proper letters of engagement. They would have to establish if I am risk-adverse and designate me as professional client or not, and they would have to understand my appetite for investing into structured products. Guardian would have to go through an extensive exercise to actually take my money and understand my financial capabilities. That's what Guardian would do if they sell directly to customers – whether I understand the products, whether I understand the risks attached to the products, whether I have enough knowledge to be able to enter into this sort of Trust or investment funds. Guardian were channelling highly complex structured funds such as New Earth (Waste Recycling), Bamboo (Eco Planet) and Lucent (Land Purchase and Planning) and therefore their responsibility to due diligence was of utmost importance.

Here, Guardian have not sold directly, they sold indirectly.

But should that mean their regulatory requirements is waived?

Absolutely not.

Directly or indirectly, the same standard applies. When they rely on a third party to sell their product, their due diligence should be as if they are coming into the market.

So therefore, they have to ensure, and it is their utmost responsibility and duty of care to their investors, that Grant and Prosperity Management Consultancy can do exactly the same function they could do if they were engaged in this market directly.

It is completely evident to all, that Prosperity Management Consultancy is a management consultancy, and not a financial consultancy. If this is not a financial consultancy how did Guardian give a mandate to Grant and Prosperity to sell their products in the market? That is a fundamental breach which goes towards the voidable element of a contract. They have not engaged properly, they are not authorised to engage, and there is a criminal conviction that says Grant and Prosperity Management Consultancy is not authorised. Guardian's assessment of whether or not Prosperity and Grant should come into the market and sell their products was woeful. If I was the chairman sat in Guardian and Prosperity made an application to me what I should have done is I should have looked at their licence and say, hang on a minute, have they got the necessary licence in that market, (i.e., Dubai) in that jurisdiction so I can rely on them to market my products?

Therefore, on the basis that there were regulatory breaches in Jersey, these contracts were therefore never entered into. These are not proper contracts, they are voidable contracts.

In light of the criminal decision, anything linked to Grant is a void contract, as they have not been entered in accordance with or in compliance with the regulatory requirements in the UAE and in Jersey and therefore all the money invested by clients should be returned.

Surely, any fraud committed by Grant visits liability back to Guardian?

The argument is very simple: if this is not the correct

legal position then for every fund – all they needed to do was set itself in one jurisdiction and sell everywhere else in the world, except in that jurisdiction. Then they don't need to be regulated. Then they can set up in say Congo and sell in the US and everywhere because Congo has the lightest legislation, and then they can hire charlatans all across the world and say, don't worry, just go abroad and collect the money.

Alongside this, Guardian have been also working with Grant under Prosperity Offshore Investment Consultants, a company that simply doesn't exist: there is no licence for that company. It's a complete misrepresentation. And no doubt, Guardian are aware of the misrepresentation when they made the Terms of Business with Grant in 2004. They were aware of the misrepresentation when I bought it to their attention in 2016. And they were aware of the misrepresentation when they received a copy of the criminal verdict on September 5th, 2017. Yet they continued on.

That is the amazing part, that they are fully aware that Grant is misrepresenting himself to the market.

Therefore, it is beyond a doubt to any reasonable person that the facts point to Guardian colluding with Grant, and they are equally liable. Those who are proactively being facilitators are at the front of my queue as much as the actual nominals of the 'organised' fraud and everything should be done to prosecute them. Unfortunately, we are living in a world where people can say and do what they like under a blanket of anonymity and don't care how it affects their target.

The message here is very clear. They OUGHT to have known.

It doesn't matter whether or not they say they did know or not – they ought to have known. They're busy collecting money. It's just a simple let me look at the licence, which they have admitted they did, and see what are they authorised to do by the Dubai Government.

I mean if you ever want a red flashing light that said Grant was acting outside his license details, his remit, his capabilities, his qualifications, to be able to do business in the UAE, that's it. And Guardian were fully aware of it, along with the fact that Prosperity Offshore Investment Consultant is a non-entity.

The notion that Van Neste didn't have any idea about that is the craziest bunch of bollocks I've ever heard in my life.

Compounded by the fact, the criminal verdict did nothing to deter Guardian from acting responsibly and correcting their position. Whilst Grant's other partners disassociated themselves from Grant and have written to their investors, Guardian, who knew all along about the trials and had a copy of the verdict in their possession since September 5th, 2017, have not taken any action and failed to inform investors allowing them and Grant to continue to profit financially. This is despite other investors warning Van Neste that they were being ill-advised by an inexperienced advisor, with the risks and illiquidity of the investments entered into, inappropriate for their risk profile and goals, plummeting the value of their Trust.

It was maddening.

If Grant had been one individual that had slipped through the net it would have been concerning, but the idea that it could be a systemic loophole that can be repeatedly exploited by fraudsters is hugely alarming.

When we were trying to learn about who Guardian and Van Neste are, we saw very little information, anywhere. That does grab your attention. I googled Guardian, and typed the names of all of the Guardian businesses into the search box, and then pressed return. First impression:

extremely shortage of results. I then put 'Philip Van Neste' into the search box, and then pressed enter. Second impression: extremely shortage of results. How is it possible that the Guardian businesses and its chairman have barely any online presence? This company handling my money was not even mainstream. It was a head-and-shoulders silhouette template of a company and people and it could be anyone for I knew.

Fantastically baffling loopholes

But what can the law do against Guardian and Van Neste, and the like?

The fundamental point in any case is convincing the court that a wrong has been committed. That is evidently so, here. But the reality is, the first hurdle, is up against a systemic problem – and they will escape all recourse on technicalities in the law.

Under English law, the argument that Guardian did not do their due diligence on Grant and his company is not strong enough and has never been successful in a court of law. In these sorts of cases, to win, we needed to show actual or what lawyers call 'blind eye' knowledge to establish liability. The more we can show Guardian actually knew Grant was operating without a license and they had actual knowledge of Grant's misconduct at the time of the investments, the greater the chance the investors have of getting their money back.

Financial legal cases are not as straightforward as other cases, in that they are complicated by jurisdiction and most likely time-bound. The Trust changed hands which protected Van Neste with the time-bound clause which means a crime is out of time to bring a claim. The problem is that by the time victims figured out what had happened it was too late to bring a claim against the first trustee, Guardian Trust Company Ltd, even though Van Neste was moving in-between and operating all the different Guardian entities at various times, playing musical chairs.

Surely, we cannot buy this idea of letting the likes of Guardian off the hook because they are pleading limitations or technicalities which Van Neste has set out many times in his correspondence to me? I trust that the courts would hate those defences, just as the judges in the criminal and civil trial did in Dubai against Grant.

I had to first detangle the legal web.

An experienced hand at Dubai legal landscape, I was a complete novice at the much more complicated legal landscape of Jersey. I had no option to relay upon a law firm recommendation for Bedell Cristin, a Jersey based law firm, highly recommended in the legal directories. They were ultra-posh, ultra-professional, and not the type for tongue in cheek conversation. They took their legal work very, very seriously, and most importantly, I felt there was commitment.

Legally, I was told by the lawyers, the trustees may have done enough to prevent them being sued.

But before we could even get started, I faced a major roadblock. All the documents and deeds related to the Trust were with my former financial advisor, and it was safe to presume Grant was not sharing. That left the trustee. For the first two months, Van Neste refused to acknowledge any of my emails on the matter, even though, as the settlor and sole beneficiary under the Trust, I was entitled to copies of Trust instruments, as well as Trust accounts. Eventually, my lawyer intervened and Van Neste received a phone call from him.

"What did you think of him?" I asked.

"Dodgy," the lawyer – who seemed to have the

perplexing gift of being able to tolerate him, summed Van Neste up in one word. What exactly was said, I am not privy to, but that same afternoon, Van Neste provided me with all Trust documentation, along with a saccharine email.

My lawyers then got to work.

Statutes of limitations are laws passed by legislative bodies in systems to set the maximum time after an event within which legal proceedings may be initiated. As the Trust changed to Guardian Global Capital (Suisse) SA three years prior, as predicted, I was essentially out of time to bring a litigation against Guardian Trust Company Ltd.

A crazy technical loophole.

My claim against Guardian Trust Company Ltd is therefore time-barred.

My lawyers argued I may have an impeachment argument with which I can extend the limitation period, however a claim letter sent to Guardian Trust Company Ltd will likely result in it raising a prescription defence (i.e., I am out of time to bring my claim). If Guardian Trust Company Ltd follows this course, I will have to issue proceedings, and argue the preliminary point of impeachment within substantive litigation. This will be an expensive process for me, and again unrecoverable costs will likely exceed any remedy that the court may award me. Moreover, when Guardian Trust Company Ltd transferred trusteeship to the trustee in 2013, the value of the Trust fund was £42,000 (albeit in reality this was an inflated figure). In any event, the majority of the loss in value of the Trust fund happened while the trustee (Guardian Global Capital (Suisse) SA was trustee of the Trust.

Guardian Asset Management's position was that I had no standing to sue it. They wrote: "Guardian Asset Management provided investment execution and nominee only services to its customers: Guardian Global Capital

(Suisse) SA (and formerly Guardian Trust Company Ltd) as Trustees of the Trust. All investment transactions executed by Guardian Asset Management were made under the authority and knowledge of your Trustees". They concluded that Guardian Asset Management has no client relationship with me.

That didn't stop us from utilising a law established in Jersey where I can make a data subject access request (pursuant to the recently enacted GDPR legislation), which my lawyer ordered via a legal discovery process. The Data Subject Access Request (DSAR), is a relatively new initiative in Jersey. Within four weeks of receipt, a company is obligated to provide you with all the personal data that it holds concerning you.

We asked John Robson, director at Guardian Asset Management, for this information. It would be interesting to see what was being said within the internal walls of the company with regards to my Trust: what actions they had taken, how did they process my data and who did they share it with as this disclosure could be helpful going forward.

Robson, however, managed to, within the law, extend that order to eight weeks at the eleventh hour: "We write to advise that your Data Subject Access Request is complex as it gives rise to a range of regulatory and legal considerations. We would advise therefore that pursuant to Article 27 (2) of the Data Protection (Jersey) Law 2018, we shall respond further to your Data Subject Access Request within 8 weeks from today".

It was all a game to them. They drag their feet in responding, and hope after a few months, people decide to 'give up'. That's how they suck the energy out of you.

Whilst we waited on that, a side line option away from Jersey was pursuing a case in the DIFC courts in Dubai.

Grant had made representations to me within the

DIFC, therefore the DIFC, whose laws are fashioned on UK laws, has jurisdiction to hear the claim against Guardian, Prosperity and myself, because of the conversations that were had, I was mis-sold a product by Guardian.

DIFC, like Jersey has laws to safeguard against these situations. A particular law is a regulatory law that somebody cannot act outside of their license and they have to have the requisite license. The courts also look at codes of conduct and that business laws have been passed. Business laws are such that you have to onboard a client properly, and understand their risk profile and understand if they are a professional client or not, and whether they have knowledge of different sorts of investment. The more complex the investment the more warning and risk analyses you have to do and give to that investor. The New Earth (Waste Recycling) fund is an example of a non-disclosure of high-risks, and I can rally up a group of investors, who can also confirm that they were not informed of the high-risks associated with investing in this fund by the trustee, by Guardian Asset Management or by Grant himself.

However, Bedell Cristin decided the best route of law for us was breach of trust against Van Neste and Guardian Global Capital (Suisse) SA, as the current trustee of the Trust. The Trust Deed contains rules which the trustee must comply with. If we can prove it acted improperly, for example allowing Guardian Asset Management to invest my money without oversight, the trustee may be responsible for losses incurred.

I'd been involved in a tediously long correspondence with Van Neste for some time, and it reached a denouement. As per Jersey law, in April 2018, we sent a notice of intent to sue to Philip Van Neste and Guardian Global Capital (Suisse) SA.

During this time, my civil case against Grant was

running simultaneously in Dubai.

Our claim letter

Now it gets legally technical. Below is a summary of the claim letter Van Neste received, which includes extracts written by Bedell Cristin.

Trust provisions.

Under the Trust Deed, the trustee has a broad power of investment reserved to it in respect of the Trust Fund. Guardian Trust Company Ltd delegated its investment powers to Prosperity under my Prescribed Direction. Prescribed Direction is defined as a 'direction given by the settlor, in relation to the exercise by the trustees of their investment powers'. Accordingly, a Prescribed Direction is a direction which informs the current trustee to undertake a discretionary (not mandatory) exercise to consider a direction given by the settlor, and considering whether or not to exercise its discretionary powers of investment / delegation. The trustee also sought to limit its liability in respect of poorly performing investments, however legislative protection prohibits a trustee from excluding all liability for losses to the Trust caused by an improper delegation of a dispositive power. By that same clause, Guardian Trust Company Ltd retained a check on the investment manager by which it could exercise its discretion (as a mere power) to seek the settlor's consent to remove or replace the investment manager.

Legislative protection.

Article 25(2)(a) of the trusts law contains a mere power by

which a trustee may delegate its powers in respect of management of trust property to an investment manager 'whom the trustee reasonably considers competent and qualified to manage the investment of trust property'. This discretionary obligation supersedes the terms of any Trust, except in circumstances where the terms prohibit a trustee from delegating its investment / other power. Mandatory discretion imposed by the Trust law requires the trustee to exercise skill and care when deciding whether or not to exercise this mere power.

Article 25(3) of the trust law exonerates a trustee for losses arising from a proper delegation of its dispositive / administrative powers, provided that delegation was made 'in good faith and without neglect' in respect of a 'delegation or appointment' or if it permits continuation of a delegation / appointment. The latter provision of the trust law adds a gloss to the discretionary exercise conducted by a trustee in considering whether or not to delegate its reserved power of investment to an investment manager, or the trustee's ongoing obligation to allow the investment manager to continue to act in that capacity; that exercise of discretion must be conducted in good faith and without neglect.

Case law.

Jurisprudence relating to wrongful delegation by a trustee dictates that not only is the trustee answerable for all the wrongful consequences of the delegation but the exercise of the discretion by the agent or attorney will also be void. Further, trustees who are donees of a mere power are not entitled to refuse to consider the desirability of exercising the power, whether it is a dispositive power of an administrative power. They cannot simply fold their hands and ignore it. Nor must they exercise it without consideration, as by doing whatever the settlor asks them to do.

Allegations of breach.

A reasonable trustee acting with reasonable skill and care would have exercised its discretion before following the Prescribed Direction of the settlor to appoint Prosperity as investment manager of the Trust. Upon its appointment pursuant to the 2013 IORA the trustee had a duty to exercise its discretion in considering the ongoing delegation of its investment powers to Prosperity by inter alia reviewing the past performance of Trust investments, conducting due diligence on Prosperity et al. Had it done so, it would have discovered that Prosperity was not competent and qualified to manage the investment of trust property, and would have brought an action against Guardian Trust Company Ltd for breach of trust.

When confirming receipt of our legal letter Van Neste made it clear that our claim was unmeritorious, and his only other comment, bizarrely, was that I had been offered my money back from Grant during the prosecution investigation.

Four weeks later, he requested an extension to respond to the claim letter within the Pre-Action Communications practice direction, based inter alia on the complexity of the dispute.

He then took a further six weeks to reply.

When his reply finally arrived, it was entirely predictable.

Endlessly, repetitively – the trustee's argument is Grant is my investment manager: "you nominated and appointed

Prosperity and Grant, not us". This, Van Neste has referred to in his various correspondence with me, is, as we know, their technical defence for Guardian to escape any liability. The investment powers were reserved to me, he went on to state, not the trustees and my investment advisor was my advisor prior to the formation of my trust. Any investments that were made were made under the Prescribed Direction which the trustees were bound to follow. This not only covered the appointment of my nominated investment manager but all investments flowing from that appointment. The investments were ultimately my investments made by me or my nominated and appointed investment manager. He also added I was free to change my nominated investment manager at any time.

The Trust Deed is absolutely clear on this point, he further states. At no time were the trustees responsible for the investment decisions made by me or my appointed manager pursuant to my reserved investment powers. Under Jersey trust law there was no breach of trust in any instances where investments were made pursuant to the investment powers reserved to me.

He thinks it's air-tight.

"Will it hold up in any court?" I ask, already knowing the answer.

"It's fifty-fifty." Lawyer-speak for not knowing which way the wind will blow.

However way you look at it, Grant and Van Neste unashamedly set us up. Van Neste knows he is pretty much legally covered on the back of the whole rogue saga.

He's not worried.

He's just pissed the administration is taking up his time.

His wealth of experience was transparent – he knew how to play the game, and he knew how to play the law. In short, he knew how to mastermind a multi-millionaire fraud scheme, and protect it.

Having principles is expensive

If I wish to issue proceedings against Guardian Global Capital (Suisse) SA, before the Royal Court in Jersey, this is done by an Order of Justice. An Order of Justice is an initiating process in which a plaintiff sets out its case against a defendant, both factually and at law. It serves as a core document for both parties and the court, showing inter alia the relationship between parties, what happened to cause a party loss and the relief sought by the injured party.

It is vital that the Order of Justice is detailed and thorough when issued, and if the plaintiff has a need to apply to amend this document at any time, it will bear the defendant's costs occasioned by any amendment.

Once drafted, the Order of Justice must be served upon the trustee by the Viscount's Department. Following service, the Order of Justice is then tabled before the Samedi Division of the Royal Court; a division of the Royal Court that sits on Friday afternoon. Proceedings are then formally commenced, and the trustee will have twenty-one days to file its defence to my claim.

Service out.

As the trustee is incorporated in Switzerland, I will need to apply to the Royal Court for permission to serve the Order of Justice upon it outside of the jurisdiction of Jersey. This may require instructing a service agent in Switzerland, which will incur costs.

The Answer.

If on receipt of the trustee's defence, known in Jersey as the Answer, contains inaccuracies, or if there is any legal or tactical reason to formally reply to any part of or all of the

Answer, I, as the plaintiff is able to do so by a Reply.

Associated work.

The pleading procedure in Jersey is malleable, and additional unforeseen costs often arise. These costs might be occasioned by Guardian Global Capital (Suisse) SA making a formal request for more detail to the Order of Justice (known as Requests for Further and Better Particulars). Similarly, the matter may have a jurisdiction issue, or there may be unforeseen issues associated with service.

Further steps.

Once the Reply is filed with the court and served upon the trustee, the pleadings stage of the dispute will conclude. It is then incumbent on me, the plaintiff, to issue a summons for directions within the following three months.

Risks.

This dispute is not without clear risks. The most immediate of these risks is that I may commence a costly action in Jersey which will ultimately not result in the reconstitution of the Trust.

Additionally, there is a risk that even if I am successful with my claim, that success may be pyrrhic; the unrecoverable element of my costs (in Jersey the usual rule is that a winning party can recover 60 percent of its legal costs from the losing party, unless exceptional circumstances apply) may be greater than any judgment sum that I am awarded.

Further, as I am not resident in the jurisdiction, and as costs of and occasioned by the dispute will be high, we would expect Guardian Global Capital (Suisse) SA to make an application for security for its costs. This would require me to pay a sum into court, which Guardian Global Capital (Suisse) SA can use to meet any adverse costs order if I ultimately lose the lawsuit. The lawyers anticipated that the sum required by Guardian Global Capital (Suisse) SA would be in the region of tens of thousands of pounds, and that the trustee is likely to be successful in such an application.

Doom and gloom.

Philip Van Neste will know for sure that they're thinking what you're thinking – for £50,000 is it really worth pursing?

DSAR: What is done in the dark will eventually come to light

As John Robson continued to fend off several exhaustive requests from my lawyers on producing the DSAR, there were suspicions that they may be putting a document holdout, which sends a signal, maybe they want to destroy some documents. A suspicion escalated, when I finally received the results.

After thirteen weeks, and with no further legal technicalities to exploit, Guardian Asset Management was forced to disclose information related to me and my Trust and it was highly insightful.

The first incredible surprise was that after eight years, since inception in 2010, I was expecting to receive a huge parcel from my DHL courier. Instead it was a misery package. When I opened the package it was equally dismal. It was so bad that they had included extra blank pieces of paper, to buff up the package. Upon closer examination, there was also a lot of repetition of copies of emails. With some pages, I squinted, trying to work out what they could be, but they were clumsily photocopied, and it was impossible to know what they represented.

The second surprise was that I didn't find one email between Grant and Van Neste. Not a single email which is substantially inconsistent with their type of relationship.

Despite what they had previously said about the reason

for their delay in providing this dossier to us ("it is complex as it gives rise to a range of regulatory and legal considerations") only some six words were redacted due to the personal details that referred to other clients: their names.

I was flabbergasted by the contents of the dossier. More tellingly, I was surprised by what it didn't show. When I actually see the extent of their non-action, I was genuinely shocked.

Overall, the paper trail in the DSAR reveal that there was no discussion on the management of my Trust or related investment management matters. There was no documentation showing the risk profile of the investments that Guardian Asset Management made, and Guardian Asset Management had never asked about the type of investments that I wanted it to make.

There was not a single correspondence on my Trust itself and its state, or concern on the selection of funds, or any concerns in relation to its continual decline. The Trust was full of start-up, short-term, high-risk, unregulated, suspended, illiquid funds and consistently losing money over the years. They had a duty to review the Trust. They had a duty to act in my best interests. There was none of that. No one had been reviewing it or taking care of the Trust. They had done no work on it.

Clearly, my Trust has been sitting on a top shelf somewhere collecting dust.

Their top priority was fees. The vast majority of their internal discussions were on the subject of fees and the messages discuss fees related to the Trust, and in other emails Guardian's senior staff discuss Grant's unpaid fees.

I then switched my focus to Van Neste and the emails he had written to his partners and colleagues within the various Guardian entities, regarding Grant's criminal court case in Dubai.

In short: a lot of backtracking going on by Van Neste.

Surprisingly – well, not surprisingly considering of what I now know of him – the DSAR reveals Van Neste hurling blame left, right and centre for all the negative emails coming his way from investors regarding the "Neil Grant situation" as he referred to it. He was carving himself out of any responsibility regarding the due diligence on Grant and his companies. At one point in his email he is reminding his colleagues that "they" not "he" had done the due diligence despite Van Neste representing the company when it came to certification issues, as demonstrated in his dealings with Grant in setting up their partnership and his name on the document authorising the Terms of Business with Grant.

The emails are dynamite. It reveals he's an extraordinary character. And not in a good way. He came across as a bit of a creep.

In one particular blunt email sent by Van Neste, he branded my accusations of Grant as baseless and that I was hoping something would 'stick'.

Then came the killer punch: he wrote: "I have not at any time provided a statement to the court in Dubai".

AAAAGGGGH! I had to reread that line and let that sink in. As part of the investigation procedures, we were handed a copy of Van Neste's statement to the prosecutor. Despite documented evidence, he was denying it which is obvious nonsense when you see the statement.

Breathtaking cheek.

I tried to imagine how he would worm his way out of it if we presented him with a copy. His response would be along the lines of, "I at no time submitted a statement to the Dubai courts … I did however write a letter addressed to them". Bizarrely, his interpretation of what he'd done, would be technically correct because Grant's lawyers submitted his statement to the prosecution.

It was clear that, according to the DSAR, Van Neste's colleagues had no idea he had written such a statement on their letterhead without informing them. They only found out when I wrote to them about it.

And there's more.

When discussing the trial and Grant, rather unsurprisingly Van Neste now plays down his relationship with his old wingman, and distances himself from him, claiming he had little to do with him. "I am not aware that Neil Grant has been convicted," he said, despite my sending him a copy of the criminal verdict one month prior to him writing that email, to which he had responded to.

Van Neste further goes on to write, "I was advised that the criminal court did not allow or agree for this case to be referred to the civil court". Which of course, doesn't make any sense. Anyone familiar with the legal profession will know a judge would never say that. Where is this information coming from? He doesn't say, but either he's telling porkies or Grant's selling him some bad porkies.

And then finally, he writes, "I have alerted the Department of Economic Development to the situation and the possibility that the wrong licence was issued," completely contradicting what he wrote and submitted to the public prosecution, and the Terms of Business he had set up with Grant.

This. Guy. Is. Unbelievable. He's orbiting on a different planet. He's making it up as he goes along. From any material I've ever read about Philip Van Neste, he largely said what he thought, what it was people wanted to hear.

It was extraordinary stuff.

There was of course no copy of a letter or email in the

DSAR package from Van Neste to the DED.

In another email he's expressing relief and sharing his findings with the rest of his team that in any event selling Trusts and policies in Dubai is not a regulated activity so "we should be OK", although in an earlier memo he had confessed that he feared the "Neil Grant situation" was "escalating" and of its potential impact. He warned colleagues to adopt a common approach when speaking to investors.

He referenced Grant's settlement offer to me in another email saying I had rejected £50,000 from Grant, although he did not say who told him that – possibly Grant.

And he kept spinning the narrative.

"I dealt with them both equally," referring to Grant and me. He had obviously slipped his mind that he had ignored my request for a statement of facts regarding my Trust and then consequently ignored all my emails during the prosecution investigation and the criminal and civil trials. Whichever way you dress that up, it indicates at least a desire to collude with Grant in damaging my case.

He went on, missing the point of the forged signature situation. It doesn't matter if it looks like my signature – it isn't my signature. That continues to be a worrying misguidance from a chairman. Forgery is forgery. With his words, Van Neste reduced a fraudulent activity to a casual, grotesquely dismissive punchline.

He was weaselling out of everything. And his colleagues never questioned the information he was sharing with them or launched an internal investigation; or at least that's what the DSAR showed.

The whole dossier offers a disturbing insight into the company's corporate culture.

Cooking the books

Ask any lawyer. If there is one thing better than breaking a great case, it's exposing a documented liar. They may give you a 'straight answer' one day, followed by many different 'straight answers' each time the same question is asked.

We discovered through a legal document that Van Neste had been cooking the valuation statements issued to me from the company.

In his response to our claim letter on September 7th, 2018, Van Neste stated that the current true value of the Trust (which I had named 'Zara') was £11,884.91 and that it was "clearly wrong to state that the investments are worthless".

Five days after receiving his response, on September 12th, 2018, we countered by asking Van Neste to provide me, as the settlor of the Zara Trust, with a breakdown of the associated costs to close the Zara Trust and to transfer the liquid cash £11,884.91 to my nominated bank account.

Reasonable enough you would think. Because I'm asking for facts, not future predictions.

After two weeks of deliberation, Van Neste carefully responded to our request: "If liquidation is an option the investments will be liquidated at this time".

If?

What happened in those five days between September 7th, 2018 and September 12th, 2018, that may affect the liquidation of the Zara Trust?

In any event why is he implying he doesn't know? Why wouldn't he know in advance if an asset can be liquidated or not, as it should be relatively easy information for him to retrieve; so why hasn't he? It's not information that one is privy to, it's standard.

By now, the investment fund Lucent (Land Purchase and Planning) was the only fund left in the Zara Trust and was suspended and had been suspended since 2016. We knew that the true value of the Trust was less than £1,000 and not of the value of £11,884.91 Van Neste had purported it to be in his reply to us.

He obviously knew that the Lucent (Land Purchase and Planning) Fund was suspended, and the papers in the DSAR showed that Van Neste knew this fact, and that the fund would not have a real value. It meant that Van Neste had knowingly concealed the true value and the poor state of the Trust from me, in a legal document. In other words, he knew the Trust was worthless.

It was a royal cock-up and proved he was manipulating valuations. Otherwise, he would liquidate the fund now, take his fees and pay me the reminder so we could all move on.

This was not his finest moment. We laid it out for him.

"In your response to our letter dated September 7th, 2018, you state that the current value of the Zara Trust is GBP 11,884.91 and that it was "clearly wrong to state that the investments are worthless". In your email dated September 26th, 2018 you state that the Trust is not of the value that you stated it to be."

Van Neste wasn't about to answer truthfully. In fact, he wasn't about to answer at all.

What followed was 24 months of intense interaction with the company, back and forth, as Van Neste tried everything to avoid being caught in a 'documented lie' and implicating himself.

From Van Neste to me, October 16th, 2018: "I have sought an update on the holdings in your portfolio and I am putting together a response which I will let you have this week".

From Van Neste to me, October 23rd, 2018. "The matter is receiving my attention and I will revert to you as soon as I can".

From Van Neste to me, November 31st, 2018: "I am

out of the office, I can be reached on guardianasset.je". This was head scratching time. Van Neste is the chairman at Guardian Global Capital (Suisse) SA and yet, he also has an active email address at Guardian Asset Management, their contracted party. As Van Neste remained silent when asked for clarification on the distinction between the two functions, more questions started building up.

Ten further emails go unanswered.

From Van Neste to me, December 12th, 2018: "I will finalise everything Monday next".

From Van Neste to me, December 21st, 2018: "I am working on this and hope to be in a position to inform you with regards to the current value and liquidity matters very shortly".

From Van Neste to me, December 28th, 2018: "I will arrange a valuation of the trust portfolio to be sent to you tomorrow by email". And to show that he graduated from the same school of dodginess as Grant he changes the email subject name, starts a new email and stops copying all the relevant people, intentionally trying to break up the links.

Three further emails go unanswered.

From Van Neste to me, January 31st, 2019: "I will attend to your email next week".

Three further emails go unanswered.

From Van Neste to me, February 14th, 2019: "I am looking into your queries and I will respond to you as soon as I have an up to date position on the holding".

Eight further emails go unanswered.

From Van Neste to me, May 1st, 2019: "You will receive a response to your emails in full very shortly".

By this time, since September 12th, 2018 I have sent Van Neste 42 emails. It's taken months, many emails and reams of patience. He's wearing me down, so I feel like giving up. That's his trick.

From Van Neste to me, May 22nd, 2018: "I shall respond later this week".

At this point, the Jersey Financial Services Commission, who had been copied in to all the emails up until now, jumped in and wrote to me with, "Thank you for copying us into your emails to Guardian Asset Management and Philip Van Neste".

That was it. That was their dramatic entrance and sliding exit.

Meanwhile Van Neste changed tactics and attempted diversionary conversations.

From Van Neste to me, June 12th, 2019: "In order for me to take matters forward, please complete and return the attached CRS form".

I knew instantly, this was to unnecessarily delay matters further and avoid answering the questions, which I was not going to fall for, and like any wronged Englishwoman, I refused to do. At this point we had not asked him to action anything, requesting information only on the Zara Trust so we can make an investment decision, as he holds all the knowledge.

From Van Neste to me, June 15th, 2019: "We are concerned that you have declined to complete the CRS self-certificate form" swiftly followed by, "I will report accordingly".

The image of him sticking his tongue out at me and flapping his hands by the side of his ears, swiftly came to mind.

The last thing Van Neste wanted was anyone looking into the matter with a fine toothcomb. It was his baggage they would uncover.

I called his bluff, "You may take whatever action you think necessary". He dropped the CRS threat like a lead balloon.

Seven further emails go unanswered between the period June 27th and August 9th, 2019.

It must be presumed, Van Neste thought nothing of his protracted silence, or, and more likely, he was trying desperately to ghost me.

If you're not familiar with the term 'ghosting', it's when someone you know suddenly cuts off all communication with you, with zero warning, and then you never hear another word from that person again.

Undeterred, I pressed on.

Van Neste finally responds within an obfuscating email: "I shall respond to your email shortly" followed by "I have requested an update on the GB Strategic Land Fund and I will send this to you". He stated that the investment in Premier New Earth (Waste Recycling) is valueless with the fund having gone into liquidation with no prospect of any value being distributable to investors.

Hang on – we knew this back in 2014. Five years later he is now telling me "this will be removed from the portfolio".

This is what mirror funds mean. They mean you cannot see or know the real value for the mirrors and smoke.

I was at a complete and utter loss how this is now the sixty-fourth email to Van Neste requesting information on my Trust in almost a year and we have not moved forward with any clarity on it.

Then came an unexpected twist.

Snookered! Here we go again

By now, I had won the civil case against Grant in the Dubai courts and Grant has exhausted all legal appeals and options.

Simultaneously, my lawyers Bedell Cristin now dropped a bombshell.

There's this thing called double recovery, I am casually told.

You can't claim twice for the same pool of money. In other words, now, I've won against Grant, I can't continue with my claim against Guardian Global Capital Suisse (SA).

Hang on a second. "Are you sure?" I ask them. "Yes," they answer, again. Casually.

Out of all the advice you have given me, *you fail to mention this crucial fact to me?*

Wasn't this the most important and relevant advice that I should have been given at the very beginning?

Obviously, if I had known that, if ANYONE had known that, they would have sensibly waited for the civil verdict before commencing anything in Jersey.

It was a U-turn I didn't see coming.

As for the lawyers – I'm all out of words! What a monumental waste of time!

It was a lawyer's job to know the law. That's why we put our trust in them. But essentially it's also a lawyer's job to advise us correctly on it. It is called 'advice of counsel' and a lawyer has great liability if a mistake is made. That is why they get paid, and paid handsomely. Although I don't think it was deliberate, it was a mistake. They hadn't advised me of this crucial fact.

In case I was reasonably expected to know this and in case I was suffering from 'intellectual poverty', which is lawyer-speak that you're being 'a bit thick', I asked a few 'men on the street' if they had heard the term 'double recovery' and knew what it meant. I sighed with relief; no they hadn't, and no they didn't know you couldn't claim from the same pool of money twice, and why didn't the lawyers tell you that at the beginning?

In a long drawn out email behind the deliberate, careful and sophisticated language, the lawyers admitted their 'mistake'. This was not by conceding that the firm may have made a mistake in not proactively advising on the law – but by not being able to identify *when* they had actually advised me on it – not even a dangle of a hint. To me, it was as good as an admission.

I only paid them for their investigatory work; at least they had done some work on the file unlike my lawyers during the criminal trial, and it had been worth it to give Guardian and Van Neste the run around.

After that they stopped responding to my emails.

I was ghosted again. So not just by Van Neste.

The lawyers ghosted me too.

It must be a 'Jersey' thing. They have a bad track record in dispensing with clients when they have either served their use, or messed things up.

Meanwhile, for now, Philip Van Neste dodged a legal bullet. Finally, he had something to thank Grant for.

Philip Van Neste wraps up

Now, Van Neste relaxed, and started wrapping things up.

A chilly antipathy now existed between the two of us following a battle for answers, a battle that only one man could win: he who holds the key to the Trust.

Initially he refused point-blank to close the Trust. He couldn't. He would be caught in a lie in a legal document and branded a documented liar, and accused of cooking the valuation statements. It's unrecoverable in terms of credibility before a court of law, should a case be filed against him.

Now, he realised that I had won in Dubai and my lawyers would not be pursuing him because of double recovery. He came up with his own plan.

Almost immediately after the civil verdict against Grant

in Dubai, on August 14th, 2018, Van Neste sent me an email with a thunderous one-liner to say, "Your Trust has been closed".

Pardon!? What? Who closed my Trust?

The answer was "the trustees", i.e., he did. He closed the Trust himself. He exercised prerogative as referred to in the Trust Deed. Yes, that damn document again, where I suspect every oleaginous word was sanctioned by him.

The trustees exercised their discretionary powers and brought the Trust to an end. They don't even need my permission to close my Trust. The most unsavoury part on this whole debacle is knowing that I really had no control over my Trust this whole time.

After one year and avoiding 57 emails and after scoffing at the notion that it was worthless, Van Neste finally had a few answers, and now confidently stated in his email to me, "The Lucent Fund has been illiquid for some considerable time".

Comedy gold. What a character.

Just like a cheater, when they're not even attempting to hide the affair you know the game is up. You have to admire his lack of compunction, the courage of his bad manners, the energy of simple cheek.

Not unnaturally, I wanted chapter and verse on what happened to my Trust and proof. A response that "the trustee decided to close my Trust" without prior warning, approval, paperwork or written confirmation will not suffice. When did he close the Trust and under which authority and clause? At the very minimum there were tax implications involved. And I also wondered how and when are they intending to transfer the suspended Lucent Fund to me?

"The assets will be transferred to you," he replied, in short.

I continued with my protracted, ongoing campaign to extract straight answers from him.

Months passed by of constant follow up before I received an off-topic reply: "Please let me have your current address," with no explanation as to why.

No one likes the tax man poking around your business, and Van Neste was using yet another tactic, wanting me to go away. Now, he continued to dodge every email I sent to him on the basis I wouldn't confirm my address to him.

Finally, after 83 emails, on December 18th, 2019, an email appeared in my inbox from him. It seems he suddenly appeared to find my address. "A letter is in the post covering all points" winning him the 'vaguest email so far' prize.

I had absolutely no faith that a) he had put a letter in the post to me and b) that it was going to arrive any time soon.

Sure enough I was right. It was another tactic to stall for time and be dismissive.

I continued to follow up throughout January 2020, confirming nothing had been received in 'the post' from him.

Van Neste finally surfaced in February 2020: "The matter is receiving my attention".

His mind is like an internet browser, nineteen tabs are open, seventeen are frozen and he has absolutely no idea where the music is coming from.

From Van Neste to me, March 26th, 2020 after 95 emails, he outdoes himself and comes up with a new excuse: "I have had the (corona) virus and I am now recovering".

Before that he had used the "We had an internet communication failure which our service provider is attending to" followed by "I was at my mother-in-law's funeral". I wouldn't be surprised if he was somehow related to her death. At this rate he was going to send us all to an early grave.

Eight further emails go unanswered.

Fast forward three months, to June 2020, and he tried to pretend again that he has sent me a letter in the post, but refusing to say when he had sent the correspondence to me, and where he had sent it and refusing to release documentary evidence of anything, including a soft copy of the said letter by email.

So began the long series of exchanges simply on this fact alone. They appear to count it a victory if they can drag out a dispute for so long that the complainant gives up in despair.

His swan farewell email, October 29th, 2020: "I had a small operation last week, general anaesthetic – and convalescing this week – back in office next week – Regards Philip".

So to cut through, at the time of finalising my book, after 125 emails over a two-year period, Van Neste dodged questions, declined to give details, answering generically. I received no proof my Trust had in fact been closed, no paperwork. For all I know, the Trust could be active and being used negligently by the Russians. I have received no paperwork on the Lucent Fund. And he knew there was nothing I could do about it.

My Trust just disappeared, with no trail. And he knows he will never be made accountable.

It made him judge, jury and executioner with zero accountability.

If I met him in the street, I would expect him to ask if I had any spare change. Perhaps even more so, if I opened a newspaper, I would expect to see him with Grant caught on CCTV sprinting out of the Fat Greek Taverna in Essex, after running up a £500 bill on cocktails and steaks. No thought about people struggling under economic and financial strain, just of feeding their own criminal avarice.

Perhaps. I thought, I've just been unlucky.

Apparently, not.

It was at this point that I burst into print, airing my woes with other victims which, incidentally, prompted a flood of correspondence from others who had suffered similar ordeals.

All this time, parallel to my emails to Van Neste, Grant's other victims were experiencing the same pattern of avoidance and the sums involved are life-changing.

Rupert had been liaising with Van Neste for about a year up until that point receiving exactly the same treatment and delays and non-descript emails as myself. He wanted to make decisions on his Trust and needed facts about his investments. He had requested Van Neste to close his Trust one and half years ago. He had requested a detailed valuation of the holdings within his Trust and he complained that the website had been inaccessible for many months, preventing him from having any visibility on his Trust. On top of that, Van Neste was dragging his feet in transferring money to him from the liquidated investments with the process taking months, instead of days.

Same story.

Eventually he received an email containing an indemnity document which Van Neste wanted him to sign, after which he will release the funds from his Trust. The 'Instrument of Indemnity' is full of gobbledegook legal jargon, that any sane person will be left struggling to understand and left Rupert questioning the purpose of the document. It seems to him to be a 'cover all' indemnity against any and all future claims against Guardian Global Capital (Suisse) SA, Guardian Trust Company Ltd and all associated parties. Van Neste was covering his back with issuing the document before the transfer of any funds.

Rupert was stuck between a rock and a hard place.

He had no legal obligation to sign this document in order to receive his money. The other danger of signing this document was that if Van Neste has over charged him, on say fees, or if he questions the amount he received from Guardian, he has no leg to stand on, to argue a case. He is effectively signing away any issues pertaining to the Trust and its mis-management.

Rupert and Van Neste have a stand-off.

Rupert understandably is reluctant to sign the indemnity document absolving all the parties and everyone connected with them from any future claim and Van Neste insists on this before he'll transfer the cash in the Trust to him.

When Rupert questioned the necessity and validity of this document to Van Neste, his response was that it was quite normal and required under Jersey law. Rupert sent an email to the Jersey Financial Services Commission, asking them to confirm that this is a legitimate document required under Jersey law in these circumstances.

Again, they made their dramatic entrance – they refused to comment as were unable to give any formal advice – and made their sliding exit.

Five months had passed and the normally laid-back English gentleman was now positively fuming, "Your behaviour continues to be unbelievable and unprofessional," he declared to Van Neste.

Roll on four months. Rupert is hit with another concern. He was shocked and annoyed to find the following previously unseen charges suddenly appear on the final statement and so far Van Neste has failed to explain what these fees are for:

GAM Sundry fees	£48.24
GAM Execution Fee R0050519 & R0060519	£100
FCM Nominee Fee to 30.06.19	£1790
FCM Nominee Fee to 30.09.19	£895
Termination Fee	£750
CRS Fee 2018	£750

It was totally unexpected.

Was it really possible that the cost of closing a Trust comes to substantial amount of £4,333.24? Or was he being taken for an expensive ride? We had been aware of the termination fee of £750, but had no idea what any of the others are.

I went to other financial advisory outfits to see if they could figure them out. They weren't sure: it's hard to work out the acronyms, they say, as they are not standard industry acronyms (quite possibly Guardian's own fee system). This is what mirror funds mean. They mean you cannot see or know real charges incurred for the mirrors and smoke.

And where there's smoke, there's Van Neste.

So, Rupert had no choice and went back to Van Neste for some clarification.

CRS stands for Common Reporting Standard. According to Van Neste, this was introduced in 2018. Apparently, clients received a CRS questionnaire as part of this process. The fee scale always provided for additional fees, including compliance related fees to be charged and by their very nature these could not have been anticipated and were chargeable under the fee scale.

Rupert had no recollection of any questionnaire on CRS and asked Van Neste for evidence of this.

No answer.

Next question: What is the link between FCM and GAM (Guardian Asset Management) companies?

Some research revealed that a company called King Street Nominees is a subsidiary of Guardian Asset Management who are used to hold 'our' investments, although under the Terms and Conditions of our Trusts, the investments are not registered in our names, they are registered in the name of King Street Nominees.

FCM is yet another company who apparently King Street Nominees use for their nominee services. We discovered FCM now owns Guardian Asset Management (previously owned by Van Neste). Van Neste claims to have no relationship with FCM however we have now discovered he briefly worked for FCM during the transition in 2018.

It's amazing how Van Neste keeps changing hats from all the Guardian businesses to try to pull a veil over the fact that, at various times, he personally is responsible for all of them.

The circle widens.

Another victim explained her story that she and her husband had opened a Trust more than a decade ago with Guardian. The couple had been sold the Trust by Grant as "safe as a bank account" and that they could take money out of it "when we like".

After a terrible loss, they had requested Van Neste to close their Trust where they had invested their tax-free pension of £85,000.

But, as it seemed, initial incompetence from Van Neste was followed by months of inaction and then apparent utter insouciance. They became frustrated and increasingly furious.

They had requested similar information I was requesting from Van Neste which Van Neste declined to provide for years. They had asked for the value of the Trust, a statement of their investments, which funds their money was placed in, and how much of their money was placed in each fund. By the time Van Neste actioned it and transferred the money to them, they came out with next to nothing. It had taken over five months to get answers after maybe 40 emails, calls, messages, everything possible.

Van Neste also refused to budge on waiving any of the fees. They were unfortunately given an amount that Van Neste simply sent with extortionate fees added to the final 'bill'. They're still arguing their case to date.

The couple had asked Van Neste for the details of his governing body to make an official complaint against him and all the entities that he appeared to be involved in. He ignored all emails.

As more and more stories were coming out, the situation acts as a cautionary tale, for most investors complain of receiving a similar response from financial institutions. The pattern is on the rise; it reveals that Van Neste's behaviour is not unusual.

What's most interesting – and sadly all too predictable to those 'in the know' – is the scant regard these companies have for their clients.

Jersey and under the bunion

At that point, we went from research to 'Now we need to turn this into a regulatory action'.

Several of Grant's victims had contacted the Financial Conduct Authority (FCA) – the financial regulatory body in the UK. The FCA regulates financial firms providing services to consumers. It operates independently of the UK Government and is financed by charging fees to members of the financial services industry.

At this time, Grant had based himself in Scotland, whilst being a resident and employee in the UAE and practising under a Dubai broker license.

When we first turned the case over to the FCA, we also provided additional victim reports.

There was very little or no information flowing from the FCA side back to us. In fact, they reminded us on several occasions that this was not a cooperative investigation. It was their investigation.

Whilst the FCA began an investigation into Grant, the financial regulatory bodies in Jersey and the Channel Island were an entirely different matter.

Guardian and Van Neste needed to be investigated. Surely?

You would think.

They didn't even entertain the idea.

First, it was a challenge to find out who the correct regulators were. For me, it was difficult to know the overriding regulator responsible for the trustee, as the Trust had changed hands. Every one of the Guardian entities that managed my Trust, and had worked with Grant, had different regulators.

It really was a tangled web.

I had discovered my trustee had changed hands in 2013 and was now Guardian Global Capital (Suisse) SA in Switzerland.

As per Guardian Global Capital (Suisse) SA and their website they appeared to be regulated by Association Romande des Intermediaries Financiers (ARIF) in Geneva. I wrote to ARIF requesting an investigation into Guardian Global Capital (Suisse) SA as my trustee.

They swiftly replied to my complaint the very next day:

"As a self-regulatory organism, we are not allowed to communicate any information to the public. Furthermore, our regulatory body has no authority to deal with complaints concerning the individual business relationships of our current or past members." This was followed by, "you should take the advice of a lawyer for any further action."

As helpful as a dried-up lettuce.

I followed up with Guardian Global Capital (Suisse) SA again, where an equally swiftly received email from them now shifted the emphasis over to the original trustees of the Trust, Guardian Trust Company Ltd domiciled in Jersey.

According to their website, Guardian Trust Company Ltd was regulated by the Jersey Financial Services Commission (JFSC) for the conduct of Trust business. The JFSA is the regulator of Jersey based companies and they are the Jersey equivalent of the FCA in the UK. Guardian Asset Management Ltd represented by John Robson at the time is regulated by the same authority for the conduct of investment business.

We are told that anyone who believed they had been mis-sold investments should contact the company that sold them the product, then proceed to the JFSA.

I wrote a complaint against Guardian Trust Company Ltd and Guardian Asset Management to the JFSA. A case handler responded asking me to complete a form in order for the JFSA to review my complaint. I was then sent a copy of the Commission's guidance on complaints, which details how you can make a complaint, and how the Commission may be able to assist you.

All looked promising so far.

Then I received a letter that the complaint was rejected on the grounds that it was outside their remit which would mean they would be unable to review it. If the case handler throws out your complaint, you typically have six months to appeal this decision from the date you receive the rejection letter. This means your case will be passed on to the Channel Island Financial Ombudsman (CIFO) Service, an adjudicator that resolves consumer complaints about a Jersey based company, for investigation and who will make a final decision on a complaint.

The next day I appealed. I highlighted the severity of the allegations, stating: "It's a pretty unpleasant situation and the allegations at the heart of it are extremely serious".

The Ombudsman took no time in getting back to me.

The encouraging aspect of the Ombudsman's letter is that he responded swiftly – too swiftly for my liking, like squatting a fly, like he wanted to shut down the matter. I received a terse letter the very next day in their normal understated manner with a belter of a one-liner regarding his services.

"While we are aware that Guardian Trust is a regulated entity, our statutory remit is defined in law and does not extend to the Trust."

Sorry, What?

Which, when you reread the letter, might just strike you, as a little odd, if not, shamefully ridiculous – especially as he offers no recourse, whatsoever.

Frankly, as Rhett Butler might say in Gone with the Wind, I don't give a damn.

And even more discouraging is to discover that again the Grant-Van Neste duo have misled me and investors into thinking that our Trust is regulated. My Trust was not even protected by the regulators. The system doesn't protect me. No wonder Van Neste was breezing through everything. An inquiry into the Guardian businesses was impossible.

Goodness me. Can this get any worse?

I double-checked on Guardian's website and nowhere was it written that the Trust itself was not regulated. Equally, Grant's website read: "The products we promote and recommend to our clients are strictly regulated to safeguard the interests of our clients". Their websites give the impression that you've got a clad-iron strong product backed by a regulated authority in a regulated jurisdiction and it's just nonsense; it's a complete misrepresentation.

Investors are pouring millions of dollars into their Trust and they are not protected. This is the irony of the whole situation. All these structures are set up in Jersey and the investors are never in Jersey; the investors are outside, and they are all unprotected. They can't even make a complaint. How many investors would deal with a company where their Trust is not regulated? Who in the world would feel relaxed about their Trust not being protected?

I thought the Ombudsman may take action on this, knowing that Guardian and the like have a duty of care to ensure that investors know exactly what they are letting themselves in for and into when opening unregulated Trusts in his jurisdiction. But as the silence continued it was clear he was stuck in his remit.

And there is root of the problem.

When they are simply not interested in what has transpired within their own jurisdiction explaining their duties away that Guardian's 'sort of set-up' is not part of their remit, then it's even more horrific. The fact that he offered no recourse, is because he knew there wasn't any. He was turning a blind eye to that issue too.

He never saw fit to investigate the risks of the unregulated parts of the financial advisory services business? Now, why? It was obvious we needed to do it.

I was annoyed with the Ombudsman. He was rejecting my complaint purely on a systemic problem and escaping all recourse on technicalities? This is why fraud victims are being let down repeatedly.

I had given the regulators first-hand knowledge. This was not an unsubstantiated claim I was sending them but a cold hard fact, along with a court judgment. They had the power to investigate. They just didn't want to.

Being aware of the problem is the first step to

correcting it. Isn't it time the regulators take responsibility? For the practice they are protecting? There should be more than public interest, they should be interested. Isn't that their job?

Because by taking no action, in their own indirect way, they are enabling this. They are indirectly supporting this 'culture of acquiescence' surrounding companies such as Guardian and a collusion to silence victims of financial fraud while offering a voice to the perpetrators.

That kind of silence isn't just wrong, it's dangerous. It sends a message to victims that it's not worth the anguish of coming forward. It sends a message about who we are as a society, what we'll overlook, whom we'll ignore, who matters and who doesn't. It's the kind of silence that has had the inevitable effect of diluting the impact of moral outrage.

All of which will be music to the ears of Van Neste, and the like, who are therefore given a free ride. In fact, I'd say there's a very good chance Van Neste will move on empowered and emboldened to what could very well be even bigger investors who have no idea what they are getting themselves into.

It dawned on me that since any losses in the Trusts were unregulated, companies like Guardian didn't have to put aside any money to cover potential losses. They knew they were protected from every angle of this highly sophisticated, yet distorted system.

How did we reach such a ridiculous state of affairs?

Barely a week goes by without some supposed new 'crisis' fuelling wall-to-wall news coverage and dire predictions of jail time for fraudulent financial advisors and their confidants.

Yet within a few days, each 'scandal' dissolves into a giant nothing.

Ombudsmen relentlessly shriek away in the media

about their hatred for anything related to fraud. And then, given the opportunity to actually make a difference, they quote technicalities for not doing anything. I am seemingly oblivious to the fact that nobody cares anymore.

When they're not even surprised it's happened, then it's even more worrying.

A comparison: The legal regulators

Are all independent regulators like this in Jersey?

I was still peeved at Bedell Cristin blindsiding me with the whole 'double recovery' thing, and then not accepting their mistake. I decided to check out the machinations of the Jersey legal profession, just out of interest, to compare it to the financial regulators.

The law firms' relevant professional body is in fact the Law Society of Jersey.

I wrote to them and I asked them to investigate into the legal advice I received from Bedell Cristin. I explained in my letter, based on their advice I instructed the firm to act on my behalf and to initiate court proceedings with first filing a claim letter against Guardian Global Capital (Suisse) SA, which they implemented. Prior to this I had provided the firm with information on the background of the case and of the ongoing civil case in Dubai against Neil Grant.

My argument was very clear. The firm simply missed giving me a crucial piece of advice. Double recovery.

Had I been given the correct advice from Bedell Cristin at the consultation stage when they were informed of the lawsuit in Dubai and before I bought their legal services, I would not have agreed to hire or paid legal fees to pursue Guardian Global Capital (Suisse) SA on my behalf.

Bedell Cristin refuses to acknowledge this fundamental fact.

I argued, no reasonable person would open a second civil case against a second party for the same pool of money if they were aware of the 'double recovery' rule. Any person would wait for the outcome of the first trial before embarking on a second trial with a second party for the same pool of money. It was simple: all I wanted was to be directed to where they had informed me of double recovery. The fact that they didn't and have said nothing – beyond the routine denial that they had not mis-advised me – leaves one to make up their own mind.

The chief executive officer of the Law Society himself replied to my letter. They would revert to me upon completion of their review. They certainly came across as professional and keen to uphold the integrity of the legal profession within their jurisdiction.

I felt optimistic.

Weeks passed.

And I did not hear back.

I followed up. I was told I would get a response early January.

He was right. A few days later I received a response. Only it was not from the Law Society of Jersey. It was from the Bedell Cristin themselves.

"We have been informed by our regulator, the Law Society of Jersey, that they will take no further action." The smug was written all over the senior associate's email.

And having administered one good slap, another was around the corner when I questioned how bizarre that the law firm is told before I am of the outcome of the investigation I requested.

Even I was not prepared for what happened next.

There had been some confusion, I am quickly told by an apologetic and rather embarrassed chief executive officer: "Bedell Cristin have misinterpreted the position in relation to the status of your complaint". Apparently, Bedell Cristin were made aware of the investigation but wrongly assumed that this meant that the complaint had been dismissed. Their response speaks volumes.

In other words, Bedell Cristin had been tipped off.

And they jumped the gun before the formal outcome announced.

It is pretty remarkable, when you think about it.

I decided to wait until I received the 'final' letter on their conclusion of their 'independent' investigation to call them out on it.

Sure enough twenty days after receiving Bedell Cristin's notification, The Law Society of Jersey confirmed the same outcome of the investigation along with the same reasons in their letter to me.

Their reaction to Bedell Cristin knowing the outcome before I did was surprising; they put the whole situation down to a dismissive, "it is unfortunate".

'Unfortunate' in that you got caught?

Although obscenely worrisome and unprofessional at the same time, this goes to the core of the integrity of regulators, as a whole. That was without doubt the stupidest thing the Law Society did and equally does not bode well for the profession.

But then again, nothing surprises me at this point.

The Law Society kept to the shadows, and the conclusion of their investigation is that if I believe the law firm has acted negligently, this type of complaint would be by way of legal proceedings against the firm. The Law Society's complaints procedure will not meet my concerns.

It only served to amplify my intrigue. Is there any professional body or regulators that is independent, unbiased and actually does anything?

The point of the exercise was to see how other

regulators in Jersey act and I now have my answer.

All of which makes me wonder: What is it with Jersey? It has almost become a competition to see who can make up the most believable excuse to get away with appalling behaviour.

Jersey as a whole and the way its regulations operate, is getting more and more ridiculous with each passing day. What is the point of them if all they ever do is redirect you to lawyers?

It is indeed an island with no bridges.

Is it any wonder, that in 2018 a construction worker killed his secret lover, before choosing to dump it on a Jersey beach, in an attempt to literally get away with murder?

Call for government support

When I started to look into this supposed 'feud' between the financial regulators and the public on the subject of lack of any action, protection and responsibility, I thought it was the newspapers and the like stirring up something that wasn't there. I didn't want to believe it. Yet, I was to learn, it most definitely exists. Actually, it's worse than anyone thinks.

That's when I decided to see what the government has to say about my situation, and put them under scrutiny.

Fraud corrodes confidence, undermines trust and damages the reputation of the UK at home and abroad. This is why I believed the British Government need to do something. It should be their mission to bring those committing this crime to justice.

I wrote to a Member of Parliament (MP) and called for the government to launch an urgent inquiry into the financial service companies and the like and their practices: "In the circumvention of the UK regulatory system by the crown dependencies – most notably Jersey. It is my belief that a systemic problem exists which enables these rogue regulatory jurisdictions to circumvent accepted UK law and practice. I understand a great deal of investigation in recent years has gone into the tax evasion, money laundering and financing of terrorism within these areas but believe a scandal of equal proportion is waiting in the wings if the flouting of basic consumer regulatory protections are allowed to continue."

I then took it further and asked for a parliamentary investigation of collusion against British citizens by Guardian Asset Management and Guardian Global Capital (Suisse) SA and I was concerned that certain fiduciary services fall outside the scope of the CIFO.

Hopes of a breakthrough increased after the chief of staff responded straight away, on behalf of the MP, and followed up with a telephone call, saying they would be pleased to assist further. They offered to write a personal letter to the relevant Minister within the Jersey Government to investigate this issue.

I provided them with everything I had – information, judgments and documentation. From that they complied a report and sent it to the Treasury Minister in the Government of Jersey.

Great, I thought. The blizzard of activity looked promising. So, I really had believed that they were going to take care of this.

Four months passed by and we hadn't received a response from the Government of Jersey, prompting a follow up by the British Government. A couple of months later, the matter had been directed to the Minister of external relations who was also responsible for financial services.

He confirmed what I had already learnt: the CIFO

provides a free and independent complaints resolution service for the financial services that are most critical for retail customers of the industry. Given its focus, some services used predominantly by high-net-worth and sophisticated investors fell outside of the CIFO's scope. This included fiduciary services.

And, in a charming touch, they, of course, responded in the way they respond to all things uncontrollable, during which the futility of the exercise was brought home to me – the only recourse was to take legal action against the likes of Guardian and Philip Van Neste.

Basically, the Government of Jersey said, despite how outrageously Van Neste and the like was behaving, there was nothing they or the regulators could do. With this realisation came a sense of hopelessness and mild panic.

Because there was. If they wanted to.

This is all now tragically familiar to me. The words are always the same: we condemn this act in the strongest possible terms; we pray these rogues are brought swiftly to justice; our hearts are with the victims who have lost their savings.

Never mind sympathising with us. How about doing something to help us?

The Minister went on to share information that the JFSC is currently investigating Guardian Global Capital (Suisse) SA for suspecting unauthorised business.

I am not even excited by that.

Currently, the likes of Guardian and Van Neste have the skilful drafting of legal documents that protect them and bypass laws.

They won't be worried about regulators or governments gently poking their noses here and there. It seems to me that we should be looking at the system itself.

I believe my experience has pointed out some pretty

gaping holes in the system and I shared an observation with the Minister that from what I can glean from his email, no authority is supervising fiduciary services, and that scope is falling out of everybody's remit. Unfortunately, that appears to be the area financial services are capitalising on, and exploiting. What is their plan to stop this, I wondered?

But the months passed, and what happened?

Never received a reply.

After his first and only email, the Minister struggled to move past distance politeness and all my emails have gone unanswered.

The silence is an excellent barometer for the Jersey Government's opinion on the subject.

Surely our type of cases should be part of a government crackdown on the roaring ocean of dodgy investments and ill-gotten gains that wash around the capital in a high spring tide of corruption. It's for the government to come up with policies that allow investors to know they're making safe judgments.

I circled back to the British Government. A thought crossed my mind. Do they even know the difference between the JFSC and the CIFO?

A MP came back to me two months later to say they would contact the House of Commons library to make enquiries. Two months later they concluded, "We have been unable to find further details regarding the distinction between JFSC and CIFO".

To which I would simply add: where can we go from here when they don't even understand the system themselves?

At this moment in time, it seems our only hope is that powerful organisations such as Guardian finally wake up to their responsibilities and simply refuse to help propagate the stuff.

As with so much of modern life, it seems we are at their mercy.

I won't hold my breath.

Knowing what I know today, Guardian and the like didn't even attempt to update their practices to more closely attempt compliance with regulatory limits. In fact, they were updating its practices to make it even better at cheating its clients.

The Mozart of the industry

The charge sheet against Philip Van Neste is long and unedifying, painting an unhealthy picture of the unsavoury internal practices of the financial advisory industry.

And yet he couldn't be nailed down.

He openly operates in very murky circumstances.

Yet, he's given a protective umbrella to do it.

His scams were proceeding flawlessly.

Yet, no one is willing to step in.

That was mystifying. This is the reality.

This industry is in such a state that a man like Philip Van Neste can hold down an incredibly privileged, responsible, powerful job as chairman of a Financial Services Provider, with no accountability whatsoever. He almost can't be bothered to cover his tracks properly or reply to anything bought to his attention. Nothing shrivels the soul like a 'customer care service', you just know couldn't care less.

Like Grant, he had a way of normalising the fraud that was going on. And that's what makes rogues so effective: hard crime is easy – outright theft, threats, robbery, assault, violence. Soft crime is difficult to prove but it's the most calculating. It's pure genius and an exercise in soft skills – trust, persuasion, sympathy. The skills of a real true con artist.

PART 3

AFTERWORD

⚮ Better to persevere than to only wish you had tried ⚮

After I lost my money, I felt very unmoored. All standards were lost at that point of reality. The unimaginable happened. The world that rogues create is an incredibly elaborate one, in which this international crime organisation has enormous power, and I was really naive and inexperienced. It creates this pervasive illusion that the only options you have are the ones that they're holding out.

Justice will not automatically happen just because you are innocent or you are a victim.

As we look at ourselves and the world today in the midst of a pandemic, one of the things that we can all commit to is to leave the world in a better shape than how we found it. And as I look at myself and where I am, I made a decision to live a life of significance at some point. A life where my presence was felt and I could make a difference. The cause that I chose was fraud. I find it quite offensive, and I became outraged.

I think there are three types of people in this world: perpetrators, victims and witnesses. And I decided that I did not want to be a witness. You have to look at the mirror at yourself and realise that you are either part of the solution or part of the problem. And I believe that witnesses who can make a difference but don't are part of the problem. It was Benjamin Franklin who said, "Until those are unaffected are as outraged as those who are affected, change will never come about". And I am against fraud of any kind, of people, man and woman being passed around as pawns to play with; and I let my voice be heard.

The search for any justice is a reversal of the normal, mundane worldly order. In the search for justice, you swim towards that which is difficult. You put your money, and your time and your effort into something with the hope (the mere hope) that some little justice will be offered in return for what you've decided to abandon your life for.

We all agree that it would be far easier to just swallow the bitter pill, and many of us do. Sometimes the scale of a crisis feels overwhelming and that individual actions can't make a difference. I've certainly felt that but I've learned that we cannot dismiss the idea of trying to do something, just because we can't do everything.

I wasn't arguing about the money. My only regret would have been if I had put money over principle, and I didn't. So, when I had the opportunity, I chose justice. It's not easy, as my story tells, but some things are worth fighting for. To me, I do not believe it to be fair, after pouring money into investments of this length and with these contributions and these assurances, for victims to be left with nothing and for the rogue financial advisor to be left with everything. It was happening way too often with no punishment whatsoever. It had become a joke. An open crime. The sad truth is that, for a certain group of people, financial advisory fraud is now so normal, so utterly unremarkable, that they feel they can do it wherever and whenever they please, without the slightest sense of embarrassment or accountability.

Our greatest defence and sometimes our only defence is our voice. No one has the right to condemn us for choosing to speak up when we have been hurt, wronged or taken advantage of.

And at times we have to use our voice for people who don't have choices, who are voiceless.

The grind of court trials, especially away from 'home', is pretty devastating to family life. Some people know they can't put themselves through it financially, mentally and physically. Or they've reached a point in their life – usually near or at retirement – where they just don't want to do it. They know their limits and it's fair enough. Others, could not subject themselves to being scrutinised and blamed all over again in the courts.

At the end of the day, everyone is doing the best they can under their circumstances.

It is important for victims of financial advisory fraud to decide at which point they feel they can walk away from the experience; that they don't look back on this point in their lives, and regret that they didn't take some action and feel they didn't do enough.

Some people decide to take the financial hit, put the experience down to an important life lesson, swallow the bitter pill, and move on with their lives completely.

However, most people are not able to do that – they try and move on from the experience, but every time they hear about a 'scam' it reignites within them those feelings of betrayal and that maybe they didn't do enough to try and get their money back. And it will always burn inside them. It's a horrible way to live.

And others decide to fight back and redirect matters to a court of law because it's purely a matter of principle to them and they want to remove a rogue from the industry to protect other people, and ultimately get their money back.

You know that there are going to be moments where something means something to you, and it connects with you.

There isn't one key to being confident in taking action. There are several, but one of them is to do difficult things in your day. To do challenging things, because every time we do a difficult thing, that's a proactive measure we can take, completely within our control. It's not something we have to think our way into. It's just the act of doing something difficult sends a message to our brain that we can do something that is hard and we don't have to listen to that resistance that says don't do this. We don't have to give in to that message our brain is telling us, that this is going to be too painful we should back away from this. Because every time we back away, that also sends a message to our brain. That when things are difficult, we're not big enough. We're not bigger than the discomfort that we're facing.

And when we do that difficult thing, face that difficult challenge, and experience that pain and discomfort, my experience has taught me one thing is true. Our confidence is massive, because now we're not looking for or need external validation. And the more we face challenges and the more our confidence grows, the less and less we need that validation from anyone else. It's like dominos. You knock down the first domino, the first difficult thing, and even if that's not as big as some of the more difficult things in your life that you have to tackle, that first domino knocks down the next one, and that knocks down another one, and each one makes you more confident in yourself, and feel more empowered, and more able to go and do the next thing. And that's where momentum comes from. Momentum isn't something that you wake up and have in your day.

Momentum is something that you gain by knocking down that first domino. Then you get the courage, then you get the confidence, then you get the momentum. Confidence, courage, momentum is the process that achieves your ultimate goal.

Grant's gamble: A cautionary tale

"I trust the UAE judicial system" Grant wrote in an email to *The National* newspaper during his trials. At the time Grant believed that all the financial advisors in Dubai were bullet proof when it comes to the law.

For a long time, he was right. They were untouchable.

But that one, reckless email he bashed out to his clients rather thoughtlessly on a day like any other, had turned out to be a colossal misjudgment. The scheme began to unravel after a mishap, ironically, by himself which led to suspicion that all was not right. In 2015, a random email sent by Grant to his client database was where he finally slipped up – accidentally referring to his company by the wrong name.

And slowly the real story behind the family's success started to unravel.

And unravel it did.

Then the roof fell in.

And he was found guilty in the eyes of the law.

He had defended himself, with expensive high-ranking lawyers, with his evidence presented in a fair and legitimate criminal court.

And he lost – three times. It's a matter of inarguable public record: he was convicted by a Dubai court and ordered to pay a fine.

He had defended himself again, and allowed himself to be seduced by more expensive high-ranking lawyers, with his evidence presented in a fair and legitimate civil court.

And he lost. Against the court-appointed expert and the judge. It's a matter of inarguable public record: he was ordered to pay damages by a Dubai court.

He gambled – on his life, his career, his reputation, and his family's future. Why?

Money.

Money is the root of all evil.

Actually no. It's the love of money is the root of all evil. Grant's love of money was his ultimate downfall.

He could have given my money back to me at any time. For a multi-millionaire, £60,000 was really not that much in the whole scheme of things. According to his wife's posts on Facebook, he spent that amount on a new kitchen during the trial. According to a manager at Friends Provident International, he had earned £100,000 in the depth of his criminal trial. Rent from his property in Scotland was netting him on average a couple of thousand pounds per week.

During his criminal trial and whilst his passport was confiscated by the public prosecution office, he told allies in his closest circle that he was alarmed by the possibility of what could happen to him. But not enough to pay up and give up his fraudulent business. He revealed that he was scared that his freedom would be taken away from him. But not enough to pay up and give up his fraudulent business. He was concerned the impact the trial was having on his wife and children. But not enough to pay up and give up his fraudulent business. He made them uproot their lives and shift back to Scotland. He wanted to take it all the way instead of paying up and giving up his fraudulent business – and now he's lost.

Had it been worth the constant stress and fear?

People would joke, pay up? Are you kidding? His arms are too short, implying he had a built-in sense of frugality and economy, despite being very wealthy.

In his memorandum to the courts, he and his lawyer wanted *me* to think about his kids and the impact the trial was having on them so that I would crumble with guilt. Hang on a second, why do I have to think about his kids when he is clearly not? He subjected them to this. It's his behaviour that got him into this mess. Why is the burden on me? I'd normally be quite sympathetic to this kind of thing, but the tone of his defence and the fact it is Grant, made me less inclined to feel bad about it. He refused to take responsibility and expected me to be responsible for his actions.

He was confident that the charges would all be dismissed. Every lawyer, including my own, had been.

He gambled – and he lost. It's as simple as that. I gambled, and one way and another, we came successfully through both trials.

Regardless of whether it's a fine or a jail sentence, it's still a criminal conviction. He still has to tick that box on any application form that asks him if he has a 'criminal conviction'. That's why Grant appealed against it repeatedly, trying to overturn both verdicts. Its relevance was so important that Grant's lawyers spent more than a half of their memorandum arguing that they don't agree with the criminal verdict in a civil court, and it is why they were playing down the significance of the conviction.

But he lost a lot more than just the court cases, and money.

Perhaps the greatest crime he committed was not one he could ever be arrested or sued for: inducing years of paranoia. He made his victims think they could trust no one. He made them doubt everything and everyone.

Time hasn't diluted his friend's anger towards his betrayal. Angry, shocked, hurt because the person that they thought was helping them, is in reality destroying their financial future. They had long been indignant that Grant had not paid the full price for his fraudulent activities against them.

His financial career is gone, and his reputation as one of the respected, and most successful, financial advisors in Dubai's history is gone too. Fired by his company, dumped by his industry friends, and not surprisingly, divorced from his childhood sweetheart.

Well there's an element of schadenfreude I suppose.

They had lived a life of glamour that is hard to reconcile with the life now facing them, with his wife now swapping their previous Dubai and Scottish mansions to living in a flat with their four sons. My distress at this development knows no start.

It's a staggering fall from grace, even by the brutal standards of the financial world. And his particular misfortune is to have his crime so painfully and widely recorded.

Given the trail of devastation he has left in his wake, it's unlikely to garner the slightest flicker of sympathy.

Two years on, he is left to ponder whether it had all been worth it.

As he hides out in Scotland, it's worth contemplating that question for a moment. Dubai is an incredibly small place, but the world is much a smaller place. *Did he really think he can just move back to Scotland as though nothing had happened?*

His story now serves as a warning to all the other rogues.

You're not untouchable.

The enablers

Many think losing investments is a hugely massive expensive

mistake made by individuals.

This mistake is not an accident.

It's caused by an out of control industry.

Since the 1980s the rise of the financial advisory services sector has led to a series of increasingly severe financial crises.

Each crisis has caused more damage, while the industry has made more and more money. The industry as a whole has become notorious for covering up. The companies refuse to stand behind their products; they promote them like crazy but when one of their customers loses their savings in poor ill-advised investments, they claim the person should have known better.

Unfortunately, Grant's scandal won't change a thing because fraud, the practice of mis-selling and misrepresentation, is acceptable by many in that industry.

The truth is that Grant was able to get away with what he did for so long because financial institutions led by 'chairmans' like Philip Van Neste, don't really give a damn about any of it. The very fact is, the industry reward, applaud and enrich people for it. They happily took Grant's financial contributions and his introductions to new clients. Well, take Van Neste, for example, and his court displays of support for his friend, Grant. He has exposed how financial companies are even helping rogues evade the law. And Grant has witnessed all this at first-hand, and doubtless calculated that nobody in his industry really cares about financial fraud. Grant believed he could simply dance away from his criminal conviction, like nothing had happened.

And the really dreadful part of this horrendous saga is that he was right, and he almost did.

His enablers even carried on as usual after they received a copy of the criminal verdict. The ghastly truth may be that it suited them to stay silent. They valued their box office earnings and status more than their integrity or their duty to their clients. At the very outset, it was clear to them all that this would be a private thing, and that nobody in the world would have any idea.

Profits first. Principles second.

Remember these companies didn't fire Grant because they found out he was a fraud, they fired him because we did.

Only after Grant was everyone's front-page news did we get a reaction and ignite some fake moral outrage.

Only then did we have a stampede of financial companies dissociating themselves from him.

Only then did his employer terminate his contract because a civil lawsuit landed on their desk. If it hadn't their contract with Grant would have carried on.

This sorry saga has not been a good advert for the industry, however much they might scream about Grant now.

Cases like this suggest we need a broader definition of culpability.

The bottom line is, in the face of such overwhelming evidence, these companies must have some responsibility and not 'constructive avoidance', exploiting loopholes.

People use the law in order to administer justice. These companies use the law, to hide their injustice.

The Financial Services industry is a service industry that should serve others before it serves itself.

A universal problem

According to Dubai newspapers, local financial experts have been quoted to say that this case is the "worst they have ever seen" in terms of the duration of the crime and the number of victims involved by the hands of a single advisor.

Interesting.

As was this fact: according to the CFA (Chartered Financial Analyst) Institute, a global association of investment professionals, 54 percent of UAE investors use a financial advisor, and only 32 percent consider them trustworthy. Those statistics are hard to ignore.

What about wider shores?

The ripple effect of the media coverage of this case has been massive, and we learnt, this case was not just limited to Grant, or Dubai.

This type of deception recurs with alarming frequency, everywhere.

However, it's so easy and convenient for 'financial experts' to point the finger and blame things on a 'poorly regulated' framework.

A simple question: Who is exploiting them?

My experience has shown that you will find rogues all round the world, no matter how tightly regulated the framework is and looks. I have had exposure to what is perceived as a 'poorly' regulated framework and what is perceived to be a more 'sophisticated' regulated framework. And the truth is, there will always be people ready to exploit other people, no matter which framework they are operating in. The government regulators who should have been protecting the citizens had done nothing in these 'sophisticated' regulated frameworks. Very well prepared, ready to kill any argument you make, my story uncovers a much more pervasive problem globally.

This is society, as a whole, today.

This is a universal problem.

The great reset

The question is: Have financial advisors made the world

riskier?

The short answer is: Yes, they have.

My concern has to do with incentives, that have just no accountability.

The incentive structures that generated huge cash bonuses based on short-term profits but which imposed no penalties for the inevitable later losses. The incentive structures that encouraged advisors to take risks that might eventually destroy their own clients or even cost lives. The incentive structures that encourage the advisors to be addicts, finding a way to make more profit with less risk, and finding a way to make more profit with more risk.

Currently the advisors themselves are trapped by a business model and industry pressure, that makes it almost impossible to 'do the right thing', to work in any other way, to work in a selfless interest, that makes it almost impossible to think of the clients' interests first.

The current way this industry works is not going in a good direction. It sounds simple that we need to change all of that but that's what we need to do. Everybody recognises that this is a problem. People are coming out and having these open conversations about their experiences, so that someone can come in and change it

Financial incentives run the world, so any solution to this problem has to realign the financial incentives.

I have spoken to many financial advisors about the subject of incentives, including very senior ones. They agreed for the need to have compensation regulated in more ways. The only way to 'clean up' this industry, to constrain the financial advisory sector and tighten standards is to introduce a whole new set of regulations.

This change is important, because investing is an increasingly large part of people's lives. As we seek financial security, currently there is no protection for us, the investors, and our hard-earned cash. Currently, the vast illogical web of rules and loopholes, increasingly impossible to understand or follow, look worryingly like an exasperated attempt to punish us, the public, for wanting to save our money and secure our future.

The Government regulators who should have been protecting the citizens, had done nothing. In fact, at the moment one of the main problems is the regulators themselves. They are not taking this seriously; they don't have a strategy whatsoever of how to deal with so many issues and problems within the industry.

Regulators will fast become irrelevant if they don't start doing something about their role. Otherwise, what is the point of them, if they can't help us? The most challenging part for me in my case was to get them to take action – any sort of action. Instead, they offer surface level assistance which never really progresses anything. Pushing paper. Looking busy. Passing the buck.

It's in need of a revolution.

The Government's role in this conversation is absolutely vital in affecting change and moving the needle. There's a huge amount of trust that we all put into government and regulatory platforms and there's an overwhelming desire for transparency, truth and protection. Government support is the birth-right of every citizen, and we treasure it as if it were. So can you imagine the fury if and when they do nothing to protect us? To which I would simply add: their purpose begins to end the day they become silent about things that matter.

Now it is time to take it to the next level. To secure our financial future and to prosper we need to evolve our financial models. Simply put: there's a lot of stuff to be focused on; a lot of work.

We need to reform the financial advisory industry.

We need a robust risk regulator.

We need a greater consumer financial protection agency.

We need to change the financial advisory culture.

It's not enough for the Governments to just acknowledge this. They have to use their folly to actively get the industry under control, and build investment communities that are more safe and trustworthy. What is happening in the financial advisory industry is affecting the world. At the moment it's a global crisis of misinformation and a global crisis of fraud.

Governments now need a reputation for being ahead of rogue financial institutions and being a 'clean' place to do business. They need to make sure that Financial Service Providers and Fund Managers and the like who are proactively being facilitators are at the front of our queue as much as the Independent Financial Advisors and they should do everything they can to prosecute them and punish anyone taking part in illegal crime – or turning a blind eye to it – by making sure those in charge of the businesses cannot continue to live their lavish lifestyles scamming clients.

Otherwise, in their own way, Governments are also enabling it by not doing enough to protect us from fraud or help us get our money back. They should stop indirectly protecting the financial world and make it crystal clear, in the most punitive way possible, that we won't tolerate such behaviour by the advisory world.

A case in point. The reason why Volkswagen finally came clean in their cheating diesel scandal is that the regulatory authority, Environmental Protection Agency (EPA), told them that if they didn't come clean, they would not certify any 2016 vehicles, including their gasoline vehicles. That meant Volkswagen couldn't sell cars.

In other words, both the Government and the regulators can be that tough with the financial advisory industry. These are choices that they can make. They could make progress if they just made more effort – preferring to skirt around the issue and deflecting it between each other, meanwhile, allowing financial companies grow stronger by the day into a financial Godzilla.

It's not the answer.

We don't need them to be just a witness and say "oh, isn't it awful". No. Their question should be "how do we protect the investor?". We need them to become a force for good. To do greater public service. To become outraged for us, and let their voice be heard with ours. For them to contribute their money, their time, and their presence to protect their citizens.

This is the time to say there is a national interest. This is the time when the interests of people, of investors, is actually more important than the profits of somebody who's already a millionaire or a company that's already a billionaire.

It's that awareness-wake up call. Wake up to the idea that if they don't change anything, nothing is going to change.

If nothing changes, nothing changes.

And the question is how long do things have to be bad before they're willing and ready to finally say "that's enough". The bigger it gets the harder it is for anyone to change.

Do I think we are going to get there?

We have to.

It's not about harming these financial intuitions, it's about reforming them, so they don't destroy us.

The killing power of a great lawyer

Love them or loathe them, we need lawyers.

But we need to find the right one.

Gone are the days that you can hand your case over to the lawyers – you have to work with them and you have to watch over them and you have to check on them, and take on a front-line role.

I can personally relate to the inability to find proper representation if you are not familiar with the profession and its framework, and for this reason I documented my journey with lawyers to show how finding a law firm is about finding the right lawyer for you. I was troubled not knowing which lawyers were genuine and which just wanted to generate some money, so they can meet their targets.

And once you find the right lawyer you have to be sure they say to you that "you go with me, it'll be me. I will never pawn you off to an associate". Yet when they do, their job will be to help them focus on winning cases, like yours. Quantity is no measure of quality. The perception of quality no true measure of relevance either.

One would be well advised to steer more towards personal recommendations than legal directories' recommendations or law firm referrals, some of which have either a formal or informal referral programme. Someone who has used the lawyer before, and can rate them on their overall service, quality, written and spoken English and of the local language, knowledge of the law and level of creativity. Someone who's been there, done it, and taken lessons from it.

Once you find 'that' lawyer, and you connect and have chemistry – well, magical is the best word I can think of to describe it. Such is the killing power of a great lawyer.

Otherwise, it can spell disaster. Compound your miseries. They can cost you lots of money, time and even lose your case for you. Such is the killing power of a poor lawyer.

When this story was first published in the media, the victims were approached by law firms in the UK, known in the legal world as 'ambulance chasers' – they see victims and rush to their aid. One lawyer approached me, and he wanted the names of all the victims and "we'll do a class action," he said. He was based in some remote place in England and he wasn't prepared for my onslaught of questions of how much he knew about Dubai local law and legal representation before the courts. I never heard from him again.

One victim was quoted AED 130,000 to take his case to court. He was ready to sign on the dotted line before I interjected, determined to thwart any attempts by law firms to over-charge vulnerable victims. It didn't include appeals, which the case will inevitably go to, or court fees, translation fees and announcement fees and the like – and what was their plan and strategy exactly?

There was one couple contemplating taking their financial advisor to court but had been told the other party's lawyers were very aggressive and will be very aggressive with them, and they were such nice people they didn't know if they could cope with it all. Yes, I agreed, it's tough. You need a thick skin. But you need a lawyer who can take them on, and take that pressure of you. That's important too.

Most victims complained the lawyers were complicating their situation by sitting on the fence. One victim said to me: "I need one that will look at the case and potentially think it's worthy. They must have seen this so many times before".

Another said: "I want to be reassured things will turn out the way I want them to".

Only, lawyers are wary of going that far and very uneasy about running so much of the transcript on the basis that there is no 'hard' evidence. They want a signed declaration from the likes of Grant, that yes he mis-sold investments to you before they are confident of anything. Until then, you case always has a fifty-fifty chance. There are lawyers who say they will take on your case because there's a strong enough case. That's usually lawyer-speak for 'the cheque's big enough'.

How do spot a flake lawyer and what to do about it?

Let's talk about the kind of lawyer who is wasting your time and money. I call them the MPI – the minimum possible investment in your case.

This is a lawyer who will you send you an email, every once in a while, shows up in your diary, every once in a while, but isn't moving things forward.

What can you do about it?

I watch their actions, not their words. When we listen to what they say, they may say everything we want to hear, and tell us positive things. But when we look beyond those words, we will see no action, we will see no real investment.

I like to think of it like a romantic movie. Does it work if you put it on mute? Eliminate all that romantic dialogue and see if it still looks like a love story. Or does it look like two people not doing very much.

Have the real conversation with that person. Send them a message or call them and say, "Listen I appreciate you're busy, and you have a lot on but I get the feeling that you're not really invested in this case, I get the sense that this isn't really progressing. Am I right about that, or have I misjudged it?"

When you say that they have two choices: either bring you more, or decide to call it a day, because you have exposed the elephant in the room.

How to protect yourself against fraud

I think this is an important juncture, because I've had,

probably like you, many realisations during this journey. What I'm afraid of is that those realisations will count for nothing if we just mindlessly go into the next chapter of our lives without finding a way to cement them.

So, I thought I'd talk about some of my realisations, and as I do it might evoke some of your realisations in a conscious way that you can record so that you don't let them go. Winston Churchill once said: "Men occasionally stumble over the truth, but most pick themselves up and carry on as if nothing happened".

Let's not be those people.

I've spoken and worked with a group of leaders and thinkers in the financial advisory industry, who have a shared goal of wanting to make this space healthier and better for all of us, who are so knowledgeable on not just what the problems are in the industry, but trying to find solutions for it, which is so important. Actively doing the work to create safe healthy trustworthy investments, and help us see what is happening with our money and to have a choice in it, so we are not controlled by this platform, not controlled by advisors.

So, if you're planning to work with a financial advisor, and if you do your homework, and know your numbers too, you will be able to spot the woods from the trees. That means there are plenty of financial advisors who are honest and hardworking who do not prey on people's desire to save for the future.

The key is to know how to spot them.

I have thirteen areas where I think questions should be asked before hiring anyone.

Qualifications. Review financial advisory credentials and certificates. The Certified Financial Planner designation (CFP) is generally considered the gold standard in the industry. Advisors must have several years of experience, take an extensive course and pass a six-hour exam to become a CFP. Once certified they must complete continuing education and are held to strict ethical standards.

The other key qualifications are Certified Public Accountant, Personal Financial Specialist, a Chartered Financial Consultant or a Chartered Financial Analyst.

However, Grant was right. Unfortunately, there are no qualifications at all required in Dubai to practice as a financial advisor, and in reality, very few advisors in the UAE will have any applicable qualification in financial services, and the vast majority of firms don't have any requirement (the salespeople are self-employed and commission only). I would say these types of firms aren't really financial advisory companies but sellers of financial products.

In comparison, in the UK the minimum qualification is Chartered or Qualifications and Curriculum Authority (QCA) level 4 but most companies in the UK will look for a level 6 Chartered Financial Advisor which is UK degree level.

Financial advisory companies of the type you get in the UK don't really exist in Dubai, unless they are UK companies that have branches in Dubai and only use qualified planners. They are Chartered or QCA Level 4, 5 and 6 and certified fiduciaries. These are the companies and advisors you need to partner with. There are only two firms I have discovered in Dubai with 100 percent qualified advisors.

Unfortunately, the advisor's qualifications are very rarely checked by their clients. The main education bodies of financial services are CII, LIBF, and CISI. You can easily check if an advisor is appropriately qualified by searching the directories on their websites. Indirectly, you will be helping to improve the standard of education for advisors in the UAE and cutting down on fake qualifications.

It is frightening to discover how many unqualified people are advising, quite legally.

How do they earn their money? This is key. As almost anyone can call themselves a financial advisor, let's start by narrowing down the financial field. Ask your advisor how he gets paid and how often. There are three basic types of advisors based on how they are paid: commission-based, fee-based and fee-only.

Commission-based advisors are not fiduciaries and are often salespeople employed by large financial institutions: investment and insurance brokerages, and are only held to suitability standards. Because of what they are paid is based on what they sell, there can be a conflict of interest. If you choose to work with a financial advisor who earns sales commissions, it is important to be aware that the temptation of commission is there and it can influence their recommendations for you. If they are paid commissions, get the details. If it's above four percent, run. The greed gets to them in the end, and before you know it, they're choosing investments that are high risk for you and high commission for them.

Fee-based advisors are typically affiliated with a broker/agent and like the commission-based advisors, generally hold a license to sell investments or insurance for a commission. Fee-based advising is confusing because like the fee-only advisor, the fee-based advisor provides financial planning for a fee. However, the important difference is they also sell products and get paid commissions. So, there is still that conflict of interest, because their fee-based recommendations could (and often do) include purchasing products they receive commissions on.

The fee-only financial advisor is the only type of

advisor I recommend because they have a fiduciary duty to act in the best interest of their clients. The fee-only model is better at aligning client interests with those of the advisor – usually either an hourly rate or a sum related to the size of the portfolio: advisors typically charge their fees by a percentage of their clients' assets, commonly one percent annually. When the portfolio's value falls, the client pays a smaller advisory fee. This model gives advisors every incentive to grow portfolios while also reducing investment risk and usually provide more comprehensive advice including real estate, retirement, investing, taxes, education funding and insurance planning.

If you don't know exactly what your advisor's fees are, or you think the advice is free, you are probably the victim of a hefty commission. If you have a Trust ask how much introductory fee your advisor is paid as well as how much they are paid directly from the Trust, as that's still your money. It's just not coming from your outside pocket, but from your inside pocket. If possible, get a copy of the payment or fee structure contract between your advisor and the Financial Service Providers, Product Providers and the Fund Managers. All in all, you need to be sure your advisor is working for you.

Prescribed Direction. If you are asked to sign this document by your financial advisor, be clear who is the overriding responsible for your money, and accountable for your investment.

The Prescribed Direction certificate legally protects financial institutions in the event a lawsuit is lodged against them should a dispute arise concerning your investment. As per your signature on the form, you agree that the company did not provide the investment advice you acted upon; and that the contract was taken out upon advice from your financial advisor, who is in no way associated with the company. Thereby accepting the company played no part in the sale of the contract of your investment funds.

Partnership Terms of Business Agreements. Ask to see a copy of the Terms of Business set up between your financial advisor and their partners, to ensure they have carried out the proper due diligence on your advisor in order to sell their products to you in your jurisdiction.

Terms and Conditions of Investment Products. Don't sign anything until you have received all the Terms and Conditions of each investment fund, policy, and Trust – or at least see a copy of it, read the small print, exercise the due diligence – just as you would for your own clients if you own or work for a business. Be clear on the eligibilities, clauses, deliverables, responsibilities and accountabilities.

Power of Attorney. Sometimes, this is embedded within the Terms and Conditions of the contract of investment products. Be clear on how much control you want your financial advisor to have in managing your investments.

Regulation. Ensure the financial advisor and their partnerships are fully regulated, and, they are regulated within your jurisdiction; and ensure the products being sold to you by your advisor is high quality regulation. Double-check with the Financial Ombudsman, and that you have a mechanism for complaint if things go wrong. Never invest a penny without checking this first.

Types of Investments. Avoid start-up companies – you're looking for a Google in a haystack of billions. The odds are against you. If you don't have the option to sell your investments at any time without a penalty, then don't sign up. Avoid such products because it means high fees and long lock-in periods. If your financial advisor is recommending these products, they do not have your best interests. Only their own. A good advisor will recommend asset allocation, diversification and rebalancing and have the skills and experience to put those into practice for you. Know where your funds are domiciled and the tax position so avoid being slapped with a hefty tax bill.

Professional License Certificate. This includes checking that your financial advisor is registered with a state licensing body and check this with the relevant bodies. Review trade licenses and check the activity they are licensed to provide. This, I would argue, is a classic example of where due diligence can provide dividends.

Court of Law. If there is any dispute between you and your financial advisor, arising out of or in connection with your agreement, including any question regarding its existence, validity or termination, insert a governing law and dispute resolution clause in your agreement subject to the court you agree for your case to be heard. For example, in the UAE, there are two options: Dubai courts under local law or the courts of the DIFC who follow English law where the agreement is governed by and construed in accordance with the laws of England.

Valuation Sheets. Review your financial position regularly, you need to understand it. The best advice is to undertake a management finance course which arms you with the knowledge to ask the right questions of your financial advisors, and demand to see a valuation sheet every month from your advisor and from your Financial Service Provider and then verify the two to each other. When an advisor explains something, you need to understand it.

Contact. Keep and maintain direct contacts with all parties: Financial Service Providers, Product Providers and the Fund Managers. Don't rely only on your advisor for information and updates on your investment portfolios.

Disclosures. Disclosures are negative reports (complaints) from clients on an advisor's compliance record.

Has the financial advisor ever been the subject of formal complaints, sued by a client or disciplined by a regulatory body?

You may be surprised to know that advisors can have multiple complaints on their record and still stay licensed to give investment advice. You can access websites such as BrokerCheck to see if they have any negative disclosures recorded against them. If an advisor has several complaints against them, it may be best to move on.

Queries. If you are querying your investments with your current financial advisor, in the first instance ideally send off an 'Information Only' letter of authority to all parties / companies requesting detailed and pertinent information on all aspects of the investments.

I would request in writing the following items:

- A signed client fact find
- A dated and signed 'reasons why' or suitability letter outlining their recommendations, all associated costs and all associated risk warnings
- A written dated proof of any risk assessment they undertook before any investment was entered into
- A written and detailed breakdown of all initial and ongoing commissions, marketing fees and advisor fees
- A written and detailed product brochure for all investments entered into
- A written and dated record of when and why any funds were changed and how that related to your experience and risk profile, and the time horizons and aims you had stated

That all sounds quite simple, doesn't it?

It might be obvious, but most people just don't follow through and actually do it; preferring to rely on a long list of client references. Yet behind each of those entreaties lies a far deeper and more complex meaning, with massive potential consequence, if, as with me and many, many others did, you are fooled.

I hope that everyone comes away with one action item that they realise they can do and they now know they can now see will have a positive effect on how they're interacting with their advisors.

Never discredit your gut instinct. You are not paranoid. Let it do its job. Your body can pick up on bad vibrations. As Morgan Freeman says, "If something deep inside of you says something is not right about a person or situation, trust it".

Financial education: the next step

For a period of time, the most dreaded words in my life were 'financial advisors'. I received financial wealth management requests every week and my response was to delete delete delete. That's what it's like for someone who has been burnt by the industry. It put me off the stock market, investment firms, Trusts – anything to do with financial services for good. My personal advice to any budding investors was to say no thank you if advisors come calling.

However, I soon realised I was going to have to pull myself out of this rut. Because at some point I will have to invest for the same reasons I invested with Neil Grant – but this time I am wiser.

If I care about my financial future, and if I never want to be financially vulnerable again, I needed to educate myself, to make myself less susceptible to disaster. My money is my responsibility and I need to take control of my money and my investments. Nobody could take care of my money as well as me.

With this in mind, financial learning and education for investors is a natural development for me. It's how we can empower all investors to have access to quality and safe education. It is needed more than ever. Part of the reason why I do this work, is to install in people a confidence in investing in the right way. And then separately, to look at the hindrances that investors were facing within the industry, really inhibiting them from being able to understand the true value of their investments. To close those gaps so investors can benefit.

When people have access to education, everyone wins and everyone succeeds. It just opens the door for success at the highest level. And that alone creates a ripple effect, for your entire life.

What I have learned from my own experience, is that supporting local financial educators and activists has a huge role in transforming societies and communities. These groups are identifying the issues that investors are facing locally, because the issues vary when it comes to lack of access to financial education – in some places it's qualification issues, in other places it is lack of infrastructure, in other places it's lack of transparency. But these local activists are now adapting to the changes and finding new ways to ensure their clients are protected and not missing out on their investments.

And the next chapter in my journey marks my first collaboration with these groups of people with the goal to give you the right investing education. In June 2021, we launched the UAE's first financial podcast with the goal to enhance financial advisory and legal services awareness so people can avoid the costly mistakes that most investors make.

So, our work is far from finished.

I'll leave a link to the podcast here:

https://businesssculpting.com/podcast/
Let's take back our power with educating ourselves.
Let's get started on securing your financial future!
Let's start there.

APPENDIX

THE WITNESS STATEMENT

The original statement has been redacted where it references various legal considerations or innocent parties with their personal information obscured.

In the CIVIL COURTS   **Case No.** ▮▮▮▮▮

AMBER WAHEED
and
NEIL RAMSAY PRINGLE GRANT
and
▮▮▮▮▮▮▮▮▮▮▮▮▮▮▮▮▮▮▮▮

STATEMENT OF
AMBER WAHEED

In this statement, I, Amber Waheed, will show that Neil Grant did the following:

(1)   He miss-used his trade license of 'management consultancy' and worked as a financial consultant/advisor under Prosperity Management Consultancy which led to me suffering financial losses.

(2)   He set up a fake financial advisory company, that is unregistered, unlicensed and unregulated called Prosperity Offshore Investment Consultants and he ran the business under Prosperity Management Consultancy's license.

(3) From February 8th, 2015, he ran both businesses under ████████████████████ (hereby referred to as ████████████ or █) license number ██

(4) He created fake company documentation and contracts to mislead and misrepresent himself and his companies to me, to conclude a contract with him, with the intention to deceive me, for personal financial gain and profit.

(5) He miss-sold investments to me which were not what we had agreed or suited to my investment profile, and he hid the reality of their poor performance from me.

(6) He benefited financially from his deceit, and was paid money directly from me and from the Product Providers and Fund Managers, and he took unauthorised fees.

(7) He used my signature on a document without my knowledge or consent.

Criminal Decision

1. A criminal judgment against Neil Grant evidences that Prosperity Management Consultancy was licensed by the Dubai Economic Development (DED) for management consulting through which it provided "consultancies and management studies for the public organisation and companies". Prosperity Management Consultancy was not licensed nor did it have competence in investment / financial advisory, or any fiduciary role (Exhibit 1).

2. However, Neil Grant represented to me and the world that he had the necessary financial advisory license, the necessary qualifications, and the necessary expertise.

3. Neil Grant introduced me to ████████ International Ltd in Guernsey and Guardian Trust Company Ltd (hereby referred to as Guardian) in Jersey in an attempt to sell their products to me. Neil Grant showed me the Terms of Business agreement he held

with Guardian to verify and convince me that he was licensed and qualified to sell Guardian's products to me. On that basis, I set up contracts. On that basis, I gave him my life-savings to invest.

4. In light of the criminal decision, anything linked to Neil Grant is void contracts as they are not proper contracts. They have not been entered in accordance with or in compliance with the regulatory requirements in the UAE and therefore all the money that was given to Neil Grant to be invested should be returned to me.

Part 1 - The Set Up

Approach by Neil Grant

(1) On May 12th, 2010, I was approached by ▇▇▇▇▇▇▇▇▇, Business Manager from Prosperity Offshore Investment Consultants inviting me to a complementary advisory consultation with Neil Grant. Her email signature read 'Prosperity Offshore Investment Consultants' (Exhibit 2), and their company website, Prosperity Offshore Investment Consultants, stated they were a financial advisory promoting "insurance linked products" (Exhibit 3).

Meeting with Neil Grant

(2) On May 16th, 2010, I attended a meeting with Neil Grant at Prosperity Offshore Investment Consultants office in the ▇▇▇▇▇▇ Hotel Office Tower. Neil Grant introduced himself to me as a Financial Consultant. His business card read 'Prosperity Offshore Investment Consultants'. The company consisted of two members of staff: Neil Grant (the owner) and ▇▇▇▇▇▇▇▇.

(3) The office signage read 'Prosperity Offshore Investment Consultants'.

(4) All stationery and stamps read 'Prosperity Offshore Investment Consultants'.

(5)   Media interviews with Neil Grant including the ███████████ and the ███████████ described Prosperity Offshore Investment Consultants as an independent financial services" (Exhibit 4).

(6)   Neil Grant showed me the Terms of Business he had set up with Guardian, based in Jersey (Exhibit 5). This document allowed Neil Grant to sell their product to me. Neil Grant had written the following in his handwriting:

    a)   Under full name of Applicant: "**Prosperity Management Consultancy**"

    b)   Against the category 'Nature of Business Activities' he wrote "**Offshore Investment Consultants**" (knowing that DED provided a license for Prosperity Management Consultancy to trade only as 'Management Consultancies' under the license number 559536)

    c)   In the category 'Regulator Authority' he wrote "**Department of Economic Development, Dubai**" (despite the fact that he was aware DED only registers a company and are not regulators)

    d)   In the category 'Business for which regulated' Neil Grant wrote "**Offshore Investment Consulting**"

    e)   In the 'Declaration of Applicant' it states "**We declare that the information furnished herewith is true and accurate**" and is signed by Neil Grant

Neil Grant's Financial Advice

1   During the meeting, I discussed my financial situation and investment objectives with Neil Grant. As a single woman with no family, I made it clear to him that I was not interested in any 'get rich quick' schemes.

2   Neil Grant wrote his recommendations on a FactFinder form (Exhibit 6). He advised me to invest in an offshore bank account with Anglo Irish; a ███████ 5 year Vision Life Insurance plan; a long-term trust with Guardian, and a Hansard

Policy (that never came to fruition due to an administration error).

3   After the meeting, on May 16th, 2010, Neil Grant sent an email to me with his 'Client Confidential' report and recommendations, and he requested another meeting with me to move things forward (Exhibit 7).

4   I agreed to purchase Neil Grant's financial advisory services because I believed that I was entering into a legal agreement with a qualified licensed financial consultant who had my best interests.

5   As per his advice I agreed to invest in the following Trust and Policy:

     a)   A long-term savings plan with Guardian. Neil Grant completed the Guardian Application Form which he stamped with Prosperity Offshore Investment Consultants and named himself the Investment Manager/Financial Advisor of the Trust (Exhibit 8 – page 3). The Trust was named 'Zara'. He told me to invest GBP 50,000 (the minimum amount required to open a trust). GBP 45,000 cash was for investment, and GBP 5,000 cash held on account for ongoing administration fees, to be deducted quarterly.

     b)   A 5 year Life Insurance plan with ███████. Neil Grant completed and signed the application form and I was to pay $1,500 (AED 5,520) per month towards the plan for the next five years (Exhibit 9).

Contract with Neil Grant and Prosperity Offshore Investment Consultants

6   I signed the Prosperity Offshore Investment Consultants Code of Conduct that formed our contract (as acknowledged by Neil Grant's email) (Exhibit 10). One of its terms states that "The investment that I am undertaking is a medium to long-term investment and is not suited to short-term trading". Under the terms of our agreement, I agreed to purchase Neil Grants'

financial services with the clear understanding that he would invest in long-term low-risk investments.

Money Transfer & Confirmation of Trust and Policy by Neil Grant

7 On May 17th, 2010, Neil Grant wrote an email of the actions needed to be taken to set up the Zara Trust and ▮▮▮▮▮ Policy. He was clever not to ask for money to be sent directly to him. He managed the money transfer process and asked me to send GBP 50,000 to Guardian in Jersey. He wrote that he will set up the Foreign Exchange Rate account from which "you will be able to transfer the GBP 50,000 to the Guardian Trust from the details I provided you with this evening" (Exhibit 11).

8 Neil Grant's office provided me with the payment and transfer details. I had no contact with Guardian (Exhibit 12).

9 On June 13th, 2010, I wrote an email to Neil Grant asking if Guardian had received my money. He replied that he had not received any confirmation but he could see that the beneficiary details he provided to me were correct. He said he will email Guardian and check the position. In the same email, he confirmed he had received the ▮▮▮▮▮ Policy documents (Exhibit 13).

10 On June 14th, 2010, Neil Grant wrote an email to me to confirm that Guardian had received my money (Exhibit 14).

11 On June 15th, 2010, Neil Grant wrote an email to me to confirm that the Zara Trust was set up (Exhibit 15).

12 In the same email correspondence, Neil Grant confirmed to Guardian that my money had been transferred through an Exchange Rate company called First Rate FX that *he* had recommended explaining that he uses them "for the benefit of our clients to avoid draconian bank charges and commissions. The client has opened an account (Barclays) with First Rate and transferred her funds "as intimated" from her own account through this exchange rate account, to the Kings Street Nominee beneficiary account" (Exhibit 15).

Investment Placements by Neil Grant

13   After the money was transferred to Guardian, and the 'Zara Trust' was set up, Neil Grant managed and placed my money into investment funds.

14   On June 24ᵗʰ, 2010, Neil Grant wrote an email to each of the Fund Managers advising them that "we will be placing a new investment of GBP 10,000 on behalf of the Zara Trust through Guardian Trusts Ltd" (Exhibit 16). He selected the following funds: Brandeaux Student Accommodation; Centurion life assurance; Prime (Burj) India and Aliquot Precious Metals.

15   Neil Grant also selected the funds for the ▇▇▇▇ Policy. They were: Aliquot Gold Bullion; Aliquot Precious Metals, HSBC GIF Brazil Equity and J.F India (Exhibit 9 – Page 5).

16   As per my agreement with Neil Grant (Exhibit 10) my understanding was that these funds that Neil Grant was investing my money into, were all long-term low-risk investment funds "not suited to short term trading" i.e. they are not high-risk funds.

Part 2 - Performance

Poor Investment Performance

17   However, it transpired that these investments were short-term, extremely risky, and unsuitable for a novice investor like myself, and each decreased in value until they were worthless.

18   Since the commencement, the Guardian Zara Trust fell from GBP 50,000 in 2010, to nil in 2016, which remains its current value.

19   On June 7ᵗʰ, 2015, the 5-year ▇▇▇▇ policy matured at a loss. After the first five months of poor performance, I stopped payments into the Policy. Neil Grant pressurised me into restarting payments otherwise, he advised, I was going to lose all

of my money. Upon his advice, I resumed monthly payments in 2013 but after 5 months, I stopped payments into the Policy. In hindsight, if I had taken Neil Grant's advice and continued to plough more money into the Policy, I would have lost more money. Upon redemption, and administration and transfer fees, I received a sum that was $6,000 less than I had paid into it, proving it to be an ill-advised investment plan. Confirmation of loss; proof of transfer of funds; full breakdown of maturity value; Policy fees and charges are detailed in Exhibit 17.

20 The constant declining value since the commencement in June 2010 in the Zara Trust and in the ████████ Policy is illustrated below, with the corresponding Valuation Statements produced by Neil Grant in Exhibit 18. In reality, these are inflated figures, because most of the funds held were suspended from redemption, performing poorly, or illiquid. The value of the ████████ Policy only increased in 2013 because I poured more money into it.

Valuation Statement Date	Guardian Zara Trust Ltd Total Value (GBP)	████████ Total Value (USD)
	(Lump Sum GBP 50,000)	(Total Investment $15,000)
June 2011	49,838.34	8,694.21
January 2012	45,365.14	7,407.77
July 2012	42,797.93	10,758.25
July 2013	42,187.95	12,009.91
November 2013	41,974.78	13,009.35
April 2014	41,757.66	13,691.97
February 2015	38,513.41	11,267.51
May 2015	37,660.00	11,678.00
September 2015	29,095.10	N/A
January 2016	28,726.13	N/A
April 2016	28,599.04	N/A
September 2017	12,336.62	N/A
January 2018	11,884.91	N/A

Reasons for the Instant and Continuous Fall in Investments

21   Under the terms of our agreement, Neil Grant was to invest in long-term low-risk funds where the increase in the value of the fund is slow over a long-term basis. I was aware that investments don't ever only go up. However, on low-risk investments, I was aware that it should not really drop more than 10%. This is the reason why I invested in the Zara Trust as part of a long-term plan to minimise the risks and did not invest in short-term trading (as per Neil Grant's advice in Exhibit 7 and our contract in Exhibit 10).

22   However, ALL the funds that Neil Grant advised me to invest into were high-risk investments for short-term gains. The risk is that the funds can be suspended and illiquid at any given time. The funds that Neil Grant selected for me were start-up companies that were always going to be high risk, as you are investing in something new that has no history or record. This is a breach of trust and of our contract and agreement. From the commencement the investments comprising the Zara Trust were in a poor state of affairs:

a)   Prime India: sharply declined in value to minus 34% by September 2013 (Exhibit 20)

b)   Brandeaux: from 1 July 2013 redemptions were suspended on the Student accommodation fund, with no certainty that the fund could restructure and realise solvency or any value for shareholders (Exhibit 21)

c)   New Earth (Waste Recycling): redemptions were suspended in January 2014 (Exhibit 22). In 2016 Guardian confirmed the value of the fund was nil.

d)   Centurion (Life Insurance Settlement): redemptions were suspended in 2012 (Exhibit 23)

e)   Lucent (Land Purchase and Planning): the fund suspended on 29th June 2016 (Exhibit 24)

f)   On October 3rd, 2016, Matt Hill from Guardian confirmed ongoing suspension on all the investment funds in the Zara

Trust (Exhibit 25). All of the Trust's investments were and are worthless.

g) On February 6th, 2018 Anna Neydar from Guardian confirmed that Lucent, the only remaining fund in the Zara Trust remains suspended (Exhibit 26).

h) Therefore the current value of the Zara Trust is nil, as the cash held on the account is for ongoing administration fees (Exhibit 19).

Reasons Why Neil Grant Picked Risky Funds

23 Neil Grant and his companies did not hold the correct Trading License. Traditional blue-chip companies such as Morgan Stanley conduct business with registered, licensed, regulated companies, and individuals who hold the correct qualifications. Any proper due diligence on Neil Grant and his companies would expose the reality that Prosperity was not licensed nor did it have competence in investment / financial advisory, or any fiduciary role.   Therefore Neil Grant purposely conducted business with new companies in need of immediate investment or who did not have the sophisticated knowledge of the correct Dubai governing bodies and laws.

24 Neil Grant and his companies were not regulated. Companies outside of DIFC are regulated by the UAE Insurance Authority for all insurance based products; and Securities and Commodities Authority (SCA) for investment based products.

a) The Insurance Authority confirm as per Article 3, Clause 8, of the 3 of 2010 concerning the code of conduct and ethics, that insurance companies were: "Not to deal with any person or entity from the professions associated with insurance that is not licensed by the IA including the business of agency, brokerage, consultation or expertise in claim settlement or actuarial expertise; and ensure that the aforesaid persons or entities have the required license" (Exhibit 27). Neil Grant manipulated the information in the Terms of Business document with

Guardian because he knew he did not have the correct license (Exhibit 5).

b) On June 12th, 2016, the SCA confirmed: **"Prosperity Offshore Investment Consultants is not licensed by SCA for any activity"** (Exhibit 28).

c) On June 13th, 2016, SCA confirmed that Prosperity Management Consultancy was not licensed by them (Exhibit 28).

25   High Commission. Neil Grant manipulated client's involvement in Trusts and Policies to generate substantial commission and fees for himself. High-risk illiquid start-up investment funds such as New Earth (Waste recycling) offer a high commission for recruiting new investors. Neil Grant's financial advice was given to me to benefit him more than me, his client. He took advantage of my trust and lack of financial knowledge and convinced me that these investments certainly 'could' give good returns without giving me the reality of the risks involved (as explained further).

Neil Grant's Fees & Commissions

26   Neil Grant's fee structure was set up directly with the Trust and Policies, and therefore difficult to calculate the true reality of the money earned by him, accept to prove he was paid fees as evidenced below:

a) Clause 2.4 of the Trust Deed (Fees) states: "A Financial Advisor fee of up to 1.25% per annum which is payable to the Investment Manager for the provision of investment advice" (Exhibit 8 – page 8).

b) Clause 2.2 of the Trust Deed (Management and Administration – Investment Management) states: "All fees and charges of the Investment Manager shall be payable out of the Trust Fund" (Exhibit 8 – page 14).

c) In the Guardian Trust Portfolio Wrap, the Financial Advisor is stamped "Neil Grant" from "Prosperity Offshore Investment Consultants" (Exhibit 8 – page 3).

27   On 7th October 2016, Matt Hill from Guardian explained the Trust fee structure (Exhibit 30). There were two separate fees applied: the financial adviser's fee and the trustee fee (also called wrap fee). The break down fees paid to Neil Grant (according to this email) as well as total fees on the account are as follows:

a)   Neil Grant's fee – he received a total of 1.5% of the value of the account at each payment interval between the inception (2010) to Q4 2012. He continued to receive the 0.25% trail fee from the trustees until Q4 2015.

b)   1.25% Financial Adviser fee – this was applied to the account between the inception (2010) and Q4 2012 (December 31st 2012). According to the email from Matt Hill, Neil Grant received the full 1.25%.

c)   1% to 0.75% Trustee (wrap) fee – this fee was charged at 1% between the inception (2010) and Q4 2015 (December 31st 2015). It was then reduced to 0.75% between Q1 2016 to the present day. According to the email from Matt Hill, Neil Grant received 0.25%.

d)   Neil Grant received the full adviser fee and 25% of the trustee wrap fee until Q4 2015 (December 31st 2015).

28   The commission structure was set up directly with the Trust and Policies, and therefore difficult to calculate the true reality of the money earned by Neil Grant, accept to prove he was paid commission as evidenced below:

a)   The Code of Conduct states Prosperity "will receive a commission from the financial institutions with which my business is placed" (Exhibit 10).

b)   Clause 2 of the Trust Deed ("Fees") states that Guardian "shall be entitled to charge the following fees of which may be shared with the Independent Financial Intermediary or Investment Manager" (Exhibit 8 – page 8).

c)   On April 27th, 2013, Neil Grant confirmed that he received a commission on placing investment funds in the Zara

Trust. This email was in reference to New Earth (Waste Recycling) and a 4% placement fee (Exhibit 29 – page 2).

d)   Industry experts predict that Neil Grant's commission for selling the ███████ plan was approximately AED 18,000 per client.

Chartered Financial Service Provider's Analysis of Neil Grant and His Advice

29   In March 2016, ███████ a Chartered Financial Consultant with ███████ Planning reviewed the Guardian Zara Trust portfolio and gave his analysis (Exhibit 31).

a)   ███████ confirmed that the investments Neil Grant had advised that I invest in were high-risk new start-up companies with no history or record.

b)   He questioned Neil Grant's academic qualifications who was grade 2 qualified and did the very basic minimum adviser qualification 20 years ago. For employment within an IFA firm in the UAE, most firms require a minimum level 3 qualification.

c)   ███████ confirmed that the risks and illiquidity of the investments I had entered into are inappropriate for my risk profile, goals and aims. I had been put into three of the commonest of these generic type of investments:-

1.   A high risk and totally illiquid Hedge Fund

2.   A "Life Settlement Fund"

3.   The Brandeaux Student Accommodation Fund

d)   ███████ advised that what I should have had was a range of publicly quoted blue-chip names that would always be liquid and that would be diversified across a number of basic asset classes such as equities or stocks & shares, gilts, corporate bonds and perhaps property but only in large safer liquid property funds (and not something like Brandeaux).

e)   The Life Settlement funds are typically an unregulated collective investment scheme made up of traded life insurance policies (TLPIs). TLPIs are investments in life assurance policies and are known to be complicated products that are unsuitable for non-experienced investors in Dubai.

f)   ████████ said he would be surprised if the total investment ever recouped its initial value, and the problem is due to the "illiquidity" of so much of it, as I am "**trapped**" in the high-risk and underperforming investments.

Part 3 – Suspicious Conduct by Neil Grant

Dissatisfaction over Neil Grant's Advice and Service

30   When the funds continued to fall in value I contacted Neil Grant on December 12th, 2012 to request a meeting to terminate our contract (Exhibit 33 – page 3 and 4). Neil Grant's response was very personal and he delayed the meeting for two months until February 12th, 2013.

31   At the meeting, Neil Grant assured me that his service will improve and be more timely and attentive. He said that as from December 31st, 2012, he had cancelled all fees to prove that he was working for my best interests alone. He convinced me to continue with the relationship and upon his assurances, I agreed. However, to his annoyance, from here-on, I regularly requested and held meetings with him.

a)   2011: – 1 meeting: June 19th

b)   2012: – 1 meeting: March 12th

c)   2013: – 3 meetings: February 12th, September 9th, and November 28th

d)   2014: – 2 meetings: May 27th and November, 24th

e)   2015: – 3 meetings: March 2nd, September 23rd, and December 1st

Difficult relationship and lack of transparency by Neil Grant

32 I had difficulty in engaging Neil Grant. Often I would send two or three emails requesting a meeting with him before I received a response.

33 I never received a true picture of the poor state of affairs with my investments. It was only at meetings that I had initiated, that I would come to know that funds were suspended such as New Earth and Centurion (as explained further).

34 Any action from a meeting, unless it was commission-related for Neil Grant, was delayed and required constant follow up e.g. the information I required to decide whether or not to exit the Zara Trust took five (5) months for him to action.

35 I repeatedly asked to see the Report of the Risk Profiling he had undertaken in selecting the funds for me. When we finally met to discuss the 'Report', he produced only the marketing flyers for each of the funds and showed no analysis.

36 He ignored questions put to him on fees and documentation. He did not respond to an (informal Legal) Notice or a Formal Complaint lodged against him.

Hiding the True Reality of the Investment Funds from Me

New Earth (Waste Recycling)

37 Neil Grant always emailed positive news on the New Earth fund to me. However, when I received the Valuation Statements, the overall value of the Zara Trust continued to fall sharply. On April 22nd, 2014, I wrote to Neil Grant that with all the positive messages on New Earth that he was sending me, this was not what I was expecting (Exhibit 34). He did not reply to my email.

38 A month later, on May 19th, 2014, I requested a meeting with Neil Grant. His Business Manager, ███████████ responded by asking why I wanted to meet him. I replied that "I'm concerned about my portfolio" and that we should have started to see some growth in the last 4 years (Exhibit 35).

39   It was at this meeting on May 27th, 2014, that I came to know from Neil Grant that the New Earth fund was suspended and the reason for the ongoing decline in the value of the Zara Trust. He informed me of the suspension only now, in May 2014 and I later discovered that the New Earth fund had been suspended with effect from January 2014 (Exhibit 22). He had hidden its true state from me by deceptively emailing me positive messages on the fund in March 2014 (Exhibit 36). When I questioned the decline in the value of the trust, he avoided responding to me (Exhibit 34) and tried to avoid meeting with me (Exhibit 35).

Request to Neil Grant to Exit the Zara Trust & a Report on Risk Profiling

40   On November 24th, 2014, I had a meeting with Neil Grant at Prosperity Offshore Investment Consultant's offices to discuss exiting from the Zara Trust altogether. At the meeting, we agreed that Neil Grant would check if there were any penalties and revert back to me as soon as possible.

41   Two months passed and I had not received a response from him. On January 16th, 2015, I emailed a reminder to him and from his reply, it was clear that he had not actioned the task he had been asked to do. I reminded him that one of the action points from our meeting back on November 24th, 2014, was that he was to look into the penalties of closing the Trust. I wrote that I was concerned he had not actioned anything (Exhibit 37 – page 2 and 3).

42   The next day, on January 18th, 2015, Neil Grant arrogantly responded to my email and wrote: **"Thanks for your concern"**. He agreed to look into closing the trust.

43   After a month passed by with no response from him, on February 12th, 2015 I wrote another reminder to Neil Grant (Exhibit 37 – page 1).

44   On February 17th, 2015, I wrote a further email to Neil Grant reminding him that I had raised several concerns over the manner in which my money is being managed by Prosperity,

and for him to explain to me how he had selected the funds in both the Zara Trust and the ▇▇▇▇ Plan, and how he has been managing my money and portfolio. I also reminded him that I was waiting for the information regarding exiting from the Zara Trust (Exhibit 38).

45   Neil Grant responded to my email with "this is **NOT something that I have delayed**". This was incorrect. The information I had requested from him was from our last meeting in November 2014. He had sent Guardian the email for the information only on January 18th, 2016, and only after I had prompted him.

46   On February 18th, 2015, I replied to Neil Grant's email, requesting to see his Risk Profiling Report. I wanted him to explain his risk analysis on each of the funds he had advised me to invest into as two (2) of the funds in the Zara Trust were now suspended (Exhibit 38).

47   Finally, five months after our last meeting in November 2014, I met with Neil Grant on March 2nd, 2015, to discuss exiting the Zara Trust and to review his Risk Profiling Report. He was now, as per his client circular dated January 29th, 2015, working under ▇▇▇▇▇▇ license (Exhibit 57). At the meeting:

a)   Neil Grant advised me to not to close the Zara Trust as it would incur penalties and that the New Earth suspension would soon be lifted. To my knowledge, Neil Grant was not receiving any fee payment and so I genuinely thought he was advising me for my best interests. However, I later discovered that he was paid fees from the Zara Trust through Guardian. Therefore he was not advising me for my best interests, but for his own (as explained further paragraphs 48 to 58).

b)   He did not produce a Risk Profiling Report and instead gave me copies of the marketing flyers for each of the funds he had selected for me.

c)   On March 31st, 2016, I wrote to Neil Grant and ▇▇▇▇▇▇ requesting a full report of the risk profiling conducted by them prior to selecting the funds for me. Neither party responded (Exhibit 39).

Neil Grant Taking Unauthorized Fees from the Trust

48   Between 2010 to December 2012 Neil Grant was paid fees from the Zara Trust.

49   From December 31st, 2012, Neil Grant and I both agreed that due to the disastrous management and status of the Zara Trust, he was not to receive any further fees (as evidenced in Exhibit 46 by Neil Grant).

50   On October 29th, 2015, I wrote an email to Neil Grant because I became aware of some fees being paid to him which he should not have received (Exhibit 40).

51   On November 3rd, 2015, Neil Grant replied and admitted that he had been paid a fee from the Zara Trust. Without any further prompt from me, he wrote: **"I will now make sure that no further broker fees are deducted"** (Exhibit 40).

52   I was shocked by his admission because we had agreed to suspend all of Neil Grant's fees from December 31st, 2012, and he assured me that he had. Furthermore, he offered no apology or explanation as to how a fee had been paid to him from the Zara Trust, unauthorized.

53   Realising he had been caught, he immediately offered to reimburse the money to me and he immediately contacted Guardian. In his email to me, Matt Hill from Guardian wrote that Neil Grant had advised them that **"there were to be no further trail fees"** to be paid to him from the Zara Trust (Exhibit 30).

54   In the same email, Matt Hill explained that from December 31st, 2012, Neil Grant was not paid any fees directly from the Zara Trust. However, as from January 1st, 2013 to January 1st, 2016, Neil Grant had continued to benefit financially by being paid fees indirectly by Guardian from the Zara Trust. Guardian confirmed that Neil Grant had given them the instruction to

cancel the indirect payments only in January 2016 (after I had caught him taking fees).

55   This is why Neil Grant advised me against exiting the Zara Trust in 2014/2015 when I had requested him to look into it, and which took him over 5 months to respond. He advised me against exiting the Trust– a Trust in which all the funds were high-risk, illiquid and suspended, whilst financially benefiting himself.

56   With the removal of Neil Grant's fees (0.25%), the fee paid from the Zara Trust was now lower (0.75% annual wrap fee rather than the previous 1% annual Wrap fee) (Exhibit 30).

57   On October 17th, 2016, I wrote to Neil Grant and ███████ requesting an explanation of the unauthorised fees. Neither party responded to me (Exhibit 41).

58   On October 31st, 2016, ███████ contacted me to arrange a settlement and agreed to pay GBP 64,800 in exchange to drop the public prosecution investigation.

Signatory Forgery

59   On March 9th, 2016, I came to know from Neil Grant that in November 2013 I had given my signed consent to the trusteeship change from Guardian Trust Company Ltd in Jersey to Guardian Global Capital in Switzerland that had led to fees being paid out of the Zara Trust.

    a)   On March 9th, 2016, I requested a copy of the consent form from Neil Grant, as I had no recollection of signing it. He replied that he would request a copy from Guardian. He wrote: "I have attached the letter that I still had on your file regarding the change from Guardian Trusts in Jersey to Guardian Global, and remember having the conversation with you". (Exhibit 42)

    b)   I asked him for a copy of the signed consent form 4 times (March 17th, 22nd, 30th, and May 3rd, 2016). Neil Grant did not respond to any of my emails.

c) I contacted Guardian, directly, requesting a copy. Guardian informed me that they had forwarded a copy to Neil Grant earlier in the year in March when he had requested a copy, yet he had not forwarded it onto me despite my repeated requests on the above dates (Exhibit 25 - under the heading "Transfer from Jersey to Switzerland").

d) Upon receiving the consent form I could see that the signature on the form was not my signature and a forgery (Exhibit 43).

e) Furthermore, the letter from Guardian that accompanied the consent form did not list a PO Box number. Therefore the letter and the consent form could not have been received by me. The only person who had a copy of that letter and consent form was Neil Grant (Exhibit 44).

f) The letter was dated September 20th, 2013. The signed consent form was received and stamped by Guardian on November 20th, 2013 (Exhibit 43). My meetings with Neil Grant had taken place on September 9th, 2013 (before the letter and consent form arrived) and November 28th, 2013 (after Guardian had received the signed consent form). Evidently, it would have been impossible for me to have signed the form, and Neil Grant could not have discussed the contents of the letter with me as he claimed.

g) On October 4th, 2016 I wrote an email to Neil Grant and ▮▮▮▮▮▮▮ entitled "Signature Query" requesting an explanation on the signature on the consent form (Exhibit 45). He was now, as per his client circular working under ▮▮▮▮▮▮▮ license (Exhibit 57).

h) On October 12th, 2016, Neil Grant replied to my email (but on a separate email and he changed the title of the email to "Guardian Letter") and he wrote **"I can assure you that neither did I sign the letter nor did I give instruction to anyone else to do the same"**. He wrote that he had discussed the letter with me **"during a meeting"**, but did not disclose the date of the meeting or that I had signed the consent form at the meeting (Exhibit 46).

i) On October 17th, 2016, I wrote an email to Neil Grant and ▮▮▮▮▮▮ outlining all the issues related to them including the signature on the consent form. I received no response to my email (Exhibit 41).

j) On October 31st, 2016, ▮▮▮▮▮▮ contacted me to arrange a settlement and agreed to compensate me GBP 64,800 in exchange to drop the public prosecution investigation.

k) On December 6th, 2016, Guardian confirmed that the original letter had been sent to Neil Grant at Prosperity's offices (Exhibit 47).

l) During public prosecution investigation it was proven that the signature on the consent form was a forgery.

m) Only after the criminal trial on September 8th, 2017 did Guardian confirm that the signed consent form had been sent to them from Prosperity's office "There can be no doubt that the transfer instruction was received by Guardian in Jersey from Prosperity by courier on 20 November 2013".

Part 4 – The Type of Funds Selected by Neil Grant

New Earth Fund (Waste Recycling) – Suspended and Lost

60 New Earth was an investment fund that was sold to me by Neil Grant as low-risk that can **"certainly"** give a good return, but was later discovered to be an extremely high-risk.

61 On April 23rd, 2013, I wrote an email to Neil Grant with regards to the dramatic fall in the price of gold: "With the recent news regarding the value of gold, has this affected my investment drastically, as I recall we have invested in this" (Exhibit 29 – page 5). He did not respond to my email.

62   On April 24th, 2013, very concerned, I wrote a further email to Neil Grant directly asking him: "Am I in high-risk investments?" (Exhibit 29 – page 5).

63   Neil Grant did not respond to that question either. Instead, he confirmed he had sold the precious metals fund two days earlier, at a loss, without informing me.

64   In his email, to me, he wrote "We are out though and the alternative to this I shall send you in a separate email as it certainly isn't Carbon Credits with your attitude to risk Amber. On a scale of 1 – 10 Carbon Credits are about a 15". Here, he showed he clearly understood and was aware of my attitude to 'risk'.

65   He went on to write "However if you like the look of the New Earth Solutions fund that I will send after this email then we can access that for you and I will forfeit the 4% fee that Prosperity would be paid".

66   That same evening Neil Grant sent me some marketing collateral and information on the New Earth fund, none of which highlighted any risks (Exhibit 48).

67   On April 25th, 2013, I wrote an email to Neil Grant asking him if he wanted me to invest in New Earth. Neil Grant replied confirming that he did and if I was "happy" with his recommendations (Exhibit 29 – page 4-3).

68   Unsure, on April 27th, 2013, I wrote back with: "I think I will pull that money out £9,100 tbc - as there's no investment that's going to give me a return right now".

69   Neil Grant immediately responded to my hesitation with "I totally refute your claim of "there is nowhere that is going to give you a return right now", as the New Earth certainly can. I don't know if you noticed that I also said I would enhance the placement by a further 4% by giving up Prosperity fee to make the placement as well". In hindsight, it was a clear persuasive tactic. He would get me to invest in the fund and offer his commission to me, but take his commission on the second investment into the New Earth fund from the sale of

Prime India, which he would go on to persuade me to sell (Exhibit 29 – page 2).

70   In the following email, he again persuaded me to invest in New Earth by offering his commission and saying "cash is a complete waste of time for interest rates".

71   On April 28th, 2013, encouraged by Neil Grant's reassurance that investing in New Earth will bring the Zara Trust into the black, I took his advice. I reminded him that "I don't want a situation where the trust is eaten up admin charges!"

72   Neil Grant's only response to my concern was that he will start the purchasing process (Exhibit 29).

73   On April 29th, 2013, Neil Grant wrote to Guardian to confirm two purchases of New Earth from the sale of Prime India and the cash in the Zara Trust from the sale of Precious Metals (Exhibit 49).

74   On May 16th, 2013, Guardian confirmed the first placement from the cash in the Trust which included Neil Grant's 4% commission (Exhibit 50).

75   On July 15th, 2013, Guardian confirmed the second placement from the sale of Prime India. This time Neil Grant took his 4% commission. By offering up the first commission as a persuasive tactic he took a commission on the second purchase through his advice to me (Exhibit 51).

76   Six months later New Earth advised trading/redemptions were suspended with effect from January 2014 (Exhibit 22). Neil Grant failed to inform me that the fund he had advised me to invest into - twice - was now suspended (reference paragraph 37 to 39 for further details).

77   On May 4th, 2015, after reviewing the Zara Trust Valuation Statement, I wrote to Neil Grant that the New Earth investment fund "has turned out to be a high-risk activity with the bulk of my investment now riding in it" (Exhibit 52). Neil Grant did not reply to my email.

Non-disclosure of High Risks in New Earth

78   I discovered that unbeknown to me at the time, Neil Grant had advised and persuaded me to invest in a high-risk investment fund that was deemed not a suitable investment for an individual investor like myself.

79   At no time during our email correspondence, and otherwise, did Neil Grant mention the high risk involved in investing in the New Earth fund and that it was not a suitable investment for an individual investor like myself.

80   Neil Grant did not discuss the risks with me highlighted in the New Earth Scheme Particulars and Supplementary Memoranda for NERR (Exhibit 53). In this document, which was never shown to me, all the risks are clearly listed and individual investors like myself are specifically advised not to invest in this fund. Neil Grants' deceit went as far as failing to share certified documents with me to obtain my signature that my financial advisor i.e. Neil Grant, had discussed the high level of risks with me and that **"investment could result in a loss of a significant proportion or all of the sum invested"** and that I understood the risk I was taking (www.premiernewearthfund.com (Exhibit 22). The only information Neil Grant had shared with me was the information in Exhibit 48 and the NERR document and risk warnings were neither included nor mentioned in his email to me. Nor was it ever mentioned during our lengthy email correspondence in Exhibit 29 when Neil Grant persuaded me to invest in the New Earth fund, twice. He had taken advantage of his position, and of my trust of his position, in most unmerciful manner.

81   On October 3rd, 2016 Guardian wrote that the likelihood of retrieving my investment from New Earth was nil: **"This fund is now in liquidation. Given the poor outlook for this fund, the asset managers have re-priced this holding to nil value"** (Exhibit 25).

82   This email confirmed to me that Neil Grant had put me into a non-mainstream, high-risk, and illiquid investment. To this day he has not responded to my requests or to a Formal Complaint

to explain what risk profiling he had undertaken and risk warnings he had given to me (Exhibit 39).

83   On October 17th, 2016, I wrote an email to Neil Grant and ███████ requesting an explanation on the New Earth fund, the NERR document and the risks associated with the fund that they had failed to disclose to me. Neither party responded to my email (Exhibit 41).

84   Two weeks later, on October 31st, 2016, ████████ contacted me to arrange a settlement and agreed to compensate me GBP 64,800 in exchange to drop the public prosecution investigation.

Centurion Fund (Life Insurance Settlement) - Suspended and collapsed

85   On September 14th, 2015, I asked Neil Grant for a meeting. He was now, as per his client circular working under ████████ license (Exhibit 57).

86   On September 16th, 2015, after not receiving a reply, I wrote another email requesting a meeting.

87   On September 17th, 2015, after Neil Grant had still not replied to my email and meeting request, I again wrote to him for the third time. He finally replied and agreed to meet me the following week.

88   On September 23rd, 2015, I attended a meeting with Neil Grant. Neil Grant gave me a copy of the Valuation Statement which showed yet another drastic fall in the value of the Zara Trust. It was at this meeting, I learned that the Centurion shares had collapsed from 159 to 27. At no point during our correspondence had Neil Grant informed me of this. I was left with no doubt that if I had initiated this meeting I would not have known about the collapse. The collapse in shares meant the value of the Centurion fund plummeted to minus GBP 8,000, bringing the overall value of the Zara Trust down to the lowest it had ever been and half the value of my initial GBP 50,000 investment.

89   I gave Neil Grant a final warning and two months to sort out the Zara Trust portfolio. As far as I was concerned it was a complete mess. I reminded him again that this was meant to be a low-risk long-term growth plan.

90   On the same day, after our meeting, I wrote an email to Neil Grant that read: **"I am absolutely horrified at the state of the trust and how overall it's been managed over the last five years. There is now only 1 active account. As agreed we will have a meeting in December 2015 which gives you time to try and fix this and give it some attention"** (Exhibit 54).

91   Neil Grant replied to my email the next day, on September 24th, 2015, and wrote: **"Fully understood"**. He acknowledged that the Trust was in a terrible state and that I was holding him responsible (Exhibit 54).

92   On November 7th, 2015, I wrote an email to Neil Grant and asked him to explain what had caused the share price to fall from 159 to 27 for Centurion, to which Neil Grant replied on November 8th, 2015. His email reveals that he had always been fully aware of the status of the fund but he had hidden the true reality of it from me (Exhibit 55).

93   During the meeting on September 23rd, 2015, Neil Grant had given me a print-out of an email sent to him from Guardian. He had erased details from the email including the date the email had been sent to him. In the email, Guardian wrote that the Centurion fund had been suspended since 2012 and that Neil Grant **"will no doubt be aware"** of it (Exhibit 23).

94   Neil Grant had not informed me that the Centurion fund had been suspended since June 2012. I only came to know in September 2015. Unbeknown to me it meant that since 2012 I had been 'stuck' in the Trust. When I had asked him to look into exiting the Guardian Zara Trust in 2014/2015 he had advised me to stay in the Trust because he knew I was trapped in it, but he had not informed me of that fact.

95   It had taken me 3 attempts to have a meeting with him. If I had not asked for a meeting I would not have known what had

happened to the Centurion fund and how it had drastically reduced the value of my Trust.

96 On December 1st, 2015, I attended a meeting with Neil Grant at the ▮ Hotel:

a) At our last meeting on September 23rd, 2015, I had given Neil Grant two months to salvage the Trust. I asked him what his plans/strategy was. He said he didn't have one.

b) It had now transpired that all the funds that Neil Grant had picked were classed as 'extremely risky' as they were start-up companies with no history/track record behind them. It seemed he was on a different strategy to which we had agreed upon, which was low-risk, long-term growth funds.

c) We were now in a situation where two of the funds in the Zara Trust were suspended (Centurion and New Earth) and only one active fund (Lucent).

d) I spoke to him about the fatal decision to reduce the number of funds within the Zara Trust from four to three and choosing all high-risk investments. I said that as a financial consultant he should have evaluated the risks and if there was a situation where 1 fund became suspended, at least the other three funds would keep the trust afloat. But by having only three funds, and all high-risk and all suspended at once, there was no income paying into the trust, and so administration fees were eating into the investment. Neil Grant acknowledged that I was right. He didn't seem to know what he was doing.

e) Neil Grant said that the situation will improve and predicted in another 5 years I will recoup my GBP 50,000 initial investment. Yet he offered no science as to how he came to that prediction. I could not see how the situation was going to improve.

f) I informed him that this matter will enter the legal space if he did not come back to me with a satisfactory strategic plan of how he was going to recoup my initial investment over the next five years.

Lucent Fund (Land Purchasing and Planning) - Suspended

97   On April 21ˢᵗ, 2015, now working under ███████████ license, Neil Grant sent an email to me recommending I invest in a fund called "Lucent" (Exhibit 56).

98   I replied to his email again reminding him that I was only looking for low-risk funds. I wrote, **"As long as this is a low risk - that can increase the overall trust over time and if you recommend that this will do this then we can look at it"** (Exhibit 56). I now realise that he had not conducted any risk assessment and had simply forwarded an e-marketing flyer to me advising me to invest in it.

99   The Lucent investment fund was suspended one year later, on June 29ᵗʰ, 2016 (Exhibit 24). Neil Grant did not inform me of the suspension. I came to know the fund was suspended from Guardian on October 3ʳᵈ, 2016 (Exhibit 25).

100   On October 4ᵗʰ, 2016, I wrote an email to Neil Grant and ███████████ asking why they had not informed me of the suspension, which now meant the true value of the Zara Trust had fallen from GBP 50,000 to approximately GBP 2,000. Neither party responded to my email (Exhibit 32).

101   On October 31ˢᵗ, 2016, ███████████ contacted me to arrange a settlement and agreed to pay GBP 64,800 in exchange to drop the public prosecution investigation.

Part 5 - Investigation into Neil Grant and ███████████

102   Between 2015 and 2016 the Guardian Zara Trust was reviewed by various chartered financial service providers in the highly-regulated DIFC free zone including ███████████ ███ and the ███████████. They all agreed that I had a right to be concerned and that there were many questions that needed answering. I had entered into an advisory agreement, and the investments recommended to me were not suitable for

my circumstances and attitude to risk, and there were questions and concerns over what exactly was disclosed to me at the time. To them, it was the worst case of a Trust they have ever seen managed which no one would ever take on.

103 My concerns about Neil Grant and the authenticity of his financial advice led me to investigate him and his company. My investigation led me to discover numerous illegal activities carried out by Neil Grant and ███████████.

Prosperity Management Consultancy (559536)

104 On January 29th, 2015, Neil Grant sent an email circular informing his clients of a change in his company license and that due to changes in the UAE law **"from 8th February 2015, I will be working under the umbrella of** ███████ ████████████ and that he was going to run his business through their license (Exhibit 57).

105 In his email, it was the first time he had mentioned 'Prosperity Management Consultancy' as he had always referred to his company as 'Prosperity Offshore Investment Consultants'.

106 On December 20th, 2015, I wrote an email to Neil Grant requesting Prosperity Offshore Investment Consultants trade license and partner details.

107 On January 9th, 2016, after eight (8) requests, Neil Grant finally responded with the following details but did not share a copy of his trade license: (Exhibit 58).

   a) The name of his company was Prosperity Management Consultancy, license number 559536, active from 18/07/2004 until 17/07/2016.

   b) Although he wrote that the name of his company was 'Prosperity Management Consultancy', the company name on his email signature on which he sent the email to me was 'Prosperity Offshore Investment Consultants'.

108 In June 2016, it was discovered that as per the DED's statement, Neil Grant was very clearly doing another activity

under Prosperity Management Consultancy and did not have either the license or competence in investment / financial advisory, or any fiduciary role (Exhibit 1).

Prosperity Offshore Investment Consultants (559536)

109 In June 2016 it was discovered that there was no record of Prosperity Offshore Investment Consultants with the DED or with the SCA (Exhibit 28).

110 It transpired that the company trading as 'Prosperity Offshore Investment Consultants' under license number 559536, was in reality registered with DED as 'Prosperity Management Consultancy', licensed to conduct a different activity (Exhibit 58).

111 It was discovered that Prosperity Offshore Investment Consultants was operating from the same office address as Prosperity Management Consultancy, first at the ▮▮▮▮▮ Hotel and then at ▮▮▮▮▮▮▮▮ (Exhibit 59).

112 Evidently, Neil Grant set up Prosperity Management Consultancy and then created a fake company, using Prosperity Management Consultancy's license number with the clear intent to deceive and for personal gain.

113 Insurance Authority confirms that as per Chapter 1, Article 2, and Clause 2 of 15 to 2013 Concerning Insurance Brokerage Regulations: **"No one may practice the Insurance Brokerage activity in the UAE without obtaining a license from the IA. Such license shall be renewed annually in accordance with the provisions of these Regulations"** (Exhibit 60).

114 The reason why the DED did not issue Neil Grant an FA license is clear from his academic qualifications - he was not qualified to give advice and meet the DED's criteria. The academic certificate Neil Grant presented to prosecution was for VISA purposes to satisfy the requirements to work for companies. This does not mean that with his academic qualification Neil Grant is qualified to set up his own advisory business. I requested the advisory qualifications Neil Grant held

and copies of those certificates. To date, Neil Grant has refused to provide them (Exhibit 39).

██████████████████████ – ██ (License Number ██)

115 On January 29th, 2015, Neil Grant distributed an email circular advising his clients of a change in license and that due to changes in the UAE law **"from 8th February 2015, I will be working under the umbrella of** ██████████████████ and that he was going to run his business through their license and be based at their offices. He wrote **"I will continue to be your financial advisor"** and **"I will simply work under the ██ brand"**. (Exhibit 57).

116 The company website stated Prosperity Offshore Investment Consultants was conducting business under ██████████████████ License ██ (Exhibit 3).

117 ██████████ company stationery and IT systems including business cards and Email ID, stated Neil Grant is a Senior Partner at ██████████ (Exhibit 61).

118 In the company's letterhead, the footer stated that Prosperity Management Consultancy is **"operating under the** ██████████████████ License no. ██ (Exhibit 62).

119 Official documents such as Financial Valuation Statements issued to clients confirmed a joint partnership between ██████████████ Neil Grant and Prosperity: ██ **Neil Grant Prosperity"** (Exhibit 63).

120 It is clear that from his email dated January 29th, 2015, Neil Grant was trading as a financial consultant with Prosperity Management Consultancy and Prosperity Offshore Investment Consultants under ██████████ license. It is impossible for one body corporate to work under the banner of another. As a UAE Insurance Authority licensed firm ██████████ should not have accepted an application from a firm that was itself not regulated as an insurance broker by the UAE Insurance Authority, breaching Articles 24 and 26 of Federal Law No 6 of

2007, Amendments of 2013. This constitutes a civil and criminal offence (Exhibit 60).

Questions Ignored by Neil Grant and ███████

121 I repeatedly asked Neil Grant and ███████ for information, explanations and transparency on the business relationship between Neil Grant, Prosperity and ███████ so I know the overriding company responsible for my investments. To this day, neither party has ever responded.

122 I wrote to Neil Grant and ███████ on February 8th, 2016, to submit a plan of how they were proposing to meet their prediction of recouping my initial investment of GBP 50,000 in the Zara Trust, over the next five years (as per paragraph 96-f). Neither party responded. (Exhibit 64).

123 I wrote a Formal Complaint to Neil Grant and ███████ on March 31st, 2016, requesting information, explanations, and transparency on the Zara Trust, fees, and risk profiling (Exhibit 39). I also requested the **"advisory qualifications Mr. Grant holds and copies of those certificates"**. Neither party responded.

124 As both Neil Grant and ███████ were failing to cooperate and forcing me to take legal action against them I wrote that any court and legal fees were to be met by them (Exhibit 65). Neither party responded.

Blind Eye Knowledge

125 ███████ denied having anything to do with Guardian and the Zara Trust. However, throughout all their correspondence with me, they never once denied that Neil Grant or Prosperity was not connected to them, or that Neil Grant or Prosperity was not working under ███████ license (Exhibit 66). It was the same pattern as other clients who also questioned their relationship (Exhibit 67).

126 On February 13th, 2016, to explain to ███████ why they were in the copy of the Notice, I forwarded Neil Grant's email circular of January 29th, 2015 to the Managing Director,

█████████ (Exhibit 68). I also sent him a copy of Prosperity's website page that stated Prosperity was conducting business under ████████████████ **License** ██. Upon receiving such emails, it is reasonable to expect a person of superior authority to have responded acknowledging they had a positive duty to make enquiries. In his email Neil Grant was stating that he is placing business through ████████ but if he was not employed by them or on their VISA this is a red flag and ████████ are in the wrong for allowing him to place business through the company without the relevant qualifications.

127 Evidently, ████████ had actual knowledge of Prosperity's marketing collateral and that ████████ name and license number are on them. I had made ████████ aware of what Neil Grant was doing and I had given them evidence of what he was doing. And yet they were turning a blind eye to it. If Neil Grant's representation was untrue, and he was misleading clients, and ████████ were aware of that, they had a duty, and ample opportunity to set the record straight or ask Neil Grant to set the record straight. However, they made a deliberate decision to avoid any confirmation despite being presented with the facts. They cannot simply fold their hands and ignore it, and then use the defence that they never confirmed or admitted anything in order to escape negligence and liability. The facts were pointing to ████████ colluding with Neil Grant.

128 On March 14th, 2016, in my email to ████████ in reference to the Notice, I wrote that Neil Grant **"is using your license which is why it involves you"** to which I received no denial. Again, ████████ deliberately refused to clarify their relationship with Neil Grant and Prosperity.

129 On April 28th, 2015, Neil Grant advised me to invest money into Lucent (Exhibit 56). As per Neil Grant's notification on January 29th, 2015, I was made to believe from both Neil Grant and ████████ that this placement was made under ████████ license number ██ a fact never denied or challenged by ████████ when presented with the fact.

130 Further questions seem to arise with each correspondence I sent to Neil Grant and ███████████

   a) Did Neil Grant work at Prosperity or ███████████ If he works for ███████ then why is he still managing non-insurance products from Prosperity?

   b) It did appear that ███████████ were now shifting the emphasis over to Prosperity as that was the company who initially offered the product Guardian Zara Trust to me, but never denying that Prosperity was working under their license.

   c) It seemed that Neil Grant had his own company but used the infrastructure of Prosperity and now the license of ███████████ to submit business.

   d) With this in mind, I became concerned that both ███████████ and Prosperity will keep passing me to each other and it was difficult to know the overriding company responsible for my investments.

   e) Neil Grant never intervened during the email correspondence between ███████████ and myself or clarified his relationship with ███████████

   f) With this in mind, it seemed that ███████████ were seeking to avoid liability for a wrongful act by intentionally keeping themselves unaware of facts that would render them liable.

131 On September 6th, 2016, I wrote another email to ███████████ pressurising them for transparency on ███████████ relationship with Neil Grant and Prosperity. I drew their attention to the DED's website and that ███████████ description of their activity under DED is 'Insurance Brokers', and it would be incorrect for them to allow anybody to be giving financial advice (Exhibit 69 – page 3).

132 Two weeks later, on September 15th, 2016, ███████████ replied that their lawyers would respond to me in a months' time

133 On October 9th, 2016, after I wrote another email prompting a response, ███████████ in-house Legal Manager, ███████████ replied stating that their lawyer had advised them that they are **"not allowed to comment or discuss this case"** (Exhibit 69 – page 1).

Settlement Offer by ███████████

Paragraphs 134 to 140 redacted.

141 On August 15th, 2017, immediately after the criminal verdict Neil Grant left the UAE and returned to the UK with his family, where he has since been working from, under the employment and VISA of ███████████. He left the UAE to escape civil litigation and ███████████ have continued to collude with him and support him with a UAE Residency VISA allowing him to work and place business under their license as evidenced in Neil Grant's client circular in February 2018 (Exhibit 74); Neil Grant's interview with the UK media on January 8th 2018 (Exhibit 75); and Neil Grant's personal email dated March 2018 (Exhibit 76).

Employment Contract between Neil Grant and ███████████

142 ███████████ submitted to the court a copy of their employment contract with Neil Grant that commenced from September 18th, 2016 (Exhibit 77). ███████████

a) Neil Grant's business card and email ID (Exhibit 61) state he is a **'Senior Partner'** at ███████████ and not a low-level manager as we are led to believe

b) ███████████ is the Managing Director of ███████████,
███████████

c) It appeared that ███████████ volunteered to submit only their employment contract with Neil Grant to the Court, but withheld the partnership contract between ███-Neil Grant-Prosperity' from February 8th, 2015 when Neil Grant and Prosperity was clearly working together and submitting business together as the Valuation Statement clearly proves

(Exhibit 63). From this policy alone, the client states the commission paid was $115,000 (Exhibit 78).

d) Despite the fact that Neil Grant had left the UAE eight (8) months prior with his family, ███████████ only terminated Neil Grant's employment contract after a civil case was filed against them, and after evidence revealed that Neil Grant, as per his own words, holds a UAE Residency VISA and is submitting business through the company email ID.

Insurance Authority, Dubai

Paragraphs 143 redacted.

Conclusion

The evidence seen altogether proves that from the moment he approached me, Neil Grant had a calculated plan to mislead and misrepresent himself to me, to extract money from me, for his own financial gain and benefit.

Neil Grant deceived financial companies, insurance authorities and government bodies as well as his clients and following the criminal verdict, an avalanche of misconduct complaints followed against him (samples of client emails and media articles: Exhibit 80).

It is clear on the facts of the matter, that knowing fraudulent activities have taken place, ███████████ actions, and lack of actions, unequivocally amount to the fact that they colluded with Neil Grant, and continue to collude with him, misrepresenting their relationship to me.

███████████ allowed Neil Grant to market and to run his businesses through their license to place business without obtaining permission from any Authority. As a result, I continued to suffer financial repercussions from their partnership as Neil Grant continued to miss-advise me. The investment fund Lucent, placed in April 2015 under ███████████ license, was suspended in 2016 bringing the overall value of the Guardian Zara Trust to nil.

Both ███████ and Neil Grant in collusion initiated settlement discussions so to protect each other, and attempt to irritate public prosecutors with a view to halting investigations. They then deliberately reneged on a settlement agreement. Their acts were premeditated, wilful and deliberate, and they should be held liable to fulfil that written agreement.

There is the financial element – I trusted Neil Grant with my life savings, but there is also the moral element. Neil Grant is morally corrupt. He took advantage of my trust in him and went as far as to use my signature on a document without my knowledge. He is the most dishonest man I have ever encountered and has shown no remorse, publicly reducing the Judge's Ruling as just a "missing activity" on his license (Exhibit 76).

███████ arguments seeking to escape the consequences of their misconduct are baseless and offensive. They took no action to rectify matters that were repeatedly brought to their attention. The only action they took was to halt the Public Prosecution investigation to escape liability.

In light of the criminal decision, and the evidence I have provided to the Civil Court, both parties are to be held liable and I respectfully ask that all the money given by me for investment (plus damages) should be returned to me.

In my evidence, I have shown that I gave Neil Grant and ███████ ample time and opportunity to provide a response and clarify and rectify matters. The behaviour of both parties is unreasonable and court action was the only option left for me to get answers and justice. Therefore as per the Judge's Summary in the criminal judgement, I respectfully ask that all costs incurred by me for both criminal and civil prosecution be reimbursed to me.

Signed

GLOSSARY AND CAST OF CHARACTERS

There are many people and companies mentioned in this book. To help you keep track of who I am talking about, you may find it useful to refer to the following cast of characters.

If you're new to the financial and legal game you may need to be au fait with the lingo – and here the experts help put together a glossary of all the terms you will encounter.

A

Abaya – traditionally, women in Dubai wear an abaya, a long, black flowing light coat over their clothing. A black scarf called a shayla is draped over the head

Abigail (Abi) Claire Grant – is the wife of Neil Ramsay Pringle Grant

Abu Dhabi – is the capital and the second most populous city of the United Arab Emirates

Abu Dhabi Court – cases relating to constitutional matters are heard only by the Abu Dhabi Supreme Court of Cassation

Advocate – a lawyer in Dubai is classified as either an advocate or a legal consultant

Allahu Akbar – is from the Arabic language meaning God is most great

Alhumdulilah – in Arabic, the word means "Praise be to Allah" or God. It is a phrase that Muslims often use in conversation, especially when thanking God for blessings

Anglo Irish Bank – was an Irish bank headquartered in Dublin from 1964 to 2011. It began to wind down after nationalisation in 2009

Glossary And Cast Of Characters

Arab – a member of an Arabic-speaking people inhabiting much of the Middle East and North Africa. Saudi Arabia, Yemen, Oman, United Arab Emirates, Qatar, Bahrain, and Kuwait are ethnically Arab

Arabic – the official language of the United Arab Emirates, and the official language of the Dubai courts. Classical Arabic is essentially the form of the language found in the Qurān

As-salamu alaykum – is a greeting in Arabic that means 'Peace be upon you'

Associate – in the context of a law firm an associate is a lawyer and an employee of a law firm who does not hold an ownership interest as a partner, or have a significant management role. Under the guidance of a partner in the firm, an associate assist with cases by conducting legal research and writing reports, legal briefs, and other documents

Association Romande des Intermediaries Financiers (ARIF) – are financial regulators in Geneva, Switzerland

Attorney – is another word for a lawyer

B

Bamboo – is an Eco planet investment fund in South America

Barrister – is one of the two types of practicing lawyers in England and Wales. Barristers mostly specialise in courtroom advocacy (trial work) and litigation

Bedell Cristin – is a law firm, in Jersey

Benjamin Franklin – was America's scientist, inventor, politician, philanthropist and business man

Brandeaux – is a student accommodation investment fund in the United Kingdom

Burj Al Arab – is a five-star hotel in Dubai, rising on a man-made island, and designed to resemble the graceful sail of an Arabian dhow

Burj Khalifa – is the tallest tower in the world since 2009, with a total height of 829.8 m (2,722 ft, just over half a mile), and is one of the top attractions to visit in Dubai

Burj India – is an investment fund

Bunny boiler – in British English, is slang and means an obsessive and dangerous female, in pursuit of a lover who has spurned her. The expression 'bunny boiler' derives from the 1987 film Fatal Attraction

Business Bay – is a central commercial, residential and business district in Dubai, United Arab Emirates

C

Common Reporting Standard (CRS) self-certificate form – regulations based on the Organisation for Economic Cooperation and Development (OECD), CRS require financial institutions to collect and report certain information about an account holder's tax residency

Candoura – see dish dash

Cardamom qahwa – a traditional Arabic coffee, made from green coffee beans and cardamom. It is often served with dates and served from a special coffee pot called dallah and the cups are small with no handle

Cassation Court, Dubai – is the third degree of litigation. If rulings made in the Court of First Instance and Court of Appeal are found to be unsatisfactory, they can be challenged before the Court of Cassation. All decisions of this court are final and binding and cannot be subjected to further appeal. This court is formed by four judges and is presided by the Chief Justice

Central Bank of the United Arab Emirates – is the state institution responsible for managing the currency, monetary policy and banking regulation in the United Arab Emirates

Centurion 101 Growth Fund – is a life insurance settlement investment fund

Channel Island – are an archipelago in the English Channel, off the French coast of Normandy. They include two Crown dependencies: the Bailiwick of Jersey, which is the largest of the islands; and the Bailiwick of Guernsey: the United Kingdom is responsible for the defence and international relations of the islands

Channel Island Financial Ombudsman (CIFO) – is the independent dispute-resolution service for complaints involving financial services provided in or from the Channel Islands of Jersey, Guernsey, Alderney and Sark

Civil Court, Dubai – resolve legal disputes between two or more people. While a criminal case always involves a government prosecutor and a defendant, the parties involved in a civil case may be private citizens, businesses or other institutions. Examples include, businesses trying to recover money they are owed or individuals seeking compensation for injuries

Civil procedure – is the body of law that sets out the rules and standards that courts follow when adjudicating civil lawsuits (as opposed to procedures in criminal law matters)

Civil judgment –is the final order of a court in a civil lawsuit

Clyde & Co – is an international law firm; with headquarters in London, United Kingdom

Complainant – in criminal cases, the prosecutor brings the case against the defendant, but the key complaining party is often called the 'complainant'

Conviction, criminal – is a formal judgment of guilt entered by a court. A criminal conviction results when a prosecutor proves in a court of law that a given individual violated the penal code or common law rules. A criminal conviction is punishment brought by the state for violating the law

Court of Appeal, Dubai – is the second degree of litigation. When an aggrieved party finds the ruling of the Court of First Instance to be not satisfactory, an appeal may be filed before the Court of Appeal. This Court is formed by three judges and is presided by one of them

Court of First Instance, Dubai – is the first degree of litigation. It has the authority to head all lawsuits pertaining to criminal and civil matters

Court privileges – is awarded in Dubai to only a local advocate to represent individuals and companies in a court of law before a judge

Court prosecutor – presents the public prosecution case and evidence before the judge in a criminal court

Council – is a title often used interchangeably with the title of lawyer. Lead council is a senior lawyer leading a team of legal representative on a particular case

Criminal defence lawyer – is a lawyer specialising in the defence of individuals and companies charged with criminal activity

Crown Dependency – three of the British Isles are in a separate political class: a Crown dependency. These islands are the Isle of Man, the Bailiwick of Guernsey and the Bailiwick of Jersey. They are not technically part of the United Kingdom, but the United Kingdom is considered responsible for them. They do have their own legislative bodies to self-govern, but the United Kingdom technically has the ability to impose its laws on them

D

Data Subject Access Request (DSAR) – a request to access personal data. The GDPR (General Data Protection Regulation) grants individuals the right to access their personal data from data controllers so that they can understand how it is processed and make sure it is processed lawfully

Defendant – is an individual, company, or institution sued or accused in a court of law

Defence lawyer – is a lawyer who represents an accused party in legal matters, including in a court of law

Deira – is an area in Dubai and is the oldest part of the city

Department of Economic Development (DED) – is the government body that registers companies in Dubai and provides companies with the appropriate business licence

Dirham – also known as simply the Emirati dirham, is the currency of the United Arab Emirates

Dish dash – is a long-sleeved, ankle length garment. It resembles a loose-fitting robe or a long shirt. It is also referred to as a thoub/thobe, or candoura. It is the main item of clothing for Arab men and is generally worn with a pair of loose-fitting trousers called sirwal, either long or short. While white is by far the favourite, they all come in different colours and styles

Downton Abbey – is a British historical drama television

Dubai – is the most populous city in the United Arab Emirates

Dubai courts – founded in 1970, Judicial courts in Dubai are divided into three stages:1-Court of First Instance: The first degree of litigation; 2-Court of Appeal: The second degree of litigation; 3-Court of Cassation: Highest and final level of litigation. All proceedings are recorded and conducted in Arabic

DEWA – is the Dubai Electricity and Water Authority, a public service infrastructure company

Dubai Financial Services Authority (DFSA) – is the financial services regulator which regulates the conduct of financial services in and from the DIFC

Dubai International Financial Centre (DIFC) – is a top ten global financial centre, and the leading financial hub for the Middle East, Africa and South Asia (MEASA). It is an independent jurisdiction under the United Arab Emirates Constitution, with its own civil and commercial laws distinct from those of the wider United Arab Emirates, and its own courts

Dubai International Financial Centre (DIFC) courts – is within the DIFC itself. DIFC laws and regulations are written in English and default to English law in the event of an ambiguity. The DIFC courts have judges taken from leading common law jurisdictions including England, Singapore and Hong Kong

Dubai Land Department (DLD) – is a department of Dubai Government that is responsible for overseeing the registration and documentation of all real estate transactions on behalf of the Government of Dubai

Dubai Police Force – is the 17,500 strong police force for Dubai. They come under the jurisdiction of the ruler of Dubai, and they cover a population of 2.8 million people

Dubai Ruler – His Highness Sheikh Mohammed bin Rashid Al Maktoum and Vice President and Prime Minister of the United Arab Emirates

E

Edinburgh – is the capital of Scotland

Eid – is a religious festival and holiday, celebrated by Muslims worldwide

Emirate – is the name the country, United Arab Emirates is sometimes referred to

Emirati – a citizen or inhabitant of the United Arab Emirates

English law – is the common law legal system of England, comprising mainly criminal law and civil law, each branch having its own courts and procedures

English law in Dubai – is practiced only in the DIFC courts by international law firms with judges taken from leading common law jurisdictions including England, Singapore and Hong Kong

Execution court, Dubai – as a means to execute a judgment regarding the payment of dues, the Execution court has the power to take certain measures

Execution judgment – is the act of getting an officer of the court to take possession of the property of a losing party in a lawsuit, called the judgment debtor, on behalf of the winner, called the judgment creditor, sell it and use the proceeds to pay the judgment

Expatriate – (often shortened to expat) is a person living and/or working in a country other than his or her country of citizenship, often temporarily and for work reason

Expert, court-appointed – are often appointed directly by the court to review documents, meet litigants and provide an expert report to the courts. Expert reports are heavily relied on by judges when issuing judgments. The expert will generally be appointed from a list of court-appointed experts which is held by the court

External counsel – is a lawyer that a company hires that is not employed by the company itself

F

Federal law – is the body of law of the common central government of a country

Financial advisor – is a professional who provides financial services to clients based on their financial situation. Sometimes they are named by their specialism such as 'investment advisor', 'pension advisor' or 'financial planner'. Sometimes they are known as 'brokers', often when dealing with products such as investments including shares

Financial Conduct Authority (FCA) – is the regulated body for all financial advisors in the UK

Financial regulators – are regulatory bodies established by governments or other organizations to oversee the functioning and fairness of financial markets and the firms that engage in financial activity

Financial Service Provider – means any provider of consumer financial products or services for the retail market which manages, invests, exchanges, or holds money on behalf of clients

Forensics – is the use of science and technology to investigate and establish facts in criminal or civil courts

Forensic expert – is someone who examines and analyses objects or substances related to a crime

Fraud Law – Fraud is a crime under the United Arab Emirate law: Article 399 of UAE Federal Law No. 3 of 1987, as amended, (the 'Penal Code') stipulates that: "Whoever captures for himself or for others transferable money or documents or signing such document or cancelling, damaging or amending it through trickery or using a false name or personality for the purpose of tricking the victim and forcing him to deliver such shall be punished". The punishment is either jail or a fine, for a period not exceeding two years or a fine not exceeding ten thousand dirhams, respectively

Francois de La Rochefoucauld – was a noted French moralist and author of maxims and memoirs

Friends Provident International – is a Financial Service Provider in the international life assurance, pensions and investment market. Head office is London, United Kingdom

Fund Manager – is a financial professional who is in charge of an investment fund

G

Gone with the Wind – is a 1939 American epic historical romance film set against the backdrop of the Civil War and one of its most famous quotes is Rhett Butler's: "Frankly, my dear, I don't give a damn"

Great Britain – is the union of the individual countries of England, Scotland and Wales

Guardian Asset Management – is a wealth management business, based in Jersey, that provides management services to financial services businesses

Guardian Global Capital (Suisse) SA – is a Fund Management Company, based in Geneva, Switzerland

Guardian Trust Company Ltd – is a Fund Management Company based in Jersey

Guernsey – is an island in the English Channel and is a British Crown Dependency

Gulf, Middle East – refers to the Arabian Gulf. The phrase Gulf Countries refers to members of the GCC (Gulf Cooperation Council), which consists of six countries: Kuwait, Bahrain, Qatar, United Arab Emirates, Oman and Saudi Arabia

Guttra – is a square or rectangular headscarf worn by men, along with a rope band (usually black) to fasten it in place

H

Habibti – comes from the Arabic root word meaning 'love', and is a term of affection for a female

Hannibal Lecter – is a fictional character and a serial killer who eats his victims

Haniff – a pseudonym

Hans Christian Andersen – was an 18th century Danish author and master of the literary fairy tale

Hansard International Limited – is a Financial Services Business and an insurance undertaking authorised to provide unit-linked life assurance products, operating out of the Isle of Man, British Isles

His Highness Sheikh Mohammed bin Rashid Al Maktoum – is the Vice President and Prime Minister of the United Arab Emirate and Ruler of Dubai

I

Illiquid – is an asset that can't be exchanged for cash easily. Illiquid assets are generally hard to sell because there is low trading activity or interest in the asset itself. As a result, illiquid assets tend to have greater price volatility

Indemnity commission – is upfront commission paid by a provider. It is normally a percentage of the first years premiums

Independent Financial Advisor (IFA) – if a financial advisor is 'independent' or advertises that it gives 'independent advice' this means that it's able to advise and sell products from any provider right across the market, giving you the very best advice and products tailored just for you

In-house lawyer – is a lawyer who looks after the legal needs of the organisation they work for

Inland Revenue – is the department of the British government responsible for collecting and administering direct taxes

Insurance Authority, Dubai – are the regulators for insurance-based products outside of the DIFC

International law firm – comprising of legal representatives, an international law firm maintains offices throughout the world, specialising in all almost all areas of law

Interpreter – is a person who provides an oral translation between people who speak different languages

Ireland – is an island in the North Atlantic and a country of western Europe

Isle of Man – is a self-governing British Crown dependency situated in the Irish Sea off the northwest coast of England

J

Jaws – is a 1975 American thriller film where a man-eating great white shark attacks beachgoers at a summer resort town

Jersey – is an island in the English Channel and a British Crown Dependency

John Robson – is the former director and board member of Guardian Asset Management

Judge Ahmad Khalid al Hamdan – a pseudonym

Jersey Financial Services Commission (JFSC) – is the financial services regulator for Jersey, Channel Islands

Jumeriah – is a coastal residential area of Dubai, mainly comprising low-rise private dwellings

K

Khalass – is an Arabic phrase that means 'end' or 'finish'

King Kong – is a film monster, resembling an enormous gorilla

L

Lady Macbeth – is a leading character in William Shakespeare's tragedy

Glossary And Cast Of Characters

Macbeth. The wife of the play's tragic hero, Macbeth, she goads her husband into committing regicide, after which she becomes queen of Scotland

Laurel and Hardy – were an English comedy duo act during the 1940s Classical Hollywood era of cinema. They became well known for their slapstick comedy

Law Society of Jersey – is the governing body of law firms and lawyers practising in Jersey, Channel Islands

Lawyer – is a person appointed to act for another in business or legal matters

Legal consultant – is a person who consults with a client to define a need or a problem and provides guidance on legal matters

Legal directory – is a directory that specifically accepts listings and published credentials from law firms and lawyers, and ranks law firms and lawyers according to a number of categories whilst being put against their peers

Legal notice – it is a way of notifying individuals or organisations about a legal matter by using a method preferred by the law courts. It's usually the first step in commencing a lawsuit against individuals or organisations

Lehman Brothers – was a global financial services firm founded in 1847. Before filing for bankruptcy in 2008, Lehman was the fourth-largest investment bank in the United States (behind Goldman Sachs, Morgan Stanley, and Merrill Lynch), with about 25,000 employees worldwide

Lincoln Lawyer – is a 2011 American legal thriller film about a brilliantly eccentric lawyer, who works out of a chauffeur-driven Lincoln Town Car rather than an office

Lionel Messi – is an Argentine professional footballer who is widely regarded as one of the greatest goalscorers of all time

Liquid – is an asset that can easily be converted into cash at little or no loss of value, within a short amount of time, and tend to have high levels of demand and security

Litigants, criminal – is a lawyer going to trial in a criminal court to either prosecute or defend their client in a criminal matter

Local – a citizen or inhabitant of the United Arab Emirates

Local law – refers to the law that operates over a particular locality. Local laws cannot conflict with state or federal laws

Local law firms – Dubai-based law firms who practice local law and are authorised to present client's cases before the judge in local courts

Local lawyers – are lawyers from the United Arab Emirates practicing local law

Long-term assets – refers to holding an asset for an extended period of time. Depending on the type of security, a long-term asset can be held for as little as one year or for as long as 30 years or more

Lucent – is a land purchase and planning investment fund

M

Man City (Manchester City) – is an English professional football club based in East Manchester, England

Man Utd (Manchester United) – is an English professional football club based in Old Trafford, Greater Manchester, England

Manager, Insurance Authority – a pseudonym

Managing partner – in the context of a law firm, a managing partner is a senior-level or founding lawyer of the firm. They are responsible for the leadership of the firm in terms of the motivation of partners and associates, and the overall operations of the firm

Marks and Spencer – is a British multinational retailer with headquarters in London, England

Marhaba – is an Arabic word, used in the Middle East to greet people, as Hello in English and Namaste in Hindi

Martha Stewart – is an American retail businesswoman, with a panache for restoring, cooking and decorating

Marshmallow test – is one of the most famous psychological experiments ever conducted, led by Walter Mischel, a professor at Stanford University, linking delayed gratification (a treat right now … or two later?) to success later in life

Matthew McConaughey – is an American actor

Matt Hill – Trust Officer, at Guardian Global Capital (Suisse) SA

Member of Parliament (MP) – is an elected member of the British Parliament: the representative of the people who live in their constituency

Memorandum – are legal or court papers. They set out the case to be presented by each party. All proceedings before Dubai courts are conducted in Arabic. Accordingly, all the court memorandums will be drafted in Arabic and official Arabic translations of all the documents upon which parties seek to rely will be necessary

Mike Tyson – is an American former professional boxer

Mis-management – to manage incompetently or dishonestly. Mis-management of funds refers to instances where a person fails to observe laws or guidelines when handling finances for another person

Mis-selling – is a sales practice in which a product or service is deliberately misrepresented or a customer is misled about its suitability. Mis-selling may involve the deliberate omission of key information, the communication of misleading advice, or the sale of an unsuitable product based on the customer's expressed needs and preferences. Mis-selling is both negligent and unethical and may lead to legal action, fines or professional censure for those who engage in it

Morgan Freeman – is an American actor, director and narrator

N

Nathan Charlson – a pseudonym, former client of Neil Grant

Neil Grant – is a convicted Independent Financial Advisor

Net Asset Value (NAV) – is the value of a fund's assets minus any liabilities and expenses. It represents the price at which investors can buy or sell units of the fund

New Earth – is a waste recycling investment fund

Nick Webster – is a journalist and a Dubai-based senior reporter for *The National*

Northern Ireland – lies in the northeastern quadrant of the island of Ireland, and is part of the United Kingdom

Notary public, Dubai – acts as the official witness in the signing (free and willing) of documents by several parties that are identified and verified by the notary. In most cases, a Power of Attorney certificate is signed in a notary public's presence

Numpty – is English slang for idiot

O

Officer Salah – a pseudonym

OJ Simpson – Orenthal James Simpson, is an American former football running back, actor, and convicted felon. He was tried for the murders of his former wife, and her friend. Simpson was acquitted of the murders in criminal court, but was later found responsible for both deaths in a civil trial

Only Fools and Horses – is a classic British television sitcom about two brothers: Del Boy (Derrick) and Rodney Trotter, set in Peckham council estate in south-east London

Opposing lawyers – are the two different sides to the case's legal representation collectively. That is, the plaintiff's legal counsel and the defendant's legal counsel would be referred to as opposing counsel because they are on the opposite sides of the case

Order for damages – if a civil lawsuit is successful, the court will issue judgment in favour of the plaintiff and make the appropriate court order for damages

P

Paralegals – are not traditionally lawyers. Indeed, their whole raison d'être is that they are not lawyers. Their job is typically to carry out the course of action suggested by the lawyer as part of a legal assistance system

Plaintiff – a person who brings a case against another in a civil court of law, seeking a legal remedy

Plea – at the start of a criminal case the person accused of the crime will be asked to plead to the charges they face. They will tell the court whether they admit the charge and plead guilty or deny the charge and plead not guilty. If the plea is not guilty, a date will be fixed for a trial when evidence in the case will be heard

Pleadings – is an opportunity for the victim and the defendant in a criminal case to orally plead their case to the judge directly

Philip Van Neste – Chairman of the Guardian businesses at various times, including Guardian Capital Global (Suisse) SA, Guardian Asset Management and Guardian Trust Company Limited

Power of Attorney (POA) – is the written authority to act for another person in specified or all legal or financial matters. A POA certificate is key for representation of clients by lawyers before the Dubai courts. A financial POA is a legal document an individual (the 'principal') can use to appoint someone (the 'agent') to act on his or her behalf regarding personal, financial and business matters

Pro bono – is the term used denoting work undertaken without charge, especially legal work for a client with a low income

Provident Providers – are life insurance companies who sell life insurance investment funds

Public Prosecution Service (PPS), Dubai – is the principal prosecuting authority in Dubai with the responsibility for taking decisions as to prosecution in all cases investigated by the Dubai police. It is the only authority that can initiate criminal cases in Dubai. It investigates, imposes charges (depending on evidence) and refers the accused to the competent court. The department also supervises the case proceedings in the criminal court

Q

Qualified investors – refer to individuals and other entities that are allowed to purchase unregistered securities. Common examples include hedge funds, venture capital funds, and private equity offerings

R

Regulators – a person or body that supervises a particular industry or business activity

Regulation – are rules made by a government or other authority in order to control the way something is done or the way people behave. The goal of regulation is to prevent and investigate fraud, keep markets efficient and transparent, and make sure customers and clients are treated fairly and honestly

Richard Flud – is the former CEO of Lehman Brothers

Rupert – a pseudonym, former client of Neil Grant

S

Sabah al khair – Arabs say good morning, although 'Sabah al khair' literally translates as 'morning of good'. The most common reply to this is 'Sabah al noor', which means 'morning of light'

Salam – is an Arabic word that literally means 'peace', but is also used as a general greeting in Arabian countries and by Muslims

Sarah – a pseudonym, former client of Neil Grant

Sami – a pseudonym

Scotland – is a country that is part of the United Kingdom, and has its own laws, court system, lawyers and judges

Securities and Commodities Authority (SEC) – are the regulators for investment-based products, outside of the DIFC

Senior public prosecutor – their main duty is to direct upon prosecution files submitted by police and government departments with a view to deciding, or advising, as to prosecution, including issues of disclosure and human rights

Settlor – is the person who puts assets into a Trust

Shakespearean – refers to anything that resembles or relates to the works of

William Shakespeare, an English playwright, poet, and actor

Sharjah – is the third largest and third most populous city in the United Arab Emirates

Sharia'h law – is the fundamental religious concept of Islam; namely, its law

Sheikh Zayed Road (SZR) – is the main artery of Dubai. The highway runs parallel to the coastline from Dubai to the border with the emirate of Abu Dhabi

Short-term assets – refers to assets that are held for a year or less

Smoke and mirrors – something that is described as smoke and mirrors is intended to make you believe that something is being done or is true, when it is not

Solicitor – is one of the two types of practicing lawyers in England and Wales. A solicitor advises clients on legal matters, and mainly prepares cases for barristers to present in the higher courts, although they can represent clients in certain lower courts

Start-up company – refers to new businesses typically aimed at resolving a real life issue with an innovative product or service. They are typically funded by a group of investors who believe in the founder or the company concept. Start-ups generally face high uncertainty and have high rates of failure

Shawarma – is one of Dubai's most popular street foods consisting of meat cut into thin slices, stacked in a cone-like shape, and roasted on a slowly-turning vertical rotisserie or spit

T

Testimony – in law, is a formal written or spoken statement and a solemn attestation as to the truth of a matter

The Blocker – a pseudonym

The National – is a private English-language daily newspaper published in Abu Dhabi, United Arab Emirates

The Scotsman – is a daily Scottish newspaper headquartered in Edinburgh, Scotland

The Times, London – is a British daily national newspaper based in London, England

Translator – is a person who translates from one language into another, especially as a profession

Trust – is a way of managing assets (money, investments, land or buildings) for people. There are different types of Trusts and they are taxed differently

Trustee – is the person who manages the Trust the 'beneficiary' and is the person who financially benefits from the Trust

U

United Arab Emirates (UAE) – is a country in the Middle East. It is a federal elective constitutional monarchy formed from a federation of seven emirates, consisting of Abu Dhabi (the capital) Ajman, Dubai, Fujairah, Ras Al Khaimah, Sharjah and Umm Al Quwain. Each emirate is governed by a ruler. The estimated population of the UAE in 2020 was 9.89 million. Islam is the official religion and Arabic is the official language

Unregulated – is an unregulated type of business or activity not controlled and directed by fixed rules or laws

Usain Bolt – is a Jamaican sprinter and world record holder dubbed "the fastest man alive"

United Kingdom (UK) – comprises four constituent countries: England, Scotland, Wales, and Northern Ireland

V

Victim – a person harmed, injured, or killed as a result of a crime, accident, or other event or action

W

Wayne Rooney – is an English professional footballer, and a record goalscorer

Whalla – in Arabic, means by God and is often used it to emphasise surprise in one's speech, and if it sounds like a question it means "really?!" or "are you serious?"

Wrap fees – are the expenses that investment managers charge to offer comprehensive management of your investment assets. The fees apply to so-called wrap accounts, which allow financial institutions to bundle together a variety of different services, including management of your assets

Winston Churchill – was Prime Minister of the United Kingdom twice: from 1940 to 1945, during the Second World War, when he led his country from the brink of defeat to victory, and again from 1951 to 1955

Witness statement – is a written account of an incident in the own words of a witness to support a legal action. It is related to the circumstances of the case

Writ notice – are court documents that are exchanged by the parties in a case

Y

Ya'ani – is more a dialect word that is more commonly used in spoken Arabic rather than the written Arabic. Ya'ani can mean 'it means' in the sense of explaining something and you want to expand on its meaning, but it also can be used as "umm", "er" or "you know, like"

Yorkshire ripper – mass murderer Peter Sutcliffe

Z

Zara Trust – all Trusts are given a name. The Zara Trust is a name of the Guardian Trust portfolio in this book

ABOUT AMBER WAHEED

*A*mber is a life, business strategist and a passionate fighter against fraud.

She was an expat living in Dubai, working for Fortune 500 companies and global law firms when she lost her life-savings after trusting a financial advisor who posed as her friend. That inspired her to invest her time to explore what is going on behind the scenes of the financial advisory industry.

Inspired by the victims of fraud, Amber has worked with a team of professionals producing legal and financial advice guides and podcasts and has become a mentor to improve the education of individuals.

Today, Amber's goal is to use her experience to help people enhance their financial advisory and legal services awareness, avoiding the costly mistakes that she and most investors make. She has immersed herself in developing Strategic Intervention Coaching and has provided coaching, management, and leadership to senior executives and Government officials.

Connect with Amber

For more information about Amber visit

https://businesssculpting.com

https://twitter.com/AmberWaheed

https://www.instagram.com/expatsindubai.behindthescenes/

Business Sculpting
Results focused coaching and consulting

PODCAST

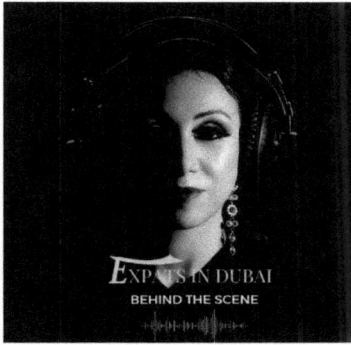

Welcome to Expats in Dubai | Behind the Scenes where it's all about helping you navigate the expat lifestyle in Dubai and enhancing your financial advisory and legal services awareness so you can avoid the costly mistakes that most investors make!

This podcast will help you understand the financial advisory pitfalls, take you behind the scenes in Dubai, highlight the supportive communities and resources available to help you along your expat journey, and also teach you how to avoid the mistakes that limit your personal and financial success.

Join me, your host Amber Waheed, to explore the deeper side of expats living in Dubai through thought-provoking interviews, vast personal experience, and insights from the trenches. Let's get started…

www.businesssculpting.com/podcast